Let The Word Speak.

A Brief Commentary of the Old Testament

By Kieron David Moore

Bible History

The Old Testament (OT) [a] was written down, mostly in Hebrew between the fourteenth century BC and the fourth century BC. The individual 'books' being written on scrolls and collected, as time went by, to form the Hebrew Bible. The first OT books very similar to what we know today were compiled into the Septuagint (otherwise known as the LXX) a Koine Greek translation in the third to second century BC.

After the split of the Roman Empire (East & West) under Emperor Theodosius (395CE) the Latin Vulgate Bible, meaning *common* (as in common language) was compiled and became the only official form. It is Jerome who did the translation for the Vulgate, with the Hebrew and the Koine Greek scriptures available to him.[b] The Koine Greek was disallowed in the Western Church after this but continued in the Eastern Church (Orthodox Church).

Thus the Vulgate became the Latin Church's Authorised Bible right through the centuries until people like Wycliffe began to dissent and believe that the Scriptures should be written in the *common* language of individual countries, in his case English. Wycliffe's bible 1382-1395CE was banned and by 1415 (Council of Constance) Wycliffe was declared a heretic and his bibles to be burnt. Those found with them were held under penalty of death. However many of these bibles and others still circulated. With the advent of the Printing Press (1440CE) Tyndale's Bible 1522 and Coverdale's Bible 1535 came into circulation and the time was now set for the Latin Church to allow English Translations. Finally in 1611 under King James 1st an authorised (by the church) copy of the Bible was produced in English, **The King James Version**. King James version remained largely the only bible within the Western Latin Church until the late 1800's when the spread of available versions began in earnest.

---

[a] Also known as Tanakh in Judaism where it is divided into the Torah (Pentateuch); Nevi'im (Prophets); Ketuvim (Scriptures).

[b] Although it might be said he had a free hand to fit the contemporary Latin Church's understanding of Christian Belief and Dogma into his translation

Bible Readership

There are presently over a hundred different English versions in circulation.[a] Commonly though, most read bibles are the KJV; International Version; Standard Version and American Bible. Many Christians today still have difficulty in really finding the time to study the larger picture of the Old Testament The bible really is the most widely bought (almost 4 billion copies in the last 50 years) but least read with less than half of its readership picking up the bible outside of the Sunday service. Hardly the life changing love affair with the Creator of the Universe in which you'd expect to see the Christian mind continually deep in meditation. In any case you may have heard it said that Jesus is the fulfilment of the Law (Torah[b]) but this has led to a whole host of favourite commonly read passages from the OT to prove the fact but the knowledge within the OT really runs so much deeper than that and is far more challenging.

Follow the Thread

Most of us look at the OT largely as a collection of writings gathered together over disparate time and place, Scripture handed to us by G-d; individual accounts of people's interaction with G-d; divine revelation; wise sayings and poems of praise .. this is not so, what is not understood is that the Bible is highly structured, both in its layout of books to the internal structure within the individual books.

If you had said to me not so long ago that there was this organisation with the OT then I would not have been in much agreement with you however with a concerted study a clearer picture emerges.

On one simple level we have the Exile of the first people Adam and Eve from an idyllic existence in Eden with G-d to the Exile of G-d's chosen people to Babylon and their continuing Exile (from G-d) on their return to the Promised Land (as described in Ezra-Nehemiah and the final three (prophetic) books of the OT, namely Haggai, Zechariah, Malachi).

G-d's plan for the restoration of Humans begins in earnest with Abraham (Noah's great grandchild) in Genesis. A great nation (although the nature of this greatness, other than number, is not specified) is to come from his seed and they will live in a plentiful Land to be shown to him. That nation does come to be eventually with Jacob (later renamed Israel) and his twelve sons. With that scene set the Israelites move to Egypt during a drought where they remain several hundred years until their oppression begins by pharaoh (largely because their numbers were significantly increasing). Now in the next book of Exodus, Moses is commissioned to save the Israelites, remove them from this oppression and return them to the Land of Israel (the Promised Land of Abraham). Moses does indeed lead the Israelites out of Egypt. Their first port of call is to be Mount Sinai where G-d is to make a

---

[a] This reflects equally the fracture of the once Catholic Christianity into as many Denomination churches. The word Catholic comes from the Greek phrase καθόλου (katholou) 'whole' or 'in general.' It is a combination of the Greek words κατά (according to) and ὅλος (holos) the whole

[b] Torah. Teaching. The Torah has at its core the 5 books of Moses (*Pentateuch* meaning five scrolls/books) but it can also refer to the entire book (Tanakh) which itself is divided into the Torah (Pentateuch); Nevi'im (Prophets); Ketuvim (Scriptures)

covenant with them. The people however don't really understand the magnitude of the events befalling them and they begin making their complaints against G-d and Moses for bringing them away from their previous lives. Moses continues on with them anyway and they arrive at Mount Sinai where G-d's Presence is.

G-d begins to speak to Moses, the people are to become a nation of priests, who will bring the knowledge of who G-d is to all the peoples and nations of the Earth. G-d will give them His Law by which they are to live their lives. In return G-d will care for and protect the people from every possible malady. The people agree and Moses receives the Law (Torah) for them. Moses returns from receiving the Ten Commandments (a summary of the Law) only to find that the people have already broken the covenant and engaged in idol worship. Although Moses does resolve that problem, it does set a president for the future of the Israelites as they continually rebel against the covenant.

G-d also agrees to come and have His Presence somewhat physically with the people as they journey on to the next stage: the entry into the Promised Land. For G-d to do this there are a number of purity Laws revealed so that the presence of a Holy G-d can exist amongst the mundane people. These Laws are revealed in the book of Leviticus including the building of a Tabernacle, and the Ark of the Covenant where the presence of G-d resides.

The book of Numbers describes the extended journey that the Israelites have in the wilderness. Moses does lead them to the borders of the Promised Land soon after the departure from Sinai but the people again mess up by refusing to enter due to the fact that there are other nations inhabiting the land when they get there and do not trust that G-d will make them succeed. The entire generation of the people are then condemned to die in the wilderness; it will be their children who enter the Land. So begins the forty year wilderness journey, all the while with the presence of G-d at the head of them and their camp.

Ultimately they do die off one by one and Moses, now an old man, brings this new generation again to the location where they will enter the Land. He is to entrust his aid, Joshua, as the next leader of the people. Moses will not enter the Land because of his own errors, but before he dies he delivers the book of Deuteronomy to the People. This book gives much advice and encouragement to them and adds a few more Laws to the existing ones as they prepare to enter the Land. Joshua (the Book of Joshua) then leads the people into the Promised Land and they begin the process of taking it from the nations living there. He sets up the Tabernacle at Shiloh and places the Ark of the Covenant there. The Israelites never do complete the task of clearing out the Land and there continues to be a corruption of the Israelites by the culture of those people. Joshua dies of old age there. Then follows the book of Judges. These Judges are the leaders of the people for the next several hundred years. The book describes the gradual descent of the people into utter corruption to a point where they are no different from the peoples they are meant to replace. The books of Samuel continue from there. The books of Samuel explain the way in which the monarchy came about. Clearly after the Judges the nation of Israel was going nowhere; there was a need for good leadership. Samuel the last Judge (also a priest at Shiloh) is asked by the Israelites to appoint a king for them. Both G-d and Samuel are dismayed by this as (YHWH) G-d has always been their king. The people insist and Saul (of Benjamin) is made king. Saul himself soon descends into madness

and David (of Judah) then becomes king. The Israelites of the tribal homeland of Saul are disgruntled by David usurping the anointed king Saul. David though has G-d's blessing to now rule. He brings peace and unity back to the Israelites and their nation begins to prosper. David captures Jerusalem from the Jebusite people and makes it his capital. He also brings the Ark of the Covenant there to a specially constructed Tabernacle. Next the 1st Book of Kings describes David's death and the coronation of his son Solomon. Solomon builds the Temple and the Presence of YHWH enters into it. Solomon is famed for his wisdom but is less well known for the heavy tax burden he placed on the people for all his building projects. He also falls into apostasy in his later life for which G-d is angered and brings enemies against him. One such enemy is Solomon's own servant Jeroboam who stirs dissent amongst the northern tribes of previous Saul supporters and those being over taxed. Solomon's son Rehoboam becomes king in Jerusalem and decides to increase the taxes. This leads to an uprising of the Northern tribes who then break away and form their own kingdom (Northern Kingdom) with Jeroboam as their king. Jeroboam sets up his own centres of idol worship and his own priesthood. The rest of the 1st Book of Kings, describes each of the kings who rule both the kingdom of Judah and the Northern kingdom.
At the end of this book the events of king Ahab of the Northern kingdom are described. Ahab's father, king Omri, has set up the capital as Samaria. It is to Ahab that Elijah (the first of a series of prophets) is sent. 2nd Kings continues with the accounts of the kings who reigned the two kingdoms, some good, many bad. 2nd Kings chapter 17 describes the ultimate downfall of the Northern kingdom as the Assyrian army invades and takes all the inhabitants away into exile. The Assyrian army also invade Judah but are unable to capture Jerusalem, then ruled by king Hezekiah and advised by Isaiah. Several further kings rule the remaining land of Judah from Jerusalem, some good and others very bad for which divine protection of the city is lost. The new empire *of the nations*, the Babylonians, invade Judah and lay siege to Jerusalem. The prophet Jeremiah advises the then kings to give in to them, but they don't listen to him. This ultimately results in the Babylonians capturing Jerusalem and taking away its inhabitants into exile. The city and the Temple are then burnt down and completely destroyed. Daniel and Ezekiel are two of the many exiles sent to Babylon. Daniel serving the king of Babylon and Ezekiel a former priest, receiving his visions as explained in the Book of Ezekiel.
The books of Chronicles, as a recap (also briefly detailing the later events of the Exiles), covers many of the same points and history as the Books of Kings, however the main themes in focus will be the arrival of the Messianic King, the rebuilding of the Priesthood/Temple and the message of hope for the future. Chronicles begins by listing a Genealogy of all the important characters of the Old Testament with the emphasis on two key areas, first the lineage of the messianic king from Adam to David and then David up to the time of the return of the Exiles. Second the family line of the descendants of Aaron and the priesthood. So with these genealogies we await the Messianic king who will come to rule Israel, rebuild the Temple and restore the priesthood. The final words of Chronicles inform us that Cyrus the Persian king has overthrown the Babylonian empire and has decreed that the Exiles are to be set free. The books of Ezra and Nehemiah pick up the story from there with the exiles returning back, or a portion of the entire Exiled people. There seems to be high hopes

amongst them that they were going to rebuild themselves, as they had been, with Jerusalem, the temple / priesthood and a king. They do manage most of that although they are unable to establish a king. The Persian authorities would not allow that and in any case the Exiles had been returned according to the decree of Cyrus for rebuilding of the Temple for YHWH. A great opportunity in fact for them to be that kingdom of priests and a holy nation (Exo19. 6). Unfortunately, the returning people still continue to disregard G-d's Law and although they are sent more prophets to advise them they are unable to maintain the level of integrity required for G-d's promises to come to fruition.
For our English versions there is no further information as to what happens in Judea from this point on till we come to the New Testament. Catholic and Orthodox bibles do include the two books of Maccabees. These accounts are of 2nd century BC events covering the Hasmonean dynasty in Judah, who did free themselves briefly from outside rule. The last of their dynasty was ended by Herod the Great when he came to power in 37 BC.
There are of course within the bible some other groups of scriptures namely the Wisdom Books and the Books of the Prophets. Wisdom Books Job, Psalms, Proverbs, Ecclesiastes and Song of Songs, which offer timeless advice on the Human condition. The books of Psalms (associated with David) and Proverbs, Song of Songs (associated with Solomon). There are also the Book of Ruth (David's great grandmother) and the Book of Ester (an Exile who became queen), both books about G-d's background intervention in Human affairs. Also the Book of Lamentations, the sorrowful aftermath following the destruction of Jerusalem.
The last books of the OT are the Books of the Prophets. They are generally understood as the three *major* [a] prophets and twelve *minor* prophets (The Book of the Twelve). These prophets were commissioned directly by G-d to various kings of Israel / Judah throughout the time of the Monarchy up until the later Returned Exiles, to advise them of the error of their ways and the consequences of disregarding G-d's wishes. Quite often the prophets were disregarded and even when they were listened to, momentum was never carried on for long.
So the Old testament ends with the last prophet (Malachi) giving hope for the future to the Exiles who have returned to Israel. I say Exiles here as even though they are now back in the Land,[b] their Exile still continues, in another way, as they continue to rebel against G-d.
The first created people, Adam and Eve, had been exiled from the Land (Eden) and G-d's Presence. Now, at the end of the OT, G-d's chosen people remain in the Land but are still exiled from Him.

---

[a] English versions have four as Daniel is included there
[b] The Land also often affected by drought. A consequence of rebellion indicated by Moses (Lev 26 / Deut. 28)

Contents

Genesis

Meaning *Beginnings.* The book begins by detailing the creation of the Cosmos, and ultimately, Human Beings. The book then goes on to describe the first people all the way through to the establishment of G-d's chosen people[a] and their translocation into Egypt.

Ch 1 & 2

Having created the world G-d then creates Human beings. These Humans are described thus

And God created man [b] *in his own image,*[c]
in the image of God created he him;
male and female created he them. (v27)

G-d then establishes them as Vicegerents of the Earth and places them in a garden (Eden) where they are commanded not to eat from a certain tree described rather enigmatically as *of the knowledge of good and evil.*[d]

Ch 3

They are tricked by another of G-d's animal creations, the serpent, into disobeying that command. This changes their self-awareness perception. When G-d's presence returns they are now scared of Him and hide. Their new found awareness disallows them to remain in the paradise made for them and they are expelled.

---

[a] One family chosen to bring about His restoration amongst Humans

[b] אָדָם ['āḏām] Gen 2.7 reads *God formed man of the dust of the ground*, the 'ground' אֲדָמָה ['ăḏāmâ] being the basis of the name Adam. The relationship between the name Adam and the ground (or land, earth) is perhaps a little more complex than that. After all were not all the creatures of the Earth made from this same stuff? An interesting viewpoint comes from the Maharal of Prague (in a homily given in 1592 and presented recently in part on the Aish.com site) which stated, that the key word is 'potential' in that any creature within the Earth has upon its coming into being a pretty much clear cut path as to what it will achieve within its lifespan. The ground has the potential to bring forth an incredible variance of plants, trees and suchlike; the 'ăḏāmâ then is *essentially* potential. Man [Adam] has that same potential in his life to bring into fruition many things including ultimately his own perfection. 2) The giving of names in the OT & NT (New Testament) invariably indicates something of the fundamental characteristics of the one named

[c] A spiritual/intellectual/cognitive image

[d] My understanding here is that the 'good & evil' are temporal terms, that is to say the 'good' (in line with Plato's 'Form of the Good') is that which is or is of the eternal whilst the 'evil' is simply that which is transient 2) Plato's Form of the Good : a perfect , eternal, changeless Form outside of space-time. 'Evil' then being described in opposite terms 3) There is another 'Tree' called the Tree-of-Life. It's description in singular terms, that is to say the creative process thus far has a series of pairs (day and night; waters below and above- Heaven and Earth; land and sea; lights of day and night) The Tree of Life without it's apparent counterpart.. *of death* (and thereby related to the tree-of-Knowledge-of-Good-and-Evil as it can bring about death) 4) The tree of Life being of G-ds domain.. of the eternal

Ch 4
Adam and Eve have their first child called Cain[a] followed by another Abel.[b] Cain murders Abel in a jealous rage. Cain is further expelled from the land and is to be a wanderer on the Earth. Adam and Eve get a another, replacement child, Seth.[c]

Ch 5
Documents the genealogy from Adam to Noah.

Ch 6
Noah has three sons Shem, Ham, and Japheth. Noah is noted as being..

> *a righteous man, and perfect in his generations: Noah walked with God.* (v9)

The people of the Earth have become very corrupt. G-d Instructs Noah to build the Ark. His family, and a single pair of all animals, are to be saved only. Noah will be a new Adam along with his family line to rule as vicegerent.

Ch 7
G-d makes it rain until a great flood covers the Earth leaving only Noah, his family and the animals in the ark alive.

Ch 8
The waters recede and Noah and all disembark into the renewed Earth.

Ch 9
G-d makes a covenant with Noah and promises never to destroy *all flesh* by flood again. The rainbow is made the visible sign of that covenant.

Ch 10
Documents the families and nations that spring from Noah's three sons.

Ch 11
The story of The Tower of Babel followed by the genealogy of Shem to Abram.
Verse 27 begins the introduction to Abram. Terah (the father of Abram) moves out of *Ur of the Chaldeans*[d] to go to Canaan, but along the way they arrive in Haran and decide to stay there.

---

[a] Meaning a possession or acquired
[b] Meaning transitory
[c] Meaning replacement
[d] Who will also be known as the Babylonians

Ch 12

Abram is then told by YHWH to leave Haran and is given *the promise…*

Now YHWH said unto Abram, Get thee out of thy country,
and from thy kindred, and from thy father's house,
unto the land that I will show thee: and I will make of thee a great nation,
and I will bless thee, and make thy name great; and be thou a blessing:
and I will bless them that bless thee, and him that curse thee will I curse:
and in thee shall all the families of the earth be blessed (v1-3)

Abram leaves Haran with his wife Sarai and their nephew Lot and enter into Canaan. They come to Shechem. YHWH again appears to Abram and promises the land where he now is to him. Abram travels through the land (places of what will become northern Judea are mentioned) though it is inhabited by the Canaanites. A drought arrives in the land, Abram leaves and travels to Egypt to stay there. Abram prospers there (though unavoidably separated from his wife) but ultimately he is asked to leave and he returns to Canaan.

Ch 13

Abram having left Egypt returns to the areas he had been before. Lot separates from Abram and takes the land to the east on the plains of the Jordan. Abram is promised again…

for all the land which thou see, to thee will I give it, and to thy seed for ever.
And I will make thy seed as the dust of the earth:
so that if a man can number the dust of the earth,
then may thy seed also be numbered (v15-16)

Ch 14

Kings of the eastern regions (Mesopotamia) are at war and Lot is taken captive. Abram comes and rescues him, defeating and plundering their armies. One of the Canaanite kings later comes to Abram..

And Melchizedek[a] *king of Salem*[b] *brought forth bread and wine:*
and he was priest of God Most High. And he blessed him,
and said, Blessed be Abram by God Most High, possessor of heaven and earth:
and blessed be God Most High, who has delivered thine enemies into thy hand.
(v18-20)

Abram gives a tenth[c] of the booty which he has just captured to Melchizedek. The king of Sodom also offers booty but Abram refuses to take anything of his.

[a] Meaning king of righteousness. An enigmatic figure who is commented on in later books of the Bible.
[b] An ancient name for Jerusalem
[c] A symbolic gesture returned to in the tithing system of Solomon's Temple

Ch 15
Verse 1 continues…

After these things the word of YHWH came unto Abram in a vision,
saying, Fear not, Abram: I am thy shield, and thy exceeding great reward.

Abram asks how this can be as he still has no offspring of his own to receive this reward. YHWH shows Abram the stars of the sky and promises so shall his offspring be in number. YHWH again promises the land to Abram but that the time is not yet as his eventual offspring will leave again for Egypt.

Ch 16
Sarai still has no child so she offers her Egyptian hand maiden Hagar to Abram to bear him a child. Hagar becomes pregnant but this causes Sarai to despise her and treat her badly. Hagar runs away but an angel of YHWH meets with her and tells her to return as her offspring too will be numerous. He is to be called Ishmael.[a] The angel goes on to say..

And he shall be as a wild ass among men;
his hand shall be against every man, and every man's hand against him;
and he shall dwell over against all his brethren. (v12)

Ch 17
YHWH again appears to Abram to make the promise as before. Abram is now to be called Abraham[b] as he will be the father of a multitude of nations. YHWH again says..

And I will give unto thee, and to thy seed after thee,
the land wherein you are a stranger,
all the land of Canaan, for an everlasting possession;
and I will be their God. (v8)

G-d then requests that the covenant between Abraham and Himself be the rite of circumcision Sarai's name is to be changed to Sarah[c] as..

And I will bless her, and moreover I will give thee a son of her: yea, I will bless her,
and she shall be a mother of nations; kings of peoples shall be of her. (v16)

---

[a] Meaning G-d hears. From the verb שמע [shama] to hear, and אל ('el), God.
[b] Of nations rather than of peoples to which he will rule
[c] שר [sar] means chief or ruler. Its feminine form, שרה (sara), denotes a princess, noble lady

Abraham laughs at this news. His laughter is of joy and incredulity that he is now to have a child in his and Sarah's old age. G-d says to Abraham that he is to call him Isaac.[a] Abraham then has his entire household circumcised.

Ch 18

YHWH then appears to Abraham. Abraham sees three men (angels) and he offers them rest and some food. They ask about Sarah and inform Abraham (again) that he is to have a son by Sarah. Sarah overhears the conversation and she also laughs to herself as she is very old by then. YHWH enquires of Abraham why had Sarah laughed as nothing was impossible with YHWH. Sarah denied laughing. In any case she is to have a child within a year. The three then go off to Sodom (within the lands of Lot) as they are intent on destroying it for its wickedness.

Ch 19

The angels come to Sodom. Lots meets them and invites them to his house. In the evening a crowd of Sodomites gather around the house and demand the men be sent out to them apparently wanting to have sex with them. Lot tries to plea with the crowd but the crowd grow hostile and are about to force their way into the house. The angels tell Lot and his family to escape as Sodom is now to be destroyed. Lot and his two daughters go to a small city called Zoar and then leave there to live in a mountain cave. There, unawares, Lot fathers children with his daughters and those children become the Moabites and the Ammonites.

Ch 20

Abraham goes to the southern areas of the land to Gerah. Another king has an interest for Sarah and a story line the same as what happened in Egypt (ch 12) with Pharaoh unravels.

Ch 21

YHWH visits Sarah and she now conceives and gives birth to a boy who is then named Isaac. Sarah says..

God has made me to laugh;
every one that hears will laugh with me. (v6)

Sarah asks Hager to leave and take Ishmael with her in a story similar to what happened earlier (ch16). Hagar wants to abandon her son to death but YHWH advises her that the child will also become a great nation so Hagar looks after the child and finds a wife for him from Egypt.

Ch 22

YHWH tests Abrahams faith. Abraham is told to take Isaac to the land of Moriah[b] where he is to sacrifice the boy on one of the mountains there. Abraham does as YHWH says and goes

---

[a] Meaning laughter

[b] Also 2 Chronicles 3:1

to Moriah. When he arrives he prepares for the sacrifice of Isaac. Just as he lifts the knife to slay him a voice from heaven tells him to stop. A goat is then seen trapped in the thicket nearby and Abraham sacrifices the goat instead. The voice again speaks saying..

because thou have done this thing, and have not withheld thy son, thine only son,
that in blessing I will bless thee,
and in multiplying I will multiply thy seed as the stars of the heavens,
and as the sand which is upon the sea-shore;
and thy seed shall possess the gate of his enemies;
and in thy seed shall all the nations of the earth be blessed;
because thou have obeyed my voice. (v16-18)

Abraham returns and stays in Beer-Sheba[a]

Ch 23
Sarah dies in her old age. Abraham mourns for her and buys a field in which to bury her.

Ch24
Abraham also is aging. He calls his faithful servant[b] and makes him swear that he will ensure that Isaac does not take a wife from among the Canaanites. The servant is to go to Abraham's kindred to search for his wife and bring her back. The servant comes to the family of Nahor, the brother of Abraham. Rebekah is chosen and she agrees to return with the servant of Abraham. She and Isaac are wed.

Ch 25
Abraham dies in his old age[c] and is buried with Sarah. Isaac continues to be blessed. Rebekah conceives with twins who struggle against each other in the womb. Rebekah is advised by YHWH..

Two nations are in thy womb,
And two peoples shall be separated from thy bowels:
And the one people shall be stronger than the other people;
And the elder shall serve the younger. (v23)

The children are born the first (therefore eldest) to be delivered is red all over and hairy he is called Esau. The other follows holding onto the first child's heel and is called Jacob. The children grow; Esau becomes a skilled hunter whilst Jacob is a quiet person remaining in the tents. Esau comes back from hunting one day very hungry and sells his birth-right under oath to Jacob for a bowl of soup.

---

[a] Meaning Well of the Oath
[b] His servant Eliezer of Damascus, as stated in 15.2. His name not mentioned as he is only a 'servant' of Abraham as Abraham is a 'servant' of YHWH.
[c] Abraham died at 175. He bore Isaac at 100

Ch 26

Another famine strikes the land and Isaac travels south to Gerah.[a] YHWH tells Isaac not to go into Egypt but to an area that YHWH will show to him. YHWH continues to promise to Isaac all the promises He gave to Abraham. Isaac fears that the men of that place will want to marry Rebekah so Isaac tells her to say she is Isaac's sister and a storyline very similar to Abraham in Gerah (ch 20) ensues. Isaac is allowed to stay in that area in safety all the same. Isaac prospered greatly there until the king of Gerah asks him to leave.
Isaac returns to Beer-Sheba where YHWH appears to him and reaffirms the promises made earlier. The chapter ends with Esau who is then noted as marrying a Hittite woman which grieves his parents Isaac and Rebekah sorely.

Ch 27

When Isaac was old, *his eyes were dim*. He called for Esau and asked him to go hunt for some food …

and make me savoury food, such as I love, and bring it to me,
that I may eat; that my soul may bless thee before I die (v4)

A point often overlooked here is that Isaac does not seem to understand the severity of the situation he is about to engage with, namely that *the seed of Abraham* will pass through Jacob not Esau.[b] It would seem that Isaac's blindness has a deeper meaning than of normal vision. He like Esau before him is now ready to give the family blessing over for his favourite dish.[c] Fortunately Rebekah overhears the conversation and contrives a plan for Jacob to imitate Esau and get the blessing. Jacob goes to Isaac and receives the blessing. Esau returns but the only blessing left for him as that he is told he will serve his brother (v40).[d] Esau is now in a mind to kill Jacob so Rebekah gets him to flee to Haran and stay there with her brother Laban. Rebekah also speaks to Isaac and compels him to send Jacob to her relatives so that he will get a wife there from among their kin. Isaac says to Jacob…

Ch 28

And God Almighty bless thee,
and make thee fruitful, and multiply thee, that thou may be a company of peoples;
and give thee the blessing of Abraham, to thee, and to thy seed with thee;
that thou may inherit the land of thy sojourning,
which God gave unto Abraham (v3-4)

---

[a] Where Abraham had gone chapter 20

[b] A clear discussion is given in The Book of Jubilees chapter 19 where Abraham has also realised this problem. Abraham is 170 years old at this blessing narrative

[c] Gen 25.31-34, there, a bowl of soup

[d] As indicated earlier by YHWH's words to Rebekah (25.23)

Jacob sets of toward Haran. At sunset he stops for the night *at a certain place*[a] and uses a stone[b] for a pillow…

And he dreamed; and, behold, a ladder set up on the earth,
and the top of it reached to heaven;
and, behold, the angels of God ascending and descending on it.
And, behold, YHWH stood above it, and said,
I am YHWH, the God of Abraham thy father, and the God of Isaac:
the land whereon thou lie, to thee will I give it, and to thy seed;
and thy seed shall be as the dust of the earth,
and thou shall spread abroad to the west, and to the east, and to the north, and to the south:
and in thee and in thy seed shall all the families of the earth be blessed. (v12-14)

YHWH further promises protection for Jacob and his safe return to the land he is now leaving. Jacob awakes afraid when he realises the importance of the place where he is. He says..

this is none other than the house of God, and this is the gate of heaven. (v16)

In the morning Jacob sets up the stone as a pillar and renames the place Beth'El.[c] Jacob vows in return to the promises of YHWH just stated..

YHWH will be my God,
then this stone, which I have set up for a pillar, shall be God's house:
and of all that thou shall give me I will surely give the tenth [d] *unto thee.* (v21-22)

Ch 29

Jacob arrives at the home of Laban. Laban has two daughters Lear (the eldest) and Rachel. Jacob falls in love with Rachel. He agrees to work seven years for Laban in exchange for Rachel's hand in marriage. At the end of the seven years Laban throws a celebration ceremony but in the evening sends Lear in to him.[e] Jacob does not notice until the morning.[f] He still wants to marry Rachel. Laban agrees to the marriage, and also for it to proceed straight after the 'bridal week' with Lear; Jacob is however to work another seven years for Laban. Laban also gives Zilpah as a handmaid to Lear and Bilhah as a handmaid to Rachel. YHWH sees that Lear isn't loved and lets her get pregnant but Rachel remains barren.

---

[a] Possibly where Abram had also stopped 13.3 and built an altar

[b] Of Abram's altar?

[c] House of G-d

[d] As Abram had promised with Melchizedek. A symbolic gesture returned to in the tithing system of Solomon's Temple

[e] Laban probably believes the elder daughter of a family should marry first

[f] Midrashim accounts indicate that the sisters were in fact twins. 2) Jacob can hardly complain after what happened with Esau

Leah's first son is called Reuben;[a] then Simeon;[b] then Levi;[c] then Judah.[d]

Ch 30

Rachel is frustrated by her inability to bear children and so offers Bilhah to Jacob so she will gain a child that way (as Sarai had done with Hagar). Bilhah becomes pregnant and gives birth to Dan[e] and then to Naphtali.[f] When Lear realises that *she* is no longer bearing any more children, she gives *her* handmaid to Jacob and so Zilpah gives birth to Gad[g] then Asher.[h] After this Lear again bears more sons and calls them Issachar[i] and then Zebulun.[j] Rachel eventually has a son and calls him Joseph.[k]

Jacob requests of Laban that he be allowed to return to Canaan. Laban suggests that he stays longer and Jacob agrees in payment of livestock. This allows Jacob to build up a great personal herd.

Ch 31

Laban's sons become envious of Jacob and his wealth; Laban too is now cold toward Jacob. Jacob decides to leave and go back home, but he does so without telling Laban as he feels he will not let him, his family and his property go. Laban comes after him and they meet near the mountain of Gilead. They then come to an agreement about their separation and set up a pillar of stones as a witness to it (named by Jacob Gilead[l] and Mizpah[m])

Ch 32

And so with the events of chapter 28 now in view, Jacob begins his return to the Promised Land.

And Jacob went on his way,[n] and the angels of God [o] met him.
And Jacob said when he saw them, this is God's camp! [p]
and he called the name of that place Mahanaim.[q] (v1-2)

---

[a] Behold a son (for now my husband will love me)
[b] He who hears (YHWH has heard that I am hated)
[c] Joined (now this time will my husband be joined unto me)
[d] G-d be praised (this time will I praise YHWH)
[e] Judge (God has judged me, and has also heard **my** voice)
[f] My wrestling (With mighty wrestlings have I wrestled with my sister, and have prevailed)
[g] Good fortune (Fortunate!)
[h] Happy (Happy am I! for the daughters will call me happy)
[i] Man of hire (for I have surely hired thee)
[j] Glorious dwelling place (now will my husband dwell with me)
[k] He shall add (YHWH add to me another son [in a doubling sense])
[l] Heap of witness. (probably from where the mountain derives its name)
[m] Watchtower (for he said, YHWH watch between me and thee, when we are absent one from another [v49])
[n] לדרכו הלך [hālak̲ derek̲] went on his way. The journey Jacob now makes along the horizontal axis in relation to the ladder of verse 12
[o] אלהים מלאכי [mal'āk̲'ĕlōhîm] Angels of G-d (same as in *the Ladder* verse)
[p] maḥănê H4264
[q] maḥănayim H4266. Plural of 'camp' – camps. 2) This chapter has several dual themes

Jacob now sends messengers to Esau, saying..

Thus shall ye say unto my lord Esau: Thus says thy servant Jacob,
I have sojourned with Laban, and stayed until now:
and I have oxen, and asses, and flocks, and men-servants, and maid-servants:
and I have sent to tell my lord, that I may find favour in thy sight (v4-5)

Jacob left Canaan in fear of Esau. Now he hopes that Esau has forgiven him and assumes a humble position in relation to his brother. The messengers go and return to Jacob only to tell him that Esau is on the way to meet him with *four hundred men.*
Jacob is afraid as he understands this to be an army coming to kill him. Jacob then divides his entire entourage into two camps[a] in the hope that if Esau attacks then half will escape
Jacob then prays to YHWH..

And Jacob said, O God of my father Abraham, and God of my father Isaac, YHWH,
who said unto me, Return unto thy country, and to thy kindred, and I will do thee good:
I am not worthy of the least of all the loving-kindnesses,
and of all the truth, which thou have showed unto thy servant;
for with my staff I passed over this Jordan; and now I am become two companies.[b]
Deliver me, I pray thee, from the hand of my brother, from the hand of Esau:
for I fear him, lest he come and smite me, the mothers and the children.
And thou said, I will surely do thee good,
and make thy seed as the sand of the sea, which cannot be numbered for multitude. (v9-12)

Jacob then makes gifts of livestock to Esau. He sends his servants ahead with large herds of various animals to give to Esau in the hope that this will appease him.

I will appease him with the present that goes before me,
and afterward I will see his face;[c] *perhaps he will accept me* (v20)

That night Jacob takes his wives, handmaids and his children and sends them across the Jabbok[d] ford.

---

[a] שְׁנֵי לְמַחֲנוֹת [š□nayim maḥănê]
[b] Allusion to the two camps of 32.2 [Mahanaim] and the split camp just stated
[c] Jacob also will see the face of G-d (v30)
[d] A tributary of the Jordan flowing from Mount Gilead

And Jacob was left alone; and there wrestled a man [a] *with him until the breaking* [b] *of the day.*
And when he saw that he prevailed not against him, he touched the hollow of his thigh; [c]
and the hollow of Jacob's thigh was strained, as he wrestled with him. [d]
And he said, Let me go, for the day is breaking.
And he said, I will not let thee go, except thou bless me [e]
And he said unto him, What is thy name? [f] *And he said, Jacob.*[g]
And he said, Thy name shall be called no more Jacob, but Israel: [h]
for thou have striven with God and with men, and have prevailed.[i]
And Jacob asked him, and said, Tell me, I pray thee, thy name.
And he said, Why is it that thou ask after my name?
And he blessed him there. And Jacob called the name of the place Peniel:[j]
for, he said, I have seen God face to face, and my life is preserved (v24-30)

Ch 33

Jacob now sees Esau coming with all his men. He now stands at the front[k] of his family and approaches him, bowing seven times as he approached but Esau upon seeing Jacob ran up to meet him and embraced him. Esau meets Jacobs family but says that he doesn't really need all the livestock Jacob has sent ahead. Jacob insists he have them..

And Jacob said, Nay, I pray thee, if now I have found favour in thy sight,
then receive my present at my hand;
forasmuch as I have seen thy face, as one sees the face of God,[l]
and thou are pleased with me.
Take, I pray thee, my blessing[m] *that is brought to thee;*
because God has dealt graciously with me, and because I have enough.
And he urged him, and he took it. (v10-11)

---

[a] In the context of this chapter Jacob's struggle is with Esau, but G-d is also involved in the dual nature of this 'man'

[b] There is an even contest having to end because of the coming of day break (give birth)

[c] The Thigh [yārēḵ] being associated with taking vows (Gen 24.2 &.9; 47.29)

[d] The struggle in the womb. *And the children struggled together within her* (25.22)

[e] Jacob has received his blessing from Isaac by deception. Now this is to be rectified

[f] Harking back to Isaac's question to Jacob impersonating Esau

[g] To receive the blessing honestly

[h] Struggle with/for G-d; upright with G-d; one who strives with G-d 2) identifying the 'man' Jacob wrestled with 3) The new name incorporating El, and deleting the former association with deception (Esau's complaint of deception. 27.36)

[i] LXX has *..but Israel shall be your name; for you grew in strength against G-d and against mighty men.*

[j] Facing / face of G-d

[k] Jacob has been noted as remaining behind or at the back until now

[l] As noted above

[m] b▯rāḵâ Baraka H1293. Jacob now gives a blessing to Esau

Jacob suggests that Esau return without him as his entourage will slow Esau down. Esau agrees and returns to Sier, his home area within Edom.[a] Jacob stays a while in a place he calls Succoth.[b] He then travels to the city Shechem in Canaan where he buys a piece of land and camps there. He also builds an altar and names it El-Elohe-Israel (G-d the G-d of Israel).

Ch 34

Leah has a daughter called Dinah. One of the leader's sons in Canaan, called Shechem, sleeps with Dinah without marriage. Jacob finds out but doesn't tell his sons. As Shechem genuinely wishes to wed Dinah Jacob says he can allow it if the males of the city all get circumcised, to which they agree and do so. However Simeon and Levi hear what happened to Dinah but not about the agreement. They come to the city and slay all the men and plunder all the goods. Jacob reprimands them for making him an enemy amongst the Canaanites whom he now says will gather against him to kill him. Jacob's sons remain unrepentant.

A disastrous episode, one where the Israelites first hopelessly fail in a chance to bring their G-d YHWH to (in this case) the Canaanite people. An opportunity opened to them that will unfortunately be wasted many times in their yet to unfold destiny.

Ch 35

Jacob is told by G-d to move the camp back to Beth'El, where he first went after escaping Esau. His sons appear to have a number of *foreign gods* in their possession. Jacob confiscates them and buries them near Shechem. They travel on to Beth'El unmolested by the Canaanites as they were fearful of Jacob. Jacob builds an altar there and calls it El-Beth-El (The G-d of Beth'El) (v7).

Verse 9 returns to the events of Jacob when he returned from Laban..

And God appeared unto Jacob again, when he came from Paddan-aram, and blessed him.
And God said unto him, Thy name is Jacob: thy name shall not be called any more Jacob,
but Israel shall be thy name: and he called his name Israel.
And God said unto him, I am G-d Almighty: be fruitful and multiply;
a nation and a company of nations shall be of thee, and kings shall come out of thy loins;
and the land which I gave unto Abraham and Isaac, to thee I will give it,
and to thy seed after thee will I give the land. (v9-12)

Jacob sets up a pillar where G-d spoke to him and called the place Beth-El. They travel from there to a place called Ephrath[c] where Rachel who is about to give birth dies whilst delivering the child. Jacob calls him Benjamin,[d] the twelfth son.

Jacob, now being also called Israel, moves to a place called the Tower of Eder, where Reuben sleeps with Bilhah, his father's concubine and Israel (Jacob) hears of it.

---

[a] To the Southeast of the Promised Land

[b] Meaning booths (makeshift shelters)

[c] The root word meaning (doubly) fruitful, probably Beth-lehem

[d] Meaning Son of the right hand

Ch 36
Genealogy of Esau

Ch37
The story of Joseph.

Now Israel loved Joseph more than all his children, because he was the son of his old age: and he made him a coat of many colours. (v3)

All of which caused the others to be hateful of him. Joseph has a dream in which his brothers bow down to him; then another dream in which they and his parents bow to him. Even Israel is surprised by this.
Joseph is at home one day with Israel. The other sons are out with the flocks. Joseph is sent by his father to see how they are faring. When they see him coming they decide to throw him into a pit from where he can't escape. Just then a caravan bound for Egypt passes nearby and Joseph is taken out of the pit and sold as a slave. The brothers return with Joseph's coat smeared in goat blood and tell Israel Joseph is probably dead. Israel is heartbroken and mourns continually for Joseph from that day on. Joseph is sold in Egypt to Potiphar, Pharaoh's captain of the guard.

Ch 38
This chapter digresses into a story in the life of Judah. He has three sons to a Canaanite woman. He eventually has the eldest son marry a certain woman Tamar. This eldest son dies so Judah gives his second son to be her husband; the second son also dies. Judah then promises he will give his third son to her, but doesn't. Tamar tricks Judah into sleeping with her by hiding her identity and pretending to be a harlot. She becomes pregnant. Judah then hears that she has engaged in harlotry and is pregnant. He decides she is to die for that. He finds out what actually happened and is ashamed of himself.

Ch 39
Returning to the story of Joseph. YHWH was with Joseph and he soon became overseer of Potiphar's household. Potiphar's wife wants Joseph to sleep with her to which he refuses. One day when they are alone she tries again but when Joseph refuses she cries for help and claims he had tried to sleep with her. Potiphar has Joseph thrown in prison. Joseph still had YHWH caring for him and soon he was put in charge by the keeper of the prison.

Ch 40
Pharaoh had his chief butler and his chief baker put in prison and Joseph is looking after them. One night they each have a dream. They don't know what the dreams mean. Joseph asks the butler to tell his dream. Joseph interprets and says he will in three days be forgiven and return to Pharaoh's household. The baker then tells his dream but the interpretation of his dream is that he will be executed, also in three days. These interpretations come true. The butler however forgets all about Joseph.

Ch 41

Two years later and now Pharaoh has dreams of seven fat cows that were eaten by seven thin cows then another dream seven healthy ears of grain grow but they also are swallowed up by seven weak ones. Pharaoh calls for all the wise men and magicians to interpret his dream but they cannot. Then the chief butler remembers Joseph and tells his story to Pharaoh concerning the young Hebrew servant Joseph in the prison. Pharaoh calls for Joseph to be brought out of the Dungeon to him. After a quick clean up Joseph is brought in and Pharaoh tells him the dreams. Joseph interprets the dreams as seven years of plenty followed by seven years of dire famine. Joseph advises Pharaoh to employ an overseer to collect a fifth of all the produce in the good years to be used in the famine years. Joseph gets the job. Joseph is renamed Zaphenath-paneah.[a] Joseph goes out into Egypt to organise everything. During the plentiful years Joseph marries Asenath and has two sons first Manasseh[b] and then Ephraim[c] Then the years of famine begin and Joseph opens the food stores to the Egyptians. The famine extends *over all the face of the earth* and soon people from all the countries roundabout come to Joseph in Egypt to buy food.

Ch 42

Jacob hears that there is grain in Egypt so he tells his sons to go there and buy some *that we may live.*[d] All but Benjamin are sent. They arrive and bow down before the governor of the land (Joseph). They don't recognise Joseph but he recognises them. Joseph accuses them of being spies and questions them. When he finds that there is a younger brother he demands they bring the lad to Joseph as proof that they are not spies. Simeon is imprisoned whilst the others are sold some grain and return to Canaan. When they arrive they tell Jacob what has happened. They are further alarmed to find their grain-money has been placed into their grain sacks. Jacob is unwilling to let Benjamin go as he would be unable to bear the grief if harm came to him.

Ch 43

Soon the food that they brought from Egypt is finished and another trip is needed. Jacob is persuaded to let Benjamin go to Egypt and they set off. They arrive and Joseph puts on a dinner for them all.

---

[a] Various translations. Josephus has Revealer of Secrets but there is also Saviour Of The Age (Jerome) or The God Speaks And He Lives; and also Head of the Sacred College (of Magicians). Although verse 41,43 and 44 and chapter 42.6 refer to Joseph as *governor of all the land* (sounds like Satrap Pana) The interpretation of Joseph's name will depend on the emphasis: was it that Joseph was able to interpret the dream or is it that he will manage the famine successfully. Worth noting is that several biblical figures have had foreign names given to them (Bel-shazzar, Shadr-Ach(u), Mesh-Ach(u), Abed-Nebu and Zerubbabel. All of which have rather straight forward meanings to their foreign names. Although Pharaoh may have emphasised that Joseph was able to interpret where no other wise man in Egypt could, the text does show greater emphasis on Joseph's Rulership role

[b] To forget. [God has made me forget all my toil, and all my father's house]

[c] Fruitful [For God has made me fruitful in the land of my affliction]

[d] From verse 1. A connection with Joseph's Egyptian name?

Ch 44

When it is time for them to leave the brothers sacks are filled with food by Joseph's servants. Joseph then instructs his servant to put a sliver cup in Benjamin's sack. Soon after the brothers have left Joseph sends his men after them to accuse them about the cup. The brothers protest their innocence but the cup is found and they are all brought back to Joseph. Joseph says only the guilty one will remain, the rest may return. Judah begs Joseph and tells the story of how it will hurt their father. Judah says he cannot return without the boy.

Ch 45

Joseph can no longer contain himself and he reveals his identity to then saying..

And Joseph said unto his brethren, Come near to me, I pray you.
And they came near. And he said, I am Joseph your brother, whom ye sold into Egypt.
And now be not grieved, nor angry with yourselves, that ye sold me hither:
for God did send me before you to preserve life. (v4-5)

Joseph then tells them to go and bring Jacob to Egypt where the whole family can stay until the end of the famine. Pharaoh is also happy for Joseph and he adds extra gifts for the brothers to take back. The brothers arrive in Canaan and meet with Jacob and they tell him that Joseph is alive and is the *ruler over all the land of Egypt.* (v26).
Jacob does not believe at first but when he sees all the gifts he begins to believe that Joseph is alive and determines to go to see him.

Ch 46

And Israel took his journey with all that he had,
and came to Beer-sheba, and offered sacrifices unto the God of his father Isaac.
And God spoke unto Israel in the visions of the night,
and said, Jacob, Jacob. And he said, Here am I.
And he said, I am God, the God of thy father: fear not to go down into Egypt;
for I will there make of thee a great nation: I will go down with thee into Egypt;
and I will also surely bring thee up again (v1-4)

And so the entire family and all their possessions went down to Egypt. Joseph arranges for them to stay in Goshen a place good for livestock and farming, When they arrive Joseph goes out in his chariot to meet Jacob. The Israelites are to stay there in Goshen as the Egyptians find shepherds detestable.

Ch 47

Joseph brings his father and some of the family to meet Pharaoh and they are given formal permission to stay.
As the famine continues the people of Egypt also run out of money to buy food. Joseph then allows them to sell livestock to Pharaoh for food. When all of the livestock have been sold the people then sell their land also. Only the priests of Pharaoh get to keep their land. Joseph

then arranges for the people to move nearer to the cities where the food is stored. Joseph also arranges that, in future, after the famine is over, the people (who will presumably return to work on their former land) are to continue giving a fifth of the produce to Pharaoh.
The Israelites stay and are *fruitful, and multiplied exceedingly* in Goshen of Egypt. After seventeen years Jacob, apparently bed ridden, calls for Joseph to come and gets an assurance from him that when he dies his body is to be buried in Canaan with his fathers in their burial place.[a]

Ch 48
Jacob is becoming weaker. Joseph brings his two sons Manasseh and Ephraim. Jacob declares that these two will be his own children. Jacob asks for the children to be brought forward that he might bless them. Jacob's personal blessing for Joseph will be given to these two instead. Jacob is almost blind by this time but as Joseph *bows down to the earth* Jacob puts his right hand on the younger's head, Ephraim and his left hand on Manasseh, the first born. Joseph notices this and tries to have Manasseh put under Jacobs right hand but Jacob says no it is correct as Ephraim will be greater than Manasseh *and his seed shall become a multitude of nations.* Jacob tells Joseph that each of them will be given a portion of the land when they return to Canaan.

Ch 49
Jacob then calls his other sons to bless them also. Each is given a blessing according to the meaning of their names, the actions of their lives thus far and the events of their future. Reuben, the first born has his pre-eminence taken away because he slept with Bilhah, Jacob's concubine (Gen.35.22). Simeon and Levi (second and third born) will be scattered because of the revengeful acts they took for Dinah (Gen.34.25-30). Judah, Jacob's fourth son then takes the eminence of the first born.

The sceptre shall not depart from Judah,
Nor the ruler's staff from between his feet, Until Shiloh [b] come;
And unto him shall the obedience of the peoples be (v10)

Jacob gives a blessing to each child and then again requests of them that after his death he be buried in Canaan in the field bought by Abraham when his wife Sarah died.[c] Jacob completes his blessings and dies.

---

[a] The famine ended 10 years ago, yet the Israelites remain in Egypt. Perhaps another opportunity lost to return to Canaan now that they were strong and the peoples of Canaan depleted

[b] A word with many interpretations. Most likely <u>That which is (rightfully) his</u> or <u>Place of rest</u>. Shiloh is where the Israelites with Joshua will set their first camp having entered the Promised Land

[c] Also buried there were Abraham, Isaac, Rebecca and Lear

Ch 50

Joseph gets permission from Pharaoh to leave Egypt to take Jacob's body back. The entire family return including servants and dignitaries of Egypt. They arrive and bury Jacob as he had wished and return to Egypt.

When they return the Brothers are fearful that Joseph will now want revenge against them. They request forgiveness. Joseph reminds them that this was all the work of G-d and that it was for the good. Joseph then assures that they remain happily in the land of Egypt. Joseph grows old in Egypt but before he dies he calls his brethren to him and says…

> *I die; but God will surely visit you, and bring you up out of this land unto the land which he swore to Abraham, to Isaac, and to Jacob.* (v24)

Joseph requests that his bones be carried back when they return. He dies in Egypt and is buried.[a]

Exodus

Meaning *the way out*; From εκ (ek), out of, οδος (hodos), way/road. The Hebrew book is named Shemot (Names) as referring to the names of the Sons of Israel coming to Egypt in the first few verses of the book. The book divides into two parts. Part 1 chapters 1-18, Israel in bondage in Egypt and their rescue. Part 2 chapters 19-40 the Israelites at Mount Sinai.

Ch 1

Israel begin to flourish in Egypt (Exodus 1.7 as a fulfilment of G-d's promise in Genesis 17.1-8). Pharaoh's power is threatened by Israel (G-d's power). The Israelites are severely mistreated. Pharaoh orders that the male children be killed at birth.

Ch 2

A man and a woman from the tribe of Levi have a boy child and keep him hidden for several months but then places the child in a waterproofed basket into the river. The basket floats away and is found by Pharaoh's daughter. She realises it is one of the Hebrew children but has compassion on him. The child's sister witnesses this and goes to Pharaoh's daughter and asks if the child's mother may come to nurse him for her. Pharaoh's daughter agrees and the child becomes her son. She names him Moses saying *because I drew him out of the water* (v10).

When Moses is fully grown he notices the wrong being done to the Hebrews. One day he sees an Egyptian beating one of the Hebrews and Moses kills the Egyptian. The next day Moses

[a] Thus ends the biblical account of the Patriarchs (Abraham, Isaac, Jacob)

sees two Hebrew people fighting and he admonishes the wrongdoer, but he then says to Moses..

Who made thee a prince and a judge over us?
Are you thinking to kill me, as thou killed the Egyptian? (v28)

Moses realises people know about what he did and he escapes just before Pharaoh hears about it and determines to kill him.
Moses escapes to Midian[a] where he stops by a well. Some shepherdesses come by to water their flock and Moses helps them. They tell their father, the priest of Midian, about it and he invites Moses to stay with him. Moses lives there and is given Zipporah the daughter of the priest as a wife. Gershom[b] is born soon after.

And it came to pass in the course of those many days, that the king of Egypt died:
and the children of Israel sighed by reason of the bondage, and they cried,
and their cry came up unto God by reason of the bondage. And God heard their groaning,
and God remembered his covenant with Abraham, with Isaac, and with Jacob.
And God saw the children of Israel, and God took knowledge of them. (v23-25)

Ch 3
Moses is tending the flock of his father in law Jethro at the mountain of G-d, Horeb.[c] Moses sees a flame of fire within a bush but the bush was not burning itself, he goes nearer to see..

And when YHWH saw that he turned aside to see,
G-d called unto him out of the midst of the bush,
and said, Moses, Moses. And he said, Here am I.
And he said, Draw not nigh hither: put off thy shoes from off thy feet,[d]
for the place whereon thou stand is holy ground. (v4-5)

G-d introduces himself as the G-d of Abraham, Isaac and Jacob and tells Moses that He has heard the groaning of the Israelites in Egypt and has now come to rescue them. G-d tells Moses that he is to go back into Egypt to Pharaoh and bring the people out.

And Moses said unto God, Who am I, that I should go unto Pharaoh,
and that I should bring forth the children of Israel out of Egypt?
And He said, Certainly I will be with thee;
and this shall be the token unto thee, that I have sent thee:
when thou have brought forth the people out of Egypt,
ye shall serve God upon this mountain. (v11-12)

---

[a] Descendants of Abraham and his wife Keturah
[b] Meaning stranger. I have been a stranger in a foreign land. (v22)
[c] AKA Sinai
[d] Shoes are an unclean thing before G-d

G-d says that Moses should tell the Hebrews that the G-d I AM THAT I AM [a] has sent him to bring them out of Egypt. Moses is then to go to Pharaoh and say..

YHWH the G-d of the Hebrews, has met with us:
and now let us go, we pray thee, three days' journey into the wilderness,
that we may sacrifice to YHWH our God.
And I know that the king of Egypt will not give you leave to go,
no, not by a mighty hand. And I will put forth my hand,
and smite Egypt with all my wonders which I will do in the midst thereof:
and after that he will let you go. (v18-20)

Ch 4

Moses is given a staff which has some of the power of G-d and can work certain miraculous events. G-d says that still Pharaoh will not believe. G-d allows Aaron, Moses, brother to assist him. Moses goes back to his father-in-law and tells him what happened and then returns to Egypt with Aaron. Moses and Aaron speak to the Israelites and are believed by them.

Ch 5

And afterward Moses and Aaron came,
and said unto Pharaoh, Thus says YHWH God of Israel,
Let my people go, that they may hold a feast unto me in the wilderness. (v1)[b]

Pharaoh says he does not know their G-d and refuses to let them go. Further he assumes the Israelites must be idle to make such a request and therefore increases their workload. The Israelites complain to Moses about it and Moses speaks to YHWH asking why he was sent in the first place as the people are now suffering even more and there is no sign of deliverance.

Ch 6

And YHWH said unto Moses, Now shall thou see what I will do to Pharaoh:
for by a strong hand shall he let them go,
and by a strong hand shall he drive them out of his land. (v1)

G-d tells Moses to go to the Israelites to encourage them and tell them they will be saved from this bondage. They will be His people and they will live in the land promised to their forefathers Abraham, to Isaac, and to Jacob. YHWH will be their G-d.
Moses goes to the people but they are dispirited and don't believe. Moses is then told to go back to Pharaoh and request the release of the Israelites. Moses replies that as the people will not listen to him how will Pharaoh. YHWH insists so Moses and Aaron continue.

---

[a] (YHWH) variously translated but fundamentally with the meaning of being; existence.

[b] The letting of the people go is not to freedom but a venture into the wilderness to worship their G-d

Ch 7

Moses and Aaron go to Pharaoh. Aaron casts down his staff and it becomes a snake but Pharaoh's magicians can do the same. Pharaoh is not impressed. Moses is then instructed to go to the riverbank when Pharaoh is there ..

And thou shall say unto him, YHWH, the God of the Hebrews,
has sent me unto thee, saying, Let my people go, that they may serve me in the wilderness:
and, behold, until now thou have not hearkened. (v17)

Moses is to tell Aaron strike the water with his staff and the water will be turned to blood. This Aaron does but again Pharaoh's magicians can replicate the same and Pharaoh walks away unmoved.

Ch 8

Next Moses returns to Pharaoh to request he let YHWH's people go, else a plague of frogs will invade Egypt. Aaron stretches forth his staff and the frogs come. However the magicians can do the same. Pharaoh does however call Moses and Aaron to him and asks them to remove the frogs, for which Pharaoh will then let the people go that they might sacrifice to YHWH. Moses asks YHWH to remove the frogs, but as soon as they are gone Pharaoh changes his mind again.

Next is a plague of lice that covers man and beast. Pharaoh's magicians cannot do this, but Pharaoh continues to ignore Moses and Aaron's request as spoken by YHWH.

The next plague follows.

And YHWH said unto Moses, Rise up early in the morning, and stand before Pharaoh;
lo, he comes forth to the water; and say unto him,
Thus says YHWH, Let my people go, that they may serve me.
Else, if thou will not let my people go, behold, I will send swarms of flies upon thee,
and upon thy servants, and upon thy people, and into thy houses:
and the houses of the Egyptians shall be full of swarms of flies, (v21-22)

Then the swarms of flies come but they do not enter the land of Goshen where the Israelites are. Pharaoh again calls Moses and Aaron and tells them that they can sacrifice to their G-d but they must remain nearby. Moses informs Pharaoh that the sacrifice of the Israelites is an abomination to the Egyptians and they may be stoned for doing so. They must travel three days into the wilderness. Pharaoh agrees but insists they not go very far away. Moses asks YHWH to remove the flies. However as soon as the flies have gone Pharaoh again *hardens his heart* and goes back on his word.

Ch 9

Next YHWH sends a plague upon all the livestock of the Egyptians and they all die. But the livestock of the Israelites are left unharmed. Pharaoh pays no heed.

Then YHWH gets Moses to sprinkle ashes in the air and a great plague of boils affect all the Egyptians, including the magicians. Pharaoh still won't listen.

For now I had put forth my hand, and smitten thee and thy people with pestilence,
and thou had been cut off from the earth:
but in very deed for this cause have I made thee to stand, to show thee my power,
and that my name may be declared throughout all the earth.
As yet exalt thyself against my people, that thou will not let them go? (v15-17)

Another disaster is sent, this time hail stones. Anyone or any animal outside will die from them. The land of Goshen is spared. Again Pharaoh pleads with Moses for the hail to stop saying *I have sinned this time: YHWH is righteous, and I and my people are wicked.* (v27) Moses stops the hail hoping that Pharaoh may know *that the earth is YHWH's* (v29) even though he is doubtful. And true to form Pharaoh again changes his mind.

Ch 10

And Moses and Aaron went in unto Pharaoh, and said unto him,
Thus says YHWH, the God of the Hebrews,
How long will thou refuse to humble thyself before me?
let my people go, that they may serve me (v2)

A swarm of locusts is next if Pharaoh refuses. Pharaoh does agree but only the men have his permission to go. This is no good as all the Israelites and their animals must go. The swarm of locusts arrive and devour everything left in the land after the hail. Pharaoh then says..

Now therefore forgive, I pray thee, my sin only this once,
and entreat YHWH your God, that he may take away from me this death only. (v17)

As soon as the locusts are gone Pharaoh changes his mind. YHWH tells Moses bring about three days of darkness over the land. Pharaoh again calls Moses and Aaron to say they may now go but the animals must remain behind. Moses explains that the animals are needed. Pharaoh tells Moses and Aaron to get out and says next time he sees them they will die.

Ch 11

YHWH has one more disaster. He informs Moses that He will go out through the land of Egypt and the first born male of every Egyptian family will die. YHWH says to Moses…

Pharaoh will not hearken unto you;
that my wonders may be multiplied in the land of Egypt.
And Moses and Aaron did all these wonders before Pharaoh:
and YHWH hardened Pharaoh's heart,
and he did not let the children of Israel go out of his land. (v9-10)

Ch 12

YHWH now tells Moses and Aaron (due to the importance of the events about to unfold) in future this month, Aviv,[a] is to be counted as the first month of the Israeli calendar.

YHWH then explains to Moses and Aaron what the Israelites are now to do.

On the tenth day of the month the Israelites are to procure a lamb, one for each household, then on the fourteenth day they are to slaughter it. Blood from the lambs is to be wiped around their doorposts and then they are to roast and eat the lamb in haste ready to move as YHWH will go through the entire land that night and kill the first born in every house of the land of Egypt but as for the houses that have the blood smeared YHWH will *Pass-over* them.

> *And this day shall be unto you for a memorial, and ye shall keep it a feast to YHWH: throughout your generations ye shall keep it a feast by an ordinance for ever.* (v14)[b]

Verse 15-20 then describe, the ordinance of the Feast of *Unleavened bread.* The feast will continue for seven days from the beginning of the Passover. No yeast (leaven) is to be used during this time. This time will commemorate the hasty escape from Egypt and the events of the first days thereafter.

Midnight comes and the firstborn male of every Egyptian household dies. Pharaoh calls for Moses and Aaron still during the night and tells them to go and take everything as they had requested previously. All the people of Egypt also urge them to go. The Israelites hastily take their half prepared (as yet unleavened) bread dough which they normally made each evening. Each Israeli family also ask their Egyptian neighbours for silver and gold before leaving, which they are given.

YHWH further instructs Moses about the actual Passover meal. It is to be eaten by the Israelites only; all foreigners must be circumcised to take part. The Israelites leave Egypt.

> *And it came to pass the self-same day, that YHWH did bring the children of Israel out of the land of Egypt by their hosts.*[c] (v51)

Ch 13

Moses is given the commandment that the first-born (when male) is to be consecrated[d] to YHWH.

> *Sanctify unto me all the first-born, whatsoever opens the womb among the children of Israel, both of man and of beast: it is mine* (v2)

---

[a] Later renamed Nisan

[b] These are the first major feasts of the Israelites to be initiated, several more will follow in due course.

[c] A mass of persons or things

[d] קָ.דַ.שׁ [qâdash] pronounce to be ceremonially clean; holy, pure, sanctified, set apart, dedicated 2) And G-d blessed the seventh day, and consecrated it (Gen 2.3)

The text then diverts back to describing the Festival of Unleavened Bread again (v3-10) This is to be as a sign and remembrance in future of what YHWH did to the Egyptians when the Israelites finally escaped.
Verse 11 returns to the first-born commandment. This is to begin when they arrive in the Promised Land. Its significance related to what was done to the first born of the Egyptians.

Verse 17 continues with the Israelite escape. Moses collects Joseph's bones and the people are led by G-d, out into the wilderness by the Red Sea. G-d's tangible presence now is leading and protecting the Israelites.

And YHWH went before them by day in a pillar of cloud, to lead them the way,
and by night in a pillar of fire, to give them light; that they might go by day and by night:
the pillar of cloud by day, and the pillar of fire by night,
departed not from before the people. (v21-22)

Ch 14
Pharaoh again changes his mind and prepares his army to go into the wilderness after them. The Egyptian army soon catch up with them. The Israelites are scared.

And they said unto Moses,
Because there were no graves in Egypt have thou taken us away to die in the wilderness?
therefore have thou dealt thus with us, to bring us forth out of Egypt? (v11)

Moses Answers..

Fear ye not, stand still, and see the salvation of YHWH, which he will work for you to-day:
for the Egyptians whom ye have seen to-day, ye shall see them again no more for ever.
YHWH will fight for you, and ye shall hold your peace. (v13-14)

YHWH tells Moses to use his staff and divide the waters of the Red Sea, which he does and the Israelites pass through on dry land. Pharaoh and his army try to pursue but are trapped when the waters of the Sea return destroying them.

Thus YHWH saved Israel that day out of the hand of the Egyptians;
and Israel saw the Egyptians dead upon the sea-shore.
And Israel saw the great work which YHWH did upon the Egyptians,
and the people feared YHWH: and they believed in YHWH,
and in his servant Moses.(v30-31)

Ch 15
The Israelites then sing a song of praise to YHWH (The Song of Moses & Miriam).
Verse 22 continues..

And Moses led Israel onward from the Red Sea, and they went out into the wilderness of Shur; and they went three days in the wilderness, and found no water.

They arrive at some water, but it's too bitter. (the watering place is called Marah.[a] The people complain about it. YHWH shows Moses how to make the water taste sweet.
YHWH then makes another statute and says if the people will listen to His voice and obey His commandments then there will be no disease amongst them as YHWH will heal them. Then in an amazing end to the chapter..

And they came to Elim, where were twelve springs of water,
and threescore and ten palm-trees: and they encamped there by the waters. (v27)

YHWH really is protecting and providing for the Israelites.

Ch 16
The Israelites continue their journey and it's now the 15th day of the 2nd month. The people are again grumbling that they are hungry and wonder why they have been brought out of Egypt just to die. They begin to reminisce on the food they had enjoyed in Egypt.

Then said YHWH unto Moses, Behold, I will rain bread from heaven for you;
and the people shall go out and gather a day's portion every day,
that I may prove them, whether they will walk in my law, or not. (v4)

The Manna[b] from Heaven falls during the evening and the Israelites collect it up and is sufficient food for them. This food will sustain the Israelites throughout their wanderings in the wilderness.

Ch 17
The Israelites continue their journey and come to another place where there is no water. They again complain. Moses tells them that they should not be testing YHWH's patience this way.

Moses cried unto YHWH, saying, What shall I do unto this people?
they are almost ready to stone me. (v4)

YHWH tells Moses to take his staff and strike the rock. Moses does so and water comes out for the people to drink. The place is called by two names, Massah[c] and Meribah[d]

---

[a] Meaning bitter
[b] Meaning - What is it?
[c] Testing
[d] Place of strife. 2) Although unusual to call a place by two names it also serves to distinguish between the Meribah of Numbers 20

Amalek[a] come against Israel to make war on them. Moses asks Joshua[b] to arrange their fighting men and Amalek is beaten. YHWH says Amalek will be as an enemy from generation to generation.

Ch 18

Moses' father-in-law hears of all his successes and comes out to him bringing Moses' wife Zipporah and two sons Gershom and Eliezer.[c] Jethro is very happy for him.
Moses is by then an acting judge, judging all matters big and small between the people. Jethro says this is too much for him and that he should appoint other judges to do this. Moses does this with only the hardest cases being brought before him. Jethro departs and goes to his own land.

Ch 19

The Israelites continue their journey arriving at the Wilderness of Sinai in the 3rd month, presumably on the first day of that month,[d] which would make their journey so far to be 47 days since leaving Egypt. They camp at the foot of Mount Sinai.

And Moses went up unto God, and YHWH called unto him out of the mountain, saying,
Thus shall thou say to the house of Jacob, and tell the children of Israel:
Ye have seen what I did unto the Egyptians,
and how I bare you on eagles' wings, and brought you unto myself.
Now therefore, if ye will obey my voice indeed, and keep my covenant,
then ye shall be mine own possession from among all peoples: for all the earth is mine:
and ye shall be unto me a kingdom of priests, and a holy nation.
These are the words which thou shall speak unto the children of Israel. (v3-6)[e]

Moses meets with the people and tells them what has been said. All the people agree to this and Moses takes back their answer to YHWH. The people are to sanctify themselves for three days[f] then YHWH will appear on the mountain (in a thick cloud). The day comes and Moses takes the people to the mountain to meet G-d.

And mount Sinai, the whole of it,
smoked, because YHWH descended upon it in fire;
and the smoke thereof ascended as the smoke of a furnace,
and the whole mount quaked greatly (v8)

---

[a] Grandson of Esau

[b] Joshua, Moses' aide, now introduced. He will ultimately lead the Israelites into the Promised Land

[c] Eliezer has not been mentioned as yet. The name means *G-d helps.* (Helping Moses to escape Egypt)

[d] The text states **in the third month……on the same day.** Or, on the same day that it became/began the third month

[e] G-d invites the Israelites into a Covenant (a two way relationship) whereby His promise to Abraham (Genesis 17.1-8) may be fulfilled.

[f] Making 50 days in total so far (assuming the interpretation of the Israelites arriving at Sinai on the 1st day of the month) then falling in line with the feast Shavuot, (Pentecost) The giving of the (Torah) Law

Only Moses and Aaron are allowed onto and to climb up the mountain.

Ch 20
Verse 3-17. Moses is given the Ten Commandments..

Thou shall have no other gods before me.
Thou shall not make unto thee a graven image.
Thou shall not take the name of YHWH thy God in vain.
Remember the Sabbath day, to keep it holy.
Honour thy father and thy mother.
Thou shall not kill.
Thou shall not commit adultery.
Thou shall not steal.
Thou shall not bear false witness against thy neighbour.
Thou shall not covet thy neighbour's house.

And all the people perceived the thundering, and the lightning,
and the voice of the trumpet, and the mountain smoking:
and when the people saw it, they trembled, and stood afar off
And they said unto Moses, Speak thou with us, and we will hear;
but let not God speak with us, lest we die.[a]
And Moses said unto the people, Fear not: for God is come to prove you,
and that his fear may be before you, that ye sin not. And the people stood afar off,
and Moses drew near unto the thick darkness where God was. (v18-21)

YHWH then tells Moses to tell the people to make an altar for sacrifices. It is to be made without hewn stones and kept at ground level.

Ch 21 through to Ch 23 verse 19.
YHWH begins to reveal The Law (Torah) to Moses.

Ch 23 verse 20 continues with the taking of the Land..

Behold, I send an angel[b] *before thee, to keep thee by the way,*
and to bring thee into the place which I have prepared.

The people are to listen to the angel and do everything that he says. He will lead them into the Promised Land. The people are warned not to worship the g-ds that they will find there but

---

[a] The people are scared
[b] As has been sent to help on other occasions thus far. (Gen 24:7; 31:11; 48:16); Exodus 14:19)

destroy them and their places of worship. Little by little they are to take the land over and remove the inhabitants as..

They shall not dwell in thy land, lest they make thee sin against me;
for if thou serve their gods, it will surely be a snare unto thee. (v33)

Ch 24

Moses, Aaron, Aaron's two sons and 70 elders are to climb up Mount Sinai. Moses alone is allowed to approach YHWH and he receives more of the Law. He then goes to the people to tell them what YHWH has said. Then..

... all the people answered with one voice, and said,
All the words which YHWH has spoken will we do. (v3)

Moses wrote down all the words of YHWH and builds an altar with twelve pillars. Moses then makes sacrifices on the altar.

And he took the book of the covenant, and read in the audience of the people:
and they said, All that YHWH has spoken we will do, and be obedient. (v7) [a]

Moses then sprinkles some of the blood of the sacrifice on the people to ratify the covenant.

Then went up Moses, and Aaron, Nadab, and Abihu,[b]
and seventy of the elders of Israel: and they saw the God of Israel;[c]
and there was under his feet as it were a paved work of sapphire stone,[d]
and as it were the very heaven for clearness.
And upon the nobles of the children of Israel he laid not his hand:
and they beheld God, and did eat and drink. (v9-11)

Moses is told to come and get the tablets of stone on which YHWH has written the Law and Commandments. A thick cloud covers the mountain for 6 days, then Moses is called to enter it. He enters the cloud and remains there forty days and forty nights.[e]

Ch 25

YHWH speaks to Moses and asks that the Israelites give freely any precious metal or other materials for the building of a sanctuary in which the Presence of YHWH may reside.

---

[a] The people, in a pivotal moment, agree to the terms with Na'aseh v'nishma, [we will do we will hear] (Exo 24.7, do first, understand later) The Israelites, three times, agree to the terms of the covenant. With the third time the agreement is ratified. [Exo 19.8; 24.3, 24.7]

[b] The two eldest sons of Aaron

[c] 'ělōhîm yiśrā'ēl

[d] YHWH shows only His feet?

[e] Chapter 25.1 through to Chapter 31.18

And let them make me a sanctuary, that I may dwell among them.
According to all that I show thee, the pattern of the tabernacle,[a]
and the pattern of all the furniture thereof, even so shall ye make it.(v8-9)

Next the Ark (a chest) is to be made 2.5 by 1.5 x 1.5 cubits (a measurement from the elbow to the end of the fingers). The exact design of the Ark is then described.

And thou shall put into the Ark the Testimony that I shall give thee (v16)

The lid (kapporet) is then described. It is to be of gold and have two cherubim, one at each side facing each other but looking toward the lid, all made from a single piece. Their wings will form a screen veiling it. Here above the lid and between the cherubim is the place where the presence of YHWH will be.

And there I will meet with thee, and I will commune with thee from above the mercy-seat,[b]
from between the two cherubim which are upon the ark of the testimony,
of all things which I will give thee in commandment unto the children of Israel. (v22)

A table is to be made and placed before the Ark,

And thou shall set upon the table showbread before me always.(v30)

A lampstand (Menôwrâh) to be made is then described. It is to have three branches each side forming seven lamp holders altogether.

Ch 26
The design of the Tabernacle itself is then described made from wooden frames overlaid with gold and beautifully woven (with more cherubim) curtains all held together with fixings of gold silver and brass.

Ch 27
An altar to be built is then described. Then the construction of a courtyard surrounding the Tabernacle. The Israelites are to bring olive oil for the Lampstand to Aaron and his sons. They are to tend to it and ensure it will burn continually.

Ch 28
Moses is then called to inaugurate the priesthood. Aaron and his four sons, (Nadab, Abihu, Eleazar and Ithamar) are chosen for that position. All their robes and special garments to be made are then described.

---

[a] Habitation; dwelling place, normally human
[b] Kappôreth; the cover of the Ark as described in Exo 25.17-21

Ch 29

A great ceremony is to be made for the consecration of Aaron and his sons into the priesthood. The altar is then to be sanctified and afterwards continual sacrifices are to be made upon it.

It shall be a continual burnt-offering throughout your generations
at the door of the tent of meeting before YHWH, where I will meet with you,
to speak there unto thee. And there I will meet with the children of Israel;
and the Tent shall be sanctified by my glory. (v42-43)

And I will dwell among the children of Israel, and will be their God.
And they shall know that I am YHWH their God,
that brought them forth out of the land of Egypt, that I might dwell among them:
I am YHWH their God. (v45-46)

Ch 30

Another altar, The Altar of Incense is to be built and placed before the Ark. Aaron is to burn incense upon it each day when he tends the Lamp.

And Aaron shall make atonement [a] *upon the horns of it once in the year;*
with the blood of the sin-offering of atonement
once in the year shall he make atonement for it throughout your generations:
it is most holy unto YHWH (v10)

Each of the Israelites are to give a half Shekel (*a ransom for his soul*) for this day.

And thou shall take the atonement money from the children of Israel,
and shall appoint it for the service of the tent of meeting;
that it may be a memorial for the children of Israel before YHWH,
to make atonement for your souls. (v16)

Moses is to make a Laver between the Tent of the Meeting and the Altar for Aaron and his sons to wash their hands and feet. Moses is then told to sanctify the whole area of the Tabernacle with specific spice incense including Aaron and his sons. Some additional spices are to be placed before the Ark.

Ch 31

YHWH tells Moses that He has appointed a certain man, Bezalel to do all the craftwork within the Tabernacle. YHWH then tells Moses to speak to the Israelites and remind them of the Sabbath.

---

[a] כִּפֵּר [kâphar] to cover over; reconciliation

It is a sign between me and the children of Israel for ever:
for in six days YHWH made heaven and earth,
and on the seventh day he rested, and was refreshed. (v17)

And he gave unto Moses, when he had made an end of communing with him upon mount Sinai, the two tables of the testimony, tablets of stone, written with the finger of God. (v18)

Ch 32
The Israelites meanwhile have noticed that Moses is a long time off on the Mountain; they come to Aaron and say..

Make us gods, which shall go before us;
for as for this Moses, the man that brought us up out of the land of Egypt,
we know not what is become of him. (v1)

Aaron simply gets on with their wish and asks them to bring all of their gold to him.[a] Aaron then has a golden calf [b] idol made. It is then presented to the people..

These are thy gods,[c] *O Israel, which brought thee up out of the land of Egypt.* (v4)

Aaron then builds an altar before it and declares that the next day there shall be a feast to YHWH.[d]

And they rose up early on the morrow, and offered burnt-offerings, and brought peace-offerings; and the people sat down to eat and to drink, and rose up to play.[e] (v6)

YHWH tells Moses to get back to the Israelites and tells him what is happening. YHWH considers destroying the people right there and instead make of Moses a great nation. Moses pleads with YHWH not to do so saying..

Why should the Egyptians speak, saying,
For evil did He bring them forth, to slay them in the mountains,
and to consume them from the face of the earth? (v12)

Moses also asks YHWH to remember the promises made to Abraham, Isaac and Jacob. YHWH repents from his intention and Moses goes down the mountain carrying with him the two tablets of the testimony written by YHWH. When Moses nears the camp and he sees the

---

[a] Bringing to mind the events of chapter 25 where Moses is to ask the people to give gold for the building of the Tabernacle

[b] The Hebrew word is עֵגֶל [ʿēḡel] meaning actually a young bull and not necessarily as young as a calf

[c] Stated in the plural. (as it was in 1 Kings 12 28). See also Psalm 106 19-20

[d] Aaron is apparently giving YHWH an image (of a calf) rather than giving a completely new god for the Israelites to worship. (In contravention to the 2nd commandment (of Ten) (chapter 20))

[e] Qûm ṣāḥaq, rise up to laugh / mock] to play. 2) As opposed to qûm šāḥâ, rise up to worship (Ex 33.10)

dancing and the golden calf, he throws the tablets down on the ground in anger breaking them.
Moses takes the idol burns it, grinds down the remains and mixes them with water. He then makes the people drink of it. Moses quarrels with Aaron for what he has allowed but Aaron says the people were intent on it and he could not stop them. Moses sees that the people have gone out of control. He stands at the gate of the camp and calls out to whoever is on the side of YHWH. To this all the sons of Levi came to him. Moses orders them to go through the camp and kill every person, even family members, who still remain in revelry. Moses says this act will bring a blessing upon them.[a] Moses returns up the mountain to make atonement for the people. Moses says to YHWH..

Yet now, if thou will forgive their sin;
and if not, blot me, I pray thee, out of thy book which thou have written
And YHWH said unto Moses,
Whosoever has sinned against me, him will I blot out of my book.[b] (v33)

Moses is then told to continue to lead the people on. YHWH's angel will continue with them. The chapter ends with the warning that some of the people are yet to be punished for the affair of the calf that Aaron made.

Ch 33
YHWH tells Moses to continue on to the promised Land with His angel leading them but YHWH now says that He will not now dwell amongst them. The people are saddened to hear this.

And YHWH said unto Moses, Say unto the children of Israel, Ye are a stiff-necked people;
if I go up into the midst of thee for one moment, I shall consume thee:[c]
therefore now put off thy ornaments from thee, that I may know what to do unto thee.
And the children of Israel stripped themselves of their ornaments from mount Horeb onward.
(v5-6)

Moses takes the Tabernacle and pitches it outside the camp and calls it *the Tent of the Meeting.*

And it came to pass, when Moses went out unto the Tent, that all the people rose up, and stood, every man at his tent door, and looked after Moses, until he was gone into the Tent. And it came to pass, when Moses entered into the Tent, the pillar of cloud descended, and stood at the door of the Tent: and YHWH spoke with Moses. And all the people saw the

---

[a] This act of allegiance will ultimately overturn the previous command from G-d for the firstborn son of each family (Exodus 13.2) to now become the Levite tribe as a whole dedicated to YHWH 2) Also against the events of Gen 34.25 where Levi (and Simeon) engaged himself in an unnecessary slaughter of the men of Shechem
[b] The book of those who will live; the righteous (Psalm 69.29); Only those guilty of sin can be held accountable
[c] The Presence of a Holy G-d being incompatible with sinful people

pillar of cloud stand at the door of the Tent: and all the people rose up and worshipped, every man at his tent door. And YHWH spoke unto Moses face to face, as a man speaks unto his friend. And he turned again into the camp: but his minister Joshua, the son of Nun, a young man, departed not out of the Tent. (v8-11)

Moses requests that YHWH's presence does continue with the Israelites and he also requests to know YHWH more, he wants to see YHWH with his own eyes to prove that YHWH shows special favour to Moses and the Israelites only of all the nations. YHWH tells Moses that no one can see Him and live.[a] YHWH does agree to pass by Moses whilst shielding him from seeing Him face to face.

Ch 34
YHWH commands Moses to bring two more tablets onto which YHWH will write again as He had the first ones. Moses returns up the mountain and YHWH descends upon it in thick cloud. Moses again requests that YHWH dwell amongst the people and to take them for His inheritance. YHWH agrees and further states that He will do great wonders amongst them. He will drive out the people who inhabit the Land as long as the Israelites make no agreements with them and also destroy their places of worship.
YHWH begins to write the Testimony again but asks Moses to write it down this time. Moses is again on the mountain for forty days. When Moses returns his face is shining because he has been speaking with YHWH. When Aaron and the people see this they are scared to come near to him. Moses calls to Aaron and the leaders of the congregation of Israel to come to him and they do. Later the people also return to him and Moses then gives them the commandments received from YHWH on Mount Sinai, after which he put a veil over his face, only removing it to talk to YWHW or the people.

Ch 35-39
Moses now calls the people to enact the commands he received earlier (chapter 25-31) as to the building of the Tabernacle under the leadership of the craftsman Bezalel (ch 31) A lot of the design imagery is of the Garden of Eden and is to remind those entering the Tabernacle that they are in G-d's Presence.[b]

And Moses examined all the work, and behold, they had done it;
as YHWH had commanded, this they had done: and Moses blessed them. (ch 39.43)

Ch 40
Now that all the work was done Moses is commanded to set it all into action. At YHWH's command, on the first day of the first month of the second year the Tabernacle begins to function.

---

[a] On Sinai, he and the 70 did apparently see G-d's feet (ch 24.9-11)
[b] As Adam and Eve had been in G-d's presence in Eden

Then the cloud covered the tent of meeting, and the glory of YHWH filled the tabernacle.
And Moses was not able to enter into the tent of meeting, because the cloud abode thereon,
and the glory of YHWH filled the tabernacle.
And when the cloud was taken up from over the tabernacle,
the children of Israel went onward, throughout all their journeys:
but if the cloud was not taken up, then they journeyed not till the day that it was taken up.
For the cloud of YHWH was upon the tabernacle by day, and there was fire therein by night,
in the sight of all the house of Israel, throughout all their journeys. (v34-38)

Upon its completion the Presence of G-d descends into the Tabernacle. The Presence then directs the movement of the Israelites as they travel on in their journey. There ends the Book of Exodus but leaves us with the odd situation of Moses no longer being able to enter G-d's Presence. It would seem, that now G-d's Presence has a dwelling place at ground level, there is further need to establish the rules for how a somewhat stubborn and rebellious people can live with that Presence amongst them.

Leviticus

The name Leviticus comes from the priestly tribe of Levi in that much of the book relates to the priests of the Israelites. The Hebrew name for the book is *Vayikra* meaning *and He is calling* (G-d to Moses) G-d from within the Tent and Moses outside.
The book has a highly structured layout although there is little consensus on that structure.[a] Most would agree the book centres on The Day of Atonement (chapter 16) with all other chapters defining how the Israelites will be able to live in G-d's Presence, avoiding the mistakes of the Nations (Gentiles) and safeguard the Presence of G-d amongst them.
The book now deals with the issue of reconciliation.[b] How do you reconcile a sinful selfish corrupt people to a holy G-d and provide for them to live in His holy presence. G-d is holy and requires a holy space around Himself (the Tabernacle) The people need to also become holy if they are to come into contact with G-d, into the Presence of G-d. The book of Leviticus deals fully with this issue.

Chapters 1-7 Laws on Sacrifice. Saying sorry and giving thanks. The blood of Animals paying for people's sin.[c] These sacrifices remind people not only of G-d's Mercy but also G-d's Justice, that is to say sin does have consequences to which some form of punishment always ensues.
Chapters 8-10. The Priesthood (as mediators). Aaron and his sons. The need to be Holy and the dangers of non-conformation to the rules when working alongside G-d's Presence (as Aaron's sons Nadab and Abihu found in ch10. v1-2)

---

[a] Liethart Kline 2015; Elliot Hartley 1992;Wenham 1979; Hill 2000; Sklar 2014; Walton 2001; Milgrum 2004; Douglas 1995. All books have differing understanding of the structure
[b] Atonement
[c] Sin. Meaning missing the (expected) mark. Falling short of the target

Chapters 11-15. Ritual purity. Sources and the cleansing thereof of unclean[a] states. Chapter 16 G-d's gift of Atonement. The Day of Atonement[b] (a general cleansing of the Israelites impurity / sin and its effect on the Tabernacle). This ceremony involves two goats one was for YHWH as a purification offering to atone for the sins of the people, sacrificed in the Tabernacle. The other for Aza'zel.[c] The priest would confess the sins of Israel whilst laying his hands on the head of the goat. This goat would then be sent away into the wilderness.

Chapters 17-25 Practical Holiness. *The Holiness Code*
Blood from sacrifices (ch 17). Moral purity (ch18-20). Qualifications for Priests (ch21-22) Feasts (ch 23-25) commemorating important events in the Israel story; how G-d continually saved them, blessed them and made them his special people [d] and ultimately how he made a way for the people to live with Him in His Presence.

Chapters 26. A call by Moses for the people to faithfulness with a series of blessings and curses applied to righteous and sinful behaviour.[e] Chapter 27 Deals with other objects, property and people, consecrated to G-d and how they are to be managed / redeemed.

G-d is now able to live with the people as their Sinful selfish corrupt nature is being dealt with by the Laws just detailed.

Numbers

The book of Numbers gets its name from the LXX chapter 1 verse 2.

Take the sum of all the congregation of the sons of Israel according to their kin, and according to houses of their patrimony, according to the ***number*** *of their names; every male according to their head count.* (LXX).

The (much more appropriate) Hebrew name is *Bamidbar - In the Desert / Wilderness;* and recounts the events of the Israelites leaving Mount Sinai to their final (second) arrival at the border of the Promised Land.

---

[a] Having had contact with death or anything corruptible
[b] Meaning cover or cover over (of sin); a pardon
[c] Aza'zel (Hebrew); ἀποπομπαῖος (LXX) . Meaning - the goat that carries away (sin/evil); escape-goat
[d] Sabbath - they are sanctified; Unleavened bread / Passover – redeemed from slavery; Festival of weeks /First Fruits – G-d's provision for them; Trumpets – He dwells amongst them; Atonement – His Holiness demands their Atonement; Booths – He brought them out of the wilderness
[e] Verse 12 ...*And I will walk among you, and will be your God, and ye shall be my people*

Ch 1

The census is now called in readiness for the next stage of the Israelite's journey, the march on to the Promised Land and the army that will be needed to take possession of it.

But first things first, the opening words of this book (verse 1) begins with...

And YHWH spoke unto Moses in the wilderness of Sinai, ***in*** *the tent of meeting...*

At the end of Exodus, as we saw earlier, Moses was unable to enter the Tabernacle / G-d's Presence, but now with the rules of Leviticus established, Moses is back in the Tabernacle able to speak with G-d. Now the people can sufficiently maintain a level of purity to keep G-d's Presence amongst them.

A pivotal moment for the Israelite people as they move forward to the Promised Land as G-d's own people and a holy nation. (Exodus 19.5-6). Although it may be noted now that the Israelites had rejected this extended calling to be a Nation of Priests when they were afraid to come into direct contact with G-d at Mount Sinai (Exodus 19.16-17).

All of the tribes are counted and their young (fighting) men numbered. All tribes that is except Levi. YHWH now commands that the tribe of Levi be appointed in charge of the Tabernacle and its furnishings. They are to move the Tabernacle from each location and reassemble it again in the next location.

Ch 2

After the census is taken a clear geometric formation of the entire camp is established by G-d. The Tabernacle at the centre with the Levite camps arranged around it. On the East side (toward the Sunrise Numbers 2.3) Judah, Issachar and Zebulun. On the South side Reuben, Simeon, Gad. On the West side Ephraim, Manasseh, Benjamin. On the North side Dan, Asher and Naphtali. Each tribe with their Leader and Standard.

Ch 3

This chapter gives some arrangements of the priesthood of Aaron and the Levites. Further the commandment concerning the first-born of the Israelites is revoked (Exo 13.2)

And YHWH spoke unto Moses, saying,
And I, behold, I have taken the Levites from among the children of Israel
instead of all the first-born that opens the womb among the children of Israel;
and the Levites shall be mine: for all the first-born are mine;
on the day that I smote all the first-born in the land of Egypt
I hallowed unto me all the first-born in Israel,
both man and beast; mine they shall be: I am YHWH. (v11-13)

YHWH then commands Moses to number the Levites. The Levite tribe is then assigned the exact places of their camp surrounding the Tabernacle.

Ch 4
Distribution of particular work necessary within the Tabernacle to the families of the Levite tribe.

Ch 5
Further rules about dealing with sin within the camp.

Ch 6
The Nazarite vow is introduced (chapter 6.1-21) for any man or woman of the children of Israel to make a special vow of dedication, holy separation and purity to G-d.

Ch 7
Moses dedicates the Tabernacle and all the tribes come up and give their gifts one tribe after another. When Moses enters the Tabernacle the voice of G-d is heard from above the *Kapporeth.*[a]

Ch 8
YHWH describes to Moses the various works of the Aaron priesthood and the Levites which they are to do within the Tabernacle.

Ch 9
More rules concerning the Passover.
Verse 15 continues with a description of the Presence of YHWH. The Cloud of G-d's Presence covers the Tabernacle (with an appearance of Fire by night) but when it lifts the people make ready to move wherever the Cloud leads them. When the Cloud resettles the Israelites stop also and make a new camp.

Ch 10
Moses is commanded to make trumpets for various alerts to be given to the Israelites as they now prepare to start their journey.
Almost one year after having arrived at Mount Sinai the Israelites are now ready to leave there and enter the next area *The Wilderness of Peran* (Num 10.12). The Israelites are to move in formation with the various tribes in positions surrounding the Tabernacle with Judah at the front. They travel on three more days.

Ch 11
But as soon as they get going again the Israelites begin to complain about their food when they remember the food of Egypt. G-d isn't too pleased by this and causes a fire to burn the outskirts of the camp. Soon after that the Israelites are again grumbling that they want to eat meat. Moses complains to YHWH that the burden of the people is too much for him.

---

[a] The specially designed lid of the Ark of the Covenant. (See Exo 25.17-21)

And Moses said unto YHWH, Why have thou dealt ill with thy servant? and therefore have I not found favour in thy sight, that thou lay the burden of all this people upon me? (v12)

Moses says to YHWH that it is all too much for him and requests that YHWH kill him. YHWH tells Moses to bring 70 of the elders to a meeting. There YHWH will share Moses' burden amongst them. YHWH then advises Moses to have the people sanctified as starting from the next day there will be meat every day, more than the people can eat and the meat shall continue every day until the people are sick of it. Moses wonders where all this meat will come from but YHWH just tells Moses to wait and see if He will do that.
Soon afterwards G-d inundates the camp with quail and the Israelites begin eating it. YHWH kills some of the people who were lusting after the meat.

Ch 12
Next both Miriam and Aaron complain to Moses because he has married a Cushite woman. YHWH defends Moses especially for his faith and then strikes Miriam with leprosy. Moses pleas on her behalf and she is healed after seven days.

Ch 13
The Israelites are soon at the borders of Canaan (the Promised Land). G-d orders Moses to send out spies, one from each tribe plus Joshua, Moses' personal aid, to enter in and explore. They return after 40 days, all but Caleb (the Judah spy) and Joshua come back with alarming reports of the people they found there who they claim to be way too strong. Caleb intervenes to request Moses that they go at once to possess the land as he believes that they are strong enough to prevail. The other spies exaggerate the strength of the inhabitants and say to the Israelites that there's no chance they can win.

Ch 14
This really gets the Israelites going and they bitterly complain against Moses and Aaron, wondering why they brought them into the wilderness just to die by the sword. Both Caleb and Joshua then try to rally the people by reminding them that they should not fear as G-d was with them and would surely give the land and it's people over to the Israelites. This only incenses the people even more who then want to stone Caleb and Joshua.
G-d then appears in the Tabernacle and says to Moses..

... How long will this people despise me? and how long will they not believe in me, for all the signs which I have wrought among them? (v11)

G-d again wants to slay the entire Israelite people and start again with Moses. Moses pleas on their behalf asking what would the Egyptians and the inhabitants of Canaan say if they found after all the wonders G-d had worked for the people then only to kill them in the wilderness. Moses says ..

...Pardon, I pray thee, the iniquity of this people
according unto the greatness of thy loving-kindness,
and according as thou have forgiven this people, from Egypt even until now. (Num 14.19)

G-d pardons according to Moses plea and replies..

...because all those men that have seen my glory and my signs
which I wrought in Egypt and in the wilderness,
yet have tempted me these ten times and have not hearkened to my voice;
surely they shall not see the land which I swore unto their fathers,
neither shall any of them that despised me see it (Num 14.12-23)

This now is the tenth time that the Israelites have been faithless to G-d and He now disallows this present generation of Israelites from entering the Promised Land.
Caleb and Joshua and their seed[a] are of course excused. G-d declares to Moses and Aaron that all this generation, 20 years and over, will die in the wilderness and they will stay there for one year for every day that the spies were in the Promised Land (40 days) and orders them to double back into the wilderness.
Moses brings the news to the people and they 'mourn greatly' and now declare that they will in fact go ahead, entering the same route as the spies, to possess the land. Moses informs them it's too late if they go they will not go with G-d's blessing and will fail. The people go anyway and are severely beaten by the inhabitants of that area.

Ch 15
Diverts somewhat from the on-going problems with the Israelite people and deals with some further laws on sacrifice; equitable treatment of strangers who stay a while with the people and the obeying of the Sabbath laws.

Ch 16
Returning right back with the again rebellious people, this time several Levites with Korah their leader and some other 250 of the elders of the people make complaint that Moses and Aaron are making themselves special to G-d and ignoring the fact that all the people are holy. Moses replies that they shall all meet on the morrow at the door of the Tabernacle and let G-d choose. G-d then causes the ground under Korah, and all the men who were in rebellion with him, to swallow them and their property down into Sheol. The earth then closes over them. Many of the people there run off in terror at the events. The following day the people gather again to complain to Moses and Aaron that *they* had killed the People of G-d. As this is happening the Glory of G-d appears at the Tabernacle and G-d asks Moses and Aaron to remove themselves from the area as He is going to destroy the people. Moses pleas on their behalf (again) and tries to make atonement for the people by calling Aaron to place incense

[a] Family kinsmen and Tribe

amongst them. G-d's anger toward the people is abated, but not before 14,700 of the people (not including the matter of Korah) die.

Ch 17

G-d gives the leaders of the people another chance to see who will be head of the priesthood by getting the leaders to each put a named staff in the Tabernacle to see which will bud. The budding staff's owner will head the priesthood. The next day it is found Aarons staff has budded. The staff was then to be left next to the Ark of the Testimony *for a token against the children of rebellion.* (v10)

Ch 18

Aaron and his sons are responsible for the Tabernacle and the altar thereof. The Levites are to do all other work within the tabernacle but not the inner sanctuary.

Ch 19

A red heifer is to be sacrificed, burnt and the ashes collected up. These ashes are to be mixed with water and used in their purification rituals.

Ch 20

The people enter the wilderness of Zin (where Miriam dies). Here there is no water and the Israelites complain again wishing they had died with the others who had died earlier with Korah. They again complain as to why had they been brought into the wilderness where there is no food or water. Moses and Aaron go to the Tabernacle and the Glory of G-d appears and directs Moses to get Aaron's staff, take it to the rock and in the presence of the Israelite Assembly *speak unto the rock before their eyes, that it give forth its water.* (v8) Moses does so but when they get to the rock Moses says unto them..

...Hear now, ye rebels; shall we bring you forth water out of this rock?
And Moses lifted up his hand, and smote the rock with his rod twice:
and water came forth abundantly, and the congregation drank, and their cattle. (v11)

Moses overstepped his authority in losing his temper calling the people rebels; assuming the power in himself to bring forth water; striking the rock twice with the staff instead of talking to it. In so doing G-d declares to Moses and Aaron that they did not believe in Him or sanctify Him in the eyes of the people, so neither of them will bring the people into the Promised Land. The place is named Meribah[a]
Moses sends a message to the king of Edom[b] as he wants to pass through their land briefly. The Israelites are refused permission. The king of Edom says if they try to pass through he will come out to fight against them. The Israelites will have to go another way.

---

[a] Strife

[b] The descendants of Esau

Aaron dies[a] of old age and his son Eleazar becomes high priest.

Ch 21
The Canaanite king Arad comes up against Israel and although he takes some prisoners at first the Israelites pray for success and then he and his places are totally destroyed by the Israelites. The people journey on but as they have been refused by the king of Edom to travel through his land there's a major detour to go around in poor travelling conditions and… the people complain again saying..

And the people spoke against God, and against Moses, Why have ye brought us up out of Egypt to die in the wilderness? for there is no bread, and there is no water; and our soul loathes this light bread. (v5)

As a punishment for this…G-d sends serpents among them which bite and kill..

And YHWH sent to the people the serpents, the ones causing death; and they bit the people, and died people many of the sons of Israel. (LXX Num. 21.6)

The people come to Moses and acknowledge they have sinned and ask Moses to plead with G-d for them. Moses enquires of G-d and is told to make a serpent and set it on a standard and anyone who was bitten could look upon the serpent and he would live.
A very odd symbol but seems to relate back to the serpent of Eden who does not listen to G-d's voice. The Israelites are doing the same (Num 14.23) continually resorting to their own thinking and appetites. Now that the serpent (who crawls on the earth) has been lifted up in the air (to the heavens) the people will be able to focus on the higher power of G-d's word. Whatever the meaning of this episode the making of the serpent on the standard works as this is the last complaint of the Israelites in the wilderness.
The Israelites then travel around for some time before G-d asks Moses to gather the people as He is going to give them water. The People break out into song..

Spring up, O well; sing ye unto it: the well, which the princes sank Which the nobles of the people dug, with the sceptre, and with their staves. (v16-17)

The chapter closes with Israel encountering king Sihon of the Amorites. The Israelites wish to pass through his land. He not only refuses but then comes to do battle against them. He and his army are completely routed and his land taken by the Israelites. Then king Og of Bashan comes to do battle against the Israelites, he meets the same fate as king Sihon.

Ch 22-24
The Israelites then travel to the Plains of Moab and encamp beyond the Jordan river near Jericho. The people of Moab are sorely afraid of them. Balak king of Moab sends for Baalam,

[a] Aaron is not to enter the Promised Land because of the events of Meribah (along with Moses)

the sorcerer, to curse the Israelites. Baalam agrees but finds that, on four separate attempts, he can only bless the Israelites each time he tries to curse them.

Ch 25

Israel stay in Moab but soon find themselves mixing with their women who then entice them to worship Moabite gods. This causes another plague amongst the people and 24,000 die before the plague is ended. This whole affair apparently instigated by Baalam who advised Balak king of Moab to let the Israelites curse themselves by coming into contact with the Moabite women. (see Num 31.16)

Ch 26

Another census is ordered by YHWH.

Ch 27

Some female descendants of Manasseh, Joseph's son, come to Moses and explain that their father Zelophehad had died and left no son for inheritance of Land. YHWH tells Moses that in future land can be inherited by daughters if there is no son.

G-d then speaks to Moses and ask him to climb Mount Abarim from where the Promised Land could be seen. G-d tells Moses that he is to die here [a] but first he is to pass on the leadership to Joshua son of Nun,[b] Moses' lifelong aid, *a man in whom is the Spirit* (v18). Moses does so before Eleazer the high priest and all the people.

Ch 28-31

Going back over the proscribed feasts of Passover; Unleavened Bread; Feast of Weeks; Feast of Trumpets; Feast of Tabernacles and other sacrifices to YHWH (Ch 28-29). Additional votive sacrifices (Ch 30). Revenge on the Midianites[c] (ch 31)

Ch 32

The tribes of Reuben, Gad and the half-tribe-of-Manasseh[d] find that the conquered lands of king Sihon of the Amorites and king Og of Bashan[e] (East of the Jordan) suitable for them as they have a lot of livestock. They ask to stay outside the Promised Land in these lands. Moses allows this but insists that their fighting men still go with the others (across the Jordan) in the fight to take control of the Promised Land. They agree to this.

---

[a] Because of what happened at the waters of Meribah

[b] The verb *Nun* means to propagate or greatly increase (become a multitude?)

[c] Concerning the events of chapter 25 (causing the Israelites to worship their gods). Moab and the Midianites were allied

[d] This first mention of Manasseh as a *half tribe* is not in reference to Ephraim as the other half but to a division of the tribe of Manasseh itself. Part (half) of Manasseh settling on the east side of the Jordan

[e] Who fought and lost against the Israelites earlier (Num 21.21-31) and (Num 21.33-35)

Ch 33
List of all the stages/journeys which the Israelites made from leaving Egypt to their arrival at the *Jordan across from Jericho* ready to cross. YHWH then gives Moses instructions concerning clearing out the land of peoples and their idols.

Ch 34
The borders of the Promised Land are stated by Moses. The Land will be divided by lot amongst the remaining 10 tribes[a] (the half tribe of Manasseh being counted again as those of Manasseh who *did* cross the Jordan). Joshua and Eleazar the priest will oversee this with the help of one leader from each of the remaining tribes.

Ch 35-36
Allocation of Levite cities, their property (livestock). Verse 9 continues with the establishment of *refuge cities* for manslayers and the rules that govern any retribution against them according to the particular circumstance involved in what they did. The refuge cities ensure the Land is kept pure. No manslayer shall return to the Land.

Ch 36
Deals again with the daughters of Zelophehad (ch 27). It is concluded that the women should only marry from their fathers tribe and therefore inheritance of ancestral land will not move to other tribes.

Deuteronomy

The name comes from the LXX as written in 17.18 *deuteronomion.*[b] Often misinterpreted as the Second Law; the meaning should be understood as a *Copy* of the Law, in the sense that Moses writes it down and it is the contents of this book which is to be followed (and duplicated as necessary in future). As such the Book of Deuteronomy [c] is a kind of abridged version of the four books to which it follows.
The Hebrew name for this book is Devarim – ' The Words' (of Moses), taken from the first line of the Book.
From Genesis to Numbers there has been a great movement of peoples and events.
From the exile of Adam from Eden (the Land; place of Rest[d]) and his expulsion from YHWH's Presence, to the culmination of YHWH's soteriological actions and His promises to

---

[a] Judah, Simeon, Benjamin, Dan, Manasseh (west), Ephraim, Zebulun, Issachar, Asher, Naphtali. 2) Levi (priesthood) are not allocated land

[b] καὶ γράψει ἑαυτῷ τὸ δευτερονόμιον τοῦτο εἰς βιβλίον [kai grapsei heauto to deuteronomion touto eis biblion] ...that he shall write him a **copy-of-this-law** in a book, (Deut 17.18) (in reference to a future king)
[c] Probably the same Book (of the Law) found by Hilkiah and given to Josiah (2 Chron 34.14)
[d] Until YHWH give rest unto your brethren, as unto you, and they also possess the land which YHWH your God gives them beyond the Jordan: (3.20); .... for ye are not as yet come to the rest and to the inheritance, which YHWH thy God gives thee (12.9)

Abraham, all now ready to come to fruition. His chosen people, in His Presence, ready for the word (from YHWH) to enter the Land.
As Deuteronomy begins, the Israelites are to the *east of the Jordan in the territory of Moab*,[a] (1.5) the place from where they will enter the Promised Land. Here they will remain until there is a re-affirmation of the Covenant,[b] (rejected earlier when the Israelites refused to enter the Land. (Num.14)

Structure of Deuteronomy[c]

1.1-5	Introduction
1.6 – 3.29	Historical recap
4.1-14	Adhere to the Covenant
4.15-24	Beware of idolatry
4.25-31	The consequences of idolatry
4.32-49	The amazing opportunity / blessing of the Covenant
5.1-5.33	YHWH spoke from Sinai and gave the Ten Commandments. The people had agreed to *listen and obey (na'aseh v'nishma)*
6.1-19	The Shema Prayer
6.20-25	Explaining to the future generations how this Covenant came about
7.1-11	Clearing the land of the people therein because the Israelites are to be a holy (separated) possession of YHWH
7.12 - 8.20	Remember YHWH, obey the Covenant and be blessed in all undertakings
9.1 - 10.22	Get ready to possess the land but remember it is for their wickedness that they are dispossessed not for your righteousness
11.1-25	Remember YHWH and His Covenant and all will be well with you
11.26-32	Blessings and Curses for obeying and rejecting YHWH
12.1-32	Removing the old places of worship and the building of a new place for the worship of YHWH
13.1-18	Punishment for those who lead the people astray
14.1 -21	Animals, birds and fish that may / may not be eaten
14.22 - 15.22	Tithing of produce to YHWH, the Levites and disadvantaged groups
16.1-17	Celebrating the Feast of Passover and Unleavened bread, Feast of Weeks and the Feast of Tabernacles
16.18 – 17.13	Rules for judges of the people
17.14-21	Instructions for a king who would rule the people
18.1-8	Caring for the Levites (who will remain landless)

[a] They did arrive there as recounted in Num 33.48 ...*on the plains of Moab by the Jordan across from Jericho*
[b] However this covenant will not be ratified fully until they cross the Jordan and the 'covenant curses and blessings' (27.1-26; 28.1-14; 28.15-68) 'are pronounced from Mount Ebal and Mount Gerazim.'
[c] Deuteronomy's structure has many similarities to contemporaneous suzerainty treaties (noting 4.8)

18.9-22	Rejecting cultic practice. Listening to YHWH's prophets
19.1-21	Rules for manslayers. Rules for witnesses
20.1-21	Rules for engaging the enemy
21.1-14	Rules for unsolved murders. Rules for female captives
21.15-23	Rule for two wife marriages; for disobedient children; death penalty procedure
22.1 - 25.19	Various laws of moral conduct
26.1-15	Bringing the first produce of the land to the priests. Tithing to the Levites
26.16-19	Affirmation of the Covenant
27.1 -28.68	The establishment of the Blessings & Curses system
29.1 - 30.20	Moses calls the Israelites to make the Covenant. He reminds them of the blessings and protection they have had and the curses those who reject the Covenant will receive
31.1-9	Moses is not to enter the land. He gives them Joshua as their new leader and tells him YHWH is now with him
31.10-13	Moses has this book placed by the Ark of the Covenant and declares that it is to be read to all the people every seventh year at the Feast of Tabernacles
31.14-23	YHWH calls Moses and Joshua to the Tent of the Meeting to give Joshua the Leadership. YHWH also warns them that the people will not obey this Covenant. Moses is called by YHWH to write down a song for all Israel to learn as a witness
31.24-30	Moses finishes writing this book and calls the elders to let them know about what YHWH has just said
32.1-47	The Song
32.48-52	YHWH tells Moses to go up Mount Abarim as the time has come for him to die there
33.1-29	Moses' blessing of the twelve tribes
34.1-8	Moses climbs the Mount Nebo, to the top of Pisgah and is shown the entire Promised Land. Moses dies and is buried by YHWH at an unknown location
34.9-12	Joshua is filled with the spirit and the people listen now to him. Moses is noted as being the greatest prophet there has ever been

The central themes from Deuteronomy are the words from Chapter 6.4-19 (G-d is One) Chapter 11.26-32 (Covenant with G-d), Chapter 26.16-19 (Blessings and Curses from G-d) The first covenant was with Noah then Abraham where their involvement with the covenant is relatively easy with G-d as initiator. Now with Moses and the Israelites the covenant is much more involved and the people must take responsibility for it. This covenant as given in Exodus (ch19-ch24) is a radical departure from the surrounding Nations. Although the notion of covenant was widespread as a peace treaty between states, the Nations have no such relationship or moral code with their gods. After all why would a god want to make a treaty to constrain himself to powerless people.

This covenant with the Israelites should have been an amazing beginning for the Israelites to enter the Land and become a *nation of priests* and an example for all nations as to how to live life the way that *the One G-d, the creator of the Heavens and the Earth*, would have the people of the Earth live.[a] Even though the Israelites did agree they never did live up to it.

Moses speaks in the first person; he gives the Law from his heart not from the stones or relaying what G-d has said. His speech now is through *Shekina* (Holy Spirit). Moses makes a series of didactic speeches to the ***new generation*** of Israelites as they are poised to enter the Promised Land; calling them to be faithful to The Covenant.

Chs 1, 2 & 3

This section stresses the rebelliousness of the people and the Grace, Provision and Faithfulness of G-d to The Covenant.

Moses now makes his first speech.[b] He recounts the main events which happened after the Israelites left Sinai. It had been only 11 days journey from there to the entry point of the Promised Land. But here we are now *in the fortieth year, in the eleventh month, on the first day of the month* (v3) and the Israelites are only now ready to make their entrance.

Moses recounts how YHWH had commanded them to leave Sinai to go to take possession of the land as promised to Abraham, Isaac and Jacob. When they arrived at the entry point the people came to Moses and suggested that spies be sent into the land to give them an idea as to how to proceed within. The spies went and returned with news that it was a good land that YHWH had given them, but the Israelites were afraid as the land was also filled with powerful people in strong cities. Moses reminded them of how the Egyptians had been beaten and that they should not fear as YHWH was with them to fight for them. The people remained scared and consequently YHWH ordered that they turn away back to the wilderness for their unfaithfulness. The people then realized their error and decided that they would go in after all, but it is was too late, YHWH would not fight on their behalf now. Moses advised them not to try but they went anyway and were easily beaten back out by the people there. The Israelites spent 38 years roaming around the wilderness within the borders of the lands of Esau, Moab and the Ammonites up until their encounter with king Sihon and king Og.[c] Moses recounts how they defeated them and their land then given to the tribes of Manasseh, Reuben and Gad. Moses further encourages them saying just as those two kings were routed so too will all other kings and people within the Promised Land be. Moses asked YHWH if he could enter the Land with the Israelites but was refused and told it would be Joshua who would lead them in. Moses will only see the Land from the top of Pisgah.[d]

---

[a] A certain verse comes to mind here. '*This is the end of the matter; all has been heard: Fear God, and keep his commandments; for this is the whole duty of man* [Adam]' (Ecc 12:13)

[b] This speech was made soon after defeating king Sihon and king Og (Num 21)

[c] Num 21

[d] Num 27.12: Deut 34.1. Mount Nebo, also mount Abarim

Chs 4 to 11. (Another call to Faithfulness)

Ch 4

Moses now exhorts the people to listen to the teaching that he is now bringing to them that they may Live and take possession of the Land. He reminds the Israelites to obey G-d's teaching as it is by this that they will be known and have the respect of the Nations.
Moses reminds them of their unique position with G-d, and the events of Mount Sinai when G-d's presence appeared there, His voice was heard and the covenant was made. Moses encourages them and their children to remain faithful and worship no graven images. He warns that if they do they will be scattered.

Ch 5

Moses calls the people together to hear the statutes and judgements of the Law and recounts the events of Sinai when the Law was being given including the Ten Commandments. He recounts their fear as G-d spoke out of the fire and their agreement (na'aseh v'nishma) with G-d and encourages them to be faithful to that.

Ch 6

Moses continues to exhort the people to fear YHWH their G-d and keep His statutes and commandments for that is what will make them successful and possess the Land.
He then gives the people the Shema[a] prayer concerning the required obedience and devotion to G-d.

Hear, O Israel YHWH is our God; YHWH is One
and thou shall love YHWH thy God with all thy heart, and with all thy soul,
and with all thy might.
And these words, which I command thee this day, shall be upon thy heart;
and thou shall teach them diligently unto thy children,
and shall talk of them when thou sit in thy house,
and when thou walk by the way, and when thou lie down, and when thou rise up.
And thou shall bind them for a sign upon thy hand,
and they shall be for frontlets between your eyes.
And thou shall write them upon the door-posts of thy house,
and upon thy gates. (Deut. 6.4-9)

Moses then continues to remind the Israelites further of the Law.

Ch 7

Moses informs the people that they are not to be afraid but to destroy the people of the land they are now about to possess and to destroy their places of worship and their idols.[b] The Israelites will be blessed and there will be no sickness or disease amongst them.

---

[a] Shema, meaning ' hear '

[b] In an action reminiscent of Noah and the flood (annihilation aimed at corruption and violence)

Ch 8
Obey the voice of YHWH

Ch 9
Moses reminds the Israelites that it is not their righteousness that will cause them to inherit the land, (because the Israelites are a stiff-necked people [a]) but the wickedness of the people who presently inhabit it. The Israelites should not forget all of their rebellious actions so far especially the affair of the *golden calf.*

Ch10
Moses recounts the writing of the second set of *Stone Tablets* and the making of the *Ark of the Covenant* and the initiation of the tribe of Levi as Priests. Another call to faith and to change their heart is made..

Only YHWH had a delight in thy fathers to love them,
and he chose their seed after them, even you above all peoples, as at this day.
Circumcise therefore the foreskin of your heart, and be no more stiff-necked. (v15-16)

The chapter ends with further calls to obey the commandments and a remembrance of the great things that YHWH their G-d has done for them.

Ch 11
The Israelites are called to remember how G-d destroyed their enemies, the Egyptian army, and how He led the Israelites through the wilderness then what He did to Korah (Lev 16) The Israelites are told again to keep the commandments and to possess the *fruitful* Land. Listening to and obeying the commandments will bring rain and fertility to the Land; falling away and serving other gods will bring drought and famine.

Therefore shall ye lay up these my words in your heart and in your soul;
and ye shall bind them for a sign upon your hand,
and they shall be for frontlets between your eyes. (v18)

By obeying the commandments and loving YHWH their G-d they will flourish in the Land; all other peoples will be in awe and dread of them. A further reinforcement is then made of the understanding that obeying YHWH will bring blessings and disobeying Him will bring curses. This blessings and curses paradigm will play heavily throughout the rest of the OT.

Behold, I set before you this day a blessing and a curse:
the blessing, if ye shall hearken unto the commandments of YHWH your God,
which I command you this day;

---

[a] Verse 9. Stubborn, headstrong, obstinate, harsh

and the curse, if ye shall not hearken unto the commandments of YHWH your God,
but turn aside out of the way which I command you this day,
to go after other gods, which ye have not known.[a] *And it shall come to pass,*
when YHWH thy God shall bring thee into the land where thou go to possess it,
that thou shall set the blessing upon mount Gerizim,
and the curse upon mount Ebal.[b] (v26-29)

<u>Chapters 12-26</u>
In the central section of Deuteronomy, Moses recounts the Law to the New Generation of the Israelites. Some of these laws may seem odd to us but when compared to the laws of nations surrounding them their radical and unique level of justice is revealed.
Ch 12
After the clearance of all the pagan worship and places, sacrifice is to be made in one central place to be chosen by YHWH. Some further laws on sacrificing and removing blood from meat to be eaten. The Israelites are encouraged to do what is right in YHWH's eyes; not what is right in their own eyes.
Ch 13
Any person whether 'prophet' or kinsman or of other cities roundabout who encourage the Israelites to worship other gods are to be killed.
Ch 14
Eating clean / unclean food. Further rules on tithing as a gift to the Levites (as they own no land) and to foreigners, fatherless and widows.
Ch 15
Every seventh (Jubilee) year all debts are to be forgiven between the people. This will ensure that there will not develop a poor underclass amongst them. Firstborn animals are to be dedicated to G-d.
Ch 16
The Israelites are commanded to make three pilgrimages each year. Passover & Unleavened Bread; Feast of Weeks; Feast of Tabernacles.[c]
Judges to be installed to judge the people in all their matters. They must remain honest.
Ch 17
Rules for the Leaders of Israel on sentencing and judgement.
When in the Land a leader[d] will be chosen to rule.

When thou are come unto the land which YHWH thy God give thee,
and shall possess it, and shall dwell therein,
and shall say, I will set a king over me, like all the nations that are round about me;
thou shall surely set him king over thee, whom YHWH thy God shall choose:

---

[a] Abandoning YHWH and entering the path of idolatry. Bringing the curse (death)
[b] These mountains are to be somehow used in the declaration of blessings and curses (Joshua 8.33)
[c] These pilgrimages as well as the given Law (Torah) were unique amongst the Nations
[d] The word מֶלֶךְ, [melek] king has a wider meaning of leadership such as Deut 11.3 ...*Pharaoh King of Egypt*. LXX has ἄρχοντα [archonta] a ruler.

one from among thy brethren shall thou set king over thee;
thou may not put a foreigner over thee, who is not thy brother. (v14-15)

Rules for that leader [a]

Only he shall not multiply horses to himself, nor cause the people to return to Egypt,
to the end that he may multiply horses;[b]
forasmuch as YHWH has said unto you, Ye shall henceforth return no more that way.
Neither shall he multiply wives to himself, that his heart turn not away:
neither shall he greatly multiply to himself silver and gold.[c]
And it shall be, when he sits upon the throne of his kingdom,
that he shall write him a copy of this law in a book,
out of that which is before the priests the Levites:
and it shall be with him, and he shall read therein all the days of his life;
that he may learn to fear YHWH his God,
to keep all the words of this law and these statutes, to do them;
that his heart be not lifted up above his brethren,
and that he turn not aside from the commandment, to the right hand, or to the left:
to the end that he may prolong his days in his kingdom,
he and his children, in the midst of Israel. (v16-20)

Ch 18
The Levite priests system of support.
Listening to prophets who have been sent by YHWH and the consequences for presumptuous (false) prophecy. There shall be no diviners or soothsayers.
Ch 19
Sanctuary for man slayers and witnesses to wrongdoing.
Ch 20-23
Rules of engagement [war]. Family problems.
Ch 24-25
Divorce.
Ch 26
The festival of First fruits is initiated. The first agricultural produce of the Land to be presented to the Priest at the Tabernacle.
Another pivotal statement as Moses brings his exhortation to a close

This day YHWH thy God commands thee to do these statutes and ordinances:
thou shall therefore keep and do them with all thy heart, and with all thy soul.

---

[a] Clearly not taken into account when Israel asked for a βασιλεὺς [basileous] leader of the people, king in 1 Sam 8.5
[b] Trading with Egypt (who had and used a lot of horses)
[c] Horses (military), women, wealth; three powers of the carnal man; enjoyed of the Gentile Nations

Thou have avouched YHWH this day to be thy God,
and that thou would walk in his ways,
and keep his statutes, and his commandments, and his ordinances,
and hearken unto his voice:
and YHWH has avouched thee this day to be a people for his own possession,
as he has promised thee, and that thou should keep all his commandments;
and to make thee high above all nations that he has made,
in praise, and in name, and in honour;
and that thou may be a holy people unto YHWH
thy God, as he has spoken. (v16-19)

<u>Chapters 27-34. Moses final speech and challenge</u>

Ch 27

Curses for not listening to G-d (losing the land and exile)

Ch 28

Blessings for listening to G-d's Commandments.

Ch 29

Verse 1 begins with a general statement applying to the whole book of Deuteronomy rather than an introduction to what follows in the chapter..

These are the words of the covenant which YHWH commanded Moses to make with the children of Israel in the land of Moab,
besides the covenant which he made with them in Horeb. (29.1)

Verse 2 continues. Moses calls all the people together and reminds them of all the great signs, care and protection YHWH has given them. (Although they have not yet fully understood them (v4)). They are again reminded to keep the words of the Covenant as it is only by adhering to it that they will prosper. They have all been called together so that ..

... you may enter into a Covenant [a] *with the LORD your God,*
and into his Curse [b] *which YHWH your God makes with you this day,*
that he may establish you today as his people, and that he may be your God (v12-13)

It is the 'system' of Curses and Blessings being announced..

And I am making this Covenant with its Curse,
with him who is standing here with us this day in the Presence of YHWH our God

---

[a] Blessing

[b] אָלָה H423 ['ālâ] curse. (The Hebrew word for 'oath' is שְׁבוּעָה H7621 - š?ḇû'â (see Num 5.21))

and with him who is not with us[a] *here this day* [b] (v14-15)

Those not there will continue in the rebellion bringing judgement on the 'moist and dry' (sinner and sinless.v19). YHWH will blot them out.

Ch 30

YHWH will use a system of *blessings and curses* upon the Israelites and they are to keep this in mind in all their actions. The Israelites are warned of the possibility of exile from the Land if they fail to listen to YHWH's Voice.

Moses says G-d will, by this system, modify the people's Hearts..

And YHWH thy God will circumcise thy heart, and the heart of thy seed,
to love YHWY thy God with all thy heart, and with all thy soul,
that thou may live (v 6)

Moses compels the Israelites to internalise the Commandments and choose Life

For this commandment which I command thee this day,
it is not too hard for thee, neither is it far off.
It is not in heaven, that thou should say,
Who shall go up for us to heaven, and bring it unto us,
and make us to hear it, that we may do it?
Neither is it beyond the sea, that thou should say,
Who shall go over the sea for us, and bring it unto us,
and make us to hear it, that we may do it?
But the word is very nigh unto thee, in thy mouth, and in thy heart, that thou may do it.

See, I have set before thee this day life and good, and death and evil;
in that I command thee this day to love YHWH thy God, to walk in his ways,
and to keep his commandments and his statutes and his ordinances,
that thou may live and multiply,
and that YHWH thy God may bless thee in the land where thou go in to possess it.
But if thy heart turn away, and thou will not hear, but shall be drawn away,
and worship other gods, and serve them; I denounce unto you this day,
that ye shall surely perish; ye shall not prolong your days in the land,
where thou pass over the Jordan to go in to possess it.

---

[a] Persisting in idolatry (The desires of the Self, which on a fundamental level, create these)

[b] The implication being that there are many amongst them still non-resolute in their faith and determination to follow YHWH. These will turn away from YHWH at any and every dilemma that faces them. The Blessings and Curses system will ultimately erode their presence whilst promoting those blessed

I call heaven and earth to witness against you this day, that I have set before thee life and death, the blessing and the curse: therefore choose life, that thou may live, thou and thy seed; to love YHWH thy God, to obey his voice, and to cleave unto him; for he is thy life, and the length of thy days; that thou may dwell in the land which YHWH swore unto thy fathers, to Abraham, to Isaac, and to Jacob, to give them. (v15-20) [a]

Ch 31. Closing to the Book

Moses speaks to the people and informs them he is soon to die and Joshua is to replace him. He further encourages them that they are not to fear as YHWH will do to the people there as He did with Sihon and Og. Moses also encourages Joshua in the same way to go and *inherit the Land* as YHWH will not fail *them.*

And Moses wrote this law, and delivered it unto the priests the sons of Levi, that bare the ark of the covenant of YHWH, and unto all the elders of Israel.
And Moses commanded them, saying, At the end of every seven years,
in the set time of the year of release, in the feast of tabernacles,
when all Israel is come to appear before YHWH thy God in the place which he shall choose,
thou shall read this law before all Israel in their hearing (Deut 31.9-11)

Moses is told he soon is to die and that he should appoint Joshua as leader. He and Joshua go to the Tabernacle and YHWH's Presence appears. YHWH then speaks to Moses and predicts that the Israelites will in fact turn away from Him, worshipping other gods. At that time much trouble will come upon the people but YHWH will not help them. YHWH tells Moses to write a *song.*

Now therefore write ye this song for you,
and teach thou it the children of Israel: put it in their mouths,
that this song may be a witness for me against the children of Israel. (v19)

When the Israelites have entered the Land and begin to forget YHWH, this song will be as a witness against them. Moses writes down the song and teaches it to the Israelites. He then hands over to Joshua.

Moses is now finished writing and he hands the book over to the Levite priests..

Take this book of the law, and put it by the side of the ark of the covenant of YHWH your God, that it may be there for a witness [against thee][b] (31.26)

Moses says that he knows how rebellious they are even now as he lives, how much more when he dies. He calls all the Elders..

---

[a] A restatement of 11.26-28

[b] The words 'against thee' not written in the Hebrew or LXX text

Assemble unto me all the elders of your tribes, and your officers, that I may speak these words in their ears, and call heaven and earth to witness against them
For I know that after my death ye will utterly corrupt yourselves,
and turn aside from the way which I have commanded you;
and evil will befall you in the latter days;
because ye will do that which is evil in the sight of YHWH,
to provoke him to anger through the work of your hands. (v28-29)

Ch 32
The Song. (v1-43)

Then Moses said to them..

Set your heart unto all the words which I testify unto you this day, which ye shall command your children to observe to do, even all the words of this law.
For it is no vain thing for you; because it is your life,
and through this thing ye shall prolong your days in the land,
where ye go over the Jordan to possess it. (v46-47)

The same day Moses is called to go up mount Abarim on Nebo to view the Promised Land. Moses is to die there.[a]

Ch 33
Moses gives a blessing to Israel..

And this is the blessing, wherewith Moses the man of God
blessed the children of Israel before his death.
And he said, YHWH came from Sinai, And rose from Seir [b] *unto them;*
He shone forth from mount Paran,
And he came from the myriads of holy ones:[c]
At his right hand was a fiery law for them.
Yea, he loves the people; All his holy are in thy hand:
And they sat down at thy feet; Every one shall receive of thy words.
Moses commanded us a Law, an inheritance for the assembly of Jacob.
And he was king in Jeshurun,[d] *When the heads of the people were gathered,*
All the tribes of Israel together (v1-5)

Moses then goes on to bless each of the tribes[e] and finishes with a commendation of G-d and Israel.

---

[a] Punishment for the affair of Meribah
[b] Probably poetic names for Sinai or part of the same range 2) Also applies to Mount Paran
[c] LXX has *And he hastened from out of mount Paran with myriads of holy ones*
[d] Poetic name for Israel. Derived from the word יָשַׁר *[Yashar]* be upright, be just, be lawful

Ch 34
Moses leaves, climbs Mount Nebo, and is shown the entire Promised Land by YHWH. He dies and is buried by G-d. Joshua son of Nun is noted (verse 9) as then being full of the Spirit of Wisdom (as Moses had laid his hands on him) and becomes leader of the Israelites.

Joshua[a]

The book of Joshua deals with the Israelites at last taking possession of the Promised Land.

The first section (chapters 1-12) gives the account of the clearance of the inhabitants.
The second section (chapters 13-22) covers the specific Land inheritance[b] and allocation to individual tribes.
The last two chapters (23-24) are final encouragements by Joshua.

Ch 1
YHWH tells Joshua that Moses is now dead and that he is now to lead the people into the Promised Land. The area is delineated as..

From the wilderness, and this Lebanon,[c] *even unto the great river, the river Euphrates, all the land of the Hittites*[d] *and unto the great sea toward the going down of the sun, shall be your border* (v4)

YHWH informs him that it all will be theirs, the people there will not be able to stand against them as He will now be with Joshua as He had been with Moses. YHWH says to Joshua..

Be strong and of good courage;
for thou shall cause this people to inherit the land (v6)

...be strong and very courageous,
to observe to do according to all the Law, which Moses my servant commanded thee: (v7)

---

[e] Simeon is missed. The main thing now happening is the occupation of the land. Simeon will not be allocated a portion but will live within Judah's portion. His actions surrounding the affair of Dinah and Shechem (Gen 36) and the Jacob's 'Blessing' (Gen 49.5-7). Levi being forgiven after the 'Golden Calf' affair (Exo 32.27-29)
[a] Joshua the new leader. He is presented in the book as a New Moses. He leads the Israelites to cross the river Jordan into the Promised Land and as the Red sea had parted for Moses, the waters of the Jordan part for Joshua and the Israelites to cross.
[b] Many surviving legal documents from this time period within other cultures (Mesopotamia) show this same framework of lands being inherited - first having any issues of other persons living on that land resolved before inheritance can take place. Also often seen is the use of lots to share the inheritance within a single group (Journal of Biblical Literature vol 119)
[c] Northern mountain range
[d] Descendants of Canaan son of Ham

Be strong and of good courage;
be not affrighted, neither be thou dismayed:
for YHWH thy God is with thee wheresoever thou go. (v9)

In verse 10 Joshua informs the people that within three days they will cross the Jordan and so they should prepare themselves for the crossing and entry.
Joshua then speaks to the Reubenites, Gadites, and the half-tribe of Manasseh concerning the agreement[a] they made with Moses to remain in the already conquered lands east of the Jordan. Joshua reminds them that their fighting men are to cross the Jordan too.

...until YHWH have given your brethren rest, as he has given you (v15)

They respond emphatically with..

..they answered Joshua, saying, All that thou have commanded us we will do, and wheresoever thou send us we will go.[b](v16)

Ch 2
Joshua sends spies up to Jericho, they stay at a harlots house, Rahab. She protects them when the king of Jericho hears that spies have been sent out. She says to them..

I know that YHWH has given you the land, and that the fear of you is fallen upon us,
and that all the inhabitants of the land melt away before you. For we have heard how YHWH
dried up the water of the Red Sea before you, when ye came out of Egypt;
and what ye did unto the two kings of the Amorites, that were beyond the Jordan,
unto Sihon and to Og, whom ye utterly destroyed.
And as soon as we had heard it, our hearts did melt,
neither did there remain any more spirit in any man, because of you:
for YHWH your God, he is God in heaven above, and on earth beneath. (v9-11)

The spies agree to save Rahab and her family in return for her saving them. They return with the encouraging news concerning how fearful the people of Jericho are.

Ch 3
On the third day they cross, led in by the Ark carried by the priests. As soon as their feet touch the water's edge the Jordan stops flowing and they pass over on dry land.

Ch 4
The Israelites cross the Jordan and make camp. YHWH tells Joshua to remove twelve stones from the river bed and bring them to the camp to be set up as a remembrance to the drying up

---

[a] Num 32
[b] Reminiscent of the na'aseh v'nishma. This time regarding the Land

of the river Jordan for the Israelites to pass over dry ground. When everyone has crossed, the waters return. They set the twelve stones at their camp near Gilgal;[a] it's the 10th day of the first month.

Ch 5

The news of these events reaches the inhabitants and they are scared further. Joshua orders all the men to be circumcised (as the generation of Israelites born in the wilderness had not been). They then celebrate the Passover (14th day of the first month). They eat the first food from the Land the day after Passover and from then on the Manna ceases.

Verse 13 opens a new section..

And it came to pass, when Joshua was by Jericho,
that he lifted up his eyes and looked, and,
behold, there stood a man over against him with his sword drawn in his hand:
and Joshua went unto him, and said unto him, Are thou for us, or for our adversaries?
And he said, Neither;[b] *but as leader*[c] *of the host of YHWH am I now come.* [d]

And Joshua fell on his face to the earth, and did worship,
and said unto him, What says my lord unto his servant?
And the prince of YHWH's host said unto Joshua,
Put off thy shoe from off thy foot; for the place whereon thou stand is holy.
And Joshua did so. (v13-15)[e]

They are near the city of Jericho and it will be their first confrontation. The Angel is the one who will do the fighting and only requires to know if Joshua will be on G-d's side. This is not Israel's battle but YHWH's.

Ch 6

Joshua is informed that Jericho is to be taken, but the army is only to march around the wall of the city with seven priests holding the Ark and seven priests blowing trumpets. This leads to success and the city is destroyed. Rahab and her family are spared and go on to live with the Israelites. Joshua says that Jericho is never to be rebuilt and passes a curse [f] on anyone who should try; it's destruction being a devotion (offering) to G-d. Nothing is to be taken from the city save precious metals, which are in turn to be placed in YHWH's treasury.

---

[a] Meaning rolled away (of reproach) in reference to the circumcision that took place. *And YHWH said unto Joshua, This day have I rolled away the reproach of Egypt* (ch. 5.9)

[b] לֹא [lô'] H3808.

[c] שַׂר [sar] H8269

[d] The promised angel of Exo 33.2?

[e] Reminiscent of Moses on Horeb Exo 2. 4-5

[f] חֵרֶם [cheremon] accursed thing

Ch 7

One of the Israelites, a certain man called Archan of the Judah tribe, takes some valuables from the destroyed Jericho. Unaware of this, Joshua sends part of the army up to the city of Ai where the Israelites are defeated.

And Joshua said, Alas, O Lord GOD,
therefore have thou at all brought this people over Jordan,
to deliver us into the hand of the Amorites, to destroy us?
would to God we had been content, and dwelt on the other side Jordan! (v7)[a]

G-d informs him of the transgression of Israel. Joshua investigates what happened. He finds the stolen booty and Archan is stoned.

Ch 8

Joshua is told to return to Ai, as it can now be taken. They lay ambush and the city is totally destroyed.

Verse 30-34 return to the directive[b] Moses in Deuteronomy 11.26-29, Joshua now builds an altar of un-hewn stones on Mount Ebal, writes the Law of Moses on them. Then in all the peoples presence..

And afterward he read all the words of the law, the blessing and the curse,
according to all that is written in the book of the law. (v34)

Ch 9-10

All the kings of the lands to be taken by the Israelites come together as one force to fight against them. The Gibeonites are scared of the Israelites and trick them into letting them live. Joshua finds out and makes of them servants. The Gibeonites (ch10) are later attacked (for joining with the Israelites) by the king of Jerusalem and his allies but are saved by Joshua. The attackers of the Gibeonites are destroyed.

Ch 11

Several other kings hear what has happened and form a huge alliance against the Israelites. YHWH tells Joshua not to be afraid as all the kings will be defeated. The Israelites destroy them all and then go on to successful battles at every point.

So Joshua took the whole land, according to all that YHWH had spoken Moses,
and Joshua gave it as an inheritance unto Israel according to their divisions by their tribes.
And the Land had rest from war. (v23)

---

[a] Joshua has a moment of faithlessness when he cries (like the Israelites in the wilderness before him)
[b] Blessings and Curses

Although the need for warfare against the kingdoms that had been in the Land had ended, there were still lots of smaller groups remaining. They are to be dealt with by individual tribes as they take their inheritance.

Ch 12
A list of all the defeated kings.

Ch 13
The second part of Joshua now begins concerning the division of the Land.
Joshua is now getting old and yet there are still a lot of Canaanite people and cities remaining in the Land. YHWH directs Joshua to leave them for now and begin to allot the ancestral homelands of the nine [a] tribes and the half tribe of Manasseh.[b] Levi received no land inheritance as they were, as the priesthood, to be catered for from the sacrificial offerings to YHWH and the Tithing system.

Ch 14-21
The Land is allocated by lot. This allows for divine intervention in the process. Caleb, one of the trusty spies of Moses requests his promised portion and is given the area of Hebron. Caleb and his clan promise to clear out the Canaanites. Judah's boundaries are established, (ch 15) however they do not clear the Jebusites who live in Jerusalem. The tribes of the children of Joseph, Manasseh and Ephraim, (ch 16-17) take their land but do not drive out the Canaanites living therein, opting instead to just have them do menial work for them. All Israel meet at Shiloh (ch 18-20) and the remaining tribes have their land decided. Then noted are the cities allocated to the Levites (ch 21) and the Priesthood.

Ch 22
The Reubenites, the Gadites and the half tribe of Manasseh leave Shiloh to go to their allocation of land on the east side of the Jordan. They build a great altar by the Jordan on their side. This almost causes a civil war but they later explain the altar is not for sacrifice of any kind but is as a *witness* between the tribes on both sides of the Jordan of their wish to worship YHWH and though their lands are cut off by the Jordan they do not want to find themselves considered as a separate people from the tribes on the west side at some point in the future. Their reasoning is accepted and the matter is resolved.
So Israel took possession of the Promised Land and although they did not clear it entirely of the Canaanites they controlled the entire area.

Ch 23
Joshua calls the Israelite leaders together to further encourage them to clear the Canaanites

---

[a] Judah, Simeon, Benjamin, Dan, Ephraim, Zebulun, Issachar, Asher, Naphtali, Manasseh (west)

[b] Moses and Joshua had already allotted to the tribes of Reuben, Gad and half of the tribe of Manasseh (Num 32.33). Verse 7 says. Manasseh had already received their land on the east side of the Jordan with Reuben and Gad. Manasseh was itself divided into two groups with one group taking land also on the west side of the Jordan (Joshua chapters 16 & 17)

out of the land and remain faithful to the Book of the Law of Moses.[a] He warns that if the Canaanites are left then YHWH will no longer protect them and that the Canaanites will become *a trap and a snare* to them. If they do not obey the commandments of YHWH then they will be removed from the land again.

Ch 24

Joshua gathers the tribes at Shechem[b] and gives a speech showing how G-d had protected them and nourished them all the way from the time of Terah the father of Abraham until now. He then continues…

Now therefore fear YHWH, and serve him in sincerity and in truth;
and put away the gods which your fathers served beyond the River, and in Egypt;
and serve ye YHWH. And if it seem evil unto you to serve YHWH,
choose you this day whom ye will serve;
whether the gods which your fathers served that were beyond the River,
or the gods of the Amorites, in whose land ye dwell:
but as for me and my house, we will serve YHWH. (v14-15)

And the people answered..

Far be it from us that we should forsake YHWH, to serve other gods;
for YHWH our God, he it is that brought us and our fathers up out of the land of Egypt,
from the house of bondage, and that did those great signs in our sight,
and preserved us in all the way wherein we went,
and among all the peoples through the midst of whom we passed;
and YHWH drove out from before us all the peoples,
even the Amorites that dwelt in the land:
therefore we also will serve YHWH; for he is our God. (v16-18)

Joshua then exhorts the people not to worship any other gods as this will lead to utter ruin. He then reaffirms the Covenant between YHWH and them. They agree and promise only to serve YHWH..

And the people said unto Joshua, YHWH our God will we serve,
and unto his voice will we hearken.
So Joshua made a covenant with the people that day,
and set them a statute and an ordinance in Shechem.
And Joshua wrote these words in the book of the Law of God;
and he took a great stone, and set it up there under the oak that was by the sanctuary of YHWH.
And Joshua said unto all the people, Behold, this stone shall be a witness against us;
for it has heard all the words of YHWH which he spoke unto us:

---

[a] Probably Deuteronomy

[b] Abram had first received the Promise of the Land in Shechem (Gen 12.6). Jacob went and lived there after his return from Paddam-Aram with his family (where he had gone to avoid being killed by Esau. Gen 33.19)

it shall be therefore a witness against you, lest ye deny your God. (v24-27)

Joshua died age 110 and was buried within the lands of Ephraim, thc land of his inheritance.[a]

And Israel served YHWH all the days of Joshua, and all the days of the elders that outlived Joshua, and had known all the work of YHWH, that he had wrought for Israel. (v31)

Verse 32 informs us that the bones[b] of Joseph are also to be buried in Ephraim at Shechem.

Judges[c]

The book of Judges tells the story of Israel's leaders from Joshua until just before the establishment of the monarchy. It is also the account of the complete failure of Israel to live up to any of the expectations of their covenant with YHWH. The book begins with the new leaders and the continuation of the taking possession of the land but ends with civil war and the Israelite nation no different from that of the Canaanites.
2.7 reads

And the people served YHWH all the days of Joshua,
and all the days of the elders[d] that outlived Joshua.

But after all those elders also died off.

...there arose another generation after them, that knew not YHWH,
nor yet the work which he had wrought for Israel. And the children of Israel
did that which was evil in the sight of YHWH, and served the Baalim. (2 10-11)

Scholars have noted that there is a clear South (Judah) to North (Dan) movement of the Judges who lead the Israelites.[e] The first judge (Othniel of Judah) is depicted as capable, but then as the movement of the Judges goes North there is a deterioration of ability to rule, and disregard of the Law (Torah)[f]
Alongside this emphasis on Judah's leadership, also in focus is the fact that the Israelites in Judges, now that they have arrived to the Promised Land, have lost their way. They have not

---

[a] Joshua 19.50
[b] Moses had carried them from Egypt (Exo 13.17)
[c] Meaning a kind of leader who is to do justice; defend the oppressed; punish the guilty.
[d] In Numbers 11 14-17 Moses requests help in the leadership of the Israelites *I am not able to bear all this people alone, alone (v14)* and although 70 elders are commissioned and given of the Spirit which is upon Moses. Their activities are not elaborated further but lays the foundation for the idea of Israel being led by Judges.
[e] This south north movement gives a structure to what is otherwise a rather unstructured collection of accounts
[f] There is no mention of the Law throughout the book of Judges

removed the Canaanites from their midst. They are often at the mercy of gentile kings and are unable to sustain any victories against them. They are without an overall leader, as is said in the last section of the book, several times *In those days there was no king in Israel: every man did that which was right in his own eyes*. This pointing forward also to the establishment of the monarchy with David as king (not Saul) [a]

Ch 1 First prologue
The opening verse has the Israelites requesting YHWH as to who will lead them. He answers that it is Judah who will take the lead (see also Jacobs blessing of Rulership for Judah, (Gen 49 8-10). A large part of the chapter is an account of how the tribe of Judah fought many successful battles having YHWH on their side. The remainder of the chapter describes how the other tribes did not remove the Canaanites from the land.

Ch 2
The Angel of YHWH comes and reminds the Israelites of the Covenant and what they were to do when they entered the Land concerning the Canaanites and their gods. YHWH goes on to say that they have not done this and consequentially He will no longer *help* them but *fight against* them.

Verse 7 Second prologue
Moves back to the death of Joshua and his burial. The new generation of people who are born after that begin worshipping the gods of Canaan. YHWH is, of course, angry with them and gives them *into the hands of their enemies round about.* (2.14)
YHWH begins to raise up Judges to free the Israelites but even then the Israelites only listen to the Judges until their freedom is achieved then they return straight away to following the Canaanite gods. In so doing YHWH allows for the Canaanites to oppress them again. The people again cry out to YHWH who feels sorry for them and again sends another Judge. This cycle repeats 6 times throughout all the accounts of the Judges.

Verse 20 returns to the theme beginning the chapter with YHWH saying He will no longer help them but leave the Gentile nations ***in*** the Land to see *whether they*[b] *will keep the way of YHWH* (v22).

Ch 3
Begins with a list of the Gentile Nations which YHWH has left in the land to *prove* Israel. The Israelites now are handed over to the king of Mesopotamia and they are made to serve him. Then YHWH sends the Judge Othniel (of the tribe Judah, brother of Caleb) to save them. Othniel prevails against the enemy and peace is achieved (40 years).

---

[a] There being some rather negative accounts made toward the tribe of Benjamin (Saul's tribe) and the town of Gibeah, where Saul reigned. .Judges 19 16-30 (Modelled on Genesis 19 1-12)
[b] The Israelites

The cycle now begins with the Israelites forgetting YHWH. Another oppressor is sent (King of Moab). The Israelites serve him for 18 years. They then begin to cry out to YHWH who has pity on them and sends another Judge (Ehud[a] of the tribe of Benjamin[b]) Ehud personally kills the Moabite king and in so doing frees the Israelites. There are then 80 years peace.

Ch 4

Ehud dies and the cycle returns with king Jabin of Canaan. Jabin has 900 iron chariots[c] and oppresses the Israelites. This leads to the remarkable introduction and making of a female judge, Deborah the prophetess. She is stated as being the '*wife of Lapidoth'* although the translation of the word *Lapidoth* equally means the '*Woman of Torches.'* therefore introducing her in her own right (not just as someone's husband). She dwells on Mount Ephraim (north of Benjamin).
She sends for Barak[d] to bring the fighting men of the tribes of Naphtali and of Zebulun to Mount Tabor, where she says Barak will win against Sisera, king Jabin's captain. Barak agrees to go but only if Deborah comes along. Sisera's army are defeated. Sisera escapes on foot but is tricked and killed by another woman Jael. The Israelites continue with their success against the king of Canaan until they *had destroyed Jabin king of Canaan.*

Ch 5

The song of Deborah. In this poetry Deborah recounts the events in parallel which have just taken place with additional details. Israel is then noted as having peace for a further 40 years.

Ch 6,7,8

The cycle repeats and this time the Midianites and the Amalekites[e] oppress Israel, specifically by destroying their crops and livestock. The people cry out and YHWH sends a prophet (unnamed) to them. He reminds them of the protection YHWH has always given them and of their continuance to ignore Him. Into this situation the story of the next judge to lead the Israelites continues..

And there came an angel of the LORD, and sat under an oak which was in Ophrah, that pertained unto Joash the Abiezrite[f] (v11)

This place then is where Gideon, Joash's son, was threshing in secret to hide it from the Midianites.
The Angel of YHWH says to him '*YHWH is with thee, thou mighty man of valour.'*

---

[a] Ehud is introduce as a left handed man which is curious as the word Benjamin means Son of the Right Hand.
[b] Benjamin's ancestral lands are immediately north of Judah
[c] The tribe of Judah were noted in 1.19 as not being able to remove some inhabitants of *the valley* (west of Judah) as they had iron chariots
[d] The name Baraq means *lightning*
[e] Grandson of Esau
[f] Of Manasseh

In a somewhat comical conversation, Gideon does not understand who he is speaking with. The Angel informs Gideon that he is the one to save Israel from the Midianites.
Gideon still is not convinced and asks the Angel to wait. Gideon goes off to cook some food (in an episode that has certain affinities with the story of Abraham on the Plain of Mamre. Gen 18). He eventually realises who it is then builds an altar to YHWH.
Gideon is directed to destroy the places of idol worship in the area and then goes on to gather the tribes of Manasseh, Asher, Zebulun and Naphtali. Gideon still requires further proofs from YHWH before fighting. When the proofs are shown he agrees to fight the Midianites. YHWH insists that the 30,000 men Gideon has mustered are too many and ultimately arranges an army of only three hundred. Gideon's small army set the Midianites in confusion and they are then destroyed by the armies of Manasseh Asher, Zebulun, Naphtali and Ephraim as they scatter. Gideon goes on to clear the entire Midianite presence in the land. The Israelites then say to him that they want him to become their Ruler[a] and his son after that. Gideon refuses and says *YHWH will rule over you.* (8.23)
Gideon then requests that they contribute some of the gold taken from the dead Midianites. He has an Ephod[b] made with it and places it in his own city of Ophrah. Thus Gideon makes a snare for himself, his family and all of Israel who end up worshipping it.
There are 40 years of peace whilst Gideon lives. He has 70 sons and many wives. He also has a concubine in Shechem, who bears him a son named Abimelech.[c]
As soon as Gideon dies the cycle begins again and the Israelites *played the harlot after the Baalim, and made Baal-berith their god* (Judges 8.33). The Israelites forget all about YHWH again and all about Gideon and the good he had done.

Ch 9
There is a movement towards making a son of Gideon the next ruler as the people had earlier indicated. Abimelech goes to his mother's brethren at Shechem and asks which is better - that the 70 sons of Gideon (now referred to as Jerubbaal) rule or that one of them rule. His family agree to have one, that is, Abimelech should rule. Abimelech then goes and kills all the other sons of Gideon save one called Jotham, who hid. All the men of Shechem then assemble and make Abimelech king.
Jotham returns to speak (from mount Gerazim) to the men of Shechem about their wicked treacherous deeds and curses them before hiding again. Abimelech rules for three years before the men of Shechem revolt against him. Abimelech and his army kill all the people of Shechem in a bloody fight against them. He then attacks another nearby city but is killed when he tries to set fire to a tower where the people of the city are barricaded in.

[a] Hebrew מָשַׁל [mashal] ; LXX ἄρχω [archō]
[b] A garment of the High Priest worn on top of a robe
[c] Meaning *my father is king* or *The Father is King 2) referring to ch 8 23*

Ch 10

After Abimelech there arose to save Israel Tola the son of Puah, the son of Dodo, a man of Issachar;[a] *and he dwelt in Shamir in the hill-country of Ephraim. And he judged Israel twenty and three years, and died, and was buried in Shamir. After him arose Jair, the Gileadite;*[b] *and he judged Israel twenty and two years. (v1-3)*

The Israelites again enter the cycle, forget about YHWH, and worship all the gods of the surrounding nations.
Now the Philistines and the *children of Ammon* (people of Ammon) oppress the Israelites. This continues for 18 years in Israel and in the Trans-Jordan area.

And the children of Ammon passed over the Jordan to fight also against Judah, and against Benjamin, and against the house of Ephraim; so that Israel was sore distressed. (v9)

And the children of Israel cried unto YHWH, saying, We have sinned against thee,
even because we have forsaken our God, and have served the Baalim.
And YHWH said unto the children of Israel, Did not I save you from the Egyptians,
and from the Amorites, from the children of Ammon, and from the Philistines?
The Sidonians also, and the Amalekites, and the Maonites, did oppress you;
and ye cried unto me, and I saved you out of their hand.
Yet ye have forsaken me, and served other gods: therefore I will save you no more.
Go and cry unto the gods which ye have chosen;
let them save you in the time of your distress.
And the children of Israel said unto YHWH, We have sinned:
do thou unto us whatsoever seems good unto thee;
only deliver us, we pray thee, this day.
And they put away the foreign gods from among them, and served YHWH;
and his soul was grieved for the misery of Israel. (v10-16)

The Israelites gather themselves together in Mizpah and try to find a leader for the fight against the children of Ammon, gathered in Gilead.

Ch 11

Now a certain Jephthah is introduced. He was the son of a prostitute, with a father called Gilead. Jephthah was a *mighty man of valour,* but Gilead's other sons drove him out of the home due to the nature of his birth.
The children of Ammon were now ready to make war on Israel. The elders of Gilead search out Jephthah and request he be their leader.[c] Jephthah thinks them all hypocrites but agrees on condition they make him their ruler in Gilead if they win against the children of Ammon.

---

[a] Northern settlement

[b] Northern, trans Jordan settlement

[c] קָצִין [qâtsîyn] chief; judge ; leader; LXX ἡγέομαι [hēgéomai] lead

The leaders of Gilead and Jephthah appear to have no knowledge of YHWH but just use his name to seal their pact.
Jephthah sends a letter to the king of the children of Ammon to ask why he has come upon the Israelites. The king of the children of Ammon complains that the Israelites have taken their land. Jephthah replies with a long history lesson about the movements of Israel in the wilderness and shows the king of the children of Ammon that the Israelites did not take their land and dealt fairly with all in their encounters. The king of the children of Ammon still wants to fight. Jephthah is filled with the spirit of YHWH and he rouses all the Israelites around the areas of Gilead and Manasseh and goes off to meet the king of the children of Ammon. Jephthah vows to YHWH that if he wins he will make a sacrifice of - *that whatsoever comes forth from the doors of my house to meet me, when I return* (v31). Jephthah wins the battle and returns home to find his only child, a daughter, come out of the house to meet him. Jephthah is sorely grieved because he must do what he swore to YHWH. He does with her according to his vow.

Ch 12

The Ephraimites turn up to complain to Jephthah as to why they were not asked to fight alongside him and threaten to kill him. Jephthah reminds them that they have been asked before and have not helped.[a] This causes the Ephraimites to battle against Jephthah and the Gileadites. The Gileadites win the battle. Jephthah rules 6 years before his death. After Jephthah there are four more judges listed but no details of their exploits are noted.

Ch 13

Again the Israelites fall away from YHWH. They are now handed over to the Philistines for forty years. Then there is a man, a Danite, called Manoah. His wife is barren.

And the angel of YHWH appeared unto the woman,
and said unto her, Behold now, thou are barren, and bearest not;
but thou shall conceive, and bear a son.
Now therefore beware, I pray thee, and drink no wine nor strong drink,
for, lo, thou shall conceive, and bear a son;
and no razor shall come upon his head;
for the child shall be a Nazirite unto God from the womb:
and he shall begin to save Israel out of the hand of the Philistines. (v3-5)

The child born is Samson. As he grows the spirit of YHWH begins to move in him.

Ch 14

Samson sees a woman, a Philistine whom he wants to marry. His parents don't want him to do so, but it is YHWH who has directed Samson to marry her. They all go off to see her. On

---

[a] The specific earlier even not mentioned in the text. The Ephraimites had also complained in a similar way against Gideon (8.1)

the way Samson kills a roaring lion with his bare hands. Samson continues to meet with the woman. Sometime later Samson returns and goes past the carcass of the lion which now has a beehive in it. Samson takes some of the honey with his hand and eats some and gives some to his parents.
Samson attends a feast for his new wife. He sets a riddle to the people there. If anyone can solve it Samson will give them 30 sets of clothes, if not they will give him. The riddle concerns what happened with the Lion. They are not able to solve it so they go to Samson's wife and get her to find out. After losing Samson realises what has happened. He then goes off and kills 30 men and uses their clothes. *But Samson's wife was given to his companion, who had been his friend* (v20)

Ch 15-16
Samson sometime later goes off to see his wife but her father won't allow it saying that he has given the woman to his companion as it seemed Samson hated her. Her father suggests Samson takes her younger more beautiful sister as his wife. Samson goes off with revenge on his mind and he uses some foxes to set fire to all the Philistine crops. The Philistines find out who did it and why; they then go off and kill Samson's wife and her father. Samson then kills the men who killed his wife and father and hides somewhere in the lands of Judah. The Philistines then come to the lands of Judah and want Samson. The men of Judah ask of Samson why he did this to their rulers. Samson says *as they did to me, I did to them.* The men of Judah tie him up and take him to the Philistines. He breaks the ropes and kills a thousand of the philistines with the jawbone of an ass. Samson goes to a prostitute in Gaza. The Philistines lay a trap but Samson escapes in the night by pulling up the city gates and carrying them off. Samson meets Delilah. The Philistines want to know the source of his strength and ask Delilah to help. She asks him several times about his strength and he tells lies each time resulting in the death of the Philistines who were arranging to trap him. In the end Samson tells her the truth about his hair. While he sleeps she has his hair cut off. Samson is captured, blinded and put in prison. Whilst in prison his hair grows back. The Philistines make a great feast to their god Dagon to praise him for freeing them from Samson. Samson is let in to the hall for them to make fun of. He gets to the pillars that support the roof and requests YHWH one more time for assistance and he topples the pillars. Many Philistines die as the building collapses. His body is taken home by his father. Samson was judge for 20 years.

<u>Appendix. Stories from Dan to Benjamin (North to South)</u>
Ch 17
Micah is introduced here, but does not say that he is or becomes a judge. There is no further mention of judges; which relates to the statement in v6 (below)[a]
A man called Micah of the hill country of Ephraim is introduced. He admits to his mother that he stole her silver and then gives it back to her. She says *Blessed be my son of YHWH,*

---

[a] YHWH is not their king. 2) Although Judge שָׁפַט [shâphaṭ] ; κρίνω [krínō] might have been more fitting to the text.

and then proceeds to make a graven image with some of the silver. She then says *I verily dedicate the silver unto YHWH from my hand for my son, to make a graven image and a molten image:* Now Micah had made, in his house, a place for worship where he kept his gods. He had also consecrated his son as priest and made an Ephod for him.
Now if all that doesn't just sound a bit crazy the next verse sets some context..

In those days there was no king[a] *in Israel:*
every man did that which was right in his own eyes. (v6)

There was a certain Levite[b] man of the family of Judah in Beth-lehem, who decides to leave and move north to the hill country of Ephraim. Micah meets the Levite and employs him to be his priest in his house.
Then said Micah, Now know I that YHWH will do me good, seeing I have a Levite to my priest.(v14)
Clearly what Micah was doing was not based on G-d's teachings. He serves YHWH the way he wants, not the way he was commanded.... *doing what was right in his own eyes*
Next verse..
In those days there was no king in Israel: (18.1)

Ch 18
Verse 2. The men of Dan seem to have not been successful with their Land inheritance and send out groups of 'men of valour' to find some other land for them to go to instead. One group come to the hill country of Ephraim and Micah's house. They recognise the Levite and ask him to enquire of YHWH if their plans will be successful. The Levite tells them they have YHWH's approval. Micah's priest tells them *what they wanted to hear*. The Danites see the city of Laish and the surrounding land (in the far North of Israel) and see the people are very peaceful. They go back to the leaders of Dan and tell them they have YHWH's blessing to go and possess the land there. So they set off with an army, passing through the hill country of Ephraim and on to Micah's house. There they enter to take the graven images and the Ephod etc. The Levite sees them do this. The Danites invite him to be *their* priest instead and the Levite gladly agrees. Micah finds out what has happened and catches up with them. He asks for his things back but the Danites threaten to kill him so he turns back. The Danites reach Laish, take the city and kill everybody there. They rename the city Dan and set up a new priesthood of a certain Jonathan (presumably the Levite priest) the son of Gershom, the son of Moses.

And the children of Dan set up for themselves the graven image;
and Jonathan, the son of Gershom, the son of Moses, he and his sons were priests

---

[a] LXX βασιλεὺς basileus (king)

[b] The Levites are a distinct tribe dedicated to service in the Tabernacle. They could not be of the family (tribe) of Judah

to the tribe of the Danites until the day of the captivity of the land.[a]
So they set up Micah's graven image which he made,
all the time that the house of God was in Shiloh.(v30-31)

Clearly the Land of Israel and most of the 12 tribes are in utter chaos and have no idea who YHWH is.

Ch 19
Again we are told *in those days, when there was no king in Israel,* there is again a Levite staying in the hill country of Ephraim. He has a concubine, from Beth-lehem-Judah. She leaves him and goes back to her father house. The Levite goes there to get back his concubine and is happily met by the woman and her father, who ask him to stay a while. He stays for the customary three days but then the father asks he stay longer. By the 5th day the Levite insists that they leave and they do but they leave late in the day. On their way they pass Jebus. The Levite's servant suggests they stay there; the Levite declines as he does not want to stay in a Gentile city and they carry on to reach an Israelite city. As the sun goes down they reach Gibeah and enter but no one takes them into their homes. Now a man, from the hill country of Ephraim, living there sees them and invites them to his house. Later in the evening some of the men of Gilead (Benjamites) come to the house and demand that the visitor be handed over to them for sex. The host declines and advises the men to do no such disgraceful thing but offers his virgin daughter and the concubine to them. The man pushes the concubine out of the house and the Benjamite men abuse her till dawn. She comes back and falls at the door. When they open the door she is dead. The Levite puts her body on his donkey and takes her home where he then cuts the body into twelve pieces and sends them to the tribes of Israel.

Ch 20
Throughout the land the Israelites are astonished at what has happened. All of Israel come together to decide what to do. The Israelites muster an army and go up to Gibeah and demand the culprits be handed over to them. The Benjamites refuse. The Israelites then go to Beth'El to enquire of YHWH what to do.

Who shall go up for us first to battle against the children of Benjamin?
And YHWH said, Judah shall go up first.[b] (v18)

They are told to fight but are beaten. They enquire a second time and are told to fight them but are again beaten. They enquire again and are told to fight; on the third attempt they utterly destroy the Benjamites and their cities.[c]

---

[a] The Assyrian captivity of the land was 733bc. Time of the Judges 1200-1000bc?
[b] In chapter 1 v1-2 the Israelites are about to begin their fight against their enemies.
Who shall go up for us first against the Canaanites, to fight against them? And YHWH said, Judah shall go up:
Now they are about to begin a civil war against their own brother
[c] And I wonder if they had YHWH's true response at any time but just kept on fighting till they got what they wanted

Ch 21
The Israelites then meet in Beth'El and lament the fact that one of their tribes is no more. They then decide to allow some Benjamite survivors to return but then note that these Benjamites have no women to become their wives.[a] So they make a plan, they find out who in Israel did not come to help them fight against the Benjamites and find one group from Jabesh-Gilead. The Israelites then send an army there to kill everyone in Jabesh-Gilead, save the virgins of that place. They take 400 virgins for the Benjamites. Then the Israelites meet with the remaining Benjamites and make peace with them. The Benjamites return but the women are still too few... It is then suggested that the Benjamites should lie in wait at the next festival at Shiloh, when the Israelite daughters come out to dance, they should kidnap them and take them for their wives; this the Benjamites do. The final verse reads, somewhat expectedly..

In those days there was no king in Israel:
every man did that which was right in his own eyes.[b] (v25)

Ruth

The book of Ruth placed in the 'Writings' section of the TaNaKh,[c] is positioned here in the LXX, at the edge of the establishment of the Monarchy. As such it forms a break from the main historical narrative in which the end of the book of Judges continues with the Books of Samuel.
Ruth will be the great grandmother of David. It tells of G-d's work in human affairs (in Moab and Israel) with faithful people. Nowhere in the book are the interventions of G-d directly mentioned, yet His actions are evident at every stage. A story of faithfulness by the actions of human agency bringing to bear G-d's law and G-d's purpose.
The Moabite Ruth[d] remains faithful to her mother-in-law Naomi and stays with her even after all family ties are severed. She returns with Naomi to Israel leaving her own family and gods for that of Naomi and the G-d she worships.
Naomi has no direct family back in Israel. Ruth becomes her companion. Ruth's self-sacrifice enables her to be the servant through which G-d can work to bring about his plans (the acceptance of the Law 1.16) She will also bring about the restoration of Naomi.
The Moabites were at the centre of the affair with Balaam when the Moabite women caused Israel to err. Ironically she now restores Israel. G-d was then working in the background to save Israel as He is now in the Book of Ruth. The book starts in sorrow and famine and ends in joy and plenty.

---

[a] The Israelites have sworn previously that none of the Benjamites would be given any of the daughters of Israel. Presumably in the last chapter. Not mentioned in the text.
[b] Against what Moses had said in Deut. 12.8 & 12.28
[c] Torah, nevi'im , ketuvim (acronym). Teaching; prophets; writings
[d] Meaning - friend; companion

Ch 1
During the time of the Judges a great famine strikes the land of Israel. A man from Beth-lehem called Elimelech,[a] takes his wife Naomi, his two sons Mahlon[b] and Chilion[c] and relocate to Moab. Elimelech dies soon after and Naomi is left with her two sons. They each marry of the women of Moab, Orpah, and Ruth. The two sons now also die leaving Naomi with Orpah and Ruth. Naomi hears that the famine is easing in Israel and decides to go back. She strongly advises Orpah and Ruth to return to their homes as she cannot guarantee any normal life for them back in Israel. Orpah leaves but Ruth refuses to leave Naomi saying..

for where thou go, I will go; and where thou lodge, I will lodge;
thy people shall be my people, and thy God my God;
where thou die, will I die, and there will I be buried:
YHWH do so to me, and more also, if aught but death part thee and me (v16-17)

They arrive back in Beth-lehem at the beginning of the barley harvest.[d] People come to meet them and enquire if this is Naomi who has returned. Naomi says..

Call me not Naomi, [e] *call me Mara,*[f] *for the Almighty has dealt very bitterly with me.*
I went out full, and YHWH has brought me home again empty (v20-21)

Ch 2
Ruth asks Naomi permission to go to where the farms are being harvested so that she may glean in one of the fields. Now it happens that Naomi had a wealthy kinsman of Elimelech's family named Boaz. Ruth chanced across his farm and began gleaning after the harvesters. Boaz visited the harvesters and asked who the woman was and they inform him. He speaks to Ruth and advises her not to go to any other field but his. He also tells her he has advised the other workers not to molest her in any way but help her. Ruth bows to him and enquires why he is being so kind. He tells her he has heard of how she came back with her mother in law. Boaz allows her to eat with the other workers and also commands them to leave extra sheaves behind for her to find. Ruth collects a lot of barley and takes it home to Naomi in the evening. Naomi finds out from Ruth that it was Boaz' farm and that he had helped her.
Naomi says..

Blessed be he of YHWH, who has not left off his kindness to the living and to the dead (v20).

---

[a] My G-d is King
[b] Meaning weak sick or wounded
[c] Meaning wasting away
[d] Naomi returns to Beth-lehem empty but at the time the Israelites are receiving harvest, their first food for a while. The Barley harvest association Shavout / giving the Law
[e] Pleasant; sweet
[f] Naomi announces her name change. It is in bitterness [marar] that the hand of G-d has come to her and she will now have no offspring (although actually not so). Naomi sees a future without promise or hope.

Boaz, is one of their *near kinsman.* [a] Naomi advises Ruth to only go to Boaz' fields for the rest of the harvest.

Ch 3[b]

Naomi has a plan. She tells Ruth to get dressed up and cleaned and find where Boaz sleeps on the threshing floor then go to him when he's sleeping. Boaz awakes to find her at his feet. She asks him to *spread therefore thy skirt over thy handmaid; for thou are a near kinsman.* (v10) in a symbolic statement in which a kinsman claims a widow as a wife. [c] He is amazed at her faithfulness that she would only go to him as a potential husband (Ruth has Naomi's restoration in mind). He agrees but there is yet a closer kinsman to her; he must be asked to marry her first. Boaz gives her more grain and she leaves before the others awake. Boaz then goes off to arrange things. Ruth goes home and tells Naomi what has happened.

Ch 4

Boaz goes to the city gate (where legal matters are settled) Just then the nearer kinsman passes by. Boaz informs him that Naomi is selling a piece of land (that had been her Husband's).[d] Therefore the land should be offered to the closest of kin first. The kinsman accepts to buy the land. Boaz goes on to tell him that the new owner of the land will also have to marry the widow of the heir of that land, Ruth.[e] The kinsman now rejects the deal as the land would become the inherited property of any son he had with Ruth and would therefore not increase his own wealth, but diminish it (by now paying for it). Boaz now announces his wish to buy it and with it take Ruth (Mahlon's widow) as a wife so that he can

..raise up the name of the dead upon his inheritance,
that the name of the dead be not cut off from among his brethren, (v10)[f]

Ruth later gives birth and the women neighbours of Naomi say..

---

[a] Boaz as a kinsman may change Naomi and Ruth's fortunes according to the Levirate marriage laws. (a redeemer) A chance to Naomi for restoration (a son).

[b] A mirroring (apart from the chiasmic structure) of chapters 2 & 3....
(1) Ruth asks Naomi if she may go to the fields and tells her what she would do; Naomi bids her go (2.2)
(2) Ruth goes to the fields (2.3)
(3) Boaz asks the identity of Ruth and is told (2.4-7)
(4) Boaz asks Ruth to stay, declares her worthy of being blessed, and gives her food (2.8-14)
(5) Ruth speaks with Naomi: Ruth tells her what has happened and Naomi gives her counsel (2.18-23)
(1) Naomi bids Ruth go to the threshing-floor and tells her what she should do (3.1-5)
(2) Ruth goes to the threshing-floor (3.6)
(3) Boaz asks the identity of Ruth and is told (3.7-9)
(4) Boaz declares Ruth worthy of being blessed, asks her to stay, and gives her food (3.10-15)
(5) Ruth speaks with Naomi: Ruth tells her what has happened and Naomi gives her counsel (3.16-18)

[c] Gen 38. Deut 25.5-10

[d] Numbers 27.9-11; Leviticus 25. 25

[e] Gen 38. Deut 25.5-10

[f] Deut 25.6

Blessed be YHWH, who has not left thee this day without a near kinsman;
and let his name be famous in Israel.
And he shall be unto thee a restorer of life, a nourisher of thine old age;
for thy daughter-in-law who loves thee,
who is better to thee than seven sons, has borne him.
And Naomi took the child, and laid it in her bosom, and became nurse unto it. (v14-16)

It is the women neighbours who name the child Obed[a] and say there is a child *born to Naomi.* Verses 18-22 conclude the book with a genealogy tracing back to Perez son of Judah and forward to David.[b]

1 & 2 Samuel

The two books of Samuel are a single continuous book (ספר שמואל, Sefer Shmuel) in the Hebrew, which seems somewhat more fitting as Samuel's death is recorded in 1 Samuel chapter 25. The books were divided by the LXX translators. Also known as the 1st & 2nd Kings in the Latin Vulgate (1 & 2 Kings as we know them becoming 3 & 4 Kings).
The books have at their core the explanation of how the monarchy begins and detail the lives of the first two kings of Israel.
The Book of Samuel now focuses in on the need for *faithful leadership* for the Israelites with the beginning of the monarchy. The book begins still within the time of the Judges and its chaos, and ends with the unified kingdom of Israel under David.
Samuel becomes the Israelite leader / judge as a high priest after Eli is rejected, but the Israelites soon want a king '*as the other nations have*' and reject Samuel. G-d sees this as a rejection of His leadership but allows their wish. Saul is made king. He starts off pretty good but rapidly begins to fail his duties, is rejected, and is replaced by David. David also begins well and does unify the tribes to a single nation with a single place of worship. David fails in his personal life and the unification is short lived (ends in the time of his grandchildren).
At key transitions of leadership in the 1 Samuel text the rejection of one leader is followed by a statement about the heart of the next: 2.34-35, Eli and family rejected; 7.2b-6 Samuel leads the people; 10.6-11, Saul chosen; 13.13-14, Saul rejected; 16.7-12 David chosen.

1 Samuel

Ch1
The story begins with Hanna. She is one of two wives of her husband Elkanah but she is barren. Elkanah worships yearly in the Tabernacle at Shiloh where Eli and his two sons are

---

[a] Servant
[b] The reference to David indicates the books final form derives from a later date than that of Ruth and Naomi.

priests. Hanna also goes to the Tabernacle and prays that if she can become pregnant she will dedicate the child G-d (with a Nazarite [a] vow).
Hanna becomes pregnant and names the child Samuel.[b] When she has weaned the child she takes him to Eli and leaves him in the Tabernacle as she had promised. Samuel will grow to be a devout priest and take the place of Eli.

Ch2
Hanna's Song (v1-10) A song with the repeated theme of God's reversal of fortune by bringing down the powerful and raising up the humble. The song is structurally similar to the Song of David (2 Sam 22) and forms a framework around the entire book of Samuel 1 & 2.

Eli's two sons are both corrupt and have no regard for G-d. One of them is expected to replace Eli after his death. However a *man of G-d* comes to Eli the priest and informs him that he is rejected by G-d (failure to act against his wayward children) also that his sons will die and his family line shall be ended (v31-33). He then tells Eli that...

.. there shall not be an old man in thy house forever.[c](v32)

And I will raise me up a faithful priest,
that shall do according to that which is in my heart and in my mind:
and I will build him a sure house;
and he shall walk before mine anointed forever.[d] (v35)

Ch 3

And the child Samuel ministered unto YHWH before Eli.
And the word of YHWH was rare in those days; visions were infrequent. (v1)

G-d is somewhat absent at this point since the High priest Eli and his family are rejected. Samuel then begins to receive visions. The first of which YHWH calls to Samuel informing him again of the prophecy against Eli.

And YHWH appeared again in Shiloh;
for YHWH revealed himself to Samuel in Shiloh by the word of YHWH. (v21)

Samuel becomes established as a prophet of YHWH at Shiloh.

---

[a] See Numbers 6 1-21

[b] Samuel [heard of G-d] Hanna asks for a male-child and G-d **hears** her plea

[c] עוֹלָם [`owlam]; αἰῶνος [aeonos]. This word mostly interpreted as ***forever***. Its core meaning seems to be ***to endure*** or ***lifelong***. The context is derived from the text (whether talking about the Earth or a man's life etc)

[d] LXX has .. *and he shall walk before My anointed all the days.*

Ch 4

The Philistines are oppressing the Israelites and having some success against them.[a] The Israelite army decide to take the Ark of the covenant out into battle.

So the people sent to Shiloh; and they brought from thence
the ark of the covenant of YHWH of hosts, who dwells [between] *the cherubim:* (v4)

Eli's two sons bring the Ark. The Israelite army hope that its presence there will give them the advantage. Unfortunately it does not, the Israelites are defeated, Eli's sons are killed, and the Ark is taken away by the Philistines. Eli is told his sons are dead; then he is told the Ark has been taken by the Philistines. Eli dies of shock at this news.[b]

Ch 5 & 6

The Ark causes plagues to come to the Philistines and they return the Ark to the Israelites and it arrives at Beth-Shemesh.[c] The presence of the Ark there causes many people who had looked upon it to die also. They say..

Who is able to stand before YHWH, this holy God?
and to whom shall He go up from us? (v20)

Then they ask the people of Kiriath-jearim.[d] to take it there.

Ch 7

The Ark is brought by the people of Kiriath-jearim to the house of Abinadab and placed under the care of his son Eleazar.[e] It will remain there for 20 years (v2)

Samuel begins to lead...

And Samuel spoke unto all the house of Israel, saying,
If ye do return unto YHWH with all your heart,
then put away the foreign gods and the Ashtaroth[f] *from among you,*
and direct your hearts unto YHWH, and serve him only;
and he will deliver you out of the hand of the Philistines. (v3)

The Israelites agree and do so. Then the Philistines are defeated.

---

[a] the Israelites are still worshipping other gods (1 Sam 7.3)

[b] Also the Glory of YHWH (which dwells there) may be assumed to have departed with it from Israel. Israel should have remained humble. They would have asked G-ds advice through Samuel. Like the events of Joshua and the Angel of YHWH, it is G-d who will win the day not them.

[c] A city given to the Kohathite Levites in the territory of North (Josh 15.10) Judah (Joshua 21:16).

[d] Also within Judah (Josh 15.9) 2) From where the Gibeonites who tricked Joshua came (Josh 9)

[e] Meaning G-d's helper

[f] Female fertility god

Samuel continues around Israel (Beth'El, Gilgal, Mizpah) as a Judge of the people. He builds an altar to YHWH at his home area of Ramah. The fate of Shiloh is not stated.[a]

Ch 8

Samuel becomes old and he makes his sons Judges. They are nothing like Samuel and are corrupt, taking bribes and seeking ill-gotten gain. The elders of Israel come to Samuel and ask for a king to lead them.[b] Samuel is disturbed by this and enquires of G-d what to do..

..and YHWH said unto Samuel,
Hearken unto the voice of the people in all that they say unto thee;
for they have not rejected thee, but they have rejected me,
that I should not be king over them.
According to all the works which they have done
since the day that I brought them up out of Egypt even unto this day,
in that they have forsaken me, and served other gods, so do they also unto thee.
Now therefore hearken unto their voice:
howbeit thou shall protest solemnly unto them,
and shall show them the manner of the king that shall reign over them. (v7-9)

Samuel warns them of the heavy burden of maintaining a king, but the people insist.

Ch 9

G-d chooses Saul.[c] He leads Samuel to him and tells Samuel that Saul is to be *nagiyd* [leader/captain] over the people[d] Saul is noted as being handsome and tall man (external attributes v2)

Ch 10

Samuel anoints Saul

Samuel took the vial of oil, and poured it upon his head, and kissed him, and said,
Is it not that YHWH has anointed thee to be leader over his inheritance?

Samuel announces to Saul he will meet a group of prophets coming from worship and ..

the Spirit of YHWH will come mightily upon thee,
and thou shall prophesy with them,

---

[a] Jeremiah 7.12 suggests it was destroyed. Psalm 78.60 says abandoned

[b] An unfortunate turn of events where the Israelites, again, find themselves unable to wait for YHWH to send them a redeemer / prophet

[c] Meaning *asked for* 2) Perhaps another lost opportunity. As Eli's two sons were corrupt, YHWH gave Samuel. Now that Samuel's two sons are corrupt, was YHWH about to intervene?

[d] LXX has the same ἄρχοντα ἐπὶ τὸν λαόν μου Ισραηλ [leader over the people of Israel] 2) YHWH does not refer to Saul as a King.; only the people do and Samuel's words reflect their wish

and shall be turned into another man. (v6)

This then comes to pass in (v9). G-d gives Saul *another heart* [a] (v11). The amazed people say.. *Is Saul amongst the prophets?* The events here become a national proverb (v12) Saul's heart is changed for one approved of YHWH. [b] Samuel calls all the people together and declares..

Thus says YHWH, the God of Israel,
I brought up Israel out of Egypt, and I delivered you out of the hand of the Egyptians,
and out of the hand of all the kingdoms that oppressed you:
but ye have this day rejected your God,
who himself saves you out of all your calamities and your distresses;
and ye have said unto him, Nay, but set a king over us. (v17-19)

Samuel presents Saul to them as *the one chosen by YHWH* (v24) . The people reply *Long live the King.* [c]

Ch 11
The Ammonites are oppressing the people of Jabesh-Gilead[d] Saul calls the entire Israeli nation to come to do battle against them. A great victory is then made. The people are happy with him and they go with Samuel to Gilgal to make Saul king there.

Ch 12
Samuel goes through some of the history and reminds the people of the times when the Israelites had been oppressed by various nations and had been saved by YHWH, who *was* their king. (v12) and goes on to say..

Now therefore behold the king whom ye have chosen, and whom ye have ***asked for****:*
and, behold, YHWH has set a king over you.
If ye will fear YHWH, and serve him, and hearken unto his voice,
and not rebel against the commandment of YHWH,
then shall both you and the king that reigns over you continue following YHWH your G-d;
but if ye will not hearken unto the voice of YHWH,
but rebel against the commandment of YHWH,
then will the hand of YHWH be against you, as it was against your fathers. (v13-15)

Then, to show the people that in fact YHWH is their G-d and King and does look after them, Samuel asks G-d to send a last bit of rain necessary for the wheat harvest and it does in fact rain. The people are ashamed and say..

---

[a] Saul was chosen because of physical attributes but his heart was *not in the right place* (state)
[b] This changing of his heart suggests a certain quality of heart is needed to function as G-ds anointed
[c] Or *'let live the King'*
[d] These people had a special relationship with the tribe of Benjamin (Saul's tribe). They refused to fight against them (Judges 21). Their women were given to the Benjamites (also Judges 21)

Pray for thy servants unto YHWH thy God, that we die not;
for we have added unto all our sins this evil, to ask us a king. (v19)

Samuel replies..

Fear not: ye have indeed done all this evil; yet turn not aside from following YHWH,
but serve YHWH with all your heart: (v20)

He then encourages them further to do the right thing and ends with..

Only fear YHWH, and serve him in truth with all your heart;
consider how great things he has done for you.
But if ye shall still do wickedly, ye shall be consumed, both ye and your king. (v24-25)

Ch 13
In the next battle Saul already goes against what G-d has commanded (offering sacrifices before Samuel arrives). Samuel informs him that his kingship is over.

And Samuel said to Saul, Thou have done foolishly;
thou have not kept the commandment of YHWH thy God, which he commanded thee:
for now would YHWH have established thy kingdom upon Israel for ever.
But now thy kingdom shall not continue:
YHWH has sought him a man after his own heart,[a]
and YHWH has appointed him to be leader over his people,
because thou have not kept that which YHWH commanded thee. (13-14)[b]

Ch14-15
Saul and his son Jonathon fight more battles against the surrounding nations, mainly the Philistines. (ch15) Samuel goes to Saul and gives very clear orders to fight and utterly destroy the people of Amelek.[c] Saul goes to fight but disregards what YHWH has commanded. Samuel tells him..

Because thou have rejected the word of YHWH,
he has also rejected thee from being king (v23)

Saul begs for forgiveness but Samuel refuses and turns to leave. Saul grabs Samuel's garment and tears it. Samuel says..

---

[a] The true qualification of the heart. This will be David
[b] Parallel with Eli (chapter 2 30-35)
[c] Descendant of Esau. Their destruction in revenge for their previous actions against Israel (Exo 17.8-16); also their actions against Israel Judges 3.12-30 & Judges 6.3

YHWH has torn the kingdom of Israel from thee this day,
and has given it to a neighbour of yours, that is better than thou. (v28)

LXX has..

And Israel shall be divided into two, and He shall not turn, nor shall change His mind,
for not as a man is He to change His mind. (v29)

Last verse says..

and Samuel came no more to see Saul until the day of his death;
for Samuel mourned for Saul:
and YHWH regretted [a] *that he had made Saul king over Israel.*

Ch 16

G-d sends Samuel to Beth-lehem where he will meet Jesse and choose one of his sons. Samuel sees Jesse's son Eliab, who he thinks will definitely be the one to be chosen..

But YHWH said unto Samuel,
Look not on his countenance, or on the height of his stature;[b]
because I have rejected him: for YHWH sees not as man sees;
for man looks on the outward appearance, but YHWH looks on the heart.

Samuel anoints Jesse's son David[c] and the spirit of YHWH comes mightily (v13) on him. Verse 14 continues..

Now the Spirit of YHWH departed from Saul, and an evil spirit from YHWH troubled him.[d]

Saul's servants then recommend…

..to seek out a man who is a skilful player on the harp:
and it shall come to pass, when the evil spirit from God is upon thee,
that he shall play with his hand, and thou shall be well (v16-17)

One of the servants recommends David whom he knows can play the harp. David is called to come before Saul to comfort him. Saul is unaware of David's anointment.

Ch 17

David and Goliath. David is on an errand to his brothers on the battlefield and ends up killing Goliath; after which the Philistines flee. Saul enquires who he is.[e]

---

[a] Strong's 3338 μετεμελήθη regret

[b] As he had done with Saul

[c] Meaning Beloved

[d] Saul from this point on suffers a mental illness akin to paranoia in which he is terrified of losing his kingship

[e] Somewhat anachronous with what we've just heard above

Ch 18
From that day Saul's son Jonathon becomes good friends with David. Saul insists that David come and stay with him.

And David went out whithersoever Saul sent him, and behaved himself wisely: and Saul set him over the men of war, and it was good in the sight of all the people, and also in the sight of Saul's servants. (v5)

David grew very popular. Saul started to hate David..

And Saul was afraid of David, because YHWH was with him, and was departed from Saul. (v12)

Saul begins to devise ways to kill David.

Ch 19-24
David manages to evade Saul with the help of Jonathon and Saul's daughter. David is protected at one point by the priests.(ch 21) He takes the Holy Bread from the Tabernacle to feed his men. Saul slays the priests because they sheltered David (ch 22). Saul pursues David trying to kill him. David has the chance to kill Saul but does not (24 3-7).

Ch 25
Samuel dies

Ch 26-27
Saul pursues David. David has the chance to kill Saul again but does not (26 5-10)
David decides to leave for his own safety and goes off with six hundred of his men to *Achish the son of Maoch, king of Gath.*[a]

Ch 28
The Philistines gather to do battle against Israel. Saul sees the army and is afraid. He tries to enquire of YHWH as to what will be the outcome but gets no answer. So Saul goes in secret to a diviner who brings back Samuel only to inform Saul he has already lost his kingdom and is to lose against the Philistines.

Ch 29
David has joined forces with *Achich king of Gath*. Achich now will be fighting alongside the Philistines. The Philistine leaders see David and his men there and refuse to let them join the battle.

---

[a] Philistine area. (Joshua 13.3); Gittite

Ch 30
David returns to his camp but it has been destroyed by the Amalekites (ch15) and everything taken as booty. David finds out where they went to. He decimates the Amalekites and gets everything back.

Ch 31
Israel battles the Philistines and are defeated. Saul and his son Jonathon are killed.

2 Samuel

Ch 1
David hears the news and sorrows over the battle, over Saul, and over Jonathon's death with a lamentation.

Ch 2
David enquires of YHWH where he should go..

And it came to pass after this, that David inquired of YHWH, saying,
Shall I go up into any of the cities of Judah? And YHWH said unto him, Go up.
And David said, Where shall I go up? And He said, unto Hebron (v2)

David goes to Hebron and is made King (over Judah) there. Saul's followers bury Saul and then make Ish-bosheth, another son of Saul, King (of the rest of Israel). A civil war breaks out between Judah and the rest of Israel (with the tribe of Benjamin (Saul's tribe) at the head of Israel).

Ch 3-4
David's position grows stronger and Ish-bosheth's is weakened. Two of Saul's fighting men sneak into Ish-bosheth's house and kill him. They bring his head to David. When David sees their wicked deed he has them killed and orders Ish-bosheth buried in Hebron.

Ch 5
The elders of Israel come to Hebron to make David their king saying..

...and YHWH said to thee, Thou shall be shepherd [a] *of my people Israel,*
and thou shall be leader [b]*over Israel*
So all the elders of Israel came to the king to Hebron;

---

[a] David, who was a shepherd of flocks now is the shepherd of Israel

[b] Nagiyd (H5057). 2) Also according to the statement of Samuel in 1 Sam 15.28 *And Samuel said unto him, YHWH has rent the kingdom of Israel from thee* (Saul) *this day, and has given it to a neighbour of thine, that is better than thou.* (David)

and king David made a covenant with them in Hebron before YHWH:
and they anointed David king over Israel
David was thirty years old when he began to reign, and he reigned forty years. (v2-4)

David then goes to the Jebusite [a] city Jerusalem and takes it from the Jebusites and establishes the City of David there. David fights on with great success with YHWH's help. Hiram, king of Tyre sends cedar and carpenters to build David a house.

And David perceived that YHWH had established him king over Israel,
and that he had exalted his kingdom for his people Israel's sake. (v12)

The Philistines come up against David to fight. David enquires of YHWH if he should fight them. YHWH says to go ahead and David beats them. A second attack by the Philistines follows. David again enquires whether he should go up against them. David receives instructions from YHWH on what to do which he follows closely and wins again.

Ch 6
David goes to get the Ark.[b] On the way back with it a man touches it and is killed by YHWH. David becomes afraid to bring the Ark to the City of David and leaves it at the house of Obed-Edom the Gittite.[c] Obed-Edom's house is blessed during the Ark's stay there. When David hears of it he goes again to get the Ark and brings it into the City of David amid much festivity and puts it in a tabernacle built for it.

Ch 7
David now asks Nathan (prophet) *See now, I dwell in a house of cedar, but the ark of God dwells within curtains* (v2). Nathan tells David to do as he thinks fit but the same night YHWH speaks to Nathan and says that He has travelled with Israelites all this time from Sinai in a Tent and never asked for the building of a *house of cedar*. So YHWH tells Nathan to say to David..

I took thee from the sheepcote, from following the sheep,
that thou should be leader over my people, over Israel;
and I have been with thee whithersoever thou went,
and have cut off all thine enemies from before thee;
and I will make thee a great name, like unto the name of the great ones that are in the earth.
And I will appoint a place for my people Israel,
and will plant them, that they may dwell in their own place, and be moved no more;
neither shall the children of wickedness afflict them anymore,
as at the first, and as from the day that I commanded judges to be over my people Israel;
and I will cause thee to rest from all thine enemies.(v8-11)

YHWH tells David that *he* will be made into a house[d]

---

[a] Canaanite group still living in the area

[b] From where it had been left with Abinadab under the care of his son Eleazar (1 Sam 7.2)

[c] The people of Gath. Whom had been friends with David when Saul wanted to kill him (1 Sam 27)

When thy days are fulfilled, and thou shall sleep with thy fathers,
I will set up thy seed after thee, that shall proceed out of thy bowels,
and I will establish his kingdom. He shall build a house for my name,[a]
and I will establish the throne of his kingdom for ever.
I will be his father, and he shall be my son: if he commit iniquity,
I will chasten him with the rod of men, and with the stripes of the children of men;
but my loving-kindness shall not depart from him,
as I took it from Saul, whom I put away before thee.
And thy house and thy kingdom shall be made sure for ever before thee:
thy throne shall be established forever. (v12-17)

David then makes a prayer of humble amazement at the works and promises of G-d for his people. (v18-29)

Ch 8
David fights a number of battles and wins much territory.

And YHWH gave victory to David whithersoever he went.
And David reigned over all Israel;
and David executed justice and righteousness unto all his people. (v14-15)

Ch 9-10
David brings Mephibosheth, Jonathan's son, to Jerusalem and treats him kindly. David continues with more successful wars against Ammonites[b] and Syrians. (ch 10)

Ch 11
The affair with Bath-sheba. David remains in Jerusalem whilst his army are out fighting. One evening he is looking out from his rooftop and he sees a very beautiful woman bathing. He asks who she is and is told that it is the wife of Uriah the Hittite (a man fighting in Israel's army). David sends for her to come and he sleeps with her. She goes back home but later sends a message that she is now pregnant. David sends for Uriah in a ruse to enquire how the battles are going. After hearing the news David sends him home for the night in the hope he will sleep with his wife. Uriah refuses to go in respect of the other men fighting. When David sees that he cannot get him to go home he sends him back to the battle with a letter to Joab, the army commander, ordering Uriah to the fiercest part of the fighting where he will surely die. Uriah does in fact get killed and Joab sends word to David. Beth-Sheba laments for her husband and then..

---

[d] The Messianic promise
[a] The Temple will have the Name of YHWH housed in it
[b] Revenge for them being constantly against the Israelites (beginning Judges 10)

when the mourning was past, David sent and took her home to his house,
and she became his wife, and bore him a son.
But the thing that David had done displeased YHWH (v27).

Ch 12
Nathan is sent by YHWH to pronounce punishment upon David..

Now therefore the sword shall never depart from thy house,
because thou have despised me,
and have taken the wife of Uriah the Hittite to be thy wife.
Thus says YHWH, Behold, I will raise up evil against thee out of thine own house;
and I will take thy wives before thine eyes, and give them unto thy neighbour,
and he shall lie with thy wives in the sight of this sun.
For thou did it secretly: but I will do this thing before all Israel,
and before the sun. (v11-12)

The child born of this affair is sickly and soon dies. David has another son with Bath-sheba and calls him Solomon.

And YHWH loved him; and He sent by the hand of Nathan the prophet;
and he named him Jedidiah,[a] *for YHWH's sake.*

David fights the Ammonites again (v26-31), captures their Capital city Rabbah and puts to death the inhabitants.

Ch 13
David's son Absalom has a sister, Tamar; she is raped by another of David's sons Amnon.[b] David does not[c] act against Amnon for this. Absalom eventually gets revenge and has him killed. Absalom then exiles himself to Geshur (the home of his mother). David longs for Absalom.

Ch14
Joab, David's General, notices that the king is pining for his son and devises a plan to get Absalom back to Jerusalem. David accepts Absalom back to Jerusalem but refuses to see him face to face. Absalom forces the hand of Joab to get him to see David and David then allows him back[d]

---

[a] Loved by G-d

[b] Eldest son of David

[c] David is angry but no action noted (v21). 2) David's response is of mercy

[d] Failure to act against Absalom's crime. 2) David's position of mercy

Ch 15

And it came to pass after this, that Absalom prepared himself a chariot and horses, and fifty men to run before him (v1)

Absalom enjoys the pomp of being next in line to the throne. He appoints himself judge at the

city gate and succeeds in gaining popularity amongst the men of Israel. He then goes to Hebron where he starts a rebellion against David. David escapes into the wilderness (again, as he had from Saul, but now not as an innocent man) with his family and household. Absalom comes to Jerusalem.

Ch 16
David in the wilderness. He remains humble in his trouble. Whilst Absalom, in Jerusalem, ingratiates himself with the lust for power.

Ch 17
Absalom gathers an army to pursue David, kill him and bring back the people who went with him. The elders are pleased with the plan. Absalom's army hunt David.

Ch18
David arranges his army and they fight against Israel and win. David requests that they *deal gently with Absalom* (v5), meaning not to harm him, saying *Beware that none touch the young man Absalom* (v12). However Absalom, whilst escaping on his mule, gets trapped by the head in a tree branch and then is slaughtered by Joab. The news of Absalom's death is given to David. David weeps for his son.

Ch19
David's army return in shame not joy when they hear of the king weeping. Joab implores David to greet the army. David removes himself from his self-pity and comes out to greet them. The Israeli army are also encouraged to return to David as their king and they do. David still does not want to force himself upon Israel as their king, after all they had rejected him for Absalom. Now that Absalom is dead he wants to be welcomed back by all the Tribes, which they do. There are still tensions between Judah and Israel as the ten other tribes[a] see that Judah holds special privilege with the king when they lead the ceremonial return of David back across the Jordan. The men of Judah state that it is *because the king is a close relative of ours* (v42). This does nothing to reduce tensions but only further contributes to the ill will that will later cause the nation to break into two.

Ch 20
As the tensions are still running high another rebellion takes place. *Sheba, the son of Bichri, a Benjamite* declares that Israel has no part with the king. This throws the whole thing up in the

[a] Verse *43 ..ten shares in the king.*

air again with Israel following him. Only Judah remains faithful to David. David gets back to Jerusalem and prepares for a swift return to pursue Sheba. He sends Joab with the mighty men of Judah after Sheba. First Sheba's army commander is killed by Joash, this turns Israel back to David. Then Sheba is killed by the inhabitants of a city where he is hiding and his head given to Joash.

Ch21-24
Conclusion

A) The Famine because of Saul's failure; David arranges atonement for it (Ch21.1-14)
B) List of David's fighting men (Ch21.15-22)
C) A rewriting of Psalm 18.[a] (Ch22- Ch23.7)
B) List of David's fighting men (Ch23.8-39)
A) Plague because of David's failure; His arrangement of atonement for it (Ch24)

1 Kings [b]

The Book of Kings will follow the lineage of the kings of Israel and Judah from first to last. The journey through the Israeli kings (Northern Kingdom) is entirely of kings who rejected YHWH and did the wrong thing (evil). In Judea the good kings ruled for about two thirds of the time from first to last, but were unable to sustain the momentum with evil kings coming after them and reversing all of their righteous governance.
Throughout the entire story of the Israeli people from Abraham till the beginning of this book, leaders of the people have been sent by YHWH. Now the Israelites (and the fractured Judea) pass on leadership from father to son. Something we already have seen had failed miserably from Abimelech, Gideon's son (Judges 8-9) to Eli and his sons (1 Sam 2-4) and Samuel and his sons (1 Sam 8).

Ch1
King David is now old and frail. His son Adonijah[c] now wants the throne, he like Absalom has chariots and 50 men to run before him. David knows about this but says nothing. Adonijah consults with some of the high officials and then decides to declare himself king. Nathan the prophet tells Bath-sheba to go to David to do something as David had promised (apparently) to Solomon[d] that he would be king after him. So she and Nathan go to David and he sends them off to get Solomon and anoint him king. When he is declared king and the cheer goes up throughout the city, Adonijah hears this and he and his supporters scarper.

---

[a] Praise to YHWH for His unfailing help and perseverance to David, king of Israel.
[b] The books of Kings 1 & 2 are a single book in the Hebrew
[c] David has 7 named sons in Hebron and 14 from Jerusalem. Of all these sons only 4 take part in the narrative. His first son Amnon was killed by Absalom. Absalom rises against David but is eventually killed by David's army commander Joash. Now Adonijah wants the throne. He will be killed by Soloman
[d] 970-931BCE

Adonijah takes refuge at the altar, but comes away when Solomon declares that he won't kill him if he behaves himself.

Ch2

Adonijah still wants the throne and tries to marry one of the kings concubines (a subversive declaration of a wish to take over from the king) Solomon has him executed ..

Now therefore as YHWH lives, who has established me,
and set me on the throne of David my father,
and who has made me a house, as he promised,
surely Adonijah shall be put to death this day. (v24)

Ch3

The main narrative of Solomon's life now follows. Though there is a clear optimistic theme that runs through there is also a veiled negative theme which ultimately rises with the downfall of Solomon in chapter 11. Worth noting here is Solomon's reign against the backdrop of Deuteronomy 17.16-20

Only he shall not multiply horses to himself, nor cause the people to return to Egypt, to the end that he may multiply horses; forasmuch as YHWH has said unto you, Ye shall henceforth return no more that way. Neither shall he multiply wives to himself, that his heart turn not away: neither shall he greatly multiply to himself silver and gold. And it shall be, when he sits upon the throne of his kingdom, that he shall write him a copy of this law in a book, out of that which is before the priests the Levites: and it shall be with him, and he shall read therein all the days of his life; that he may learn to fear YHWH his God, to keep all the words of this law and these statutes, to do them; that his heart be not lifted up above his brethren, and that he turn not aside from the commandment, to the right hand, or to the left: to the end that he may prolong his days in his kingdom, he and his children, in the midst of Israel.

Solomon marries Pharaoh's daughter.[a]

Solomon loved YHWH [b] *walking in the Statutes of David* (v3a) [c]
But he also *sacrificed in the High Places* (v3b) [d]

---

[a] The daughter of Pharaoh may well have been a proselyte to Israel's G-d, but the alliance between Egypt and Israel sets Solomon into a contravention of Deut 17.16

[b] In chapter 11 v1 he will *love many strange women*

[c] Why does he not walk in the statutes of YHWH or Moses? (Deut 17.18-19) 2) Does Solomon hold the Psalms of David as statute?

[d] Former Israeli sites of worship such as Gibeon. But Solomon will ultimately build High Places for the worship of Gentile gods (Ashtoreth, Milcom, Chemosh, Molech) (11.4-8)

Solomon usually goes to Gibeon[a] to sacrifice to YHWH as that is where the Great High Place was (although the Ark was in Jerusalem). When he is there he has a dream by night. YHWH asks him his wish. Solomon's request is..

Give thy servant therefore an understanding[b] heart to judge thy people,
that I may discern between good and the bad;
for who is able to judge this thy great people? (v9)

Solomon's wish is granted..

..behold, I have done according to thy word:
lo, I have given thee a wise and discerning[c] heart;
so that there has been none like thee before thee,
neither after thee shall any arise like unto thee. (v12)

And I have also given thee that which thou have not asked, both riches and honour,
so that there shall not be any among the kings like unto thee, all thy days. (v13)

Then follows the judgment of the two women and the stolen child (v16-27)

And all Israel heard of the judgment which the king had judged; and they feared the king:
for they saw that the wisdom of God [d] was in him, to do justice. (v28)

Ch 4
Solomon is king over all Israel. He appoints an administration including twelve (tax) officers over the whole of the land; each one to supply his necessities for one month each.

Judah and Israel were many as the sand which is by the sea in multitude, eating and drinking
and making merry. And Solomon ruled over all the kingdoms from the River[e]
unto the land of the Philistines, and unto the border of Egypt:
they brought tribute, and served Solomon all the days of his life. (v20-21)

For he had dominion over all the region on this side the river, from Tiphsah [f] even to Gaza,
over all the kings on this side the river: and he had peace on all sides round about him.
And Judah and Israel dwelt safely, every man under his vine and under his fig-tree,
from Dan even to Beer-sheba, all the days of Solomon. (v24-25)

---

[a] Tribal lands of Benjamin 5 miles north of Jerusalem. A Levitical city (Joshua 21.17). The tabernacle which Moses had made was then there (1 Chronicles 21. 29; 2 Chronicles 1. 3-5)
[b] Shama [hearing]

[c] בִּין [bîyn, bene] H995. Understanding; ability to distinguish

[d] אֱלֹהִים ['elohiym] often used when ordinary people make reference to YHWH
[e] Euphrates
[f] West Euphrates, a crossing point

Thereby fulfilling G-d's promises to the Israelites. Judah and Israel having peace but at the expense of a huge military force.

And Solomon had forty thousand stalls of horses [a] *for his chariots,*
and twelve thousand horsemen. (v26)

And God [b] *gave Solomon wisdom and intelligence exceeding much, and largeness of heart,*
even as the sand that is on the sea-shore. (v29)

Solomon becomes exceedingly wise..

And there came of all peoples to hear the wisdom of Solomon,
from all kings of the earth, who had heard of his wisdom. (v34)

Solomon's wisdom is largely that of intellectual rather than spiritual pursuit. (v31-33)

Ch5

Hiram king of Tyre, who had built David's house sends greetings to Solomon. Solomon asks of him..

And, behold, I purpose to build a house for the Name of YHWH[c] *my God,*
as YHWH spoke unto David my father,
saying, Thy son, whom I will set upon thy throne in thy room,
he shall build the house for My Name. (v5)

Hiram agrees to send workmen and cedar wood and Solomon gives him food supplies. Solomon calls tens of thousands Israeli men to work on the project (v13)

Ch6

And the house which king Solomon built for YHWH,
the length thereof was threescore cubits, and the breadth thereof twenty cubits,
and the height thereof thirty cubits.(v2)

A word of warning follows to Solomon saying that it is obeying the Law which is the main objective..

And the word of YHWH came to Solomon, saying,
Concerning this house which thou are building,
if thou will walk in my statutes, and execute mine ordinances,
and keep all my commandments to walk in them;

---

[a] Solomon ignores the commandment Deut 17.16

[b] אֱלֹהִים ['elohiym]

[c] The Temple providing a dwelling place for The Name

then will I establish my word with thee, which I spoke unto David thy father.
And I will dwell among the children of Israel,
and will not forsake my people Israel. (v11-13)

And in the eleventh year, in the month Bûwl, (which is the eighth month),
was the house finished throughout all the parts thereof,
and according to all the fashion of it. So was he seven years in building it. (v38)[a]

Ch 7

And Solomon was building his own house thirteen years,
and he finished all his house.(v1)

Solomon's house takes twice as long as the Temple and is nearly twice the size. He also builds his wife (Pharaoh's daughter) a house adjoining it. His house is described as..

For he built the house of the forest of Lebanon;
the length thereof was a hundred cubits, and the breadth thereof fifty cubits,
and the height thereof thirty cubits,
upon four rows of cedar pillars, with cedar beams upon the pillars. (v2)

Solomon brings Hiram, a metalwork craftsman from Tyre to work on the Temple. He makes an extensive array of items throughout.

Thus all the work that king Solomon wrought in the house of YHWH was finished.
And Solomon brought in the things which David his father had dedicated,
even the silver, and the gold, and the vessels,
and put them in the treasuries of the house of YHWH. (v51)

Ch8
Solomon assembles all the leaders of Israel in Jerusalem; then the priests bring the Ark to the Temple and then the Glory of YHWH fills the Temple.[b]

Then spoke Solomon, YHWH has said that he would dwell in the thick darkness.[c]

---

[a] This verse not present in the LXX

[b] This Temple, now built, houses a Living Presence of G-d. Now of all the temples across all times and places in the world there were hundreds of gods placed, metal, stone, wood, all kinds, but this Temple alone actually has a god, The G-d of the Heavens and the Earth. (this point could also be said with Moses and the Tabernacle he made). YHWH wanted to live amongst His people, and here He does, but there is also the amazing didactic example to all the nations of the Earth, and probably is part of the reason why it is done by YHWH 2) The Presence of YHWH fills the temple as it had done with Moses' Tabernacle (Exo 40.34)

[c] Exo 20 21 *And the people stood afar off, and Moses drew near unto the* ***thick darkness*** *where God was. (ii)* Deut 4.11 *And ye came near and stood under the mountain; and the mountain burned with fire unto the heart of heaven, with* ***darkness, cloud, and thick darkness****. (iii)* Lev 16.2 *and YHWH said unto Moses, Speak unto Aaron thy brother, that he come not at all times into the holy place within the veil, before the Kapporeth which*

I have surely built thee a house of habitation, a place for thee to dwell in forever. (v12-13)

Solomon then says..

Blessed be YHWH, the God of Israel,
who spoke with his mouth unto David thy father, and has with his hand fulfilled it, saying,
Since the day that I brought forth my people Israel out of Egypt,
I chose no city out of all the tribes of Israel to build a house,
that my Name [a] *might be there; but I chose David to be over my people Israel*
Now it was in the heart of David my father to build a house for the Name of YHWH, the God of Israel. But YHWH said unto David my father,
Whereas it was in thy heart to build a house for my Name,
thou did well that it was in thy heart, nevertheless thou shall not build the house;
but thy son that shall come forth out of thy loins,
he shall build the house for my Name.[b] (15-19)

And YHWH has established his word that he spoke;
for I am risen up in the room of David my father,
and sit on the throne of Israel, as YHWH promised,
and have built the house for the Name of YHWH, the God of Israel.
And there have I set a place for the ark,
wherein is the covenant of YHWH, which he made with our fathers,
when he brought them out of the land of Egypt. (v20-21)

Solomon then makes a humble impassioned prayer that G-d continues with the promises made to David. He also requests that the prayers of the people are ever heard.

On the eighth day he sent the people away; and they blessed the king, and went unto their tents joyful and glad of heart for all the goodness that YHWH had showed unto David his servant, and to Israel his people. (v66)

Ch 9
G-d appears to Solomon a second time and says..

And as for thee, if thou will walk before me,
as David thy father walked, in integrity of heart, and in uprightness,
to do according to all that I have commanded thee,
and will keep my statutes and mine ordinances;
then I will establish the throne of thy kingdom over Israel for ever,
according as I promised to David thy father (4-5)

---

is upon the ark; that he die not: for I will appear in ***the cloud over the Kapporeth*** (the cover of the Ark of the Covenant.

[a] Ordinarily specific idols were placed in temples dedicated to them. Here it is the *Name* that is there

[b] 2 Sam 7 13. YHWH's statement that David's son will build the temple

Followed by the warning to Solomon of the dire judgement for failing to follow the Law (Torah).

..then will I cut off Israel out of the land which I have given them;
and this house, which I have hallowed for My Name, will I cast out of my sight
and Israel shall be a proverb and a byword among all peoples.
And though this house is so high, yet shall every one that passes by it be astonished,
and shall hiss; and they shall say,
Why has YHWH done thus unto this land, and to this house? (v7-8)

Solomon continues with the building project..

And it came to pass at the end of twenty years, wherein Solomon had built the two houses,
the house of YHWH and the king's house (now Hiram the king of Tyre had furnished
Solomon with cedar-trees and fir-trees, and with gold, according to all his desire),
that then king Solomon gave Hiram twenty cities in the land of Galilee. (v10-11)

Solomon repays Hiram with 20 cities from Galilee.[a] Hiram is unimpressed as he *had sent to the king six-score talents of gold.* (v14). Solomon increases taxes to pay for it (v15). Solomon continues with building projects and expanding his army with chariots and horsemen. The Israelite men are called up into his army. He uses the remaining gentiles in the land to work as bondservants. (v21) [b]

Ch 10
Solomon gets much wealth. He makes for himself a great luxurious throne. The queen of Sheba visits to confirm for herself the fame of Solomon[c]

So king Solomon exceeded all the kings of the earth in riches and in wisdom.
And all the earth sought the presence of Solomon,
to hear his wisdom, which God [d] had put in his heart. (23-24)

Solomon gets more horses and chariots from Egypt[e] (v28-29)

Ch 11
Solomon's time as king has thus far brought about great wealth, peace and respect amongst the nations. Unfortunately, from this pinnacle of power, Solomon now rapidly begins his downfall and descends into serious transgression and adultery against YHWH.

---

[a] Solomon cedes cities of the Promised Land
[b] The ideal of Exo 19.6 (nation of priests) & Exo. 34:11-12 (.. they will become a snare) abandoned
[c] Solomon is elevated above his countrymen (Deut 17.20)
[d] אֱלֹהִים ['elohiym]
[e] Solomon's peace seems to be enabled by a huge army

Now king Solomon loved many foreign women, together with the daughter of Pharaoh,
women of the Moabites, Ammonites, Edomites, Sidonians, and Hittites;
of the nations concerning which YHWH said unto the children of Israel,
Ye shall not go among them, neither shall they come among you;
for surely they will turn away your heart after their gods:
Solomon clave unto these in love.
And he had seven hundred wives, princesses, and three hundred concubines;
and his wives turned away his heart. For it came to pass,
when Solomon was old, that his wives turned away his heart after other gods;
and his heart was not perfect with YHWH his God,
as was the heart of David his father. (v1-4)

Solomon builds places of worship for his foreign wives and goes after their gods.

And YHWH was angry with Solomon, because his heart was turned away
from YHWH the God of Israel, who had appeared unto him twice,
and had commanded him concerning this thing, that he should not go after other gods:
but he kept not that which YHWH commanded.
Therefore YHWH said unto Solomon, Forasmuch as this is done of thee,
and thou have not kept my covenant and my statutes, which I have commanded thee,
I will surely rend the kingdom from thee, and will give it to thy servant. (v9-11)

G-d declares Solomon's kingdom is to be taken from him, not in his lifetime but of his sons.

However I will not rend away all the kingdom; but I will give one tribe[a] *to thy son,*
for David my servant's sake, and for Jerusalem's sake which I have chosen. (v13)

Only Judah (with Jerusalem) and Benjamin will remain with one of his sons as king. YHWH then begins to raise up adversaries for Israel in the surrounding regions. Jeroboam, (Ephraimite) one of Solomon's officials also rises up against him. He had been informed by Ahijah, a prophet, that the kingdom was to be torn and ten[b] tribes given to him; with one[c] tribe remaining with Jerusalem..

Howbeit I will not take the whole kingdom out of his hand; but I will make him prince all the
days of his life, for David my servant's sake whom I chose,
who kept my commandments and my statutes
but I will take the kingdom out of his son's hand,
and will give it unto thee, even ten tribes.

---

[a] Benjamin

[b] The actual division of the twelve tribes is unclear here. Judah and Benjamin are adjoining areas. The tribe of Simeon was allotted their land within Judah (Joshua 19.1). Levi also is associated with Judah / Jerusalem. This leaves Reuben, Issachar Zebulun, West & East Manasseh, Ephraim, Dan, Naphtali, Gad, Asher.

[c] Judah including Benjamin [chapter 12 v21]

And unto his son will I give one tribe,
that David my servant may have a lamp always before me in Jerusalem,
the city which I have chosen me to put my Name there.
And I will take thee, and thou shall reign according to all that thy soul desires,
and shall be king over Israel.
And it shall be, if thou will hearken unto all that I command thee,
and will walk in my ways, and do that which is right in mine eyes,
to keep my statutes and my commandments, as David my servant did;
that I will be with thee, and will build thee a sure house, as I built for David,
and will give Israel unto thee. (v34-38)

Solomon hears of this and wants to kill Jeroboam. Jeroboam flees to Egypt and awaits the death of Solomon. Solomon eventually dies and his son Rehoboam is to reign.

Ch 12
Rehoboam goes off to Shechem to be made king of Israel. Jeroboam hears of it and also travels there. They all meet with the Elders of Israel. The Elders complain to Rehoboam that Solomon's tax burden had been great throughout the land and request a lowering of it. Rehoboam ignores the advice of the Elders to reduce the tax but he takes the advice of his age-mates who say increase the tax. So Rehoboam did not change his position (as it had been decreed by G-d anyway (v15).

There is a break up again of Israel

And when all Israel saw that the king hearkened not unto them,
the people answered the king, saying, What portion have we in David?
neither have we inheritance in the son of Jesse:
to your tents O Israel: now see to thine own house, David.
So Israel departed unto their tents. (v16)

But as for the children of Israel that dwelt in the cities of Judah,[a]
Rehoboam reigned over them. (v17)

All Israel hear that Jeroboam has returned and they make him their king.
Rehoboam returns to Jerusalem to muster an army but stops when the man of G-d Shemaiah declares it is against G-d's wishes.
Jeroboam, now as king, thinks that if the people of Israel go up to Jerusalem to worship they will return to Rehoboam so he makes two golden calves one in the tribal lands of Dan[b] and one in Beth'El.[c]

---

[a] יְהוּדָה [Yehuwdah] The beginning of the Jewish nation
[b] In the most northern part of the kingdom of Israel. Probably Laish
[c] South Ephraim. Most southern part of the kingdom of Israel

Whereupon the king took counsel, and made two calves of gold;[a]
and he said unto them, It is too much for you to go up to Jerusalem:
behold thy gods, O Israel, which brought thee up out of the land of Egypt. (v28)[b]

He also sets up his own priesthood and the people begin to worship their new gods. Jeroboam sets up his own festival times.

Ch 13
A man of G-d comes up to Beth'El to condemn Jeroboam and the priests. Jeroboam continues in his way making more priests for the high places.

And this thing became sin unto the house of Jeroboam,
even to cut it off, and to destroy it from off the face of the earth. (v34) [c]

Ch 14
Jeroboam's son, Abijah, becomes sick and he wanted to know what would happen to him. Secretly he sent his wife to enquire of the prophet Ahijah (who told him he would be king[d]). Ahijah tells her that the boy plus Jereboam's entire family line will die and another king will rule Israel. Also the whole of Israel will be punished with exile for the idolatry of Jereboam. After Jeroboam's death his son Nadab rules.

Meanwhile in Judah, with king Rehoboam,

And Judah did that which was evil in the sight of YHWH,
and they provoked him to jealousy with their sins which they committed,
above all that their fathers had done.
For they also built them high places, and pillars,
and Asherim, on every high hill, and under every green tree;
and there were also sodomites in the land: they did according to all the abominations of the nations which YHWH drove out before the children of Israel. (v22-25)

God sends Shishak king of Egypt up against Jerusalem and he loots the Temple and the kings house. There is also continuing war between Judah and Israel. Rehoboam dies and is replaced by his son Abijah

---

[a] Repeating the error of Exodus 32

[b] As Aaron had said Exo. 32.4 'These are thy gods, O Israel, which brought thee up out of the land of Egypt.' 2) as with the Exo 32.4 event the golden calves are not necessarily another god to worship but an image applied to YHWH

[c] Jeroboam had been promised the kingdom but only if he obeyed YHWH's commandments (11.38)

[d] 1 Kings 11

Ch 15

King Abijah of Judah is not a righteous king. Wars continue between Judah and Israel. Abijah dies and is replaced by his son Asa.

King Asa of Judah is a righteous king and does away with all the sinful things of Abijah. He is at war with the now king Baasha of Israel. Asa gets the last of the treasures in the Temple and the kings house and uses them to make a pact with Ben Hadad the king of Aram in his fight against Baasha.
Asa dies and his son Jehoshaphat takes his place.
Picking up from chapter 14 (v20), verse 25 continues with an account of Israeli kings.
A somewhat chaotic period of assassinations ensues with one king after another being replaced in Israel, leading to the arrival of Elijah the prophet.
Nadab (Jeroboam's son) rules as an evil king following in his father's footsteps. A certain Baasha (of the house of Issachar) rises up and kills him. Baasha becomes king. He then continues to kill Jeroboam's entire family (as Ahijah the prophet had prophesied would happen (in chapter 14) for leading Israel into idolatry). Baasha however still continues his own rule in the idolatry of Jeroboam.

Ch 16

A prophet (Jehu) declares to Baasha that he and his family are also to die for this sin. Baasha dies and Elah, his son, succeeds to the throne in Israel. Zimri, a chariot commander, kills him and becomes king in Tirzah.[a] Zimri has Baasha's entire family assassinated. When the Israeli army hear about it, they make Omri the Captain of the army, their king. Omri takes the city of Tirzah. When Zimri finds out he goes to the palace, sets fire to it and dies in the process. Israel are split with half of them wanting a certain (otherwise unknown) Tibni king and the others Omri. Omri prevails over Tibni and reigns in Tirzah. Omri is as bad or worse than Jeroboam. Omri buys a hill to build his own city to rule from and calls it Samaria, after the previous owner.

And he bought the hill Samaria [b] *of Shemer for two talents of silver;*
and he built on the hill, and called the name of the city which he built,
after the name of Shemer, the owner of the hill, Samaria. (v24)

He eventually dies and is replaced by his son Ahab. Ahab marries Jezebel.[c] He builds a temple to Baal in Samaria and builds an Asherah pole. He is the worst king so far. During his rule the city of Jericho is rebuilt.[d]

---

[a] The capital city of the kingdom of Israel from where Jeroboam ruled first
[b] Meaning watchtower
[c] Daughter of the Sidonite king
[d] Against the curse/ directive of Joshua (Joshua 6.26)

Ch17

Elijah[a] the prophet. He is sent to Ahab first to tell him that there will be a drought in the land. Elijah hides in the desert for a while where he is fed by the ravens. Elijah is told by G-d to go to the Widow of Sidon.[b] Elijah stays with her and her meagre food supply miraculously does not run out. The widows son becomes sick and dies. The widow blames Elijah. Elijah brings the boy back to life.

Ch 18

Elijah is sent to Ahab. Ahab blames Elijah for Israel's trouble. Elijah says it is because Ahab has led Israel away from YHWH. They meet on Mount Carmel for a showdown between their gods. Elijah wins and the priests of Baal are all killed by the people watching at Elijah's request. It then starts to rain. Ahab rides back to Jezebel. Elijah follows.

Ch 19

Jezebel declares she will kill Elijah. Elijah escapes into the wilderness where he is fed by the Angel of YHWH. He eventually arrives at mount Horeb and stays in a cave.

..and, behold, the word of YHWH came to him, and he said unto him,
What are you doing here, Elijah?
And he said, I have been very jealous for YHWH, the God of hosts;
for the children of Israel have forsaken thy covenant,
thrown down thine altars, and slain thy prophets with the sword:
and I, even I only, am left; and they seek my life, to take it away.
And he said, Go forth, and stand upon the mount before YHWH.
And, behold, YHWH passed by, and a great and strong wind rent the mountains,
and broke in pieces the rocks before YHWH; but YHWH was not in the wind:
and after the wind an earthquake; but YHWH was not in the earthquake:
and after the earthquake a fire; but YHWH was not in the fire:
and after the fire a still small voice.
And it was so, when Elijah heard it, that he wrapped his face in his mantle,
and went out, and stood in the entrance of the cave.
And, behold, there came a voice unto him, and said,
What are you doing here, Elijah?
And he said, I have been very jealous for YHWH, the God of hosts;
for the children of Israel have forsaken thy covenant,
thrown down thine altars, and slain thy prophets with the sword;
and I, even I only, am left; and they seek my life, to take it away. (v9-14)[c]

G-d tells Elijah that there are actually seven thousand who have still been faithful to him.[d]

---

[a] With Elijah now starts a series of prophets sent to the kings of Israel and Judah to warn them of their errors

[b] Whilst Elijah is bringing true worship to the Sidonites, the Sidonite Jezebel is doing the opposite in Israel

[c] A teaching to Elijah toward his unnecessary harsh judgement (excessive zeal) upon the Baal priests

[d] Such as Obadiah and the 100 prophets he protected from Jezebel (1 Kings 18)

Elijah is told to go and anoint Elisha in his place.[a] Elisha begins to minister to Elijah.

Ch 20
King Hadad of Aram goes to war against Ahab. Elijah helps Ahab to win. Ahab forgives Hadad but Elijah says he should not have.

Ch21
Ahab wanted the vineyard of another man but he refused. Ahab is angry and tells Jezebel. She arranges for the man to be killed. G-d sends Elijah to the king to tell him that for what he has done disaster is to befall him and his house and that of Jezebel.

Ch22
King Jehoshaphat of Judah (became king in chapter 15.24) came to Ahab and requested that they fight together to get back a certain city[b] from Ben-Hadad. Ahab agrees to help and fight together. They enquire of YHWH if they should go and they are told to do so by his prophets. One prophet, whom Ahab dislikes, (for being truthful) tells him that he will die in the fight. Ahab is in fact killed in the battle and is replaced by his son Ahaziah.

2 Kings

The book of Kings is a single book in the Hebrew. This *2nd* book forms a direct continuation from 1 Kings. Also known as Kings 4 in the Latin Vulgate (Samuel 1 & 2 named there Kings 1 & 2).

Ch 1
Ahaziah falls through a lattice window and is injured. He sends messengers to enquire of the god Baal-Zebub, the god of Ekron,[c] if he will recover. The Angel of YHWH says to Elijah..

Arise! go up to meet the messengers of the king of Samaria, and say unto them,
Is it because there is no God in Israel, that ye go to inquire of Baal-zebub, the god of Ekron?
Now therefore thus says YHWH,
You shall not come down from the bed where you have gone up, but shall surely die. (v3-4)

Ahaziah sends one of his captains with 50 soldiers to bring Elijah to him but Elijah calls down fire on the troop and they are consumed. This happens a second time and a third, except the third time the captain begs for his and his soldier's lives and pleads for Elijah to come to

---

[a] G-d ends Elijah's prophet-hood for the unnecessary killing of all the prophets of Baal? That earthquake and thunder do not contain G-d; But just a small voice does/is enough

[b] An unfulfilled promise made by Ben-hadad from 1 Kings 20.34

[c] Philistine city (Joshua 13.3)

the King. Elijah is told by the Angel of YHWH not to be afraid and he goes to the king, only to tell him again that he will die. He does die and as he had no son Joram[a] another son of Ahab becomes king (of Israel).

Ch 2

This chapter returning to the narrative of the prophets Elijah and Elisha. (1 Kings 19) Elijah visits various places in Israel with Elisha ever following him. Elijah uses his cloak to part the waters of the Jordan, which they then cross. Elijah tells Elisha that he (Elijah) is about to be taken away and asks what Elisha would like. Elisha requests a double potion of Elijah's spirit. Elijah says that will only be possible if Elisha is able to see him as he leaves. Elijah is then swept up into heaven (which Elisha does witness) leaving only his cloak. Elisha picks up the cloak and wears it. Elisha then has the powers that Elijah had[b]

Ch3

Joram[c] is noted as being an evil king, and although he stops the Baal worship he continues with the sin of Jeroboam.[d] The king of Moab rebels against paying Israel an annual tribute. Joram and Jehoshaphat king of Judah and the king of Edom come together to fight against Moab. They enquire of Elisha what would be the outcome of the war. Now because Jehoshaphat has favour with Elisha,[e] he informs the kings that they will prevail and they do.

Ch4

Elisha helps a widow by giving her an unending supply of olive oil. Elisha meets another woman, a widow of one of *the sons of the prophets* [f] who had previously died. She looks after him at her home whenever he is in the area. She has no son but Elisha tells her that she will have one and she does. Later the boy child falls ill and the woman calls for Elisha. Before Elisha arrives the boy dies but Elisha prays to YHWH and brings him back to life.[g]
Later there is a famine in the land and Elisha feeds his followers.

Ch5

Naaman the captain of the Aram army is noted as being a good man. He has leprosy and hears of the prophet of Samaria who could heal him. The king of Aram sends him with a letter to the king of Israel asking for him to be healed by the prophet. Elisha hears of it and asks Naaman be sent to him. Elisha has him wash in the river Jordan and Naaman is cured. Elisha takes no reward from Naaman but Gehazi, Elisha's servant, thinks that he should have and so follows Naaman to tell him that Elisha has changed his mind about the gift and so

---

[a] There appears to be some confusion in the text regarding Jehoram and another royal son Joram.

[b] The spirit of prophesy. 2) Elisha receives a double portion (Elisha will do exactly double the miracles as Elijah did. 3) Elijah had been the prophet of fire; Elisha will be known as the prophet of peace and healing

[c] Jehoram

[d] 1 Kings 12. 28

[e] For enquiring of him the outcome of the war just stated. The enquiry instigated by Jehoshaphat

[f] Followers / disciples of prophets

[g] Similarities in the miracles of Elijah and Elisha 2) Similarities between Elisha's miracles and those of Jesus

Naaman gives Gehazi the gift. When Gehazi returns, Elisha knows what has happened. The leprosy of Naaman comes to Gehazi.

Ch6

The king of Syria is at war with Israel and makes his camp in wait of the Israeli army. Elisha knows about this and informs the Israeli king. The king of Syria sends his army to capture Elisha, but when they arrive Elisha prays that the army be struck blind and they are. The now blind army is first led back to Samaria where their sight is regained and instead of killing them Elisha orders that they be fed a feast and allowed to go back. After that the king of Syria left Israel alone. Later king Ben-Hadad of Syria came to lay siege on Samaria. There is such hunger in the city that there is cannibalism. The king of Israel is distraught when he hears this and blames Elisha and YHWH. He now orders Elisha to be killed.

Ch7

When the king's messenger arrives at Elisha's house. Elisha tells him that he will eat in Samaria in plenty as from the next day. When the next day comes the Syrian army have fled their camp leaving behind all their food and possessions.

Ch 8

King Ben-Hadad falls sick, and sends Hazael, his servant, to enquire of Elisha if he will recover. Elisha says that he will but that he will die anyway. Hazael is told by Elisha that he will become king in Ben-Hadad's stead. Hazael brings the message to the king in his bed and then suffocates him. Hazael becomes king of Syria.

Verse 16 returns to the account of the kings of Judah.
King Jehoram son of Jehoshaphat[a] now rules. Although he was an evil king, YHWH allows him to continue due to the promises to David. This time the king of Edom rebels against paying tribute to Judah and set up their own king. Jehoram attacks Edom but is beaten back. After that, hostilities between Edom and Judah become continuous.
Jehoram's son Ahaziah [b] rules after him. Also an evil king, following the error of Ahab. He rules in Jerusalem for 1 year only.

Ch 9

Elisha sends one of the *sons of the prophets*[c] to Ramoth-Gilead[d] to anoint Jehu[e] as the new king over Israel. It seems that Jehu's anointing as king is specifically brought about so that he

---

[a] 1 Kings 15.24. The account of Jehoshaphat's death is found in 2 Chron 21.18)

[b] Some confusion here with Azariah as there is an ***Ahaziah the son of Jehoram*** *king of Judah*. (2 kings 8.25) and an ***Ahaziah the son of Ahab*** who *began to reign over Israel in Samaria in the seventeenth year of Jehoshaphat king of Judah* (1 kings 22. 51)

[c] מִ.בְּ.נֵי [ben] H1121; LXX υἱῶν [vios] G5207. Son of the Prophets (a follower of the prophet)

[d] One of three refuge cities (Deut 4.43) east side of the Jordan

[e] Elijah had been told to do this (1 Kings 19.16)

may exact revenge on Ahab's entire surviving family. He begins with Jezebel (v30-37), Joram (v24) and king Ahaziah of Judah. (v27)

Ch 10
Jehu kills all of Ahab's remaining sons (v1-11) and then kills the brethren of king Ahaziah of Judah. Jehu continues on into Samaria to find and kill any of Ahab's kinsmen. Jehu clears Israel of Baal worship but does not destroy the two temples built by Jeroboam (with the golden calves)[a] and for whatever his reasons..

> *Jehu took no heed to walk in the law of YHWH, the God of Israel, with all his heart: he departed not from the sins of Jeroboam, wherewith he made Israel to sin.* (10.31)

King Hazael of Syria returns to make war on Israel along their border.

> *In those days YHWH began to cut off from Israel: and Hazael smote them in all the borders of Israel;* (v32)

Jehu dies and Jehoahaz (of Israel) his son rules in his place.

Ch 11
Athaliah was the mother Ahaziah (killed by Jehu. Ch 9.27). When she heard that her son was dead, she took the throne for herself and then also embark on a killing spree to ensure there is no one to usurp her. However Joash, a son of Ahaziah is hidden by his aunt in the Temple for six years. Jehoiada, the priest, then arranges an uprising and has the boy crowned king.

> *And Jehoiada made a covenant between YHWH and the king and the people, that they should be YHWH's people; between the king also and the people.* (v17)

The people then go through the land and destroy all the Baal worshipping places amid great celebration. Finally the boy Joash, now called Jehoash, is crowned king at seven years of age.

Ch 12
King Jehoash rules in Judah assisted by Jehoiada. He does the right thing in the eyes of G-d although the high places are allowed to continue. He makes repairs to the Temple.
King Hazael of Syria wants to capture Jerusalem. Jehoash has to clear out all the valuables from the temple to pay him off . Jehoash is assassinated and his son Amaziah reigns.

Ch 13
Continuing on from the end of chapter 10, King Jehoahaz (son of Jehu) is noted as continuing to do wrong. YHWH therefore *delivered Israel unto king Hazael continually*. Jehoahaz makes a plea to YHWH to help them. His plea is accepted and king Hazeal leaves off

---

[a] 1 Kings 12

oppressing them. The people however continue in idolatry. Jehoahaz dies and is replaced by his son Joash.
Now Elisha is dying and Joash comes to see him. Elisha tells Joash that they are to succeed over Hazael king of Syria for a while only. The Moabites now begin to attack Israel.
Joash continues with the idolatry (the sin of Jeroboam[a])

Ch14
King Amaziah (son of Jehoash (ch 12) begins his rule in Judah. There is another civil war between him and Joash of Israel. Joash comes up to Jerusalem and breaks down the wall. He then takes away the remaining treasures within the Temple and the kings palace plus hostages and carries them to Samaria. Joash dies and Jeroboam II succeeds in Israel.[b] Jeroboam II is no better than his namesake although YHWH has some mercy on him.
Amaziah is assassinated and, his son Azariah (Uzziah) becomes king in Judah.
Jeroboam II dies and is replaced by his son Zechariah.

Ch15
King Azariah/Uzziah of Judah.[c] He tried to do what was right in YHWH's eyes but did not take away the *high places.* He was afflicted with leprosy and his son Jotham ruled publicly for him until his death.
Zechariah ruled in Israel but did the same evil as the kings before him. A certain Shallum killed him and made himself king. Shallum ruled six months only before another unknown man, Menahem came up from Tirzah,[d] killed him and made himself king. Menahem travels to a city called Tiphsah in Israel; they refuse him entrance. He eventually forces his way in and brutally kills all the pregnant women as their punishment. King Menahem rules in Israel (during Azariah's rule in Judah). He clearly did evil in the sight of YHWH.
Israel now will become a vassal state to Assyria..

There came against the land Pul the king of Assyria; and Menahem gave Pul a thousand talents of silver, that his hand might be with him to confirm the kingdom in his hand. And Menahem exacted the money of Israel, even of all the mighty men of wealth, of each man fifty shekels of silver, to give to the king of Assyria. So the king of Assyria turned back, and stayed not there in the land. (v19-20)

Menahem's son Pekahiah rules after him for two years. Then…

... Pekah the son of Remaliah, his captain,[e] conspired against him, and killed him in Samaria (v25)

---

[a] Worshiping the golden calves
[b] Hosea and Amos were the prophets active during this period
[c] Isaiah begins to prophesy during his reign up to king Hezekiah
[d] The capital city of the kingdom of Israel from where Jeroboam ruled first
[e] Pekahiah's captain

Pekah begins his rule (at the end of Azariah/Uzziah's rule in Jerusalem) in Pekahiah's place. Pekah forms an alliance with Rezin the king of Syria[a] and is against Judah.
The king of Assyria[b] makes war on Israel. It's not clear if this war is in response to Ahaz' request (as noted ahead in ch16) or another earlier event.

In the days of Pekah king of Israel came Tiglath-pileser king of Assyria, and took Ijon, and Abel-beth-maacah, and Janoah, and Kedesh, and Hazor, and Gilead, and Galilee, all the land of Naphtali [c] *and he carried them captive to Assyria.* (v29)

A certain Hoshea kills Pekah and becomes king (of Israel). King Azariah/Uzziah dies and his son Jotham[d] (Judah) begins to rule. He tried to do what was right. Jotham made some extensions to the Temple complex. He did not, however, remove the worship in the *high places.*

In those days YHWH began to send against Judah, Rezin the king of Syria,
and Pekah the son of Remaliah (v37)

Ch 16
Jotham died and his son Ahaz[e] became king in the 17th year of Pekah. He did the wrong thing again, including child sacrifice.[f] Pekah and Rezin come up against Judah (again?)

Then Rezin king of Syria and Pekah son of Remaliah king of Israel came up to Jerusalem to war: and they besieged Ahaz, but could not overcome him. (v5)

So Ahaz sent messengers to Tiglath-Pileser king of Assyria, saying,
I am thy servant and thy son: come up, and save me out of the hand of the king of Syria,
and out of the hand of the king of Israel, who rise up against me.
And Ahaz took the silver and gold that was found in the house of YHWH,
and in the treasures of the king's house, and sent it for a present to the king of Assyria.
And the king of Assyria hearkened unto him; and the king of Assyria went up against
Damascus,[g] *and took it, and carried the people of it captive to Kir, and slew Rezin.* (v7-9)

Israel now is a vassal state to Assyria. Judah has also, in the process, become a vassal state to Assyria. Ahaz modifies the Temple to make it appeal to the king of Assyria (v18). Ahaz dies and is replaced by his son Hezekiah.

---

[a] Capital Damascus
[b] Capital Nineveh
[c] Galilee and Naphtali. See Isaiah 9.1. All the northern region of the kingdom of Israel
[d] Jotham had been in command for some time already as his father had leprosy (v5)
[e] Micah prophesies to Jotham, Ahaz and Hezekiah
[f] 2 Kings 16 3-4; 2 Chronicles 28: 1 – 4
[g] Syria

Ch17

In the twelfth year of Ahaz, Hoshea[a] became king of Israel. Shalmaneser king of Assyria still holds Israel as a vassal state. Hoshea tries to make a pact with Egypt but Shalmaneser finds out and invades Israel. Samaria is besieged three years until it is overrun. The inhabitants thereof and of the entire northern kingdom of Israel are removed from the Land and taken away in captivity as slaves into Assyria and Media.[b]

In the ninth year [c] *of Hoshea the king of Assyria took Samaria,*
and carried Israel away unto Assyria,
and placed them in Halah, and on the Habor, the river of Gozan,
and in the cities of the Medes. (v6)

And it was so,
because the children of Israel had sinned against YHWH their God,
who brought them up out of the land of Egypt
from under the hand of Pharaoh king of Egypt,
and had feared other gods, and walked in the statutes of the nations,
whom YHWH cast out from before the children of Israel,
and of the kings of Israel, which they made.
And the children of Israel did secretly things that were not right against YHWH their God:
and they built them high places in all their cities,
from the tower of the watchmen to the fortified city;
and they set them up pillars and Asherim upon every high hill, and under every green tree;
and there they burnt incense in all the high places,
as did the nations whom YHWH carried away before them;
and they wrought wicked things to provoke YHWH to anger;
and they served idols, whereof YHWH had said unto them, Ye shall not do this thing.
Yet YHWH testified unto Israel, and unto Judah, by every prophet, and every seer, saying,
Turn ye from your evil ways, and keep my commandments and my statutes,
according to all the law which I commanded your fathers,
and which I sent to you by my servants the prophets.
Notwithstanding, they would not hear, but hardened their neck,
like to the neck of their fathers, who believed not in YHWH their God.
And they rejected his statutes, and his covenant that he made with their fathers,
and his testimonies which he testified unto them;
and they followed vanity, and became vain,
and went after the nations that were round about them,
concerning whom YHWH had charged them that they should not do like them.
And they forsook all the commandments of YHWH their God,

---

[a] Hoshea becomes king when he assassinates Pekah in ch 15.30 (although somewhat anachronistically stated)
[b] 2 Chron ch 30 indicates that there were many of the Israeli tribes/people who escaped the exile to Assyria
[c] 721BC

and made them molten images, even two calves, and made an Asherah,
and worshipped all the host of heaven, and served Baal.
And they caused their sons and their daughters to pass through the fire,
and used divination and enchantments, and sold themselves
to do that which was evil in the sight of YHWH, to provoke him to anger.
Therefore YHWH was very angry with Israel, and removed them out of his sight:
there was none left but the tribe of Judah only. (v7-18)

And the king of Assyria brought men from Babylon,
and from Cuthah, and from Avva, and from Hamath and Sepharvaim,
and placed them in the cities of Samaria instead of the children of Israel;
and they possessed Samaria, and dwelt in the cities thereof. (v24)

The people have been removed from the *Holy Land* but it should be noted that the land itself is holy, that is to say it is not just the presence of the people that makes it holy. The Land remains Holy. The presence now of peoples from all over the Assyrian empire with their pagan worship is another unacceptable situation for YHWH, who then sends lions amongst them to slay them. The new inhabitants then complain to the king of Assyria that the (previous) god of the land is causing this because that god is not being worshipped now. The king of Assyria allows one priest of YHWH to return to *teach them the law of the god of the land.* (v27). The priest goes to Beth'El to teach anyone who wants about the G-d of the Israelites. However, this has little effect on the new people and most continue to worship their own gods in the existing High Places and continue with the culture they brought with them..

Unto this day they do after the former manner: they fear not YHWH,
neither do they after their statutes, or after their ordinances, or after the law or after the
commandment which YHWH commanded the children of Jacob, whom he named Israel;
with whom YHWH had made a covenant, and charged them, saying,
Ye shall not fear other gods, nor bow yourselves to them,
nor serve them, nor sacrifice to them: (v34-35)

So these nations feared YHWH and served their graven images;[a]
their children likewise, and their children's children,
as did their fathers, so do they unto this day (v41)

Judah is now the only remaining tribe in their land of the former Israeli nation. All Israel[b] have been carried off into exile.

---

[a] The new inhabitants allow for a bit of YHWH worship presumably just enough *to keep the lions off*
[b] Reuben, Issachar, Zebulun; Manasseh, Ephraim; Dan, Naphtali; Gad, Asher. 2) Simeon was allocated their land within Judah and therefore not part of the Northern Kingdom of Israel. This would also leave the possibility that Benjamin was one of the Ten tribes carried off. Also possible is that the (half) tribe of Manasseh (Num 32.23; Josh 13.6-8) is counted as two tribes (East & West Jordan) therefore giving the Ten tribes as

Ch18

Picking up now from the end of chapter 16, Ahaz's son Hezekiah, is now king of Judah. He was a great king in the eyes of YHWH.

And he did that which was right in the eyes of YHWH,
according to all that David his father had done. (v3)

He cleared out all the worship of foreign gods from Judah.

He trusted in YHWH, the God of Israel;
so that after him was none like him among all the kings of Judah,
nor among them that were before him.
For he clave to YHWH; he departed not from following him,
but kept his commandments, which YHWH commanded Moses.
And YHWH was with him; whithersoever he went forth he prospered. (v6-7)

In the fourteenth year of Hezekiah,[a] the new king of Assyria, Sennacherib, invades Judah and takes all the cities of the land except Jerusalem. The spokesman for the Assyrians calls up from outside the wall of Jerusalem for the people to surrender. Hezekiah refuses as he believes that YHWH will protect them.

Ch 19

The servants of Hezekiah enquire of the prophet Isaiah what to do. Isaiah tells them that they will prevail and Sennacherib will die in his own land. Isaiah says..

And the remnant that is escaped of the house of Judah
shall again take root downward, and bear fruit upward.
For out of Jerusalem shall go forth a remnant,
and out of mount Zion, survivors:
the zeal of YHWH shall perform this. (30-31)

An Angel of YHWH puts a plague in the Assyrian camp and they all die. Sennacherib is killed in Nineveh and Esar-Haddon his son rules in his place.

Ch 20

Hezekiah becomes sick. He enquires if he will die. Isaiah says he will. Hezekiah prays to YHWH and Isaiah returns to tell Hezekiah that he will not die (for 15 more years) and will continue to defend Jerusalem against the Assyrians. A get-well delegation are sent from

---

Reuben, Issachar Zebulun, West Manasseh, East Manasseh, Ephraim, Dan, Naphtali, Gad, Asher. Therefore leaving Judah with Simeon (scattered within; Gen 49.70), Levi and Benjamin

[a] Samaria fell in the sixth year of Hezekiah (ch 18.10)

Babylon to Hezekiah. He foolishly shows them all the king's treasures. Isaiah informs Hezekiah that now the Babylonians will one day return and take everything away to Babylon including Hezekiah's own sons.

Ch21

Hezekiah's son Manasseh becomes king after him. He reverses all the work of his father and rebuilds the places of idol worship. He sets up altars to these idols in the Temple of YHWH and returns to child sacrifice. We are then reminded (v7-8) …

... in the house of which YHWH said to David and to Solomon his son,
In this house, and in Jerusalem, which I have chosen out of all the tribes of Israel,
will I put my Name for ever; neither will I cause the feet of Israel to wander any more out of the land which I gave their fathers,
if only they will observe to do according to all that I have commanded them,
and according to all the law that my servant Moses commanded them.

G-d's judgement..(v13-14)

And I will stretch over Jerusalem the line of Samaria,
and the plummet of the house of Ahab; [a]
and I will wipe Jerusalem as a man wipe a dish, wiping it and turning it upside down.
And I will cast off the remnant of mine inheritance,
and deliver them into the hand of their enemies;
and they shall become a prey and a spoil to all their enemies;

Manasseh dies and is replaced by his son Amon. He follows in his father's ways. He is killed in his house by his own servants and is replaced by his son Josiah.

Ch 22

King Josiah [b]

And he did that which was right in the eyes of YHWH,
and walked in all the way of David his father,
and turned not aside to the right hand or to the left. (v2)

Josiah has workmen in to repair the Temple. A Book of the law is found and taken to the king. He reads it and is shocked to find how they have been disobeying the commandment therein. Josiah asks the high priest to enquire of YHWH. They go to unto Huldah the prophetess and she informs them it is too late, G-d's judgement is coming; only Josiah will reign till his death peacefully without witnessing what will happen.

---

[a] Extend the same fate thereof - Exile

[b] Jeremiah is noted as beginning his prophet-hood in the 13th year of his reign. The prophet Zephaniah and Habakkuk also prophesied at this time

Ch 23
Josiah calls a meeting of all the elders at the Temple and...

And the king stood by the pillar, and made a covenant before YHWH,
to walk after YHWH, and to keep his commandments, and his testimonies,
and his statutes, with all his heart, and all his soul,
to confirm the words of this covenant that were written in this book:
and all the people stood to the covenant. (v3)

Josiah then clears away all the idol worship from within the temple, Jerusalem and Judah (and there was a lot!). He then goes into Israel to Beth'El and destroys their altars and continues on through the whole of Israel.

He then reinstates the Passover..

Surely there was not kept such a Passover
from the days of the judges that judged Israel,
nor in all the days of the kings of Israel, nor of the kings of Judah;
but in the eighteenth year of king Josiah
was this Passover kept to YHWH in Jerusalem. (v22-23)

And like unto him was there no king before him, that turned to YHWH
with all his heart, and with all his soul, and with all his might,
according to all the law of Moses; neither after him arose there any like him. (v25)

Notwithstanding, YHWH turned not from the fierceness of his great wrath,
wherewith his anger was kindled against Judah,
because of all the provocations wherewith Manasseh had provoked him.
And YHWH said, I will remove Judah also out of my sight, as I have removed Israel,
and I will cast off this city which I have chosen, even Jerusalem,
and the house of which I said, My Name shall be there. (v26-27)

Pharaoh Necoh of Egypt is passing through the land on his way to help the king of Assyria.[a] Josiah picks a fight with him but is killed in the battle against him at Megiddo. Josiah is replaced briefly by his son Jehoahaz. He does the wrong thing again. Pharaoh soon returns and takes control of the region. Judah now is paying tribute to him.

And Pharaoh-Necoh made Eliakim the son of Josiah king in the room of Josiah his father,
and changed his name to Jehoiakim:
but he took Jehoahaz away; and he came to Egypt, and died there. (v34)

[a] The Assyrians are being attacked and beaten by the Babylonians

Jehoiakim is a puppet king and just there to collect taxes for Pharaoh.

Ch 24

The Babylonian empire shortly thereafter expands into Israel / Judah and Jehoiakim switches allegiance to Nebuchadnezzar. Jehoiakim then again rebels against Nebuchadnezzar (switching back allegiance to Pharaoh). Nebuchadnezzar returns to besiege Jerusalem.

In his days Nebuchadnezzar king of Babylon came up, and Jehoiakim became his servant three years: then he turned and rebelled against him.
And YHWH sent against him bands of the Chaldeans, and bands of the Syrians, and bands of the Moabites, and bands of the children of Ammon, and sent them against Judah to destroy it, according to the word of YHWH, which he spoke by his servants the prophets.
Surely at the commandment of YHWH came this upon Judah, to remove them out of his sight, for the sins of Manasseh, according to all that he did, and also for the innocent blood that he shed; for he filled Jerusalem with innocent blood: and YHWH would not pardon. (v1-4)

Shortly before the Babylonians break into the city, Jehoiakim dies and his son Jehoiachin becomes king. Jehoiachin's reign is short lived (three months); he will be taken into captivity.

King Jehoiachin of Judah.

At that time the servants of Nebuchadnezzar king of Babylon came up to Jerusalem, and the city was besieged. And Nebuchadnezzar king of Babylon came unto the city, while his servants were besieging it; and Jehoiachin the king of Judah went out to the king of Babylon, he, and his mother, and his servants, and his princes,[a] and his officers: and the king of Babylon took him in the eighth year of his[b] reign. And he carried out thence all the treasures of the house of YHWH, and the treasures of the king's house, and cut in pieces all the vessels of gold, which Solomon king of Israel had made in the temple of YHWH, as YHWH had said. And he carried away all Jerusalem, and all the princes, and all the mighty men of valour, even ten thousand captives, and all the craftsmen and the smiths; none remained, save the poorest sort of the people of the land. And he carried away Jehoiachin to Babylon; and the king's mother, and the king's wives, and his officers, and the chief men of the land, carried he into captivity from Jerusalem to Babylon. And all the men of might, even seven thousand, and the craftsmen and the smiths a thousand, all of them strong and apt for war, even them the king of Babylon brought captive to Babylon. And the king of Babylon made Mattaniah, Jehoiachin's father's brother, king in his stead, and changed his name to Zedekiah. (v10-17)

---

[a] Daniel (Belteshazzar) and his three companions, Hananiah (Shadrach) Mishael (Meshach) Azariah (Abed-nego) are amongst these

[b] Nebuchadnezzar

King Zedekiah of Judah. Zedekiah also rebels against Nebuchadnezzar. He, like Jehoiakim before him takes the advice of false prophets (ignoring Jeremiah who is in Jerusalem at this time). Zedekiah therefore believes the Babylonians will not / cannot prevail against the city of Jerusalem.

Ch 25[a]

And it came to pass in the ninth year of his reign, in the tenth month, in the tenth day of the month, that Nebuchadnezzar king of Babylon came, he and all his army, against Jerusalem, and encamped against it; and they built forts against it round about. So the city was besieged unto the eleventh year of king Zedekiah. On the ninth day of the fourth month the famine was sore in the city, so that there was no bread for the people of the land. Then a breach was made in the city, and all the men of war fled by night by the way of the gate between the two walls, which was by the king's garden (now the Chaldeans were against the city round about); and the king went by the way of the Arabah. But the army of the Chaldeans pursued after the king, and overtook him in the plains of Jericho; and all his army was scattered from him. Then they took the king, and carried him up unto the king of Babylon to Riblah; and they gave judgment upon him. And they slew the sons of Zedekiah before his eyes, and put out the eyes of Zedekiah, and bound him in fetters, and carried him to Babylon.
Now in the fifth month, on the seventh day of the month, which was the nineteenth year of king Nebuchadnezzar, king of Babylon, came Nebuzaradan the captain of the guard, a servant of the king of Babylon, unto Jerusalem. And he burnt the house of YHWH, and the king's house; and all the houses of Jerusalem, even every great house, burnt he with fire. And all the army of the Chaldeans, that were with the captain of the guard, broke down the walls of Jerusalem round about. And the residue of the people that were left in the city, and those that fell away, that fell to the king of Babylon, and the residue of the multitude, did Nebuzaradan the captain of the guard carry away captive. But the captain of the guard left of the poorest of the land to be vinedressers and husbandmen.(v1-12)

Nebuchadnezzar leaves Gedaliah[b] as governor of Judah in Mizpah,[c] over the remaining people he has left behind in the land. Some army officers[d] arrive back and meet Gedaliah in Mizpah. Gedaliah promises amnesty to them. One of them, Ishmael, of *royal seed* kills Gedaliah. They then escape with all the remaining people to Egypt for fear of the Babylonians.
At the last verse of 2 Kings, the exiled former (last descendant) king Jehoiachin is brought out of prison in Babylon, given an allowance and allowed to eat at the king's table,[e] and so

[a] The Fall of Jerusalem 586-7 BC
[b] An Israelite. 2) These events are also covered in Jeremiah (who was in Jerusalem at the time) chpts 40 to 43
[c] Mizpah in Benjamin (immediately north of Judea) where many important meetings took place amongst the Israelites including the election of Saul
[d] Probably some of the officers who escaped with Zedekiah
[e] 2 Kings 25.29

with him the last hope for the continuation of the monarchy according to the promise of 2 Sam 7.12-16.

1 Chronicles

Now many of us might just look at the books of Chronicles and assume that they can safely be skipped as they really only cover the books of Kings again. Not so. There is a portion which covers same people same events but the writers viewpoint differs.
Chronicles will recount the entire story of the Old Testament / Torah from Adam to the returning of the Exiles from Babylon. The main themes in focus will be the arrival of the Messianic King and the rebuilding of the Priesthood/Temple and the message of hope for the future.

Ch 1-9
Genealogy of all the important characters of the Old Testament / Torah with the emphasis on two key areas, first the lineage of the Messianic king from Adam to David and then David up to the time of the return of the Exiles. Second the family line of the descendants of Aaron and the Priesthood he headed. So with these genealogies we await the Messianic king who will come, rebuild the Temple and restore the Priesthood.

Ch 10
Saul and his sons are killed when the Israelite army is defeated by the Philistines. The chronicle does not describe any other events of Saul as king.

Ch 11
David made king in Hebron. He takes the city Jebus from the Jebusites and renames it Jerusalem. He enters the stronghold thereof and renames that *the City of David.*[a] There then follows an extensive list of the *mighty men* of Israel's army who helped David become king.

Ch 12
Further acknowledgement to those men who helped David become king. Verse 23-37 details all the men of the tribes[b] of Israel who came to Hebron to affirm David as king.

Ch 13
David gathers the people and they agree to get the Ark of the Covenant from Abinadab in Kiriath-Jearim. On the way back a certain man Uzza touches the Ark to steady it and is killed by YHWH. David then fears bringing the Ark back to Jerusalem and it is left in the house of Obed-Edom. Obed-Edom's household receives blessings from YHWH whilst it is there.

---

[a] Zion
[b] Judah, Simeon, Levi, House of Aaron, Benjamin, Ephraim, Half tribe Manasseh, Issachar, Zebulun, Naphtali, Dan, Asher, (and from the other side of the Jordan) Reuben, Gad, the other Half tribe of Manasseh

Ch 14

David builds his house with help of Hiram king of Tyre. The Philistines attack when they hear that David has been made king. David enquires of YHWH what to do and he is told to fight them as he will overcome them. The Philistines are beaten and Israel becomes feared amongst the nations.

Ch 15

David prepares the Tabernacle and then sends the priests to get the Ark. A great jubilant possession then brings the Ark to the Tabernacle in the City of David in Jerusalem.

Ch 16

David brings the Ark into Jerusalem and appoints Levite priests to administer within the Tabernacle. David then gives an explanation of the way the praise will be conducted within the Tabernacle by way of a song (v7-36). The song itself made up from several Psalms[a] in praise to YHWH for all he has done with Israel and the entire Earth. The High Place at Gibeon[b] is still allowed to continue with Zadok as High Priest.

Ch 17

David, now living in his house, wants to build a House for YHWH. Through the prophet Nathan, YHWH says ..

Thou shall not build me a house to dwell in:
for I have not dwelt in a house since the day that I brought up Israel, unto this day,
but have gone from tent to tent, and from one tabernacle to another. (v 4-5).

YHWH says that He has never asked for a house to be built. He gives the message to David that as David was a shepherd before he will now be the leader of the Israelites and his name will be great amongst the nations.

And I will appoint a place for my people Israel, and will plant them,
that they may dwell in their own place, and be moved no more. (v9)

YHWH then promises to build David a house (of lineage) through which David's son will rule.

He shall build me a house, and I will establish his throne for ever.
I will be his father, and he shall be my son. (v12-13)

David then goes to the Tabernacle and makes a humble prayer of thankfulness to YHWH for all the great things He has done.

---

[a] Psalm 105 v1-15; Psalm 96 v1; Psalm 96 v13; Psalm 106 v1; Psalm 106 v47-48.
[b] The tabernacle which Moses had made was still there (1 Chronicles 21:29)

Ch 18-20
David subdues his enemies and there is peace and righteousness in Israel.

Ch 21

And Satan stood up against Israel, and moved David to number Israel (v1)

David orders Joab, his army commander to conduct a census of fighting men of the entire nation. Joab thinks it wrong to do so but it's the kings order and does so.

And God was displeased with this thing; therefore he smote Israel.
And David said unto God, I have sinned greatly, in that I have done this thing:
but now, put away, I beseech thee, the iniquity of thy servant;
for I have done very foolishly. (v7-8)

YHWH then is to send great trouble upon Israel. He gives David a choice between three catastrophes to choose one from that will befall the Israelites. David chooses pestilence and 70,000 people die. G-d also sends an angel to Jerusalem to destroy it.

And David lifted up his eyes, and saw the angel of YHWH standing between earth and heaven, having a drawn sword in his hand stretched out over Jerusalem. (v16)

David then pleads with G-d that he only should die as it was his command alone to number the troops. The angel tells David to build an altar on the same place (the threshing floor of Ornan)[a] where the angel was standing. David speaks to Ornan and buys the threshing floor from him and builds an altar there. After this YHWH withdraws the angel. David then began to sacrifice there as he was scared to go to the High Place of Gibeon.[b]

Ch 22
Continuing straight on from the above events, the site for the House of G-d is decided.

Then David said, This is the house of YHWH God,
and this is the altar of burnt-offering for Israel. (ch22 v1)

David prepares all the materials required for the Temple and speaks to Solomon to encourage him in the work ahead. David also encourages Israel's leaders to help Solomon and says..

Now set your heart and your soul to seek after YHWH your God;
arise therefore and build ye the sanctuary of YHWH God,
to bring the ark of the covenant of YHWH and the holy vessels of God,

---

[a] On Mount Moriah adjacent to The City of David
[b] Burnt offerings were not done at the Tabernacle

into the house that is to be built to the name of YHWH. (v19)

Ch 23-26

David is now very old. He makes Solomon king. The entire priesthood are to assist in the construction. It's organisation and running, when completed, is established.

Ch 27

The arrangement (division) of the men of Israel who will work for the king throughout the year. The administration for the nationwide running of Israel is set up. (v25-34)

Ch 28

David gathers the elders and recaps the events since chapter 17 (when he first wanted to build a house for G-d). He then says..

Now therefore, in the sight of all Israel, the assembly of YHWH,
and in the audience of our God,
observe and seek out all the commandments of YHWH your God;
that ye may possess this good land,
and leave it for an inheritance to your children after you for ever.
And thou, Solomon my son, know thou the God of thy father,
and serve him with a perfect heart and with a willing mind;
for YHWH searches all hearts, and understands all the imaginations of the thoughts.
If thou seek him, he will be found of thee; but if thou forsake him, he will cast thee off forever.
Take heed now; for YHWH has chosen thee to build a house for the sanctuary:
be strong, and do it. (v8-10)

David gives Solomon the plans of the Temple building and it's running by the priests.[a]

All this, said David, have I been made to understand in writing from the hand of YHWH, even all the works of this pattern. (v19)

And David said to Solomon his son,
Be strong and of good courage, and do it: fear not, nor be dismayed;
for YHWH God, even my God, is with thee; he will not fail thee, nor forsake thee,
until all the work for the service of the house of YHWH be finished. (v20)

[a] David as a new Moses received instructions as to the details of the Temple building

2 Chronicles

David dies and the chronicler continues with the focus on the kings of Judah only.
The kings are qualified, as in the Book of Kings, by them being obedient to G-d bringing success and blessings or disobedient bringing about much trouble, self-made suffering and ultimately exile.
Through this study of the Judean kings who follow David, the reader is given an understanding of why Israel failed. It also gives a clear picture of who they are as a people and what they would expect from a righteous (messianic) king and encourages them in their own faithfulness.

Ch 1

And Solomon the son of David was strengthened in his kingdom,
and YHWH his God was with him, and magnified him exceedingly. (v1)

Solomon calls all the leaders of Israel together and they go off to The High Place of Gibeon to worship and make sacrifices there before the Altar. That night G-d appeared to Solomon and asked him his wish. Solomon requests wisdom and it is granted. [a]

Ch 2
Solomon arranges a huge workforce, mostly of foreigners living in Israel.

Ch 3-4

Then Solomon began to build the house of YHWH at Jerusalem on mount Moriah,
where YHWH appeared unto David his father,
which he made ready in the place that David had appointed,
in the threshing-floor of Ornan the Jebusite. (v1)

Solomon then starts the building of the Temple in all its splendour.

Ch 5
The Temple is completed and the Ark of the Covenant brought in to the inner sanctuary. All of the holy items from the Tabernacle are set in place within the Temple and a great celebration ensues conducted by the priests. The Glory of YHWH fills the House.

Ch 6
Solomon then stands before the people and blesses YHWH for all He has done for Israel. He then makes an impassioned prayer[b] for YHWH to uphold the promises made for David's throne[c]

---

[a] This episode covered in 1 Kings 3. There it is followed by an account showing Solomon's wisdom (the two women and the child), Here it is followed by an account of Solomon's army (equipped with Egyptian horses and chariots) and an account of the great wealth he brought to Jerusalem

Solomon then says..

But will God in very deed dwell with men on the earth?
Behold, heaven and the heaven of heavens cannot contain thee;
how much less this house which I have built.
Yet have thou respect unto the prayer of thy servant, and to his supplication, YHWH my God,
to hearken unto the cry and to the prayer which thy servant prays before thee;
that thine eyes may be open toward this house day and night, (18-20)

Solomon then makes a series of pleas for the prayers of the Israelites and of foreigners to be heard at the Temple, their sins be forgiven and assistance given.

Ch 7
The glory of YHWH again fills the Temple. A great feast is made celebrating the blessings of YHWH toward Israel. YHWH appears to Solomon to answer his prayers just made. If the people continue to humble themselves before G-d and seek Him earnestly then their prayers will be answered, but if they do not they and the Temple will be destroyed..

then will I pluck them up by the roots out of my land which I have given them;
and this house, which I have hallowed for my name, will I cast out of my sight (v20)

Ch 8
Solomon restores the cities formerly given to king Haran.[a] He makes all the non-Israeli people living in the Land into bondservants. He marries Pharaoh's daughter and establishes the order of the Levite priests as king David had proposed.

Ch 9
The queen of Sheba visits Solomon. All the kings roundabout bring riches to Solomon. He has a huge collection of chariots and gets horses for them from Egypt.

So king Solomon exceeded all the kings of the earth in riches and wisdom.
And all the kings of the earth sought the presence of Solomon,
to hear his wisdom, which God had put in his heart. (v22-23)

Solomon dies and is to be replaced by his son Rehoboam.

---

[b] Folllowing the events of 1 Kings 8.
[c] 2 Sam 7. 13 *He shall build a house for my name, and I will establish the throne of his kingdom forever*
[a] Which Solomon had given to Hiram (1 Kings 9.11)

Ch 10

All of Israel follow Rehoboam up to Shechem where he is to be made king. Jeroboam also goes.[a] The Israelite leaders are keen to discuss the tax burden Solomon had imposed upon the nation. Rehoboam agrees to look into it. He first speaks with the elders who advise him to *reduce* it. He then speaks with some of his age-mates who advise him to *increase* the tax. Rehoboam takes the latter advice (a decision influenced by YHWH). When he informs the elders of his decision all Israel rebels against his becoming king. Only Judah[b] remain with him. Rehoboam has to flee for his life back to Jerusalem.

Ch 11

Rehoboam wants to make war on Israel but Shemaiah, the man of God, tells him not to. He therefore fortifies all the cities of Judah instead. All the Levite priests within Israel come to Judah (and Benjamin). Jeroboam, now as Israel's king, sets up *the golden-calves* [c] again and establishes his own priesthood. Rehoboam appoints his son Abijah chief with the mind of passing the throne to him.

Ch 12

Rehoboam's power and wealth cause him and the people with him to forget YHWH. Shishak king of Egypt is sent by YHWH to attack Judah. Although Rehoboam repents Shishak is allowed to capture all the fortified cities and takes away all the treasures of the Temple and the kings house in Jerusalem. Rehoboam further repents and continues his rule in Jerusalem, strengthening his position again. He dies and is replaced by his son Abijah

Ch 13

Abijah makes war on Jeroboam. He musters a great army and..

Abijah stood up upon mount Zemaraim, which is in the hill-country of Ephraim, and said, Hear me, O Jeroboam and all Israel: Ought ye not to know that YHWH, the God of Israel, gave the kingdom over Israel to David for ever, even to him and to his sons by a covenant of salt? [d] (v4-5)

Jeroboam doesn't listen and comes out to fight Abijah but is completely routed. Jeroboam never recovers his position and eventually YHWH kills him.

Ch 14

King Abijah dies and is replaced by his son Asa. He is a good king and restores worship of YHWH throughout Judah. The king of Ethiopia comes against him. Asa requests YHWH for victory and the Ethiopian army is destroyed.

---

[a] From 1 Kings chapter 11&12. Jeroboam's role so far is not described here. A former high official of Solomon. He had been in exile hiding from Solomon

[b] Chapter 11 will include the tribe of Benjamin (as accorded in the prophecy of Ahijah (2 Kings 11.29-32))

[c] As the Israelites had done in the wilderness (Exo 32)

[d] A sure thing. Leviticus 2:13; Numbers 18:19

Ch 15

A prophet meets with Asa and encourages him to remain firm in the worship of YHWH. Asa then continues to re-establish YHWH worship in all of Judah / Benjamin and in the cities of the hill country of Ephraim which he had taken. Many people from the tribes of Ephraim, Manasseh and Reuben join with Judah and a great celebration is held where they reaffirm their faith by oath to YHWH. Judah has peace for thirty five years during his rule.

Ch 16

King Baasha comes up against Judah. Asa, this time decides to ask Ben-Hadad king of Syria for help. He brings out some of the treasures from the Temple to give to him for his help. Ben-Hadad comes and Baasha retreats.

Hanani the seer comes to Asa to inform him that because he did not trust YHWH to solve this problem he will now be beset with wars. Asa has Hanani put in prison for saying that. Asa becomes ill and dies.

Ch 17

Asa's son Jehoshaphat becomes king. He walks in the ways of David and is very successful. He refortifies the cities of Judah and clears out any idol worship. He sends teachers of the Law (Torah) out to the people in all the cities of Judah. All the surrounding nations fear and respect Judah and bring gifts to Jehoshaphat.

Ch18

Jehoshaphat makes friends with king Ahab of Israel. When they meet Ahab asks him to join forces to fight for Ramoth-Gilead.[a] Jehoshaphat agrees but want to hear from the prophets first. He enquires if there is a prophet of YHWH. Ahab says there is a certain Micaiah but he doesn't like him. Jehoshaphat has him called anyway. Micaiah tells them that they will be beaten and Ahab killed. Which is exactly what happens. Jehoshaphat escapes with YHWH's protection.

Ch19

Jehoshaphat returned in peace to Jerusalem. Jehu (son of Hanani the seer) meets him and says..

Should thou help the wicked, and love them that hate YHWH?
for this thing wrath is upon thee from before YHWH.
Nevertheless there are good things found in thee, in that thou
have put away the Asheroth out of the land, and have set thy heart to seek God. (v2-3)

Jehoshaphat continues as a good king and sets judges in all of the fortified cities of Judah demanding of them honesty before YHWH. He also set the priests up to judge in Jerusalem.

---

[a] A refuge city (Deut 4.43) east side of the Jordan, being held by the king of Aram (1 Kings 22.3)

Ch 20

Moab and Ammon come up to fight Judah. It's a huge army. Jehoshaphat goes to the Temple to enquire of YHWH what to do. The spirit of YHWH comes upon one of the Levites there who informs him of victory. He is told to take the army to meet the enemy but not to fight; only stand still and let YHWH do the fighting. All the inhabitants of Jerusalem worship YHWH when they hear this. When they meet at the battle place the Judeans begin to sing praises to YHWH. The Moab and Ammonite army is destroyed. Fear returns to the nations roundabout and there is peace in Judah. Jehoshaphat does not clear out all the high places as the people were not fully convinced of YHWH. Jehoshaphat later made another pact with Ahaziah to build ships to go to Tarshish. Another prophet informs Jehoshaphat that because he has made another pact with an evil king his works will be destroyed. The ships were in fact broken and could not travel to Tarshish.

Ch21

Jehoshaphat dies and is replaced by his son Jehoram. He begins his rule by slaughtering all of his brothers and other leaders. He married one of Ahab's daughters and walked in the evil ways of the kings of Israel. He built many High Places and caused Judah to sin. A writing of Elijah the prophet is brought to him stating that for what he has done a plague of disease will be brought on his people and himself. YHWH causes the Philistines and the Arabians to come against Judah. They break through and take all the treasure from the kings house including his sons and wives as prisoners leaving only Jehoahaz the youngest son. Jehoram dies in the way the prophet Elijah had said and the people buried him in the city of David but not in the tombs of the kings.

Ch22

The people make Jehoahaz, now called Ahaziah, king. He rules for one year only and follows the council of Jehoram's advisers and does evil. He joined forces with Joram son of Ahab to fight Hazael king of Syria at Ramoth-Gilead. They also go out to fight against Jehu.[a] Jehu is on a mission to destroy Ahab's entire family, which he does, including Joram. Jehu then slaughters Azariah and his brothers. Athaliah, Azariah's mother becomes queen. She begins by killing all the royal-seed of the house of Judah. However the daughter of Ahaziah saved one boy, Joash, and hid him in the temple. He was there six years whilst Athaliah ruled. Jehoiada, the high priest (2 kings 11) arranges for Joash to be crowned king and Athaliah is killed.

Ch 23

Jehoiada makes a covenant between himself, the people and the king to return to the worship of YHWH only. All of Judah rejoice.

[a] Anointed by Elijah (1 Kings 19.16) / Eilsha (2 Kings 9) as king

Ch 24

Joash is a good king (being advised by Jehoiada). He restores the Temple, which had been degraded by Athaliah. As long as Jehoiada lived he did good. When Jehoiada died the other leaders of Judah became advisers to him. Their advice however was to abandon YHWH and worship the Asherim. The Spirit of God came upon Zechariah the son of Jehoiada. He tried to reason with them that they cannot prosper unless they follow YHWH. The people, at the request of Joash, stone him in the Temple court. The same year YHWH sends the Syrian army to invade Judah. They destroy the leaders and take their wealth as booty to Damascus. Joash who is left sick on his bed is killed by his servants. He too, like Jehoram, is not buried in the tombs of the kings. Joash's son Amaziah rules after him.

Ch25

Amaziah, sometimes a good king and sometimes an evil king, that is *he did that which was right in the eyes of YHWH, but not with a perfect heart.* (v2) He begins his reign by killing the servants who had killed his father, although he seems to be following the Law of Moses in this. Amaziah plans to make war on Edom. He musters 300,000 fighting men from Judah and also hires 100,000 men from Ephraim Israel. A man of G-d comes to him and advises him that he should not fight with the Israeli men as G-d is not with them and therefore they will not be able to help Judah's army. Amaziah asks what he should do about the fee paid to them to which the man of G-d reminds him that YHWH can give him much more than that. Amaziah tells the Israeli army to return home, and although they have been paid they are fiercely angry. Amaziah goes to battle and makes a decisive win. The Israeli army attack and plunder Judean cities on the way back. Amaziah brings back some of the captured Edomite idols and sets them up to be worshiped. A prophet of YHWH is sent to Amaziah to ask him if it is a good thing to worship gods that were unable to help the Edomites. Amaziah tells the prophet he is not that kings adviser. The prophet then tells Amaziah that G-d has therefore determined to destroy him. Amaziah then decides to make war with Israel and sends a message to king Joash[a] for them to meet in battle. Joash does advise Amaziah that he cannot win against Israel.

But Amaziah would not hear; for it was of God,
that He might deliver them into the hand of their enemies,
because they had sought after the gods of Edom. (v20)

Amaziah goes out to meet Joash anyway and is beaten. He is taken back to Jerusalem where Joash and the Israeli army break down the wall of Jerusalem. They take all the treasure from the Temple, the kings house plus captives and return to Samaria. Amaziah continues to rule but eventually has to flee Jerusalem and is killed in Lachish.

[a] Of Israel. Grandson of king Jehu, son of Jehoahaz (2 Kings 10)

Ch 26

Amaziah's son Uzziah is made king. He rules for 52 years and is noted as doing *what was right in the eyes of YHWH as his father Amaziah had done.* (v4) although clearly there is some flexibility in that statement.

> *And he set himself to seek G-d in the days of Zechariah,*[a] *who had understanding in the vision of G-d and as long as he sought YHWH, God made him to prosper.* (v5)

Uzziah makes many victorious battles against the surrounding nations who begin to fear him and pay tribute. He also did many building projects all over Judea and his name spread abroad. Unfortunately this fame causes him to trespass against YHWH. Uzziah went into the Temple to burn incense upon the Altar. The priests come in to tell him this is only for the priests to do. Uzziah was angry with them for chastising him but immediately his head became leprous. He was rushed out of the Temple but the leprosy remained with him for the rest of his life. He has to remain in a separate house, being a leper, and his son Jotham was in charge of affairs. Uzziah died and was buried in a field belonging to the kings (as he was a leper)

Ch27

Jotham becomes king. Verse 2 reads..

> *he did that which was right in the eyes of YHWH, according to all that his father Uzziah had done: howbeit he entered not into the temple of YHWH. And the people did yet corruptly.*

His non entry into the temple is probably in relation to what his father did and the corruption of the people is likely that they still worshiped in the high places (2 Kings 15.35). Jotham continues with the building projects that were being done when his father lived. He has successful battles against the Ammonites. He dies and is buried in the city of David. Ahaz, his son, then reigns.

Ch28

Ahaz is an evil king.

> *..he walked in the ways of the kings of Israel, and made also molten images for the Baalim. Moreover he burnt incense in the valley of the son of Hinnom, and burnt his children in the fire, according to the abominations of the nations whom YHWH cast out before the children of Israel. And he sacrificed and burnt incense in the high places, and on the hills, and under every green tree.* (v2-4)

Judah then begins to be attacked and overcome by all the neighbouring nations. The end for Jerusalem / Judah now is in sight. The events of Ahaz' rule mark a major collapse in the

---

[a] Son of Jehoiada

fortunes of Judah and Israel. Events during his rule (see 2 Kings 16-17) are second only to those that led to the destruction of Jerusalem by the Babylonians. The book of Isaiah also has a large section covering his rule (Chapters 7-10). Ahaz will see the fall of Samaria and the end of the kingdom of Israel as they are exiled by the Assyrians. Only the city of Jerusalem will remain with the tribes of Judah, Benjamin and Levi.
The king of Syria attacks and carries off many captives to Damascus; the king of Israel attacks and kills 120,000 of the Judean army, then they carry off 200,000 captives from the city of Jerusalem to Samaria. A prophet of G-d advises the Israelis that they should not take their brethren as slaves. The Israelis agree and return them to Jericho. The Edomites then attack and take away captives; the Philistines too invade the lowlands and overrun many cities and towns there. Ahaz asks the king of Assyria for help. The Assyrian king does come but only to help himself to the remaining treasures of the kings house and the Temple. Ahaz further falls as he decides the gods of the Syrians must be the stronger and so begins to worship them. He removes precious metal from the Temple to build altars to these new gods around Jerusalem and in the cities still within his control. Further it is noted that he *shut up the doors of the house of YHWH* (v24).[a] Ahaz dies and is buried in the city of Jerusalem somewhere, but not in the tombs of the kings.

Ch 29
Ahaz is replaced by his son Hezekiah. He is a good king. In his first act he *opened the doors of the house of YHWH* (v3) again and called the Levites back into service. He says that the reason for recent troubles in Judah [b] is that the people have turned their backs on YHWH. The priests enter into the Temple and bring out all the unclean things there and burn them in the valley of Kidron. They then restore the Temple and all the vessels therein ruined by Ahaz. They go to Hezekiah to tell him that they have finished their preparations. Many sacrifices are then made on the altar to atone for the sins of *all Israel.*

So the service of the house of YHWH was set in order.
And Hezekiah rejoiced, and all the people, because of that which God had prepared for the people: for the thing was done suddenly (v35-36)

Ch 30.
Verse 1 reads..

And Hezekiah sent to all Israel and Judah, and wrote letters also to Ephraim and Manasseh,[c]
that they should come to the house of YHWH at Jerusalem,
to keep the Passover unto YHWH, the God of Israel.[d]

---

[a] 2 Kings 16.18 indicate that he modified the Temple to suit the king of Assyria
[b] He also has events in Samaria / Israel in view. Hezekiah sees that the whole of Israel is now under threat of collapse.
[c] House of Joseph sometimes distinguished from Israel
[d] It would seem by this action of Hezekiah that there was not a complete removal (into exile) of all the people / tribes of Israel. Also mentioned are the tribes of Asher, Zebulun (v10) Issachar (v18)

Bearing in mind that the people of Israel had been taken into captivity during Ahaz' rule, a decree is made by Hezekiah that all (the remaining people) of Israel should come from now on to Jerusalem to celebrate the Passover. This Passover is to be held late (in the second month) as the priests and the people were not ready in time.[a] Hezekiah arranges for letters to be sent to all of Israel saying..

Ye children of Israel, turn again unto YHWH, the God of Abraham, Isaac, and Israel,
that he may return to the remnant that are escaped of you
out of the hand of the kings of Assyria.
And be not ye like your fathers, and like your brethren,
who trespassed against YHWH, the God of their fathers,
so that he gave them up to desolation, as ye see.
Now be ye not stiff-necked, as your fathers were; but yield yourselves unto YHWH,
and enter into his sanctuary, which he has sanctified for ever,
and serve YHWH your God, that his fierce anger may turn away from you.
For if ye turn again unto YHWH, your brethren and your children shall find compassion
before them that led them captive, and shall come again into this land:
for YHWH your God is gracious and merciful,
and will not turn away his face from you, if ye return unto him. (v6-9)

When these letters arrive in the cities of Israel they are laughed at and scorned upon. Only some from the tribes of Asher, Manasseh, Ephraim Asher, Issachar and Zebulun take heed and come to Jerusalem. Judah all come together *as one* to obey. Any other altars within Jerusalem are removed and thrown into the Valley of Kidron.[b] The Passover Feast is then held with a great multitude, followed by the Feast of Unleavened Bread. Many of the people attending are not ceremonially clean but due to the situation they are allowed to participate.

And all the assembly of Judah, with the priests and the Levites, and all the assembly that came out of Israel, and the sojourners that came out of the land of Israel, and that dwelt in Judah, rejoiced. So there was great joy in Jerusalem; for since the time of Solomon the son of David king of Israel there was not the like in Jerusalem. Then the priests the Levites arose and blessed the people: and their voice was heard, and their prayer came up to his holy habitation, even unto heaven. (v25-27)

Ch 31
As soon as the celebrations are over all the people present go off, first with Judah to break down every pillar, altar and high place within Judah. They then proceed into Benjamin, Ephraim and Manasseh to do the same. Then all the *children of Israel* return to their own

[a] A delayed Passover was allowed, according to Numbers 9.6-13 for persons who had been in an unclean state at the normal time for holding the Passover (14th day first month)
[b] Meaning place of darkness

places. Hezekiah then re-establishes *the courses* of the priests, a system of rotational service proscribed by David, and the sacrificial duties of the Temple (according to the way it had been ordained by Moses in Deuteronomy). All the people of Jerusalem brought food to the Levites in abundance and store rooms were arranged for the excess.

And thus did Hezekiah throughout all Judah;
and he wrought that which was good and right and faithful before YHWH his God.
And in every work that he began in the service of the house of God,
and in the law, and in the commandments, to seek his God,
he did it with all his heart, and prospered. (v20-21)

Ch 32
The new king of Assyria Sennacherib invades Judah. He begins attacking the cities therein. Hezekiah fortifies Jerusalem and blocks the water supplies outside the city. He then gathers the people and says..

Be strong and of good courage, be not afraid nor dismayed for the king of Assyria,
nor for all the multitude that is with him; for there is a greater with us than with him:
with him is an arm of flesh; but with us is YHWH our God to help us, and to fight our battles..
(v7-8)

The people believe Hezekiah's words. Sennacherib sends his messenger to Jerusalem where he calls up to the people on the wall to give in the king of Assyria. He tells them that Hezekiah is deceiving them as they cannot withstand Sennacherib. The messenger then taunts them asking how they think their god will save them when all the other gods of the nations have failed them and had been captured. The Assyrians see the God of Jerusalem as any other they have encountered, and as they are aware that Hezekiah has just demolished the places of worship of many of these they now think that Jerusalem is now in a weaker position.

And they spoke of the God of Jerusalem, as of the gods of the peoples of the earth,
which are the work of men's hands. (v19)

Hezekiah and the prophet Isaiah pray to heaven. YHWH sends an angel to destroy the Assyrian army and the king retreats back to his own land where he is killed by his own children. Hezekiah wins the respect and is *exalted in the sight of all nations from thenceforth* (v24). They then begin to send precious gifts.
Hezekiah is stricken down with a mortal disease [a] Hezekiah prays to YHWH and is given a sign.[b] He repents again[c] and is given fifteen more years to live. Hezekiah continues to receive from YHWH great wealth of every kind. However..

---

[a] See Isaiah 38 & 2 Kings 20. His disease in 2 Chron 20.6 appears to be at the time Jerusalem was being attacked by Assyria
[b] Isaiah 38.7; " Chron 8-11
[c] Isaiah 38.9-20

..in the business of the ambassadors of the princes of Babylon,[a] *who sent unto him to inquire of the wonder that was done in the land, God left him,*[b] *to try him, that he might know all that was in his heart* (v31)

Hezekiah dies and is replaced by his son Manasseh.

Ch 33

Manasseh is an evil king he completely reverses all the acts of his father Hezekiah, rebuilding all the altars in Judea and placing graven idols within the Temple. He returned to child sacrifice (in the valley of Hinnom)[c] and all kind of sorcery. Judah becomes more evil than the nations surrounding them. YHWH ties to speak to Manasseh and the people but they take no heed. YHWH then sends the Assyrians to Jerusalem and Manasseh is taken to Babylon. Manasseh repents and prays to YHWH to help him. His wish is granted and he is returned to Jerusalem, *then Manasseh knew that YHWH, he was God* (v13). Manasseh then has a total turn around and follows directly in his father's footsteps clearing out all the idol worship and engaging in building projects within Jerusalem. He commands Judah to serve YHWH only. The people do but their worship of YHWH goes ahead in some of the High Places as well as the Temple. Manasseh dies and is replaced by his son Amon. He rules for two years only and returns again to the idol worship that his father had but he is unrepentant and trespasses more and more. He is killed by his servants, who are in turn killed by the people. Josiah, his son rules after him.

Ch 34

And he did that which was right in the eyes of YHWH,
and walked in the ways of David his father,
and turned not aside to the right hand or to the left. (v2)

Josiah destroys every altar and graven image of all the idol worship in Judea and then moves out into Israel into Manasseh, Ephraim, Simeon and Naphtali to do the same there. A collection of funds is then made throughout Judah and Israel to make repairs to the Temple. There is need of hewn stones and timber to repair damages done by former kings. All the craftsmen and the priests come to attend to the works. Whilst this is going on, a *book of the law of YHWH given by Moses* is found in the Temple and is taken to the Josiah. The scribe reads of it to Josiah who is deeply disturbed by the contents. It would seem at this point that there were no remaining Books of the Law extant and with the contents now being read to Josiah, he orders the priests to..

---

[a] Hezekiah again became proud of his wealth. (2 Kings 20.12-19)

[b] In a way such as with Job

[c] As Ahaz had done

Go ye, inquire of YHWH for me, and for them that are left in Israel and in Judah,
concerning the words of the book that is found;
for great is the wrath of YHWH that is poured out upon us because
our fathers have not kept the word of YHWH,
to do according unto all that is written in this book. (v21)

The high priest and others go off to consult Huldah the prophetess. She informs them that evil is to be brought upon Jerusalem and all the curses written in the Book will now come to be because of what the former kings have done. Josiah, however, because of his own actions of righteousness, will not see the trouble to come but will die in peace. The word is brought back to Josiah. He calls everyone in the city together and reads them the Book of the Law and makes a covenant to do all that is written in the book.

And Josiah took away all the abominations out of all the Land [a] *that pertained*
to the children of Israel, and made all that were found in Israel to serve, YHWH their God.
All his days they departed not from following YHWH, the God of their fathers. (v33)

Ch 35
Josiah celebrates the Passover feast. The Passover is arranged in accordance with the Book of the Law. Verse 18 reads..

The Passover had not been observed like this in Israel since the days of the prophet Samuel;
and none of the kings of Israel had ever celebrated such a Passover as did Josiah, with the
priests, the Levites and all Judah and Israel who were there with the people of Jerusalem.

The king of Egypt with his army are on their way to Carchemish to help the Assyrians against the Babylonians.[b] He has to pass through Israel / Judah but Josiah refuses him passage. The king of Egypt tells him that it is G-d's request that he continue. Josiah still refuses and goes up to do battle against him at Megiddo. Josiah is killed. Having killed Josiah, Pharaoh is now in control of Judah. He will assume this control when he returns from battle.

Ch 36
The people take Jehoahaz, Josiah's son as king. He had ruled for three months only when Pharaoh returns..

The king of Egypt made Eliakim, a brother of Jehoahaz,
king over Judah and Jerusalem [c] *and changed Eliakim's name to Jehoiakim.*
But Necho took Eliakim's brother Jehoahaz and carried him off to Egypt. (v4)

---

[a] אֶרֶץ ['erets] H776

[b] The Babylonians will end the Assyrian empire at this battle and begin their own

[c] The death of Josiah at the hand of the king of Egypt effectively makes Judah/Jerusalem a vassal state of Egypt. After the (unsuccessful) battle at Carchemesh, the king of Egypt returns via Jerusalem

Jehoiakim is an evil king. After 11 years rule, the king of Babylon, Nebuchadnezzar attacks Jerusalem. Jehoiakim is put in fetters and taken to Babylon with treasure from the Temple. Jehoiakim's son Jehoiachin is made king. He rules for three months before Nebuchadnezzar had him brought to Babylon with more treasures from the Temple. Nebuchadnezzar makes Zedekiah, Jehoiachin's brother king.

Zedekiah was twenty and one years old when he began to reign;
and he reigned eleven years in Jerusalem:
and he did that which was evil in the sight of YHWH his God;
he humbled not himself before Jeremiah the prophet speaking from the mouth of YHWH
And he also rebelled against king Nebuchadnezzar, who had made him swear by God:
but he stiffened his neck, and hardened his heart
against turning unto YHWH, the God of Israel.
Moreover all the chiefs of the priests, and the people,
trespassed very greatly after all the abominations of the nations;
and they polluted the house of YHWH which he had hallowed in Jerusalem.
And YHWH, the God of their fathers, sent to them by his messengers,
rising up early and sending, because he had compassion on his people,
and on his dwelling-place: but they mocked the messengers of God, and despised his words,
and scoffed at his prophets, until the wrath of YHWH arose against his people,
till there was no remedy. (v11-16)

The final section covers three components describing 1) the fall of Jerusalem to the Babylonians, 2) the 70 years prophecy of Jeremiah and 3) the Decree of Cyrus [a]

Therefore he brought upon them the king of the Chaldeans, [b]
who slew their young men with the sword in the house of their sanctuary,
and had no compassion upon young man or virgin, old man or hoary-headed:
he gave them all into his hand. And all the vessels of the house of God,
great and small, and the treasures of the house of YHWH,
and the treasures of the king, and of his princes, all these he brought to Babylon.
And they burnt the house of God, and broke down the wall of Jerusalem,
and burnt all the palaces thereof with fire, and destroyed all the goodly vessels
thereof. And them that had escaped from the sword carried he away to Babylon;
and they were servants to him and his sons until the reign of the kingdom of Persia:
(v11-20)

to fulfil the word of YHWH by the mouth of Jeremiah,[c]

---

[a] Of Persia, who has recently overthrown the Babylonian Empire

[b] The Fall of Jerusalem 586-7 BC

[c] Jer 25.12; 29.10

(until the land had enjoyed its Sabbaths:
for as long as it lay desolate it kept sabbath,)[a]
to fulfil threescore and ten years. (v21)

Now in the first year of Cyrus king of Persia,
that the word of YHWH by the mouth of Jeremiah might be accomplished,
YHWH stirred up the spirit of Cyrus king of Persia,
so that he made a proclamation throughout all his kingdom, [b]
and put it also in writing, saying, Thus says Cyrus king of Persia,
All the kingdoms of the earth has YHWH, the God of heaven, given me;
and he has charged me to build him a house [c] *in Jerusalem, which is in Judah.*
Whosoever there is among you of all his people,
YHWH his God be with him, and let him go up.[d] (v22-23)

Ezra-Nehemiah[e]

This book picks up immediately where 2 Chronicles leaves off. And so it is that Judah and Benjamin (at least) mobilise for the return to Judah, Jerusalem and the Temple.
Also worth noting here is the fact that the last two verses of 2 Chronicles (above) are copied almost exactly as the first two verses of The Book of Ezra. The events taking place now in Judah (Ezra) follow on from 2 Chronicles. Those Israelites of the diaspora who wish to return to be part of the 'promise' again are recorded as part of the restoration of both place and people.
This era contains a dense population of the events of various biblical books including the ending of 2 Kings and 2 Chronicles; Jeremiah (chapters 26-52); Lamentations (1-5); Isaiah (40-66);[f] Ezekiel, who is carried away as an exile before his prophet-hood begins; Daniel, also an exile, who is brought into King Nebuchadnezzar's palace; Book of Haggai & Book of Zechariah, the prophets who advise Zerubbabel and Joshua when the exiles return to Jerusalem; Book of Ester; Book of Obadiah a prophecy against Edom (who

---

[a] Lev 26. 34-35. The Chronicler here associating/understanding Jeremiah's 70 years as compensation to the **Land** for its improper use. (Sabbatical years, Lev 25.2-4). 2) Within the larger Blessings (v1-13) and Curses (v14-38) context of Lev 25. 3) The Babylonian administration leaving just a few of the poor people in the conquered area of Judea [2 Kings 25.12]. (The Assyrians had repopulated the Northern Kingdom after their conquest there [2 Kings 17.24]) And had left their people in Judea around Jerusalem which they also conquered (2 Kings 18.13)

[b] The Decree of Cyrus 538 BC

[c] As David and Solomon had

[d] But they do so at the wishes of a Gentile king. There's a certain irony in the situation as Israel, by now, had they been faithful to G-d, would occupy Cyrus's seat, rightfully theirs as they had had in 1 Kings 4.21 with Solomon.

[e] An interesting feature of this section is the pairing of leading role persons; Ezra Nehemiah pair; the Zerubbabel Joshua pair and the Haggai Zechariah pair. The roles and actions often blurring through the text.

[f] [Deutero] Isaiah (ch 40-55) the exiles in Babylon & [Trito] Isaiah (56-66) the returned exiles.

assisted the Babylonian army in their assault on Jerusalem) That said there is only the Book of Malachi remaining historically of the OT after the return of the exiles.[a]
The book of Ezra is part of the separated,[b] originally single book including Nehemiah (Scroll of Ezra). It has the account of the events of the returning Exiles and their restoration of the Temple and the city of Jerusalem and ultimately themselves as a people.
The chiastic structure of the book reveals this..

A Zerubbabel's return and list of returnees (Ezra 1-2)
    B Building of the temple and opposition (Ezra 3-6)
        C. Return of Ezra (Ezra 7-8)
            D Centre: Purification of the people (Ezra 9-10)
        C Return of Nehemiah (Neh. 1-2)
    B Building of the walls and opposition (Neh. 3:1-7:3)
A Zerubbabel's list of returnees; final reforms (Neh. 7:4-13:31)

The book is divided into three main sections covering the actions of the leading characters of the book - 1) Joshua & Zerubbabel,[c] 2) Ezra and 3) Nehemiah.
Each section beginning with the orders of the Persian king for a group of Exiles to return.
Also noted from the chiastic structure is that the book is 'framed' by the lists of the returnees, they also form a part of the restoration as they are now the 'restored' people who will live in Judah/Jerusalem, worship at the Temple and live by the Law.

Section 1
Ch 1-6 Joshua & Zerubbabel lead the rebuilding of the Temple.

Ch 4-6 has another internal structure with 2 segments. These 2 segments also define the Aramaic language switch over evident in The Book of Ezra.

Seg. 1	Seg. 2	
4.1-5	5.1-5	Encounter
4.6-16	5.6-17	Request
4.17-22	6.1-12	Decree
4.23-24	6.13-15	Enactment

Section 2
Ch 7-10 Ezra leads the teaching of the Torah

Section 3
Ch 1-13 Nehemiah leads the rebuilding of the city wall of Jerusalem.[d]

---

[a] Malachi's era normally understood as shortly after Nehemiah. Malachi also begins (1.1-4) with a condemnation of Edom)
[b] Separated in the first printed versions (16th century)
[c] The grandson of king Jehoiachin. Zerubbabel (a Babylonian name) does not claim his Hebrew Name? There will be no separate house of the monarchy?

The book begins by raising our hopes with regard to the Temple, Jerusalem, the Israelite people and their hoped for Kingdom (of G-d) and all the promises of G-d thus far, but by the end of the book none of it has happened; again the people fail to obey the Commandments of G-d and consequently fail to attain the divine approval necessary for this to take place. Although left unaddressed the fact that at the end of this restoration the final missing component, the actual return of the Presence of YHWH to the new Temple does not take place.

Ezra

Ch 1

Cyrus[a] tells all those Exiles..

Whosoever there is among you of all his people, his God be with him,
and let him go up to Jerusalem, which is in Judah,
and build the house of YHWH, the God of Israel (v3)

Cyrus allows them to collect donations of valuables and he himself gives back the Temple treasures that the Babylonians had taken away.

Then rose up the heads of fathers' houses of Judah and Benjamin, and the priests, and the Levites, even all whose spirit God had stirred to go up to build the house of YHWH which is in Jerusalem. (v5)

Ch 2

A list of the families who returned. Some 50,000[b] people altogether. Verse 70 mentions that ... *and all Israel* [dwelt] *in their cities.* Which is the only indication thus far that there were people from all tribes returning at this time.

Ch 3

Joshua and Zerubbabel build an altar and celebrate the feast of Tabernacles. They pay for craftsmen and send for materials for the building of the Temple. In the 2nd month of the 2nd year of their coming they lay the foundation of the Temple.

And they sang one to another in praising and giving thanks unto YHWH,
saying, For he is good, for his loving-kindness endures for ever toward Israel.
And all the people shouted with a great shout, when they praised YHWH,

---

[d] Which ultimately restores the city itself

[a] Babylon falls to the Persian Empire (539 BC) with Cyrus as emperor. His decree (538 BC). Cyrus sets up an administration for this empire. (Daniel is one of three top level administrators below him. [Daniel 6 1-3]). In the 1st year of Cyrus Daniel prays to G-d for the forgiveness of the Israelites [Daniel 9]

[b] This figure a fraction of the total population of the Israelites who, presumably, remained in the Diaspora

because the foundation of the house of YHWH was laid.
But many of the priests and Levites and heads of fathers' houses, the old men that had seen the first house, when the foundation of this house was laid before their eyes,
wept with a loud voice; and many shouted aloud for joy:
so that the people could not discern the noise of the shout of joy from the noise of the weeping of the people; for the people shouted with a loud shout, and the noise was heard afar off.
(v11-13)

Some of the older men (who had been young men when they were exiled some 50 years earlier) remember the glory of the former Temple. This foundation is somewhat smaller (see Haggai 2.3) and sorrowfully cry; others who had not known the former glory, cried for joy.

Ch 4
The people who have lived in Israel since the Assyrians conquered the cities surrounding Jerusalem (2 Kings 17.24) offer their help to build the Temple as they say they too have worshiped YHWH. Zerubbabel, and Joshua, and the rest of the heads of fathers' houses of Israel reject this request and say to them..

Ye have nothing to do with us in building a house unto our God.(v3)

Something of a lost opportunity for Judah and Israel to bring YHWH to the nations. The disgruntled people go off and begin to hinder the building project. They send a letter to the King Ahasuerus / Artaxerxes[a] (1st Aramaic section[b]) to inform him that the people of Jerusalem are a rebellious people and are not building their city with the intent of paying tribute to him but setting themselves up against him. They ask him to check through the court annals to see why the city was destroyed in the first place. The king finds the records of Nebuchadnezzar and orders the work in Jerusalem to stop. The work is halted until the second year of a new Persian king, Darius[c]

---

[a] Verse 5-6... 'Artaxerxes' should be understood not as a given name but as an honorary title such as 'Emperor' or 'His Majesty'. Same applies to Ahasuerus (ruler). Ahasuerus is the Hebrew title and Artaxerxes the Aramaic There's something of a mixture here between royal titles, dynasties and actual names (also Persian/ Median and Hebrew titles for the same adding to the confusion) 2) Cyrus ruled as king of Persia from 559BC and of Babylon 20 years later from 539BC. Cyrus' son Cambyses II ruled after him (530-522BC) . It is likely that Cambyses is the king their letter goes to, but still possible is Cyrus

[b] Verse 8 to chapter 6 verse 18 2) Also worth noting here is that the writers of the letter Bilsham and Mithredath (v7) have names of the same basic meaning (across languages) of Rehum and Shimshai (v8) [Transition point to Aramaic]

[c] Darius the Great (522- 486BC) 2) The name Darius also an honorary title 'holder/possessor of the good' (empire) 3) Darius becomes king at the time that the Persian Empire was fraught with rebellion in various parts. He is engaged in several military campaigns to regain full control. It is in this milieu that the Israelites find a degree of freedom to continue their work

Ch 5

Now the prophets, Haggai the prophet, and Zechariah the son of Iddo,
prophesied unto the Jews that were in Judah and Jerusalem;
in the Name of the God of Israel, prophesied they unto them. (v1)

Now the prophets Haggai and Zechariah begin to prophesy. (continuing Aramaic section)
An interesting point about these two is that Haggai's date of beginning to prophesy is detailed to the day as 1st day 6th month 2nd year Darius (Haggai 1.1). He advises Zerubbabel and Joshua of the word of YHWH. Haggai's last prophecy is 24th day 9th month 2nd year Darius. A period of less than 4 months. Zechariah begins his prophecy in the 8th month 2nd year Darius and covers the same topics. They *almost could be* the same person.
It makes you look at the affinity between Zerubbabel[a] and Joshua[b] who also are closely associated in Ezra. After all the returning Exiles are not working for the exultation of the Kings of Persia but are in fact, as the other settlers in Judah have claimed, resetting their kingdom with the hope and expectation of G-d's promises to His chosen people to be realized. Clearly the Jews/Israelites have a difficult situation to build that kingdom of dominance whilst serving a Persian king. That said, is Zerubbabel the clear candidate for the new monarchy or is it Joshua as the priest king[c] (Melchizedek). Either way both 'hidden' from plain view of the Persian king.[d]
So Haggai & Zechariah now prophesy to Zerubbabel & Joshua and tell them to restart the work of building the Temple. This attracts the attention of the Persian governor who asks them who gave them permission. They request that the Persian king search through *the kings treasure house in Babylon* (v17) for the Decree of Cyrus and then decide what to do.

Ch 6
Darius orders a search and they find the scroll it reads in part..

Concerning the house of God at Jerusalem, let the house be build, the place where they offer sacrifices, and let the foundations thereof be strongly laid; the height thereof threescore cubits, and the breadth thereof threescore cubits; with three courses of great stones, and a course of new timber: and let the expenses be given out of the king's house. And also let the gold and silver vessels of the house of God, which Nebuchadnezzar took forth out of the temple which is at Jerusalem, and brought unto Babylon, be restored, and brought again unto the temple which is at Jerusalem, everyone to its place; and thou shall put them in the house of God. (v3-5)

---

[a] Royal line
[b] Priestly line
[c] Zech 6 11-13.. yea, take of them silver and gold, and make crowns, and set them upon the head of Joshua the son of Jehozadak, the high priest; and speak unto him, saying, Thus speaks YHWH of hosts, saying, Behold, the man whose name is the Branch: and he shall grow up out of his place; and he shall build the temple of YHWH, even he shall build the temple of YHWH; and he shall bear the glory, and shall sit and rule upon his throne; and he shall be a priest upon his throne; and the counsel of peace shall be between them both.
[d] Whose own name is hidden? The reign of Cyrus moves directly to the reign of Darius yet there was another king between them, Cyrus' son Cambyses

Darius then issues a decree in which he offers all possible help to the construction of the Temple. A decree is also made for severe punishment to anyone interfering with the progress of the work. (v11-12) The temple is completed on the 3rd day of the month of Adar [a] in the 6th year of Darius (516BC) The rededication of the temple is 70 years[b] after its destruction. The Israelites make a great feast and make sin offerings for the twelve tribes and set up the order of the priesthood and Levites according to the Laws of Moses.[c]

And the children of the captivity kept the Passover
upon the fourteenth day of the first month.
For the priests and the Levites had purified themselves together;
all of them were pure: and they killed the Passover for all the children of the captivity, and for their brethren the priests, and for themselves.
And the children of Israel that were come again out of the captivity,
and all such as had separated themselves unto them from the filthiness of the nations of the land, to seek YHWH, the God of Israel, did eat, and kept the feast of unleavened bread seven days with joy: for YHWH had made them joyful,
and had turned the heart of the king of Assyria [d] unto them, to strengthen their hands in the work of the house of God, the God of Israel. (v19-22)[e]

---

[a] 6th month of the civil calendar

[b] Jer. 29 10 *For thus says YHWH, After seventy years are accomplished for Babylon, I will visit you, and perform my good word toward you, in causing you to return to this place.* 2) Jer 52 12-13 *Now in the fifth month, in the tenth day of the month, which was the nineteenth year (586-7BC) of king Nebuchadnezzar, king of Babylon, came Nebuzaradan the captain of the guard (who stood before the king of Babylon) into Jerusalem. And he burned the house of YHWH, and the king's house; and all the houses of Jerusalem, even every great house, burned he with fire.*

[c] It can be noted here that *the Glory of YHWH*, which had 'filled' Solomon's Temple did not fill this second temple. Also the Ark of the Covenant is missing, it's whereabouts unknown.

[d] An odd way to address Darius. Perhaps because he set his capital Susa in the old Assyrian territory of Elam

[e] These four verses returning to Hebrew text and continuing with the following list of returnees.

Ch 7

Ezra a well versed priest of the line of Aaron comes to Jerusalem[a] with another wave of exiles. Artaxerxes has issued a decree [b]

I make a decree, that all they of the people of Israel, and their priests and the Levites, in my realm, that are minded of their own free will to go to Jerusalem, go with thee (v13)

Artaxerxes gives him a large quantity of treasure and says..

And thou, Ezra, after the wisdom of thy God that is in thy hand, appoint magistrates and judges, who may judge all the people that are beyond the River, all such as know the laws of thy God; and teach ye him that know them not.
And whosoever will not do the law of thy God, and the law of the king, let judgment be executed upon him with all diligence, whether it be unto death, or to banishment, or to confiscation of goods, or to imprisonment. (v25-26)

Ezra gives praise to YHWH for what is unfolding..

[c]*Blessed be YHWH, the God of our fathers, who has put such a thing as this in the king's heart, to beautify the house of YHWH which is in Jerusalem;*
and has extended loving-kindness unto me before the king,
and his counsellors, and before all the king's mighty princes.

---

[a] During the reign of Artaxerxes [verse 8] Following on from the events just covered with Darius and the Temple being completed in his 6th year one might expect that in the 7th year a cohort of priests might return. However as the king (in his 7th year) mentioned here (v7) is named Artaxerxes, a common misunderstanding amongst scholars arises that this year and king are in reference to Artaxerxes 1st (465-424) His seventh year would be 458 BC, a jump of 58 years until Ezra's arrival, where no further developments take place in Jerusalem!
This point in Ezra does mark a major disagreement between scholars as to the timing of events here and the following section of Nehemiah. Personally I would think that the now introduced Ezra, a priest, is referring to the king in the generic sense, mentioned above, therefore becoming the seventh year of Darius, (515BC) the following year of the Temple's completion and 23 years after the Cyrus Decree.
There are three lines of defence for the 58 year lacuna view

1) The Elphantine Letters from the Jewish Temple of Elphantine. One such letter dated 407BC refers to Jehohanan the high priest and Sanballat the Horonite. (moving the Lacuna even further). (The names could be honorary titles or official positions rather than people as some scholars have proposed)
2) The genealogy of Nehemiah 12. 10-11 mentioning several generations of high priests covering the Lacuna and beyond. However, 1 Chronicles 3.19 has a similar type of chronological extension (later insertion), carrying the genealogy of Zerubbabel down to Maccabees)
3) The 490 years of Daniel chapter 9. Counting back 490 years from the crucifixion of Christ we arrive near the Lacuna date (458 BC) and therefore the decree for Ezra to return (7.13) should refer to this king Artaxerxes 1st mentioned above and as such relates to ***the going forth of the word*** (Dan 9.25). -(See notes in Daniel 9)

[b] Aramaic continuing from verse 12 to 26

[c] Return to Hebrew text

And I was strengthened according to the hand of YHWH my God upon me,
and I gathered together out of Israel chief men to go up with me. (v27-28)

Ch 8

A list is made of those who are coming back with Ezra from Babylon. Ezra assembles them together before the journey begins and finds there aren't any Levites amongst them. Ezra sends out to bring some temple servants. Many arrive and are registered. A fast is called in aid of safe journey to Jerusalem. All the silver and gold they have to take to the Temple is divided for the Levites to carry. When they arrive they rest three days then on the fourth they hand in the treasure and begin a great sacrifice of animals to the G-d of Israel YHWH.

Ch 9

When Ezra arrives he hears the bad news that the Israelites and the priests already there have adopted the customs of the local people and taken wives from among them. Ezra says..

And when I heard this thing, I rent my garment and my robe, and plucked off the hair of my head and of my beard, and sat down confounded (v3)

Ezra makes an impassioned prayer to G-d reminding the Israelites present of the history which had led the Israelites into destruction and exile. It was only by G-d's mercy they had been allowed to return to the land, and already they had forgotten one of the main reasons they were sent away, namely the intermarriages which led the people away from YHWH and his Law to the custom and practice of the Nations. Ezra ends his prayer with..

YHWH, the God of Israel, thou are righteous; for we are left a remnant that is escaped,
as it is this day: behold, we are before thee in our guiltiness;
for none can stand before thee because of this. (v15)

Ch 10

Now while Ezra prayed and made confession, weeping and casting himself down before the house of God, there was gathered together unto him out of Israel a very great assembly of men and women and children; for the people wept very sore. (v1)

The people make a covenant to divorce all the foreign wives and the children born with them. All the People of the Captivity are called to Jerusalem for them to swear to this covenant. The people say..

Now therefore make confession unto YHWH, the God of your fathers, and do his pleasure;
and separate yourselves from the peoples of the land, and from the foreign women.
Then all the assembly answered and said with a loud voice,

'as thou have said concerning us, so must we do' (v11-12)[a]

Still some of them refuse (v15). It is then noted..

And the children of the captivity did so. And Ezra the priest, with certain heads of fathers' houses, after their fathers' houses, and all of them by their names, were set apart; and they sat down in the first day of the tenth month to examine the matter. And they made an end with all the men that had married foreign women by the first day of the first month. (v16-17)

Nehemiah

Ch 1

We are now introduced to Nehemiah. He meets with his brethren and some of the Jews who have been in Jerusalem since the Cyrus decree. They have travelled to Shushan.

Now it came to pass in the month Chislev [b] *in the twentieth year,*[c] *as I was in Shushan* [d] *the palace that Hanani, one of my brethren, came, he and certain men out of Judah; and I asked them concerning the Jews that had escaped, that were left of the captivity, and concerning Jerusalem. And they said unto me, The remnant that are left of the captivity there in the province are in great affliction and reproach: the wall of Jerusalem also is broken down, and the gates thereof are burned with fire.*(v1-3)

---

[a] Another *na'asey v'nishma* moment

[b] Nehemiah's dating method differs from Ezra's. Nehemiah uses the Persian secular calendar

[c] Although not clarified here, the twentieth year is stated again as of Artaxerxes in chapter 2 verse 1. As noted in Ezra 4 this can be an honorary title

Now Nehemiah has just been told there has been no building in Jerusalem and so the twentieth year will relate to the end of the period between Cyrus Decree and Darius Decree. Probably the 20th year of Persian rule so 519BC (as it is understood by Nehemiah). This places Nehemiah in Jerusalem 2-3 years before Ezra. (this is also in accordance with the chiastic structure mentioned above. The book of Ezra / Nehemiah does not require a linear reading). Other correspondences between Ezra & Nehemiah are that Nehemiah finishes the work on the wall on the 25th day of Elul (6th month) after 52 days (Neh 6.15), Therefore the work began on the 4th day of the 5th month (the day Ezra is noted as arriving at the Temple (Ezra 7.8; 8.33) Both Ezra and Nehemiah are present at the Jerusalem wall dedication festival (Neh 12. 36;38) . Ezra also reads the scroll in (Neh 8.8)

Also noted below are some of the returnees contemporary with Ezra and Nehemiah

Ezra 8.33 ..into the hand of **Meremoth the son of Uriah**

Neh 3.4 And next unto them repaired **Meremoth the son of Uriah**

Ez 10.31 And of the sons of **Harim**: Eliezer, Isshijah, **Malchijah**,

Neh 3 11 **Malchijah** the son of **Harim**,

2) Bearing in mind what has just been noted in 'Ezra's Lacuna,' Nehemiah is now, according to common assent, in the 20th year of Artaxerxes I (445BC). The first wave of returnees have now been in Judah / Jerusalem for 93 years! They have had the Decree of Darius of help and protection since his decree till now, a period of over 70 years Ezra has been there 13 years. Still the city is a burnt out ruin with apparently a gleaming new very active Temple within!

[d] The palace of Shushan (Elam) Darius' main residence

Nehemiah prays asking for forgiveness in a similar prayer confessing the sins of Israel in a similar way as Ezra's in Ezra chapter 9.

Ch 2

Nehemiah is working in the kings presence *in the twentieth year of Artaxerxes the king* [a] (v1) on this occasion serving wine to him. The king notices Nehemiah is downcast and asks him what's wrong and he answers..

the city, the place of my fathers' sepulchres, lies waste,
and the gates thereof are consumed with fire (v3)

The king gives him leave to go and do the work and gives him letters to various governors along the way to help him. Nehemiah arrives at Jerusalem and goes covertly around the city examining the damage to the walls. He later says to them there..

Ye see the evil case that we are in, how Jerusalem lies waste,
and the gates thereof are burned with fire:
come, and let us build up the wall of Jerusalem, that we be no more a reproach [b]
And I told them of the hand of my God [c] *which was good upon me,*
as also of the king's words [d] *that he had spoken unto me.*
And they said, Let us rise up and build.
So they strengthened their hands [e] *for the good work.* (v17-18)

Again local people scorn the Israelites for building. Nehemiah answers them..

and said unto them, The God of heaven, he will prosper us;
therefore we his servants will arise and build:
but ye have no portion, nor right, nor memorial, in Jerusalem. (v20)

...further antagonising and distancing them from more people groups.

Ch 4

The locals are still angry that the Israelites are building the wall and decide to come together and fight against the workers. The workers then arm themselves for the work to continue..

---

[a] Although Artaxerxes is mentioned here again (in the single book of Ezra-Nehemiah), many commentators declare this to be a later king 465-424 BC and the' twentieth year' therefore would be 445 BC. But Artaxerxes is mentioned in Ezra chapters 4,6,7,8. Darius is also mentioned as king in Ezra 4,5,6. Though you may wonder why it took 90 years before the 50 day enterprise of completing the walls was begun

[b] The reproach is the result of the pre-exilic Israelite sin. The solution to that is obeying the Commandments of YHWH Ezekiel 5.15; Dan 9.16; Jer 42.18; Lam 2.15

[c] Nehemiah uses the word **elohiym**

[d] Nehemiah appealing to the power of the Persian king

[e] By their own hands they will do this. Zechariah (2.4-5) has said there will be no wall built by men

everyone with one of his hands wrought in the work,
and with the other held his weapon; and the builders,
everyone had his sword girded by his side, and so built (v17-18)

Ch 5

The work stops because of in-fighting. There has been no rain[a] and the price of food is rising. The Israelites are charging high prices for profit to their fellow Israelites. Nehemiah reminds them this is not the way forward.

Ch 6

Locals continue to harass the building project and try to get at Nehemiah, presumably to kill him. They do not succeed. The wall is finished in 52 days.

Ch 7

Nehemiah organises the people according to their genealogies.

Ch 8

All the people are gathered together to hear Ezra [b] read the Law of Moses to them. The book was read to them in such a way that they all understood. The feast of Tabernacles is reinstated.

Ch 9

Now in the twenty and fourth day of this month the children of Israel
were assembled with fasting, and with sackcloth, and earth upon them.
And the seed of Israel separated themselves from all foreigners,
and stood and confessed their sins, and the iniquities of their fathers.
And they stood up in their place, and read in the book of the law of YHWH their God
a fourth part of the day; and another fourth part they confessed,
and worshipped YHWH their God (v1-3)

The priests then stand up and bless G-d for who he is and what He has done for the Israelites from Abraham through Moses and to the Promised Land and all the way to the present day. Including all the stories of unfaithfulness of the people and YHWH's faithfulness to them. [c]

---

[a] G-ds promise of plentiful food is unfulfilled due to the continuing sin of the people

[b] Nehemiah is clearly contemporary with Ezra. (Nehemiah 8.8) Ezra reads from the scroll

[c] A beautiful walk through the Israelite history (v5-37), with certain aspects reminiscent of Steven's speech

Ch 10

And the rest of the people, the priests, the Levites, the porters, the singers, the Nethinim, and all they that had separated themselves from the peoples of the lands unto the law of God, their wives, their sons, and their daughters, every one that had knowledge, and understanding; they clave to their brethren, their nobles, and entered into a curse, and into an oath, to walk in God's law, which was given by Moses the servant of God, and to observe and do all the commandments of YHWH our Lord, and his ordinances and his statutes; (v28-29)

Ch 11

And the princes of the people dwelt in Jerusalem: the rest of the people also cast lots, to bring one of ten to dwell in Jerusalem the holy city, and nine parts in the other cities. And the people blessed all the men that willingly offered themselves to dwell in Jerusalem. (v1-2)

Ch 12

These were in the days of Joiakim the son of Jeshua, the son of Jozadak, and in the days of Nehemiah the governor, and of Ezra the priest the scribe. And at the dedication of the wall of Jerusalem they sought the Levites out of all their places, to bring them to Jerusalem, to keep the dedication with gladness, both with thanksgivings, and with singing, with cymbals, psalteries, and with harps. (v26-27)

And they offered great sacrifices that day, and rejoiced; for God had made them rejoice with great joy; and the women also and the children rejoiced: so that the joy of Jerusalem was heard even afar off. (v43)

Ch 13

Further clarifications of what was written in the Law of Moses concerning the separation of Israel from the nations followed by a rather amazing downer after what has just passed. Nehemiah has had to return to the king, oddly noted as the king of Babylon,[a] when he returns after a year he finds a chaotic degeneration within and without Jerusalem. Priests are setting up their houses in the Temple courts; the Levites were not being cared for and had gone off to work their farms for food; the Sabbath day was being ignored with much trading markets and movement of goods on that day. Even after Nehemiah chased out the traders they just continued to hold market outside the wall until he threatened them to be beaten; he also finds the intermarriage again of the Israelites with the local women.

---

[a] Cyrus had given the overthrown provinces certain autonomy. As long as they kept the tribute and the taxes flowing to him they were allowed puppet kings and self-rule. Also Ezra 6.22- King of Assyria

Nehemiah ends with..

Remember me, O my God, for good. (the good that he has done) (v31)[a]

Esther [b]

Set at the beginning of the Persian period that began with Cyrus, the book explores the hidden power of G-d in human affairs. G-d is not mentioned directly but the book shows how His ‘hidden’ actions are at every stage, (and you should look for the signs) as He cares for his people even in the diaspora. The Tetragrammaton appears in acrostic form four times 1.20; 5.4 (first letter of four words) and 5.13; 7.7 (last letter of four words). In 5.4 & 7.7 the Tetragrammaton is spelled forwards. (spoken by Esther and the Narrator). 1.20 & 5.13 it is spelled backwards (spoken by the king and Haman [Gentile]).
The book has a structure of coincidental and ironic reversals throughout with a matching structure built around the central chapter 6 which covers Haman’s humiliation and Mordecai’s exaltation.

1&2 the kings splendour, feast, decree;.
3 Haman’s elevation 3.1, edict 3.12-14, banquet 3.15;
4 Ester and Mordecai planning
5 Ester’s banquet
6 Haman’s humiliation, Mordecai exalted.
7 Ester’s banquet
8 Ester and Mordecai planning (v3-6)
8 Mordecai’s elevation 8.15-16, edict 8.9-14, banquet 8.17
9&10 Mordecai’s splendour, feast, decree

Ch 1

Set in Susa,[c] the capital of Persia. King Ahasuerus[d] decrees a feast to show ....*the riches of his glorious kingdom and the honour of his excellent majesty*[e] (v4) The king at some point during the festivities is having a banquet and he requests ..

..to bring Vashti the queen before the king with the crown royal,
to show the peoples and the princes her beauty; for she was fair to look on. (v11)

---

[a] Also 5.19; 13.22. remember me, O my God [zakar 'elohiym] 2) The new remnant/branch theology?

[b] Deut.31.18.. I will hide [אַסְתִּיר] and the name Esther [אֶסְתֵּר].

[c] Shushan. From where the Book of Nehemiah also begins

[d] 2) LXX has Artaxerxes [Αρταξέρξου] 2) Of Ezra 4?

[e] As Solomon had done?

She refuses to come. The king is angry and is advised to get another queen.

Ch 2

A search is announced throughout the kingdom for the new queen. Mordecai,[a] a Jew [b] working in the palace has a female cousin whom he has brought up; her parents were dead.

And he brought up Hadassah,[c] that is, Esther,[d] his uncle's daughter:
for she had neither father nor mother, and the maiden was fair and beautiful;
and when her father and mother were dead, Mordecai took her for his own daughter. (v7)

Esther is taken to the palace as one of the possible maidens to become queen.

Esther had not made known her people nor her kindred;
for Mordecai had charged her that she should not make it known. (v10)

Esther is chosen and made queen. Mordecai overhears a conversation between two palace door-keepers who were plotting to kill the king. Mordecai goes off to tell the king and the door-men are questioned and executed. Mordecai is given a commendation which is recorded in the kings chronicles. (v23)

Ch 3

A man called Haman is made the king's second in command. He requires that all the king's servants bow to him. Mordecai refuses to do this. When Haman finds out about it, and also finds out that he is a Jew, he decides to kill not only Mordecai but the entire Jewish people. Haman draws a lot to see when the date shall be for his revenge on the Jews..

In the first month, which is the month Nisan, in the twelfth year of king Ahasuerus,
they cast Pur, that is, the lot, before Haman from day to day, and from month to month,
to the twelfth month, which is the month Adar. (v7)

Haman informs the king that there are a people within his kingdom who do not obey his laws. Haman then asks for them to be destroyed. The king agrees and letters are issued throughout the kingdom that all Jews are to be killed and their property taken. With all this in place Haman and the king sit down to drink. (v15)

---

[a] Nehemiah 7.7 ....*who came with Zerubbabel, Jeshua, Nehemiah, Azariah, Raamiah, Nahamani, Mordecai*; 2) also (Ezra 2.2)

[b] יְהוּדִי [y?hûḏî] Yehuwdee; of the Jewish nation; of the Tribe of Judah

[c] Meaning myrtle [Hebrew name]

[d] Meaning star [Persian name]

Ch 4

There is great sorrow throughout the kingdom amongst the Jews. Mordecai gets one of the letters and shows it to Esther and asks her to go to the king and make a request on behalf of her people. Esther replies that..

All the king's servants, and the people of the king's provinces, do know, that whosoever, whether man or woman, shall come unto the king into the inner court, who is not called, there is one law for him, that he be put to death,
except those to whom the king shall hold out the golden sceptre, that he may live:
but I have not been called to come in unto the king these thirty days. (v11)

Mordecai says to Esther..

Think not with thyself that thou shall escape in the king's house, more than all the Jews.
For if thou altogether hold thy peace at this time,
then will relief and deliverance arise to the Jews from another place,
but thou and thy father's house will perish: and who know whether thou are not come to the kingdom for such a time as this? (v13-14)

Esther answers..

Go, gather together all the Jews that are present in Shushan,
and fast ye for me, and neither eat nor drink three days, night or day:
I also and my maidens will fast in like manner; and so will I go in unto the king,
which is not according to the law: and if I perish, I perish. (v16)

Mordecai does as Esther has said.

Ch 5

Ester then dresses in her royal attire and goes to the king. The king accepts her intrusion.. *and the king held out to Esther the golden sceptre that was in his hand* (v2). He enquires what troubles her. Esther requests that the king and Haman first come to a banquet she has arranged the same day. They come to the banquet and again the king enquires of what Ester wants. She requests only that the king and Haman come to another Banquet the next day. The king agrees. Haman goes home happy, especially pleased with the important place he has in the kings retinue. On the way he sees Mordecai, who again does not bow. This angers Haman to a point where he cannot enjoy his position anymore. He speaks to his wife and friends about it and they advise him to immediately have a gallows built, then in the morning go to the king and ask that Mordecai be hanged there. Then, they say, he will be able to go happily in the afternoon to the banquet. Haman likes this plan and goes ahead with it.

Ch 6

That same night the king can't sleep and he asks for a book of records to be read to him. In the records read to him is the account of how Mordecai had saved the king.

The king then asks what reward was given him to which they find out he had not been rewarded anything. The king then requests for an official in the courts to come – just as Haman is arriving with his plan. Haman is called in to the king.

So Haman came in. And the king said unto him,
What shall be done unto the man whom the king delights to honour?
Now Haman said in his heart,
To whom would the king delight to do honour more than to myself?
And Haman said unto the king, For the man whom the king delights to honour,
let royal apparel be brought which the king uses to wear,
and the horse that the king rides upon, and on the head of which a crown royal is set:
and let the apparel and the horse be delivered to the hand of one of the king's most noble
princes, that they may array the man therewith whom the king delights to honour,
and cause him to ride on horseback through the street of the city, and proclaim before him,
Thus shall it be done to the man whom the king delights to honour.
Then the king said to Haman, Make haste, and take the apparel and the horse,
as thou have said, and do even so to Mordecai the Jew,
that sits at the king's gate: let nothing fail of all that thou have spoken.
Then took Haman the apparel and the horse, and arrayed Mordecai, and caused him to ride
through the street of the city, and proclaimed before him,
'Thus shall it be done unto the man whom the king delights to honour. (v6-11)

Haman returns home utterly humiliated. His wife and advisers then tell him..

If Mordecai, before whom thou have begun to fall, be of the seed of the Jews,
thou shall not prevail against him, but shall surely fall before him. (v13)

Whilst they are still talking some officials arrive to take Haman to the banquet.

Ch 7
They come to the banquet and again the king asks Esther her request; this time she says ..

...let my life be given me at my petition, and my people at my request for we are sold,
I and my people, to be destroyed, to be slain, and to perish. (v3-4)

Then spoke the king Ahasuerus and said unto Esther the queen,
Who is he, and where is he, that does presume in his heart to do so?
And Esther said, An adversary and an enemy, even this wicked ...Haman.
Then Haman was afraid before the king and the queen. (v5-6)

The king walks away in anger, then Haman makes a plea to Esther for his life.

Then the king returned out of the palace garden into the place of the banquet of wine;
and Haman was fallen upon the couch whereon Esther was.
Then said the king, Will he even force the queen before me in the house?
As the word went out of the king's mouth, they covered Haman's face. (v8)

One of the officials there informs the king that Haman has had a gallows built at his home ..*And the king said, Hang* [a] *him thereon.* (v9) Haman is hanged there.

Ch 8

Mordecai is given Haman's position. Esther begs the king to revoke the decree to destroy the Jews. The king informs her that a decree once made cannot be changed so he issues another decree instead whereby the Jews are allowed to defend themselves.

Wherein the king granted the Jews that were in every city to gather themselves together,
and to stand for their life, to destroy, to slay, and to cause to perish,
all the power of the people and province that would assault them, their little ones and women,
and to take the spoil of them for a prey, (v11)

And Mordecai went forth from the presence of the king in royal apparel of blue and white, and with a great crown of gold, and with a robe of fine linen and purple: and the city of Shushan shouted and was glad. The Jews had light and gladness, and joy and honour. And in every province, and in every city, whithersoever the king's commandment and his decree came, the Jews had gladness and joy, a feast and a good day. And many from among the peoples of the land became Jews; for the fear of the Jews was fallen upon them. (v15-17)

Ch 9

On the 13th day of Adar the day when the Jews were to be slaughtered the Jews kill all their enemies throughout the kingdom. The date is declared as a feast day for the Jews and is called *Purim* after the way the first date of Haman had been set.

Ch 10

Has only three verses in which the king collects a *tribute* (tax) from his entire kingdom, presumably to go to Mordecai for the assistance of the Jews.

For Mordecai the Jew was next unto king Ahasuerus, and great among the Jews,
and accepted of the multitude of his brethren,
seeking the good of his people, and speaking peace to all his seed. (v3)

---

[a] LXX has eipen de ho basileus Staurotheto epí autou!. And said the king, Let him be crucified upon it! (the single use of the word σταυρός stauros)(crucify) outside the NT)

Job [a]

The testing of Faith.[b] That is on what basis is ones faith founded. Is it love, respect, awe or for the hope of blessings, wealth, health? Centred around the question of G-d's wisdom and justice, the question is also asked why is there suffering in the world and why also do the righteous suffer.
The book of Job forms part of the Wisdom literature alongside Proverbs and Ecclesiastes.
The geographical setting is not clarified but is unimportant to the content Teaching.
The story begins with a brief description of Job. He is described as being perfect, upright, one that feared God and turned away from evil.[c] (ch1 v1) and very wealthy, in fact the greatest of all the children of the east (v3)
After a brief description of Job sacrificing on behalf of his children[d] the scene shifts to G-d's Divine Council. The Divine council appears in diverse scriptures throughout the OT and is where witnesses are gathered and judgement made.

---

[a] Chiastic structure of Job –

1 Job's fortunes
 2 Job's friends arrive (ready to chastise) **[FRAME]**
  3 Job curses
   4 Eliphaz and Job
   8 Bildad and Job
   11 Zophar and Job
   15 Eliphaz and Job
    18 Bildad and Job
    20 Zophar and Job
    22 Eliphaz and Job
    25 Bildad and Job
   27 Job's final words to the friends
     28 **Where is wisdom found** ?
   29 Job restates his case
    32 Elihu
    34 Elihu
    35 Elihu
    36 Elihu
   38 The LORD
   40 The LORD
   40 Job withdraws
   40 The LORD
  42 Job repents
 42 Job's friends leave (chastised) **[FRAME]**
42 Job's fortunes

[b] And its integrity in a crisis 2) Also covering theodicy. The vindication of divine providence in view of the existence of evil
[c] [Job 28.28] And he said to man, 'Behold, the fear of the Lord, that is wisdom; and to depart from evil is understanding.' 2) Proverbs 9.10 3) Psalms 111.10
[d] Jobs actions might raise the question can one sacrifice on behalf of another. However it does show his concern for the lives of those beyond his own.

Within the OT there is:-

A scene from **1 Kings 22 19-23** has Micaiah prophesying that he saw G-d *sitting on his throne, and all the host of heaven standing by him on his right hand and on his left. And YHWH said, Who shall entice Ahab, that he may go up and fall at Ramoth-Gilead? And one said on this manner; and another said on that manner. And there came forth a spirit, and stood before YHWH, and said, I will entice him. And YHWH said unto him, Wherewith? And he said, I will go forth, and will be a lying spirit in the mouth of all his prophets. And He said, Thou shall entice him, and shall prevail also: go forth, and do so.*

Jeremiah 23 *18 For who has stood in the council of YHWH, that he should perceive and hear his word? who has marked my word, and heard it?*

Job 15.8 Do you listen in on God's council? Do you have a monopoly on wisdom?

Psalm 89 v 5-7 *And the heavens shall praise thy wonders, YHWH;*
Thy faithfulness also in the assembly of the holy ones.
For who in the skies can be compared unto YHWH?
Who among the sons of the mighty is like unto YHWH,
A God very terrible in the council of the holy ones,
And to be feared above all them that are round about him?

Psalm 82 *God stands in the congregation of God; He judges among the gods.*

Isaiah 14 13 *And thou said in thy heart, I will ascend into heaven, I will exalt my throne above the stars of God; and I will sit upon the mount of congregation, in the uttermost parts of the north; I will ascend above the heights of the clouds; I will make myself like the Most High.*

So the idea of the Divine Council is common enough although the appearance of the *Adversary* (Satan) is not otherwise mentioned. The use of the word Adversary occurs over twenty times in the OT it can be used for one of G-d's angels as in Numbers 20.22 where an angel of YHWH stands in Balaam's way to be an *adversary* to him. Its use generally as any opposing force.

The Adversary[a] says to G-d that the only reason Job worships G-d is because he is blessed by Him with wealth and substance. Let it be taken from him then *he will renounce* [b] *thee to thy face* (1.11). He is given permission to test Job and goes off to begin. In four disasters, Job's family and possessions are taken away. Job's reply to this is..

Naked came I out of my mother's womb, and naked shall I return there:
YHWH gave, and YHWH has taken away; blessed be the Name of YHWH. (1.21)

---

[a] Spends a lot of time walking through the earth. 2) He believes he knows why people worship G-d

[b] The Hebrew text actually says *Bless* in this verse (although the interpreters chose to use '*renounce*.' The original text appears to use antiphrasis here and *curse* is actually the word intended. The scribes of the text being unable to place that word next to G-d's name. The same occurs in chapter 1 verse 5, Jobs sacrifice for his children *It may be that my sons have sinned, and renounced God in their hearts*; also chapter 2 verse 5 *But put forth thy hand now, and touch his bone and his flesh, and he will renounce thee to thy face*; and Jobs wife (chapter 2 verse 9) *Then said his wife unto him, Do you still hold fast your integrity? renounce God, and die*.
2) The use of the word ***curse/bless*** being central to the book's insight into Faith and Belief

The Divine Council returns; this time the Adversary requests the test be increased to Job's own health. G-d gives permission and Job's health is taken away. His entire body is covered with sores..

Then said his wife unto him,
Do you still hold fast your integrity? renounce G-d, and die![a]
But he said unto her, Thou speak as one of the foolish women speak.
What? shall we receive good at the hand of God, and shall we not receive evil?
In all this did not Job sin with his lips. (2 9-10)

Job effectively passes the two tests but now three friends arrive[b] to console him in his plight. The central poetic section of their speeches and Jobs then begins.[c] Job now curses[d] his life and wishes he had never been born.
The friends Eli'phaz,[e] Bildad and Zophar, begin their answers and engage Job in arguments using their understanding about G-d and how His Justice works in the Cosmos. Arguing through legalism, they say that Job must have done something to deserve that which has befallen him.[f] Their assumption that all things in the universe operate on the principle of justice. That is, be good and good will happen to you; be evil and evil things will happen to you.[g] Job's argument is that he is innocent and his suffering therefore cannot be divine punishment (which is true). Job accuses God of *injustice…*

Though I am perfect; I regard not myself,[h]
I despise my life. This one thing therefore I said,
He destroys the perfect and the wicked.
If the scourge[i] *slay suddenly, He will mock at the trial of the innocent.*
The earth is given into the hand of the wicked;
He covers the faces of the judges thereof:
If it be not he, who then is it? (ch 9 21-24)[j]

---

[a] Jobs wife's understanding is, it appears, if there's nothing to be gained from worshipping G-d then give it up.
[b] The three friends arrive in continuation of the Adversary's test. The Adversary believes that all people serve G-d for selfish reasons. The three should learn from Job but they are lost in religious dogma and inherited notions

Remember the days of old,
Consider the years of many generations:
Ask thy father, and he will show thee;
Thine elders, and they will tell thee. (Deut 32.7)

[c] Two cycles of four speeches with a central summary prayer (chapter 28) at the end of the discourse with the three friends
[d]Job **curses** his life. H7043 qālal [וַיְקַלֵּל]
[e] Meaning G-d is fine (refined) Gold. His name linked to that of Eli'hu (G-d is He). The link to ch 28 (mining)
[f] Retribution doctrine. The Adversary's belief that Job's faith also is based upon this
[g] Proverbs 11.21, 10.16; Ecc 8.11; Psalm 1
[h] To claim innocence and provoke divine wrath. He doesn't care
[i] Calamities and misfortunes sent upon men by G-d
[j] Similarities with psalm 22 *…my G-g my G-d why…*

Job's friends insist that he must have done something wrong. Job's mind is tormented as he wants to accuse G-d but knows that it is wrong to do so. Job dismisses their claims and upholds his innocence. The friends begin their speeches somewhat proactively but then when Job rejects their knowledge they become frustrated and finally in their last speeches plainly annoyed.

There are two cycles[a] of four speeches in which Job first speaks and then is answered by one of the friends, then he answers to their speech and so on. Eli'phaz begins and ends the first cycle (chapter 4-5 and 15). Bildad begins and ends the second cycle (chapter 18 and 25). Job's answer to Bildad (ch 26) followed by a final reply to all three friends (ch 27).[b] Chapter 28 forms a thematic prayer of the entire book and Job's position thus far.[c]

Then through Chapter 29-31 Job restates his case. He ends up reminiscing on his past good deeds and justifying himself. Stating..

For calamity from God is a terror to me,
And by reason of his majesty I can do nothing. (31.23)

Job, in all his actions has had the fear of G-d's retribution for sinful action; and fear of His majesty that disallowed him to do anything wrong..

Oh that I had one to hear me!
Lo, here is my signature, let the Almighty answer me
And that I had the indictment which mine adversary has written! (31.35)

Job demands G-d to come up and explain.

Then the youthful[d] Eli'hu[e] enters into the discourse. His Hebrew name giving a dimension to the book representing their dominant/advanced theology.

Then was kindled the wrath of Elihu
the son of Barachel[f] *the Buzite,*[g] *of the family of Ram*[h]

---

[a] The majority of commentators discern 3 cycles (although the last cycle is incomplete) But they rarely take into account the Chiastic structure of this and other OT books. This unfortunately has led to many believing the text to be corrupted having missing sections / additions

[b] Job reaffirms his commitment to the truth and acknowledges also that G-d does punish the wicked and reward the righteous. He chastises the three for failing to find the wisdom that encompasses Job's experience

[c] The failure of the human mind to arrive at hidden wisdom. Wisdom remains with G-d

[d] A common theme of a god to arrive in the form of a youth? Raphael in Tobit? 2) Al Khidr

[e] His name means God is Yahu or My God Is He. The name is also the same as Elijah. Elijah אליה ; Elihu אליהו

[f] Meaning G-d has Blessed or Blessed of G-d

[g] Meaning lifted or lift and take away

[h] Meaning High or at the Apex

against Job was his wrath kindled,
because he justified himself rather than God. (32.2)

Eli'hu begins by admonishing the three for not being able to answer Job.[a] He then goes on to make four [b]speeches. He says G-d is Just and operates the Cosmos on the principal of Justice. He draws on a different conclusion than that of the three speakers and says G-d's punishment may not be for sin of the past, it could be a warning to avoid sin in the future; or pain and suffering could be used to build character and valuable lessons.[c] Job is admonished by Eli'hu, who says G-d is a *Great Teacher..*

Take heed, do not turn to iniquity,
for this you have chosen rather than affliction.
Behold, God is exalted in his power; who is a teacher like him? (36.21-22)

Eli'hu talks of the wonders of G-d's creation and asks Job if he knows how any of it works. Eli'hu doesn't say he knows why Job is suffering but he knows he is wrong to accuse G-d of injustice and so ends the discussion.

Chapter 38. G-d shows up and in four speeches[d] answers from a whirlwind[e] to respond to Job's accusation of injustice and incompetence. He takes Job on a tour of the universe and questions Job about the order of the Cosmos. Has Job ever been involved in any of that? G-d asks Job if he would like to run the universe and goes on to describe Leviathan and Behemoth.[f]

There is a perspective that humans have not conceived. To one human life it may seem like injustice but it needs to be seen in an infinitely larger context. Job is simply not in a position to accuse G-d.

So why is there suffering in the world? It's a complex picture, but the world is a wild and dangerous place and it has not been designed by G-d to prevent suffering.[g]

G-d simply asks for Job to trust in him and so except suffering when it happens and trust G-d in His Justice, care and knowledge.

Job says..

I had heard of thee by the hearing of the ear but now my eye sees thee
Therefore I abhor myself, and repent in dust and ashes.. (42 5-6)

Job's admission here that his understanding of who and what G-d is has been until now flawed. Job had only heard from others who G-d is. Now he has had personal experience. Job repents.

---

[a] 32.6-22;
[b] Ch 33; ch 34; ch 35 ch 36-37
[c] Which ultimately is the answer to Job's suffering
[d] Ch 38-39; ch 40.1-2; ch 40.6 – 41.34; ch 42. 7-8
[e] 2 Kings 2 11........and Elijah went up by a whirlwind into heaven.
[f] Symbols of disorder and danger within creation
[g] Pain and pleasure as part of the human condition that contribute to the growth of physical and spiritual being

G-d says to Eli'phaz that he and his two friends were wrong in their arguments, and orders them to bring sacrifices to Job that he may offer them on their behalf.[a] G-d approves of Job with his struggle for understanding throughout the trial.
Job is restored with more children and double the possessions he had before. He lives for a further 140 years.[b]

Psalms

A highly organised book. We tend to think of it as a hymn book filled with poems and ceremonial songs. Many scholars have studied the structure of Psalms but its complexity goes beyond the present study. For the basics we have that David is accredited to writing/compiling[c] Psalms, just as Moses received and wrote down The Law and David's son Solomon wrote the Wisdom books of Proverbs and Ecclesiastes. It forms the new covenant with G-d and his King. David's rule and his sons[d] greater rule.
The themes of the Wisdom of G-d and the Rule of G-d are central and are woven throughout the entire book.
Like Deuteronomy and The Law (Pentateuch) it has 5 parts -

Opening		1 & 2	
	Book I [e]	3-41	Rise of Davidic throne
	Book II	42-72	The Davidic throne
	Book III	73-89	Fall of the Throne
	Book IV [f]	90-106	The Exile and Rescue
	Book V	107-145	Restoration with the Son of David
Ending		146-150	5 Hallelujah psalms

Psalms is not an anthology but a structured historical chronological narrative.
Psalms begins *The New Covenant* between G-d and His anointed King.

---

[a] Job offers sacrifices. He had done this for his children having *sent* (for) *and sanctified them* (1.5). This time they come from those that know they have done wrong
[b] Double lifespan also?
[c] About half of the psalms are noted as by David. Psalms clearly relate to Rulership and covers the making dissolution and renewal of the covenant with David.
[d] His Greater Son
[e] Books I, II, III, IV, end with :-
Book I (psalm 41) *Blessed be YHWH, the God of Israel, from everlasting and to everlasting.* Amen and Amen.
Book II (psalm 72) *And blessed be his glorious name for ever; and let the whole earth be filled with his glory. Amen and Amen.*
Book III (psalm 89) Blessed be YHWH for evermore Amen and Amen.
Book IV (psalm 106) Blessed be YHWH, the God of Israel, from everlasting even to everlasting. and let all the people say, Amen Praise ye YHWH
[f] Isaiah 40-55 covering the same theme.
2) Moses is mentioned 8 times in Psalms, 7 times in this section

Psalm 1
Blessings on they who meditate on the Torah, reading and obeying it. (The Torah in this case applying to the 5 books of Moses and the Torah of the complete OT).
Psalm 2
A reflection on G-d's promise of 2 Sam 7 where the Messianic king is established and all who rail against him are defeated *Blessed are all they that take refuge in Him.* (v12)

Psalm 1-2	Opening
<u>Book I</u>	
Psalm 3-41	Davidic group
<u>Book II</u>	
Psalm 42-49	7 Psalms from the Sons of Korah
Psalm 50	YHWH speaks (Psalms of Asaph)
Psalm 51-53	Three types of sinners (Psalms of David)
Psalm 54-60	7 Psalms of David
Psalm 61-67	7 Psalms of David
Psalm 68-72	David and Solomon (5 Psalms)
<u>Book III</u>	
Psalm 73-83	The Temple desecrated (Psalms of Asaph)
Psalm 84-88	Sons of Korah.
Psalm 89	The King / Kingdom, Temple end
<u>Book IV</u>	
Psalm 90-92	Moses[a] & G-d's refuge
Psalm 93-100	YHWH Reigns as king
Psalm 101-103	The faithful Servant
Psalm 104-106	Hallelujah Psalms
<u>Book V</u>	
Psalm 107-110	The Suffering Servant. Melchizedec their leader
Psalm 111-117	Egyptian Hallel (7 Psalms 3-1-3)
Psalm 118-119	3rd King-Torah Pair (1st- ps1–2, 2nd-ps18–19, 3rd-ps118–119)
Psalm 120-134	Song of Ascents
Psalm 135-137	Praise and Thanksgiving
Psalm 138-145	Davidic group
Psalm 146-150	Doxology

[a] Links in these Psalms to Deut 32;33 and Exodus 32

Chiastic arrangement Book 1

Psalms 1-14 [2x7 Psalms]

1-2 wisdom folly personal and national[a]

3-7 (5 Psalms) lament

8 hymn (1st Hymn of the psalter) [b]

9-13 (5 Psalms) lament[c]

14 wisdom and folly

Psalms 15-24 [10 Psalms] [d]

15 liturgical. Approaching G-d

16 trust

17 lament

18 royal

19 hymn (2nd Hymn of the psalter) [e]

20-21 royal

22 lament

23 trust

24 liturgical. Approaching G-d

---

[a] From a chiastic point of view psalms 1 & 2 form a single psalm

[A] wise man1 1-3;

[B] Foolish man 1 4-6;

[B] Foolish nation 2 1-3;

[A] Wise nation 2 10-12

[b] *What is man that you are mindful of him or the son of Adam that you care for him?*

[c] Psalm 9 & 10 are half acrostic together forming one full acrostic. They seem to have been split to fit the chiastic order. LXX psalm 9 is not split. The numbering of LXX Psalms is therefore different from the Hebrew

[d] Symbolic number [10 Commandments]

[e] *The heavens declare the glory of God; the skies proclaim the work of his hands.*

25-34 [10 Psalms]

25 acrostic[a]

26 I wash my hands in innocence

27 safety in G-d

28 hear my cry…I call for help

29 hymn (3rd Hymn of the psalter) [b]

30 I called to you for help and you healed me

31 safety in G-d

32 I acknowledge my sin

33 song of praise (22 verse)[c]

34 acrostic

35-41 [7 Psalms]

35 betrayal

36 praise

37 trust in G-d. The wicked will perish (acrostic)

38 The suffering servant's[d] plea to G-d for help

39 trust in G-d. The wicked will perish

40 thanksgiving and trust

41 betrayal

So ends Book I of the Psalms. It has been my intention here with Book I to show the amazing hidden structure within. This structure does continue right through the Psalter. There are many online resources which cover the entire book but for now it's enough to make known and open up any further study by those interested.
What does it all mean for the reader? That the central meaning - key verse - vital elements - will be found at the centre of the Psalm with verses before and after forming a carefully designed shell.
As we've seen, Book 1 exhibits chiastic structure, but this is also true for the other four books of the Psalms. This chiastic structure extends to the individual psalms as well.[e]

---

[a] Each verse starting with a successive letter of the alphabet
[b] *The voice of the LORD is upon the waters*
[c] Symbolic 22 letters of the Hebrew alphabet
[d] David
[e] Often exhibiting an ending and a beginning with the same verse

Here is one well known Psalm (Psalm 8) – What is Man?

A YHWH, our Lord, How excellent is thy Name in all the earth,

B Who have set thy glory upon the heavens[a]
Out of the mouth of babes and sucklings [b]

C You have established strength, because of your adversaries,
That thou might silence the enemy and the avenger.[c]

D When I consider thy heavens, the work of thy fingers,
The moon and the stars, which thou have ordained;

E What is man, that thou are mindful of him?
And the son of man, that thou visit him?

E For thou have made him but little lower than God,
And crown him with glory and honour.

D Thou make him to have dominion over the works of thy hands;
Thou have put all things under his feet:

C All sheep and oxen,
Yea, and the beasts of the field,[d]

B The birds of the heavens, and the fish of the sea,[e]
Whatsoever pass through the paths of the seas.[f]

A YHWH, our Lord, How excellent is thy Name in all the earth!

---

[a] G-d's dominion in the heavens
[b] G-d's mastery over babbling suckling humans
[c] G-d ultimate dominion over 1 adversary [ṣārar], 2 enemy ['ōyēḇ] and 3 avenger [nāqam]
[d] Man's ultimate dominion over 1 sheep [ṣōnē'] 2 oxen ['elep̄] and 3 beasts of the field [b?hēmâ]
[e] man's dominion over chirping and gulping creatures
[f] Man's dominion on the Earth

Proverbs

Proverbs is a collection of wise sayings made by Solomon.[a] Solomon was understood to be the wisest man of his time and part of this collection are his own (Section II). The calling of the book Proverbs is perhaps somewhat simplistic as they are, as the LXX has in verse 6, παραβολὴν, [parables] principles placed side by side with common situations to illustrate moral social and spiritual concepts. Wisdom is not law but human experience reflecting G-d's wisdom.

As with Psalms, the book of proverbs is written as poetry. Hebrew poetry, the form thereof being mirrored parallelisms (Chiasm).

Proverbs has a number of independent collections as follows:-

Introduction (1.1-1.7)

The book begins with an outline of its intended purpose (v2-6)

To know wisdom and instruction;
To discern the words of understanding;
To receive instruction in wise dealing,
In righteousness and justice and equity;
To give prudence to the simple,
To the young man knowledge and discretion:
A wise man will hear, and increase in learning;
And a man of understanding will acquire sound counsels:
To understand a proverb, the interpretation,
The words of the wise, and their dark sayings.

Verse 7 sets the theme for the first section and the entire book..

The fear of YHWH is the beginning of knowledge

Followed immediately by the antithesis of this..

but fools despise wisdom and instruction.

Pursuit of wisdom and the Fear of YHWH[b] is the highest good as we do live in a moral universe. Wisdom and knowledge are different. Wisdom – a skill; knowledge a practical ability. Wisdom is used for a disciplined life in G-d's world.

---

[a] Link of Solomon to wisdom (1 Kings 3.9) Solomon makes a request for wisdom to be given him so that he may lead. Solomon knew 3000 proverbs (parabolḗs LXX) (1 Kings 4.32) and 1000 songs (not Psalms). Solomon begins the Wisdom tradition in Israel

[b] Reverential respect and awe for G-d and acknowledgment to human humbleness. Recognition of the wise saying's correctness and our humble acceptance that we don't have that higher understanding

Section I, (1.8- 9.18) a series of speeches from a father to a son on the listening to wisdom and its ultimate benefits and rejecting folly and its ultimate failure.[a]
This is often wound around the symbolic figures of *Lady Wisdom* and *Lady Folly.*
Clearly throughout the OT thus far the effects of Israel's unhelpful interaction with foreign women has been at the core of their downfall not the least of which is Solomon himself making the appearance of the Adulteress / loose / Lady folly all the more poignant here. Her wider interpretation is as the opposing counterpart to Lady wisdom and is to a degree a symbolic character as is Lady Wisdom.
There are in fact ten[b] speeches / lectures within this section.
They are divided over the chiastic structure..

A. Invitation of folly (1:8-19)
B. Invitation of wisdom (1:20-33)
C. Invitation to call out for wisdom (2:1-1-9)
D. the loose woman (2:10-22)
E. Good consequences of wise living (3:1-20)
F. Right social behaviour (3:21-35)
G Embrace wisdom (4:1-27)
G Don't embrace the adulteress [folly] (5:1-23)
F. Wrong social behaviour (6:1-19)
E. bad consequences of adultery [folly] (6:20-35)
D. the loose woman (7:1-27)
C. Invitation of wisdom who calls out (8:1-36)
B. Invitation of wisdom (9:1-12)
A. Invitation of Folly (9:13-18)

Section II (10.1 to 22.16) The proverbs of Solomon. A collection of proverbs directly associated with Solomon. Mainly dealing with righteous and sinful human conduct.

Section III (22.17-24.22). The words of the wise.
Begins with..

Incline thine ear, and hear the words of the wise,
And apply thy heart unto my knowledge.

There are thirty parts to this section. LXX states..

Have I not written to you three times of counsels and knowledge, (22.20)

Possibly referring to 3 x 10 sayings (commandments).

---

[a] The two paths
[b] Referencing to Commandments

Section IV (24.23-24.34) Also belonging to the wise ones. An additional collection of proverbs relating to Judges and their need to give honest judgement and also to the poverty that befalls the lazy.

Section V (25.1- 29.27) More proverbs of Solomon. Compiled by the men of Hezekiah king of Judah. For the proper conduct of a righteous King.

Section VI (30) Words of Agur.[a] A model for one reading the scripture. The writer struggles to understand what G-d is and concludes that the knowledge of such is beyond human understanding.

Section VII 31.1-9 Words of king Lemur. This section details guidance for leaders.

Epilogue. The wife of noble character. Acrostic (22 verses) 31.10-31. This section is also chiasm, the centre being verse 23..

Her husband is known in the gates, When he sits among the elders of the land.

Which is odd as here the emphasis is on the man not the wife. But here we have the man (once a son himself) who has listened to Lady Wisdom (from the beginning of Proverbs) throughout his life and now he, his wife and children are a focal point of the entire community.

Ecclesiastes

Written by Solomon[b] the book explores what makes for a meaningful life here on Earth (under the Sun) facing that ultimate fact that you will eventually die and that which you worked for will pass to another.
Kohelet acknowledges that the work of creation[c] is already complete; is only this work that will endure, and is in the hands of G-d only.

The sun also arises, and the sun goes down,
and hastens to his place where he arose.
The wind goes toward the south, and turns about unto the north;

---

[a] Meaning 'gatherer'. It's not quite sure whether this is a personal name or the simple noun (a gatherer). LXX has *My son, revere my words, and receive them, and repent.; Thus speaks the man to the ones trusting in Elohim. And now I shall cease.*
[b] The writer of Ecclesiastes refers to himself as Kohelet. A term used of a teacher or speaker in the Assembly. This is also where the name of the book comes from as the LXX refers to the speaker as Ἐκκλησιαστής [eklaysayastays]. The Hebrew book is called Kohelet
[c] Gen 2.2 And on the seventh day G-d finished his work which he had made... 2) Psa 19.1 *The heavens declare the glory of God; the skies proclaim the work of his hands.*

it whirls about continually, and the wind returns again according to his circuits.
All the rivers run into the sea; yet the sea is not full;
unto the place from where the rivers come, there they return again.
All things[a] *are wearisome;*[b] *man cannot utter it:*
the eye is not satisfied with seeing, nor the ear filled with hearing.
The thing that has been, it is that which shall be;
and that which is done is that which shall be done: and there is no new thing under the sun.
Is there anything whereof it may be said, See, this is new?
it has been already of old time, which was before us. (1.5-10)

A key word used in the book is הֶבֶל [heḇel] [c] translated somewhat unfortunately as Vanity. It is a word which gives a sense of *transience* or *fleeting* such as a breath or a vapour or without lasting quality (separated from the eternal), the fleeting nature of our own mortality. Not to be confused with a meaning of *pointless or futility* as although the Vapour's existence is fleeting it can still be nevertheless fulfilling. Therefore we have..

Fleeting transience says the teacher fleeting transience, all is transience (1. 2)

This statement then is not one of despair or sorrow but of acknowledgment of the truth and a foundation from which Kohelet will examine the Life *under the Sun*, and draw his conclusions as to what will be a meaningful Life and what will be a meaningless one.

The use of Hebel in the first half of the book is generally in association with negative statements but as the book progresses the use of the word becomes more positive and reflects Kohelet's teaching that in fact love, joy and the pursuit of wisdom do give meaning to the human life and it is through these that the transience in life will be reordered into an overarching inspiration and guidance. And once we accept our fleeting lives as such the fleeting *Toil* that we engage in takes new meaning. In the end the transience of life is the focus and the teaching that makes us aware of the eternal. It is Love and joy that fulfil human lives and wisdom[d] that enables it.

Hebel is also used in conjunction with idolatry..

They have moved me to jealousy with that which is not God;
They have provoked me to anger with their vanities: (Deut 32.21)

---

[a] דָּבָר dâbâr H1697 word; speech

[b] יָגֵעַ yâgêaʻ H3021

[c] הֶבֶל [heḇel] The word appears 38 times throughout Ecclesiastes. 2) the name also given to Adam's second son Abel whose life was transient but not pointless as his actions were accepted by G-d. Abel like the patriarchs who followed him were shepherds their lives a journey and their spirituality an ongoing search
[d] Wisdom is not transient

As such Hebel becomes *the work of their hands* (Isaiah 2.8) which surely is a worthless toil, a service paid to ourselves.

Another key word is Vexation..

I perceived that this also was a vexation of spirit. (1.17) KJV
I perceived that this also was a striving after wind. (1.17) ASV

The word Vexation actually interprets two different words in the Hebrew text - H7475 רַעְיוֹן [raʿyôn] (three times) and H7469 רְעוּת [r□ʿûṯ] (seven times). These words appear only in the Book of Ecclesiastes and as such do give a problem for interpretation. Their root words give the assumed meaning *longing, striving, desire*. LXX also interprets them as one word προαίρεσις [pro-hai-resis]. Prohairesis is a word first used by Aristotle taking the root word hairesis (choice). For Aristotle the Prohairesis is a communicating influence/voice within the human soul influencing and committing it to rational action. As such the ASV interpretation is correct in the use of *striving* (but not in the use of the word wind).

Spirit (human) H7307 [רוּחַ rûaḥ] too is a key word. Although it can be used for the actual (North, South) wind, it is the fundamental motivating power that animates the entire Cosmos, *the breath of G-d*. It appears 23 times and is unfortunately interpreted as wind (9 times) as with the saying *striving after wind*. (eg.1.14). Better *the striving of the spirit.*

Although Kohelet does not understand this spirit he knows it is it which directs life..

I have seen all the works that are done under the sun;
and, behold, all is fleeting and the striving of spirit. (1.14)

Then I looked on all the works that my hands had wrought,
and on the toil that I had toiled to do; and, behold,
all was fleeting and a striving of the spirit,
and there was no profit under the sun. (2.11)

As he came forth from his mother's womb, naked shall he go again as he came,
and shall take nothing for his toil, which he may carry away in his hand.
And this also is a grievous evil, that in all points as he came, so shall he go:
and what profit has he that he toiled for the spirit? (5:15-16)

Another key word is Labour/Toil it appears 27 times [a]
We do all die eventually and all our work passes on, then knowing that, why do men toil so in their lives? It would seem that Men are compelled by their spirit to toil, a fundamental characteristic of the Human to labour or strive for something. Kohelet is driven to find meaning/purpose but all remains incomprehensible, yet still, *he* is driven on.

Kohelet's (Solomon) search for meaning is all the more pertinent in the light of his own life where he writes from a position of great wealth, influence and wisdom, as many understand a fulfilled life in such terms. It seems even this does not guarantee a feeling within oneself of accomplishment.

Kohelet gives advice..

Live joyfully[b] *with the wife whom thou love*
all the days of thy transient life, which he has given thee under the sun,[c]
all thy fleeting days: for that is thy portion in life,
and the toil which you take under the sun. (9.9)

The Song of Solomon

An amazing book within the OT / Torah. I would argue a central book, that when understood in its overarching context it brings into focus the entire OT / Torah. There has been much interpretation of the book throughout history but it seems that many who do interpret, take the book as something *quite different* within the OT and probably shows the difficulty people have in reading/understanding the entire OT (as attempted in this present book). The interpretation in recent times as literal exemplifies this lack of understanding and reflects more of our own selves and culture than its core teaching.[d] After all Solomon was renowned for his riddles. (1 Kings 4.29-34; 1 Kings 10.1-9)

There are several levels to the book which entwine their way throughout.

If I would ask you which book in the OT is about a man and a woman in a garden, naked and without feelings of shame, then most would bring to mind the Genesis 2-3 story of Adam and Eve and their ultimate *exile* from that garden (paradise). Now we are not given any detail as to the life of the couple between their creation and their exile but we can assume it is an idyllic existence in perfection. Although the relationship between Adam and Eve may well have been filled with the Love and desire for each other's company, the focus here is not

---

[a] H5998 עָמַל & H5999 עָמָל

[b] Joy, love being of the true labours of man Under the Sun? (2.10 Joy as the portion/reward of Labour)

[c] In the material realm

[d] Even then the tendency to overlook the spiritual dimension, the desire of a man to reunite with that from which he was separated in the formation of Eve

necessarily on their interpersonal relationship but the one they enjoy with G-d, of being in His *Presence,* up to their separation when they ultimately *hide* from Him. Exile ensues; paradise is lost. Song of Songs rediscovers that paradise.

There is a dream-like quality of the narrative. The movement from scene to scene, filled with the language of emotion. Changes in events within the book exhibit a kind of *disorder* consistent with dreaming.

2.17 *till the day break and the shadows flee*
3.1 *By night on my bed I sought him whom my soul loves:*

Chapter 5 has a very dream like progression, interpreted symbolically we have the love language between G-d and his people, He and his Beloved are separated, G-d seeks them but they're lost in sin to His Presence. They seek G-d in repentance but He can't be found.
A common feature of OT prophecy and communication between G-d and man is that it is often received in dreams. ... *In thoughts from the visions of the night, When deep sleep falls on men..* [a]
Joseph's dreams and Pharaoh's dreams. It seems too that Adam and Eve were in a dreamlike state until *..their eyes were opened.*

<u>The Land</u>

Often overlooked in interpretations is the importance of the Land itself. The Promised Land of Abraham. It was to that Land which Moses, initially, was to lead the Israelites. A Land of milk and Honey[b] beautifully fertile. A land of freedom.

6.11 LXX has..

Into the garden of walnuts I went down to behold
among the produce of the valley of the rushing streams;
to see if bloomed the grapevine, blossomed or if the pomegranates.
There I shall give you my breast. [c]

The Song of Songs details the landscape in which the lovers play out their attempts to unite, as much as the lovers themselves. The lovers are mostly described in/as features of the landscape. A literary device also used by Isaiah where Israel is compared to a vineyard..

Let me sing for my beloved a song of my love touching his vineyard.
My beloved had a vineyard in a very fruitful hill: (Isa 5.1) [d]

---

[a] Job 4.13 The dreams of the wise

[b] Deut 11.9 *And that ye may prolong your days in the land, which the LORD swore unto your fathers to give unto them and to their seed, a land that flows with milk and honey.*

[c] Abundance

[d] Parable of the vineyard (5.1-7)

<u>Sacred Marriage</u>

Isaiah 54.4-6

Fear not; for thou shall not be ashamed: neither be thou confounded;
for thou shall not be put to shame: for thou shall forget the shame of thy youth;
and the reproach of thy widowhood shall thou remember no more.
For thy Maker is thy husband; YHWH of hosts is his name:
and the Holy One of Israel is thy Redeemer;
the God of the whole earth shall he be called.
For YHWH has called thee as a wife forsaken and grieved in spirit,
even a wife of youth, when she is cast off, says thy God.

Isaiah 62.5

For as a young man marries a virgin, so shall thy sons marry thee;
and as the bridegroom rejoices over the bride, so shall thy God rejoice over thee.

Isaiah 66.10-13

Rejoice ye with Jerusalem, and be glad for her, all ye that love her:
rejoice for joy with her, all ye that mourn over her;
that ye may suck and be satisfied with the breasts of her consolations;
that ye may milk out, and be delighted with the abundance of her glory.
For thus says YHWH, Behold, I will extend peace to her like a river,
and the glory of the nations like an overflowing stream: and ye shall suck thereof;
ye shall be borne upon the side, and shall be dandled upon the knees.
As one whom his mother comforts, so will I comfort you;
and ye shall be comforted in Jerusalem.

Ezekiel 16.7-14

I caused thee to multiply as that which grows in the field,
and thou did increase and wax great, and thou attained to excellent adornment;
thy breasts were fashioned, and thy hair was grown; yet thou were naked and bare.
Now when I passed by thee, and looked upon thee, behold, thy time was the time of love;
and I spread my skirt over thee, and covered thy nakedness:
yea, I swore unto thee, and entered into a covenant with thee,
says the Lord YHWH, and thou became mine.
Then washed I thee with water; yea, I thoroughly washed away thy blood from thee,
and I anointed thee with oil.
I clothed thee also with broidered work, and shod thee with sealskin,
and I girded thee about with fine linen, and covered thee with silk.
And I decked thee with ornaments, and I put bracelets upon thy hands,
and a chain on thy neck. And I put a ring upon thy nose, and ear-rings in thine ears,

and a beautiful crown upon thy head. Thus were thou decked with gold and silver;
and thy raiment was of fine linen, and silk, and broidered work;
thou did eat fine flour, and honey, and oil; and thou were exceeding beautiful,
and thou did prosper unto royal estate.
And thy renown went forth among the nations for thy beauty;
for it was perfect, through my majesty which I had put upon thee, says the Lord YHWH.

The book of Hosea. Chapters 1, 2 and 3 (Marriage theme throughout)

Ultimately the book Song of Songs is, like love, something which can only be *experienced* and not explained. It does require a degree of spiritual maturity to read but can only be read in solitude with your own soul. *By night on my bed I sought him whom my soul loves:* (3.1)

That said I would venture to interpret the first few lines of the book as..

Let him kiss me with the kisses of his mouth; (1.2)[a]
The desire for an intimately close relationship with G-d. The kisses being His Words.

Thine oils have a goodly fragrance; (1.3a)
Draw me; we will run after thee: (1.4a)
The desire to follow and be in that Presence

The king has brought me into his chambers (1.4b)
G-d brings to Himself, not as a servant but as a bride, in union.

And finally, a warning against entering into that relationship with G-d prematurely[b] (as with the affair of the Golden Calf) without the knowledge of who G-d is and what He requires..

I adjure you, O daughters of Jerusalem, by the roes, or by the hinds of the field,
That ye stir not up, nor awake my love, until she[c] *please* (3.5)[d]

Isaiah

The name Isaiah means *YHWH Is Salvation* or *Salvation of YHWH*. Clearly stated *The Book of the Salvation of G-d*. This name for the book really does give us an accurate description of the contents within. G-d is the redeemer and His people Israel. They need only, at any time,

[a] LXX adds.. *for your breasts are better than wine.*
[b] impatiently
[c] Love
[d] This verse repeated in 2.7 and 8.4

repent and conform to His Commandments (Torah) for His full Power and Glory to be revealed / bestowed upon them.

The book covers a period of Israeli history from the death of king Uzziah, until the rebuilding of the 2nd Temple, some 240 years later. The *prophet* Isaiah begins his commission in ch 6.

Outline

Chapter 1-5

The first 5 chapters set the themes which will continue throughout the rest of the book, namely that YHWH is the only saviour and those who follow and obey Him will prosper and those who don't will perish; and that Israel are to take up the challenges given at Sinai and bring the knowledge of the One True G-d to all nations.

Chapter 6-39

Isaiah, the prophet begins his prophecy during the time of King Uzziah of Judah (788-736BC) and continues through to the events of King Hezekiah of Judah (726-697BC).

Chapter 40-55

Chapter 40 picks up around the time of the Decree of Cyrus (538BC). This section covering the prophecies of Isaiah towards the end of the Babylonian captivity.

Chapter 56-66

The prophecies of Isaiah during the period of the returning exiles as they begin to re-establish themselves within the Promised Land.

Ch 1

The vision of Isaiah the son of Amoz, which he saw concerning Judah and Jerusalem, in the days of Uzziah, Jotham, Ahaz, and Hezekiah kings of Judah. (chapter 1 v1)

Isaiah accuses Judah and Jerusalem of rebellion, corruption and idolatry and condemns them for their utterly evil ways. But G-d still encourages them to repent and be obedient as then they will again prosper. G-d promises to remove all the dross and return Jerusalem to purity. All who follow G-d will prosper all who rebel will perish.[a]

Wash yourselves, make yourselves clean;
put away the evil of your doings from before my eyes;
cease to do evil; learn to do well; seek justice, relieve the oppressed,
judge the fatherless, plead for the widow.
Come now, and let us reason together, says YHWH:

---

[a] The strong link between righteousness and salvation

Zion shall be redeemed with justice, and her repentant ones with righteousness (v27)

though your sins be as scarlet, they shall be as white as snow;
though they be red like crimson, they shall be as wool.
If ye be willing and obedient, ye shall eat the good of the land:
but if ye refuse and rebel, ye shall be devoured with the sword;
for the mouth of YHWH has spoken it. (v16-20)

Ch 2
Another vision concerning Judah and Jerusalem. Although the vision is directed to Jerusalem and Judah, the entire nation of Israel is included.

O house of Jacob, come ye, and let us walk in the light of YHWH.
For you have forsaken thy people the house of Jacob, (v5-6a)

They will eventually be restored to glory and the peoples of the world will come to be taught about the One True G-d and peace will be brought to the entire earth. The arrogance of Man will be humbled and G-d will prevail and be exalted. Do not trust in Man..

Cease ye from man, whose breath is in his nostrils;
for wherein is he to be accounted of? (v22)

Ch 3
Jerusalem and Judah are to be cut off and left without leadership. They have brought the ensuing disaster upon themselves and are collapsing. G-d's judgment comes to the leaders as it is they who have led the people astray and oppressed them. The women too are to be humbled as they also are totally immoral and parade their beauty. Jerusalem will be left destitute for all this.

Ch 4
Women will be left without husbands, but the righteous (Branch) will be victorious. Those who are left will be holy. They will be cleansed *by the spirit of justice, and by the spirit of burning* (v4). G-d's glory will return to Jerusalem as He had been when they were led through the wilderness with Moses..

And YHWH will create over the whole habitation of mount Zion,
and over her assemblies, a cloud and smoke by day,
and the shining of a flaming fire by night;
for upon all the glory shall be a defence. (v5)

Ch 5
The parable of the vineyard (verse 1-7)
The House of Israel is compared to the produce of a vineyard. The produce is very poor. G-d says He will destroy the vineyard and it will be a rainless wasteland of weeds. Verse 8 continues saying the leaders have oppressed the people and made themselves rich. None

respect the laws of G-d. The people are left unprotected for lack of understanding. The leaders are again condemned. G-d then calls to the nations to come and destroy Israel.

Ch 6

Although we are now in chapter 6 it is here that the commissioning of Isaiah by YHWH is recorded. He is to warn the people, although they will not listen. It's too late for them; they are to be like trees chopped down with only stumps remaining. It is these stumps that will be as a *Holy Seed* remaining in the land.

Isaiah's Vision. (in the year that King Uzziah died. v1)
Isaiah sees a vision of G-d on his throne surrounded by the Seraphim at the Temple. Isaiah is scared by this and believes he will now die.

"Woe to me!" I cried. "I am ruined!
For I am a man of unclean lips, and I live among a people of unclean lips,
and my eyes have seen the King, the Lord Almighty." (v5)

One of the Seraphim takes[a] a burning coal from the Altar, brings it to Isaiah and touches his mouth with it, proclaiming to Isaiah 'that *your guilt is taken away and your sin atoned for.'*

Ch 7

This chapter explains the historical situation now facing Judah/Jerusalem..

And it came to pass in the days of Ahaz the son of Jotham, the son of Uzziah, king of Judah,
that Rezin the king of Syria, and Pekah [b] *the son of Remaliah, king of Israel,*
went up to Jerusalem to war against it. (v1)

Their alliance comes together in hope of capturing the city for themselves and to end the succession of the Davidic line by installing the *Son-of-Tabeal* [c] on the throne. When the people of Jerusalem hear of it they are terrified.

The importance of this event should not be underestimated.[d] Commentators mostly focus in on the ultimate destruction of Jerusalem by Nebuchadnezzar (586BC) but Jerusalem is here inches away from the same fate. What began with the promises to Abraham[e] and followed through with Moses and the events of Sinai; [f] then with the establishment of the monarchy

---

[a] The angel uses tongs to do this
[b] 737-732BC (Albright chronology)
[c] Verse 6. Meaning God is good/pleasing. A slight variation of this name gives לא ('al) [the Hebrew particle of negation] instead of אל ('el) therefore giving the meaning 'not good'
[d] As is often the case in favour of future Divine intervention in Israel's destiny
[e] Gen 17.1-8
[f] Exo 19 & 20

and the promise to David,[a] is here and now under threat of complete destruction. Jerusalem is all that's left..

And the daughter of Zion is left as a booth in a vineyard,
as a lodge in a garden of cucumbers, as a besieged city. (Isaiah 1.8)

Israel has split into two kingdoms[b] and the Northern Kingdom of Israel, long departed from the worship of YHWH, has now turned on the Southern Kingdom of Judah, making *alliances with the nations.* It has destroyed all the cities of Judah bar Jerusalem, has killed and taken captive the inhabitants thereof.[c] Now, it's sights are on the last two extant things, the city of Jerusalem itself and [to end] the Davidic line. It is now we see king Ahaz when the news reaches him of the army against him.

...And his heart was moved, and the heart of his people,
as the trees of the wood are moved with the wind. (7.2)

Isaiah is now called to go, with his own son *Shear-jashub,*[d] to meet[e] Ahaz and inform him that he is not to be scared of this army, they will not succeed. In fact the country of Syria and the land of Israel (Ephraim/Samaria as its seat of power) soon will be themselves conquered.[f]

YWHW then asks King Ahaz (regarding as to whether he believes in what Isaiah has said)

"Ask YHWH your God for a sign,
whether in the deepest depths or in the highest heights."
But Ahaz said, "I will not ask; [g] *I will not put YHWH to the test."* (v11-12)

YHWH says that He will give a sign anyway and says..

Therefore the Lord [h] *himself will give you a sign: behold, a virgin* [i] *shall conceive,*

---

[a] 2 Sam 7
[b] 1 Kings 11.21-12.35
[c] 2 Chronicles chapter 28
[d] Meaning.. a remnant shall return. The prophetic name Isaiah gave to his son. The significance explained in Isa 10..20-23
[e] The same location as where Rabshakeh, the Assyrian General, speaks to Hezekiah's top advisers (Isa 36.2)
[f] According to 2 Kings 16 7-9, Ahaz (who does not have sufficient faith in Isaiah's words) requested help from the king of Assyria, giving a large gift of treasure to which the King of Assyria responds by conquering Damascus (Syrian capital) and killing King Rezin. The account does not say what happens to Pekah king of Israel but 2 Chron 28 indicate that the King of Assyria does not help Ahaz, (at least against the Israeli part of the army)
[g] Ahaz is not known for his piety towards YHWH. His intention is to rely on Assyria anyway
[h] אֲדֹנָי ['ădōnāy] H136
[i] עַלְמָה [Alma]. A young woman of marriageable age. LXX has παρθένος [parthenos] virgin. The Hebrew word בְתוּלָה [b?thûwlâh] is virgin as in Genesis 24.16. These events occur shortly before the birth of Hezekiah.

and bear a son, and shall call his name Immanuel.[a] (v14)

For all the troubles now facing Ahaz and the people of Jerusalem they must wonder is this the end? The naming of this child ʿimmānû'ēl [G-d is with us] is the sign that G-d will defend Jerusalem and the Davidic lineage. G-d then says before the child grows the present enemy will be destroyed. The king of Assyria will be called upon by G-d to do this (7.17-18). Ahaz' son Hezekiah will be a great and faithful king in Jerusalem.

Ch 8

Isaiah has another son.[b] G-d directs him to call the boy *Maher-shalal-hash-baz* [swift is booty, speedy is prey] [c] Isaiah reaffirms G-d's promise against the pact between Samaria and Damascus..

Take counsel together, and it shall be brought to nought;
speak the word, and it shall not stand: for God is with us. [d] (v10)

Isaiah reaffirms the overall picture which includes all of the Israeli nation..

And I will wait for YHWH, that hides his face from the house of Jacob,
and I will look for him. Behold, I and the children whom YHWH has given me are for signs
and for wonders in Israel from YHWH of hosts, who dwells in mount Zion. (17-18)

Isaiah warns the Northern Kingdom of Israel who are attacking Jerusalem..

And they shall pass through it,[e] *sore distressed and hungry;*
...and it shall come to pass that when they shall be hungry, they shall fret themselves,
and curse by their king and by their God,
and turn their faces upward and they shall look unto the earth,
and behold, trouble [f] *and darkness,*[g] *gloom of anguish* [h]
and into thick darkness [i] *they shall be driven away* (v21- 22)[j]

---

2) Isaiah's prophesy spoken to Hezekiah concerning the king of Assyria [2 Kings 19 21] *This is the word that YHWH has spoken concerning him: The virgin daughter of Zion has despised thee and laughed thee to scorn.* Isaiah 37.22 *The virgin daughter of Zion has despised thee and laughed thee to scorn* (same event described)

[a] The name Immanuel appears again in Isaiah 8.8. (an exclamation of hope – O G-d be with us!) Also 8.10 where the literal meaning is written

[b] With a prophetess. Presumably his wife

[c] In reference that Damascus and then Israel are soon to be looted by the Assyrians.

[d] ʿimmānû'ēl

[e] Pass out of the land

[f] צָרָה [tsârâh] H6869. Affliction

[g] חֲשֵׁכָה [ḥăšēḵâ] H2825. Spiritual emptiness

[h] צוֹק [tsôwq] H6695 Distress

[i] אֲפֵלָה ['ăphêlâh] H653. Angst

[j] Note that these people are in darkness

Ch 9

[a] But there shall be no gloom [b] to her that was in anguish.[c]
as in the former time when he lightly [d] afflicted the land of Zebulun
and the land of Naphtali; and afterward did more grievously [e] afflict her
by the way of the sea, beyond the Jordan, Galilee of the nations.[f] (9.1)[g]

The people that walked in darkness have seen a great light:[h]
they that dwelt in the land of the shadow-of-death,[i] upon them has the light shined. (9.2)[j]

The Israelites have been made into a great numerous nation according to G-d's promise to Abraham. The nations which oppress them will be broken and their armies easily defeated.[k] (v3-5)

Continuing to verse 6, the reaffirmation of the Davidic promise of 2 Samuel 7. 8-16.

For unto us a child is born, unto us a son is given;
and the government shall be upon his shoulder: and his name shall be called

---

[a] The original Hebrew Isaiah includes this verse at the end of chapter 8, (English versions 9.1) as it does in fact continue with the theme of the distressed people taken into captivity

[b] מוּעָף [h4155] mûʿāp̄. (of the root) darkness. Used only once in OT

[c] This line in reference to the Assyrian forces (i*n their oppression of Jerusalem)* ... *there is no weariness to the one who oppresses her* (Hebrew Bible). LXX has *Drink this first. Act quickly, O land of Zebulon, land of Nephthalim* continuing the sense of urgency from *Maher-shalal-hash-baz* [*Τοῦ ὀξέως προνομὴν ποιῆσαι σκύλων· the swiftly plunder made of spoils]*

[d] קָלַל [h7043] Qâlal lightly

[e] כָּבַד [h3513] (kāḇaḏ) heavier

[f] The inhabitants are taken into captivity by Assyrian forces.

In the days of Pekah king of Israel came Tiglath-pileser king of Assyria, and took Ijon, and Abel-beth-maacah, and Janoah, and Kedesh, and Hazor, and Gilead, and Galilee, all the land of Naphtali; and he carried them captive to Assyria (2 Kings 15.29)

[g] Hebrew Isaiah 8.23

[h] The Hebrew text begins the next paragraph with the answer to the promise to David in 1 Kings 15.4 (also 2 Kings 8.19; 2 Chron 21.7; Psa 132.17)

Nevertheless for David's sake did YHWH his God give him a lamp in Jerusalem,
to set up his son after him, and to establish Jerusalem;

2) Israel has heard of the new king (Hezekiah) in Jerusalem 3) Irony. The Israeli people have been taken captive by a <u>great power</u> Assyria, their god Assur is depicted as a flaming sun with wings

[i] צַלְמָוֶת [h6757] tsalmâveth death-shadow/darkness. 2) Close to death

[j] Hebrew Isaiah 9.1

[k] As when Gideon, with 300 men routed the Midianite army (Judg. 7.2-8)

Wonderful, Counsellor,[a] *Mighty God,*[b] *Everlasting Father, Prince of Peace.* [c]
Of the increase of his government and of peace there shall be no end,
upon the throne of David, and upon his kingdom, to establish it, and to uphold it
with justice and with righteousness from henceforth even for ever.
The zeal of YHWH of hosts will perform this. (v6-7) [d]

The prospect of Jerusalem being destroyed and the throne usurped by the combined armies of Israel and Syria has filled the city with much anguish. Ahaz has also been doing what was wrong in YHWH's eyes throughout his reign. It is of some relief to hear that Assyria will be sent by G-d to crush those armies.
Israel is further condemned for their actions and defiance against YHWH. They are informed that they are going to be routed by the surrounding nations.

Ch 10
Assyria will be used by G-d for His purposes; but Assyria will also fall into ultimate judgement for their own idolatry and pride.

...and under his glory there shall be kindled a burning like the burning of fire.
and the light of Israel [e] *will be for a fire, and his Holy One for a flame;*
and it will burn and devour his thorns and his briers [f] *in one day.* (v16-17)

Israel will one day be at the head of the nations and as such will also rule Assyria. Isaiah introduces the term *the remnant of Israel.* He also includes *all Israel* (house of Jacob)..

---

[a]Also Isa 25.1 ...wonderful counsels (from afar)
[b] Also 10.21 ... Mighty G-d
[c] Verse 6. The literal Hebrew for this verse is

And he-shall-call name of him
one-marvellous, one-counselling, G-d masterful, Father-of-future, chief-of well-being

or (without translating as with the previous names)

and his name shall be called pele'yā ʻaṣ-gibôr'ēl-aḏʼāḇ-śaršālôm

LXX has simply

and is called his name, 'of great counsel Messenger,'
For I shall bring peace upon the rulers, and his health. [v5]

[d] This prophecy in the same way applies to later kings/leaders who attempt to reinstate G-ds purposes. Most notably Jesus. 2) Ahaz' child Hezekiah will be a great king and will obey the Laws and Testimonies of YHWH. Hezekiah will also have his own section in the Book of Proverbs (25-29) dedicated to 'the righteous king'
[e] *let us walk in the light of YHWH* [Isa 2.5] 2) *that put darkness for light, and light for darkness* [Isa 5.20} 3) *behold, darkness and distress; and the light is darkened in the clouds thereof.* [Isa 5.30] 4) *The people that walked in darkness have seen a great light: they that dwelt in the land of the shadow of death, upon them has the light shined.* [Isa 9.2]
[f] enemies

And it shall come to pass in that day, that the remnant of Israel,
and they that are escaped of the house of Jacob,
shall no more again lean upon him that smote them,[a]
but shall lean upon YHWH, the Holy One of Israel, in truth.
A remnant shall return, even the remnant of Jacob, unto the mighty God.[b]
For though thy people, Israel, be as the sand of the sea,[c] *only a remnant of them shall return:*
the destruction decreed shall overflow with righteousness. (v20-22)

YHWH encourages His people further and says His anger against them is soon to be over. Assyria will be destroyed.

For yet a very little while, the indignation against thee shall be accomplished,
and mine anger shall be directed to his destruction. (v25)

Ch 11
A totally righteous leader will come..

And there shall come forth a rod out of the stem of Jesse,
and a Branch shall grow out of his roots:
And the Spirit of YHWH shall rest upon him, the spirit of wisdom and understanding,
the spirit of counsel and might, the spirit of knowledge and of the fear of YHWH. (v1-2)

Ushering in an era of world peace and the understanding/knowledge of G-d..

for the earth shall be full of the knowledge of YHWH, as the waters cover the sea.
And it shall come to pass in that day, that the root of Jesse, that stands for an ensign of the peoples, unto him shall the nations seek; and his resting-place shall be glorious. (9-10)

G-d will return the Remnant of Israel from all over the world..

And there shall be a highway for the remnant of his people that remains from Assyria;
like as there was for Israel in the day that he came up out of the land of Egypt. (v16)

Ch 12
A song of praise to G-d for all the comfort and salvation he has given to His people..

Praise YHWH with songs, for he has done glorious things;

---

[a] Alliances with the nations
[b] *The mighty G-d*, a title used in 9.6 [gibôr'ēl]
[c] The original blessing to Abraham (Gen 22.17)

let this be known to all the world. (v5)

Ch 13

A prophecy against the nations. *The Day of the Lord* [a] is soon coming. They will be overthrown and humbled in a great tumultuous event.

Ch 14

Verse 1-27 All of Israel[b] will be brought back where they will rule those who have ruled them. All the haughty nations will be brought low including the Assyrians who will be trampled down with the rest of them.

Verse 28-32 A prophecy which came in the year Ahaz died. Specifically against the Philistines; they will be destroyed with the others. Ch 15-16 A prophecy against Moab. They also will be destroyed. Ch 17. A prophecy against Damascus, it's destruction assured. Ch 18. A prophecy against Cush. Ch 19. A prophecy against Egypt.

Ch 20

In the year that the supreme commander came to Ashdod, [c]
when Sargon the king of Assyria, sent him and he fought against Ashdod and captured it
at that time YHWH spoke through Isaiah son of Amoz (v1-2)

Isaiah is told to strip naked for three years as a sign that the King of Assyria will come to Egypt and lead them off as captives, naked, with the Cushites[d] who trusted in them.

Ch 21 A prophecy against Babylon, Edom and Arabia. Ch 22. A prophecy against the Valley of Vision (Jerusalem). The inhabitants of Jerusalem are condemned for not trusting in G-d. Ch 23. A prophecy against Tarshish, Sidon and Tyre.

Ch 24

A prophecy against the Land. It will be emptied and laid waste. G-d will punish all the kings of the earth. They will be gathered together and shut up as prisoners..

Then the moon shall be confounded, and the sun ashamed;
for YHWH of hosts will reign in mount Zion, and in Jerusalem;
and before his elders shall be glory.[e] (v23)

---

[a] The point at which G-d enacts his judgement on the people of the earth

[b] Verse 1 ..House of Jacob

[c] West of Jerusalem on the coast

[d] A people south of Egypt

[e] Greater than the Sun and Moon. LXX has
And shall melt away the brick, and shall fall the wall, for YHWH shall reign...

Ch 25-27

A song of praise to G-d who rules all the nations from His Holy Mountain. Israel will return there as a vineyard and will fill the world with fruit.

Ch 28

Ephraim will be destroyed. Judah should not become complacent. G-d will act against her for any transgressions. The troubles she has endured have been as a teaching to her.

Ch 29

Woe to Ariel[a]

A severe warning to Jerusalem that in the same way that irreverent people have surrounded G-d in his Temple, He will now surround Jerusalem with the nations to oppress and besiege her. They will, however, be unsuccessful (this time) and will vanish *like in a dream.*

The people of Jerusalem/Judah have become arrogant and prideful of their honoured position with YHWH. They have become blind to and ignorant of G-d's instruction. Their worship has become a meaningless religious show and their festivals pleasing to themselves only. Righteous people are oppressed but will eventually be the successful. G-d reminds them they are His redeemed people (through Abraham) and ultimately it will be the patriarchs (Jacob) who, although presently ashamed of what has become of the people of Israel, will be eventually proud of them.

But when he sees his children, the work of my hands, in the midst of him,
they shall sanctify my Name; yea, they shall sanctify the Holy One of Jacob,
and shall stand in awe of the God of Israel.
They also that err in spirit shall come to understanding,
and they that murmur shall receive instruction. (v23-24)

Ch 30

Woe to the children of apostasy.[b]

The prophecy against the Northern Kingdom of Israel. The time period being covered thus far in Isaiah is mainly[c] between Ahaz and his son Hezekiah. (742 to 697BC). Now, Hoshea king[d] of Israel (730-721BC) has rebelled against the Assyrian king (to whom Israel has become a tributary) [Verse 2 Walk *down* to Egypt] and has made a pact with Pharaoh against Assyria [Verse 6 The burden of the beasts] Hoshea sends tribute (treasure) to Pharaoh instead.

Isaiah says..

---

[a] Hôy 'ărî'ēl . Ariel. A double meaning ... Judah the Lion of G-d, and... the Altar of G-d. The lion is supposed to protect and uphold YHWH's Law, but has become proud of themselves

[b] Hôy [woe] bēn [children] sārar [turn back morally]. LXX has οὐαὶ τέκνα ἀποστάται [children of apostasy] The word for rebellious is as in verse 9 (H4805) מְרִי [m?rî] mer-ee'

[c] Chapter 6 on

[d] Began his reign in the twelfth year of Ahaz (2 Kings 17.1)

For Egypt helps in vain, and to no purpose:
therefore have I called her Rahab[a] *that sits still.* (v7)

Isaiah prophesies..

For it is a rebellious people, lying children, children that will not hear the law of YHWH;
that say to the seers, See not! and to the prophets, Prophesy not unto us right things!
speak unto us smooth things, prophesy deceits,
get out of the way, turn aside out of the path,
cause the Holy One of Israel to cease from before us. (v9-11)

G-d says it is only in Him that they will be saved, not in military might.

For the people shall dwell [b] *in Zion at Jerusalem; thou shall weep no more* (v19)

G-d Himself is the one who will defeat the Assyrians.

Ch 31
Do not trust in Egypt they cannot help.

Now the Egyptians are men, and not God; and their horses flesh, and not spirit (v3)

Turn ye unto him from whom ye have deeply revolted, O children of Israel. (v6)

And the Assyrian shall fall by the sword, not of man. (v8)

The ultimate consequences of Hoshea's actions are not described here. Assyria will carry off Israel into captivity.[c] Perhaps chapters 33-34 given as prophecy against this.

Ch32 Verse 1-8
Isaiah shifts somewhat here to a future idealised description of a period of restoration of true leadership and the return of justice; an end to corrupted leaders.
Verse 9-20 is directed to the people[d] who are at ease living comfortably; they will soon be mourning. The city is to be destroyed, the land left uncultivated. Following from chapters 30-31, with the immanent invasion of the Assyrians into Israel, this prophecy suits better the fate of the Northern Kingdom and Samaria and *its* daughters. The mention of *...the hill and*

---

[a] Pride. Egypt [poetic]

[b] yāšaḇ [remain]. All of the people of Israel will worship there

[c] 2 Kings 17.6; " Kings 18.9-11

[d] Poetically Women and daughters. The people of Jerusalem (with YHWH as their husband) rather than specifically directed to women

the watch-tower.. in verse 14 would then relate to the city of Samaria as its name means *..hill of the watchtower.* [a]
However many commentators attribute this to a further-in-the-future event to which Jerusalem will succumb for its sin and joyful celebrating when they should have been mourning (29.1). They will remain that way until..

until the Spirit be poured upon us from on high,
and the wilderness become a fruitful field,
and the fruitful field be esteemed as a forest. (v16)[b]

Verse 16-20 continue with hope for the future.

Ch 33
Woe to the plunderers. Assyria will be destroyed. G-d will ultimately be the plunderer of assailants. G-d will rule in Justice and Righteousness. At G-d's Judgement all are brought low. G-d announces his Judgement *of fire.* Sinners are afraid but the righteous are happy.

Look upon Zion, the city of our solemnities:
your eyes shall see Jerusalem a quiet habitation,
a tent that shall not be removed, the stakes whereof shall never be plucked up,
neither shall any of the cords thereof be broken.
But there YHWH will be with us in majesty…(v20-21)

Ch 34
The Day of Judgement for the nations as G-d brings about eschatological destruction on them all. Edom is singled out but its name is probably emblematic of the nations generally.

For YHWH has a day of vengeance, a year of recompense for the cause of Zion (v8)

Only animals and birds will live in their cities.

Ch 35
The wilderness will blossom and the deserts rejoice; all the lands will see the glory of G-d who comes and saves the people who have been faithful.

Then the eyes of the blind shall be opened, and the ears of the deaf shall be unstopped.
Then shall the lame man leap as a hart, and the tongue of the dumb shall sing;
for in the wilderness shall waters break out, and streams in the desert.
And the glowing sand shall become a pool, and the thirsty ground springs of water:

---

[a] 1 Kings 16.24
[b] Is it not yet a very little while, and Lebanon shall be turned into a fruitful field, and the fruitful field shall be esteemed as a forest? (29.17)

in the habitation of jackals, where they lay, shall be grass with reeds and rushes.
And a highway shall be there, and a way, and it shall be called The Way of Holiness;
the unclean shall not pass over it; but it shall be for the redeemed:
the wayfaring men, yea fools, shall not err therein.
No lion shall be there, nor shall any ravenous beast go up thereon;
they shall not be found there; but the redeemed shall walk there:
and the ransomed of YHWH shall return, and come with singing unto Zion;
and everlasting joy shall be upon their heads: they shall obtain gladness and joy,
and sorrow and sighing shall flee away (v5-10)

Ch 36-37
A return to a prose section. Hezekiah is now king and is ruling in the footsteps of David, following the statutes of YHWH. He rebels against Assyrian rule. Soon after that, the Assyrian Chief army commander arrives at Jerusalem, ahead of his army, with the conquering of the city in mind.

Now it came to pass in the fourteenth year of king Hezekiah, that Sennacherib king of Assyria came up against all the fortified cities of Judah, and took them. (36.1)

The Assyrians have earlier taken Samaria and exiled the entire people of the Northern Kingdom of Israel.[a] The Assyrian Chief commander now advises the inhabitants of Jerusalem to surrender. Hezekiah enquires of Isaiah what to do and is told not to give in. He listens to Isaiah and repents and humbles himself before G-d. When the Assyrian army arrive at Jerusalem the city is miraculously saved..

... And the angel of YHWH went forth, and smote in the camp of the Assyrians a hundred and fourscore and five thousand; and when men arose early in the morning, behold, these were all dead bodies. So Sennacherib king of Assyria departed. (v36-37)

Ch 38-39
Hezekiah becomes seriously ill. G-d says he is to die. Hezekiah makes an impassioned plea/prayer and his life is extended. Hezekiah's downfall follows as he hosts, in Jerusalem, a Babylonian delegation, who have heard of his illness. He shows to them the treasures of the entire city. Isaiah hears about this and predicts that this new ally will one day return and conquer Jerusalem taking away all of its treasures.[b] Hezekiah is comforted that at least in his lifetime there will be peace and security.

Thus ends the …*vision of Isaiah the son of Amoz, which he saw concerning Judah and Jerusalem, in the days of Uzziah, Jotham, Ahaz, and Hezekiah, kings of Judah.* (1.1)

---

[a] 2Kings 18.9-11. Fall of Samaria 721

[b] This prediction ultimately comes true when the Babylonians conquer Assyria and then go on to Judah / Jerusalem and destroy the entire city and carry off all the people into slavery in Babylon.

Now obviously the book of Isaiah does continue on from here; there are those who believe that Isaiah wrote the following chapters / scriptures and then sealed them for the future as perhaps stated in ..*Bind thou up the testimony, seal the law among my disciples* (8.16) and there are those who believe that another unnamed prophet (given the name Second Isaiah or *Deutero Isaiah*) has written them and that the title Isaiah has the wider context in the sense of the *Book of the Salvation of YHWH*. Either way the prophesies do continue with the concern for Israel, their purpose as a chosen people, and their G-d.
A major point, although seldom commented on, is that this Deutero Isaiah has no interest in the monarchy.[a] He makes no further mention of it but in its place has the establishment of the *Servant of YHWH.* [b]

Ch 40[c]
A new section begins more than a hundred years later at some time toward the end of the Babylonian Exile [586BC-538BC]. YHWH announces that the iniquity of Jerusalem has been paid for and pardoned and in a kind of *second* Exodus the Israelites are to be freed from slavery *again* and are to return to The Promised Land. A way is to be made through the land for Israel's return.

The voice of one that cries, Prepare ye in the wilderness the way of YHWH;
make level in the desert a highway for our God. (v3)

YHWH now continues with His purposes for His People by bringing them back..

He will feed his flock like a shepherd, he will gather the lambs in his arm,
and carry them in his bosom, and will gently lead those that have their young. (v11)

The ultimate power and glory of YHWH the creator of everything is then extolled..

Who has measured the waters in the hollow of his hand,
and meted out heaven with the span,
and comprehended the dust of the earth in a measure,
and weighed the mountains in scales, and the hills in a balance? (v12)

And the foolishness and vanity of worshipping the *things created* exposed..

---

[a] David is mentioned in 55.3-4 with the emphasis on faithful promises of G-d to the righteous humble servant...

Incline your ear, and come unto me; hear, and your soul shall live:
and I will make an everlasting covenant with you, even the sure mercies of David.
Behold, I have given him for a witness to the peoples, a leader and commander to the peoples.

[b] Abraham is first to be called Servant of YHWH (Gen. 26.24) . By faith and works he becomes the father to all the believers and the servants who follow 2) From the seed of Abraham
[c] Isaiah 40-55. A reversal. From captivity within the nations to leadership of the nations

The image, a workman has cast it,
and the goldsmith overlays it with gold, and casts for it silver chains.
He that is too impoverished for such an oblation chooses a tree that will not rot;
he seeks a skilful workman to set up a graven image, that shall not totter. (v19-20)

G-d further reminds and admonishes Israel that His plan, though it is difficult to comprehend by humans, will continue..

Why say thou, O Jacob and speak thou, O Israel 'My way has been hid from YHWH?
And from my God my judgment passes over.'
Have you not known? Have you not heard? The God of the age -- YHWH,
Preparer of the ends of the earth, Is not wearied nor fatigued,
There is no searching of His understanding. (v27-28)

Ch 41
YHWH declares..

But thou, Israel, my servant,[a] *Jacob whom I have chosen, the seed of Abraham my friend,*
thou whom I have taken hold of from the ends of the earth,
and called from the corners thereof, and said unto thee, Thou are my servant,
I have chosen thee and not cast thee away; fear thou not, for I am with thee;
be not dismayed, for I am thy God; I will strengthen thee; yea, I will help thee;
yea, I will uphold thee with the right hand of my righteousness. (v8-10)

YHWH declares his overall rule and his chosen people Israel who will bring YHWH to the nations. Israel is encouraged not to fear as YHWH is with them and will uphold them with inexhaustible power. YHWH calls Himself *King of Jacob*[b] and makes further statements against the weakness of Idols and their inability to predict the future of Israel. (v21)

Ch 42
In a rewriting of Psalm 2,[c] YHWH now calls on *His Servant* the New Israel and explains how they will be..

Behold, my servant, whom I uphold; my chosen, in whom my soul delights:
I have put my Spirit upon him; he will bring forth justice to the Gentiles.
He will not cry, nor lift up his voice, nor cause it to be heard in the street.
A bruised reed will he not break, and a dimly burning wick will he not quench:
he will bring forth justice in truth. He will not fail nor be discouraged,

---

[a] A return to the ideal of Exo.19.6 *and ye shall be unto me a kingdom of priests, and a holy nation*
[b] The return to the rejected ideal of 1 Sam 8.7 (the people reject YHWH as their King). Also 43.15
[c] The establishment of the messianic king with David

till he have set justice in the earth; and the isles shall wait for his law.[a]
Thus says God YHWH, he that created the heavens, and stretched them forth;
he that spread abroad the earth and that which comes out of it;
He that gives breath unto the people upon it, and spirit to them that walk therein:
I, YHWH, have called thee in righteousness, and will hold thy hand, and will keep thee,
and give thee for a covenant of the people, for a light of the Gentiles;
to open the blind eyes, to bring out the prisoners from the dungeon,
and them that sit in darkness out of the prison-house.
I am YHWH, that is my name; and my glory will I not give to another,
neither my praise unto graven images.
Behold, the former things are come to pass, and new things do I declare;
before they spring forth I tell you of them. (v1-9)

The servants are called in humility to bring G-d's truth to the nations (and within the Israelite people) who have been blind and deaf to the ways of the One true G-d.

Ch 43
G-d encourages the Israelites not to fear as they have been redeemed. G-d is their saviour. Israel have not listened and have gone their own way. G-d has punished them. Now He has forgiven them, they should make their return back from all the areas in which they have been captives, and in this *New Exodus*, YHWH will *..make a way in the wilderness* (v18)

Behold, I will do a new thing; now shall it spring forth; shall ye not know it? (v19)

Ch 44
G-d further encourages Israel His chosen one..

I will pour my Spirit upon thy seed, and my blessing upon your offspring (v3)

G-d is the only God and all the events of the world are under His control..

Thus says YHWH, the King of Israel,[b] *and his Redeemer, YHWH of hosts:*
I am the first, and I am the last; and besides me there is no God.
And who, as I, shall call, and shall declare it,
and set it in order for me, since I established the ancient people?

---

[a] Verse 1-4 set out the way of the Servant; not one of arranging armies to conquer nations but peacefully, lovingly and patiently, in the spirit of YHWH bring them to the truth. 2) This sets post Constantine Christianity (Battle of Milvian Bridge 312AD) at odds with that ideal. Jesus is the suffering servant. The focus of the servant of Isaiah both here and chapter 53 is not the three days of Jesus crucifixion but the lifetime of 'turning the other cheek' and in so doing slowly teaching the oppressor of their error and allowing G-d to act on one's behalf (as with Hezekiah)
[b] YHWH as King and sole true G-d

and the things that are coming, and that shall come to pass, let them declare.
Fear ye not, neither be afraid: have I not declared unto thee of old, and showed it?
and ye are my witnesses. Is there a God besides me?
yea, there is no Rock; I know not any. (v6-8)

G-d explains that's the idols are worthless/useless and serve only to lead people astray. G-d, again declares that Israel are His people and that He has forgiven them.

All creation join in with the praise of this..

Sing, O ye heavens, for YHWH has done it; shout, ye lower parts of the earth;
break forth into singing, ye mountains, O forest, and every tree therein:
for YHWH has redeemed Jacob, and will glorify Himself in Israel. (v23)

G-d then declares of Jerusalem..

...She shall be inhabited; and of the cities of Judah,
They shall be built, and I will raise up the waste places thereof;
that says to the deep, Be dry, and I will dry up thy rivers;
That says of Cyrus, He is my shepherd, and shall perform all my pleasure,
even saying of Jerusalem, She shall be built;
and of the temple, Thy foundation shall be laid. (v26-28)

Ch 45

G-d reminds them that Cyrus[a] was brought in at His request. It is through leaders like him that He makes his wishes known and enacts His purposes.

Only in YHWH, it is said of me, is righteousness and strength; even to him shall men come;
and all they that were incensed against him shall be put to shame.[b]
In YHWH shall all the seed of Israel be justified, and shall glory. (24-25)

Ch 46

G-d further dismisses the idols Bel and Nebo of the Babylonians (who are also carried off into captivity) and reminds Israel that it is He who cares for the Israelites..

... my salvation shall not tarry; and I will place salvation in Zion for Israel my glory. (v12)

Ch 47

G-d has used Babylon to bring about justice to His people. The Babylonians assumed, in error, that it was their gods who had delivered Israel into their hands. They dealt severely

[a] See Ezra 1

[b] Shall admit their guilt, admitting their oppression of a nation who actually bore salvation

with them unaware of this. Now the Babylonians will be taken into captivity and treat the same way.

Ch 48
Israel have had YHWH as their God, but in truth they have not followed Him. YHWH has declared to them in the past what would happen if they continued in error. Now it has happened and still they remain obstinate. YHWH has freed them from Babylon, which has surprised the Israelites somewhat. They are unable to say that any Idol or god of the nations told them this would happen. Now it is known YHWH has done this and the reason why is given..

I have refined thee, but not as silver; I have chosen thee in the furnace of affliction (v10)

YHWH says that if only the Israelites had listened in the first place none of this would have happened and in fact the reverse would have come to be. The Israelites are then commanded..

Go ye forth from Babylon, flee ye from the Chaldeans;
with a voice of singing declare ye, tell this, utter it even to the end of the earth:
say ye, YHWH has redeemed his servant Jacob!
And they thirsted not when he led them through the deserts;
he caused the waters to flow out of the rock for them;
he clave the rock also, and the waters gushed out. (v20-21)[a]

Ch 49
Israel now declares to the nations their awareness of their/His mission..

Thou are my servant; Israel, in whom I will be glorified. (v3)

But admit the time thus far has been wasted..

But I said, I have laboured in vain, I have spent my strength for nought and vanity;
yet surely the justice due to me is with YHWH, and my recompense with my God (v4)

YHWH then says that this act of restoring Israel back as a nation is yet a light thing compared to what He has in mind..

I will also give thee for a light to the Gentiles,
that thou may be my salvation unto the end of the earth (v6)

YHWH says (of Israel)..

---

[a] The ransomed people now return with similar miraculous events taking place as they make their return through the lands. Alluding to the miracles in the wilderness of Sinai (Exodus 17:6)

to him whom man despises, to him whom the nation abhor, a servant of rulers:
kings shall see thee and stand up; princes shall bow down; because of YHWH who is faithful,
the Holy One of Israel, who has chosen thee. (v7)

The Israelites are encouraged to return..

They shall not hunger nor thirst; neither shall the heat nor sun smite them:
for he that has mercy on them will lead them, even by springs of water will he guide them.
And I will make in all my mountains a way, and my highways shall be raised.
Lo, these shall come from far; and, lo, these from the north and from the west;
and these from the land of Sinim.[a] (v10-12)

Again all creation is filled with joy for the unfolding events..

Sing O heavens; and be joyful O earth; and break forth into singing O mountains:
for YHWH has comforted his people, and will have compassion upon his afflicted. (v13)

The voice of Zion speaks..

But Zion said, YHWH has forsaken me, and my Lord [b] *has forgotten* me (v14)

YHWH says she will be restored and all those enemies who surrounded her in aggression will now surround her in homage.

Ch 50
YHWH continues to say it was for Israel's sin and iniquity that he/she was exiled. No one had listened to Him, and not because He was without power to act.

Verse 4 begins a speech from the (true) Servant of YHWH[c]

The Lord YHWH has given me the tongue of them that are taught,
that I may know how to sustain with words him that is weary:
he wakens morning by morning, he wakens mine ear to hear as they that are taught.
The Lord YHWH has opened mine ear,
and I was not rebellious, neither turned away backward.
I gave my back to the smiters, and my cheeks to them that plucked off the hair;
I hid not my face from shame and spitting. For the Lord YHWH will help me;
therefore have I not been confounded: therefore have I set my face like a flint,
and I know that I shall not be put to shame.

---

[a] The furthest known inhabited lands of the Earth

[b] אֲדֹנָי ['Ădônây]

[c] The faithful Remnant of Israel who are also taken away into captivity (including the prophets)

He is near that justifies me; who will contend with me?
let us stand up together: who is mine adversary? let him come near to me.
Behold, the Lord YHWH will help me; who is he that shall condemn me?
behold, they all shall wax old as a garment; the moth shall eat them up. (v4-9)

A statement from the narrator to those who listen..

Who is among you that fears YHWH, that obeys the voice of his servant?
he that walks in darkness, and has no light,
let him trust in the Name of YHWH, and rely upon his God. (v10)

And to those who don't..

Behold, all ye that kindle a fire, that gird yourselves about with firebrands;
walk ye in the flame of your fire, and among the brands that ye have kindled.
This shall ye have of my hand....ye shall lie down in sorrow. (v11)

Ch 51
The servant of YHWH extorts the reader to emulate the faithfulness of Abraham. Although he was one person, the faith he had is the same faith that all have. Israel is asked to listen as the Law and Justice of YHWH are to go out *for a light* [a] to all the nations. G-d's salvation and righteousness will never be abolished. Righteous people should not fear the reproach of men.
G-d is called to return to Zion amid joy and gladness. Jerusalem has lain in destruction and desolation. Now she is to be restored and those who afflicted her will themselves be afflicted.

Ch 52
The captives are told to cleanse themselves ready for the return to Jerusalem. They have been captives in Egypt and Assyria, now with the Babylonians. The news comes that the people are to return to Zion..

How beautiful upon the mountains are the feet of he that brings good tidings,
that announces peace and brings good tidings of happiness,
who announces salvation and says unto Zion, Thy God reigns! (v7)

The waste places of Jerusalem sing for joy as she has been redeemed..

YHWH has made bare his holy arm in the eyes of all the nations;
and all the ends of the earth have seen the salvation of our God. (v10)

[a] Verse 4

Depart! Depart! Go out from there, touch no unclean thing; go out of the midst of her;
purify yourselves, ye that bear the vessels of YHWH.
for ye shall not go out in haste, neither shall ye go by flight:
for YHWH will go before you; and the God of Israel will be your rear-guard. (11-12)

Behold, my servant shall deal wisely,
he shall be exalted and lifted up, and shall be very high.[a]
Like as many were astonished at thee (his visage was so marred more than any man, and his form more than the sons of men), so shall he sprinkle[b] *many nations;*
kings shall shut their mouths at him: for that which had not been told them shall they see;
and that which they had not heard shall they understand. (13-15)

Ch 53

Who has believed our message?[c] *and to whom has the arm*[d] *of YHWH been revealed?*
For he grew up before him as a tender plant, and as a root out of a dry ground:
he had no form nor comeliness; and when we see him,
there is no beauty that we should desire him.
He was despised, and rejected of men; a man of sorrows, and acquainted with grief:
and as one from whom men hide their face he was despised; [e] *and we esteemed him not.*
Surely he has borne our grief, and carried our sorrows;
yet we did esteem him stricken, smitten of God, and afflicted.
But he was wounded[f] *for our transgressions, he was bruised* [g] *for our iniquities;*
the chastisement of our peace was upon him; and with his stripes we are healed.[h]
All we like sheep have gone astray; we have turned everyone to his own way;
and YHWH has laid on him the iniquity of us all.

---

[a] The verbs used here (רוּם [rûm] H7311 and נָשָׂא [nāśā'] H5375) parallel the Throne vision in 6.1 and the description of YHWH in 57.15. The majestic status of YHWH applied to the Servant

[b] In expiation

[c] The return of a (or any) nation from exile. A nation apparently destroyed by G-d, now given opportunity for restoration

[d] YHWH has made bare his holy arm in the eyes of all the nations; and all the ends of the earth have seen the salvation of our God. (51.10)

[e] *Thus says YHWH, the Redeemer of Israel, and his Holy One, to him whom man despises, to him whom the nation abhors.* (Isa 49.7) 2) This chapter esteemed by the early Christians. Their emphasis on the faith and the way of non-aggression expressed. See notes chapter 42

[f] חָלַל (ḥālal) profaned. A word used 7 times in Second Isaiah.

[g] דָּכָא (dâkâ') crushed; broken into pieces

[h] Lamentations 3. (actually the entire chapter v1-66) verse 1-4 below

I am the man that has seen affliction by the rod of his wrath.
He has led me and caused me to walk in darkness, and not in light.
Surely against me he turns his hand again and again all the day.
My flesh and my skin has he made old; he has broken my bones

He was oppressed, yet when he was afflicted he opened not his mouth;
as a lamb that is led to the slaughter,[a]
and as a sheep that before its shearers is dumb, so he opened not his mouth.
By oppression and judgment he was taken away;
and as for his generation, who among them considered that he was cut off out of the land of the living for the transgression of my people to whom the stroke was due?

And they made his grave with the wicked, and with a rich man in his death; [b]
although he had done no violence, neither was any deceit in his mouth.
Yet it pleased YHWH to crush[c] *him; he has put him to grief:*
when thou shall make his soul an offering for sin,
he shall see his seed, he shall prolong his days,
and the pleasure of YHWH shall prosper in his hand.
He shall see of the travail of his soul, and shall be satisfied:
by the knowledge of himself shall my righteous servant justify many;
and he shall bear their iniquities.
Therefore will I divide him a portion with the great,
and he shall divide the spoil with the strong;

---

[a]A curious parallel in the book of Jeremiah which seems to allude to Isaiah
Jeremiah 11.19

But I was like a gentle lamb that is led to the slaughter;
and I knew not that they had devised devices against me,
saying, Let us destroy the tree with the fruit thereof,
and let us cut him off from the land of the living,
that his name may be no more remembered.

[b]Other scripture alluding to the raising of the 'dead'
2) Isaiah 26.19

Thy dead shall live; my dead bodies shall arise. Awake and sing, ye that dwell in the dust;
for thy dew is as the dew of herbs, and the earth shall cast forth the dead.

3) Hosea 6 1-2

Come, and let us return unto YHWH; for he has torn, and he will heal us;
he has smitten, and he will bind us up.
After two days will he revive us: on the third day he will raise us up, and we shall live before him.

4) Hosea 13.14

I will ransom them from the power of Sheol; I will redeem them from death:

5) Ezekiel 37 12-14

Therefore prophesy, and say unto them, Thus says the Lord YHWH:
Behold, I will open your graves, and cause you to come up out of your graves,
O my people; and I will bring you into the land of Israel. And ye shall know that I am YHWH,
when I have opened your graves, and caused you to come up out of your graves,
O my people. And I will put my Spirit in you, and ye shall live,
and I will bring you to the land of Israel:
and ye shall know that I, YHWH, have spoken it and performed it, says YHWH.

[c] דָכָא (dâkâ') crushed; broken into pieces

because he poured out his soul unto death, and was numbered with the transgressors: yet he bare the sin of many, and made intercession for the transgressors.

Ch 54
Israel is compared to a childless wife..

Sing, O barren, thou that did not bear; break forth into singing, and cry aloud, thou that did not travail with child: for more are the children of the desolate than the children of the married wife, says YHWH [a]

Because her offspring shall possess the nations and the cities of Israel re-inhabited. YHWH calls Israel His wife, who has been cast off. Now she is to return to her husband..

For this is as the waters of Noah unto me;
for as I have sworn that the waters of Noah shall no more go over the earth,
so have I sworn that I will not be angry with thee, nor rebuke thee.
For the mountains may depart, and the hills be removed;
but my loving kindness shall not depart from thee,
neither shall my covenant of peace be removed,
says YHWH that has mercy on thee. (v9-10)

She is to be beautifully rebuilt and all her children taught the peace of YHWH. No one will oppress her in the future as those who try will fall. Every weapon raised against her will fail and every tongue that speaks against her will be condemned. This will be the heritage of the Servant of YHWH.

Ch 55
A final encouragement to Israel to come back to the Promised Land[b] where they will again be in covenant with YHWH and will be totally cared for. The nations will all come to Israel's assistance..

For ye shall go out with joy, and be led forth with peace:
the mountains and the hills shall break forth before you into singing;
and all the trees of the fields shall clap their hands.
Instead of the thorn shall come up the fir-tree;
and instead of the brier shall come up the myrtle-tree:
and it shall be to YHWH for a name,
for an everlasting sign that shall not be cut off. (v12-13)

---

[a] The returning exiles. Isaiah 49.21 (the sorrow of the childless wife)

[b] Psalm 18.43 *Thou hast delivered me from the strivings of the people; Thou hast made me the head of the nations: A people whom I have not known shall serve me*. Isaiah 25.3 *Therefore shall a strong people glorify thee; a city of terrible nations shall fear thee.*

Ch 56

A third section, generally held to begin here, referred to as Third Isaiah or *Trito Isaiah*. The exiles[a] have made their return and are making a beginning to understand who they now are as a people after all the events which have befallen them. The books of Ezra & Nehemiah give a somewhat clear idea of where the people are and what they are doing, but this section of Isaiah, although running contemporaneous with Ezra Nehemiah, deals only with the larger vision of the destiny and purpose of the Servants[b] of YHWH. Isaiah describes a universal salvation to *All* people of righteousness somewhat at odds with the *Israel only* perspective of Nehemiah / Ezra (and of the Ezekiel restoration vision of Ezra ch 40-48). Exactly where Isaiah and his visionary movement are is not elaborated upon. Some commentators (i.e. Hanson) also see this as the beginning of a rivalry for authority between the hierocratic and the prophetic groups (which would extend to John the Baptist & Jesus) as the nation moved forward with their emerging identity as a returned people.

This section brings together the themes from the entire book: Divine salvation and human righteousness. Verse 1 begins with the introduction of the key themes of Justice Righteousness and Salvation. The individuals who live their lives by justice and righteousness are tied to G-d's act of granting Salvation.

Thus says YHWH, Keep ye justice,[c] *and do righteousness;* [d]
for my salvation [e] *is near to come, and my righteousness to be revealed.*

YHWH also offers salvation to all mankind..

Also the foreigners that join themselves to YHWH,
to minister unto him, and to love the Name of YHWH, to be his servants,
every one that keeps the Sabbath from profaning it, and holds fast my covenant; (v6)

..for my house shall be called a house of prayer for all peoples (v7b)

It is individual righteousness, not nationality which qualifies one for salvation. The division between Israel and the nations is swapped for the division between those who serve G-d and those who rebel against Him.

---

[a] According to Ezra chapter 2 there are 42,360 returnees in the first wave, a small fraction of the entire nation
[b] Used now on in the plural
[c] מִשְׁפָּט [mishpâṭ] mishpat; justice; judgement
[d] צְדָקָה [tsᵉdâqâh] tsadaqah; righteous acts
[e] יְשׁוּעָה [yᵉshûwʻâh] yeshuah; salvation, deliverance

Ch 57

And he will say, Cast up, cast up,[a] *prepare the way, take up the stumbling-block out of the way of my people.* (v14) [b] [c]

The ‘cast up’ or ‘build up’ refers to the actual building of a highway. A highway which leads to Mount Zion. YHWH’s offer of salvation to the people and their response to step up to the challenge. A pathway in which the people must walk but also the pathway which will bring YHWH back to the Holy place.

For thus says the high and lofty One (v15) as with ch 6.1, the same two verbs are used (also 52.13) to describe the Servant. The majesty of YHWH is shared with the Servant.

YHWH promises to forgive them and help and heal them..

I have seen his ways, and will heal him:
I will lead him also, and restore comforts unto him and to his mourners.
I create the fruit of the lips: Peace, peace, to him that is far off and to him that is near,
Says YHWH; and I will heal him. (v18-19)

Ch 58
G-d explains what exactly is the righteousness He requires.

Ch 59
G-d explains it is not His lack of power but the peoples sin which has brought disaster on them. However He will still save them.

And a Redeemer will come to Zion,
and unto them that turn from transgression in Jacob, says YHWH.
And as for me, this is my covenant with them, says YHWH:
my Spirit that is upon thee, and my words which I have put in thy mouth,
shall not depart out of thy mouth, nor out of the mouth of thy seed,
nor out of the mouth of thy seed’s seed,

---

[a] סָלַל סָלַל [sālal ! sālal !] H5549

[b] Also

Go through, go through the gates; prepare ye the way of the people;
cast up, cast up the highway; gather out the stones;
lift up an ensign for the peoples. (62.10)

[c] Also

The voice of one that cries, Prepare ye in the wilderness the way of YHWH;
make level in the desert a highway for our God.
Every valley shall be exalted, and every mountain and hill shall be made low;
and the uneven shall be made level, and the rough places a plain: (40.3-4)

says YHWH, from henceforth and for ever. (v20-21)

Ch 60
Isaiah's glorious vision, the promise of salvation of the people and of the restoration of Jerusalem (as the capital of Israel) and all the cities of the land and of course the rebuilding of the Temple to which YHWH's presence will return. Nations and their wealth will serve Israel. Any nation that tries to afflict Israel will perish.. Former enemies will come in total reverence.

Arise, shine; for thy light is come, and the glory of YHWH is risen upon thee.
For, behold, darkness shall cover the earth, and gross darkness the peoples;
but YHWH will arise upon thee, and his glory shall be seen upon thee.
And nations shall come to thy light, and kings to the brightness of thy rising. (60.1-3)

Israel's name amongst the nations will be transformed from scorn to excellency. The Israelites themselves will *All* serve YHWH in righteousness..

Thy people also shall be all righteous; they shall inherit the land for ever,
the branch of my planting, the work of my hands, that I may be glorified. (v21)

Ch 61
Begins with..

The Spirit of the Lord YHWH is upon me;
because YHWH has anointed me to preach good tidings unto the meek;
he has sent me to bind up the broken-hearted, to proclaim liberty to the captives,
and the opening of the prison to them that are bound;
to proclaim the year of YHWH's favour and the day of vengeance of our God;
to comfort all that mourn; to appoint unto them that mourn in Zion,
to give unto them a garland for ashes, the oil of joy for mourning,
the garment of praise for the spirit of heaviness;
that they may be called trees of righteousness, the planting of YHWH,
that he may be glorified.
And they shall build the old wastes, they shall raise up the former desolations,
and they shall repair the waste cities, the desolations of many generations.
And strangers shall stand and feed your flocks,
and foreigners shall be your ploughmen and your vine-dressers.
But ye shall be named 'the priests of YHWH;'

men shall call you the ministers of our God (v1-6)[a]

Israel still maintains a high position to the nations..

And their seed shall be known among the nations,
and their offspring among the peoples; all that see them shall acknowledge them,
that they are the seed which YHWH has blessed. (v9)

The servant rejoices in his exalted position..

I will greatly rejoice in YHWH, my soul shall be joyful in my God; for he has clothed me with the garments of salvation, he has covered me with the robe of righteousness, as a bridegroom decks himself with a garland, and as a bride adorns herself with her jewels.
For as the earth brings forth its bud, and as the garden causes the things that are sown in it to spring forth; so the Lord YHWH will cause righteousness and praise to spring forth before all the nations. (v10-11)

Ch 62
For the sake of Zion, YHWH will not rest until her righteousness and glory spread through the entire Earth. Zion will be the desire of all.

Thou shall no more be termed Forsaken;
neither shall thy land any more be termed Desolate:
but thou shall be called Hephzi-bah,[b] *and thy land Beulah;*[c]
for YHWH delights in thee, and thy land shall be married.
For as a young man marries a virgin, so shall thy sons marry thee;
and as the bridegroom rejoices over the bride, so shall thy God rejoice over thee. (v4-5)

---

[a] LXX has

Spirit of YHWH is upon me, because he anointed me
to announce good news to the poor. He has sent me
to heal the ones being broken in the heart; ;to proclaim to captives a release,
and to the blind recovery of sight; to call year of YHWH the acceptable,
and day of recompense; to comfort all the ones mourning;
to give to the ones mourning for Zion glory instead of ashes;
an anointing of gladness to them that mourn; according to an apparel of glory
instead of a spirit of indifference. And they shall be called
generations of righteousness, a thing planted of YHWH for glory.
And they shall build up wildernesses everlasting being made quite desolate prior.
They shall rise up and shall revive cities of wildernesses
having been made quite desolate for generations.
And shall come foreigners tending your sheep,
and Philistines as ploughmen and vine dressers.
And you priests of YHWH shall be called. Ministers of the El (v1-6)

[b] Delightful

[c] Married

Behold, YHWH has proclaimed unto the end of the earth,
Say ye to the daughter of Zion, Behold, thy salvation comes;
behold, his reward is with him, and his recompense before him.
And they shall call them The holy people, The redeemed of YHWH:
and thou shall be called Sought out, A city not forsaken. (v11-12)

Ch 63
Begins with a bloody vision of G-d returning from battle where He has destroyed all Israel's enemies. YHWH has done this himself without help (as he had done with Cyrus and other leaders of nations previously).

Ch 63.7-64.11 - The Servants Lament
In this powerful Lament the loving kindness and faithfulness of G-d, the saviour of Israel through the ages is remembered. Also remembered is the faithlessness of the people ultimately resulting in the destruction of the nation, of Jerusalem, and the Temple.
The speaker humbly requests forgiveness and restoration.

Ch 65
After the lament there is a turning point in Isaiah with the vision of the new people of G-d. YHWH laments the rebelliousness of the people and condemns them to destruction. Those who have served faithfully, His servants, will be saved and shall live joyfully and in peace throughout the Land enjoying G-d's protection.

For, behold, I create new heavens and a new earth;
and the former things shall not be remembered, nor come into mind.
But be ye glad and rejoice for ever in that which I create;
for, behold, I create Jerusalem rejoicing, and her people gladness. (v17-18)

Ch 66
YHWH declares that it is not necessarily to the Temple[a] that He will look to accept the penitence of men but to he that..

.. *is poor and of a contrite spirit, and that trembles at my word.* (v2)

Now YHWH's children are fully grown and Jerusalem is ready to receive them. YHWH is also coming to enact his Justice against the evildoers. G-d gathers all people from all nations and tongues to see his glory and they will congregate at His Holy Mountain[b] in Jerusalem. In this new heaven and new earth this new people will remain..

---

[a] The Temple, here described in the unusual less than central position. Perhaps an allusion to the priesthood who control it as a position rather than a calling

[b] The Temple wherein will be YHWH's Presence (as it had been in Solomon's temple (2 Chronicles 7)

and it shall come to pass, that from one new moon to another, and from one Sabbath to another, shall all flesh come to worship before me, says YHWH (v23)

Jeremiah

A priest from Anathoth[a] in the tribal land of Benjamin (about 3 miles from Jerusalem). The word of G-d came to him in the 13th year of the reign of Josiah[b] and continued until the Babylonian exile of the people of Jerusalem.

Jeremiah is somewhat afraid of the commission reminiscent of both Moses and Isaiah..

But YHWH said unto me, Say not 'I am a child'
for to where ever I shall send thee you shall go,
and what ever I shall command thee you shall speak.
Be not afraid because of them; for I am with thee to deliver thee, says YHWH
Then YHWH put forth his hand, and touched my mouth;
and YHWH said unto me, Behold, I have put my words in thy mouth. (v7-9)

Jeremiah is also given a position by YHWH somewhat akin to kingship..

see, I have this day set thee over the nations and over the kingdoms,
to pluck up and to break down and to destroy and to overthrow, to build and to plant. (v10)

Jeremiah is informed that a nation from the North is being called to attack Jerusalem because of the idolatry of the leadership and people of Jerusalem and Judah. YHWH is to pronounce His judgements against them; Jeremiah is to deliver them fearlessly as YHWH will protect him as a *fortified city, and an iron pillar, and brazen walls* (v18)

All the rulers and priests and people will fight against him, but..

they shall fight against thee; but they shall not prevail against thee:
for I am with thee, says YHWH, to deliver thee. (v19)

Ch 2

Jeremiah is to remind the people of what G-d has done for them when He brought them out of Egypt, through the wilderness and into the Promised Land. Now they have forgotten Him and are following every other god of the surrounding nations. Israel has become *their* servant. The people had promised not to do so but has failed utterly.

---

[a] A city allocated to the Levite priests (Joshua 21.18)

[b] King Josiah of Judah (640-609BC)

In his prophecy, Jeremiah describes their idolatry in terms of sexual misconduct. Here described in the way of wild animals reacting to a mating opportunity (v23-24). YHWH rejects the people and their rulers. They have not accepted that they are doing anything wrong, yet they follow that which has already been rejected by G-d a long time since.

Ch 3
Israel is described as a prostitute for all of the idolatry. The rain has been withheld and there is drought in the land.

Therefore the showers have been withheld, and no spring rains have fallen.
Yet you have the brazen look of a prostitute; you refuse to blush with shame.
Have you not just called to me: 'My Father, my friend from my youth,
will you always be angry? Will your wrath continue forever?'
This is how you talk, but you do all the evil you can." (v3-5)

Both Judah and Israel[a] are equally corrupt. G-d implores them to return..

Return, O backsliding children, says YHWH; for I am a husband unto you:
and I will take you one of a city, and two of a family, and I will bring you to Zion.
And I will give you shepherds according to my heart,
who shall feed you with knowledge and understanding. (v14-15)

G-d says that at some point in the future, the Ark of the Covenant will no longer be the focal point of His presence, but the entire City of Jerusalem will be his Throne and all nations will gather to it. Judah and Israel will come back together.[b]

Ch 4
G-d wishes..

If you will return, O Israel, says YHWH, if you will return unto me,
and if you will put away your abominations out of my sight; then shall you not be removed;
and you shall swear, as YHWH lives, in truth, in justice, and in righteousness;
and the nations shall bless themselves in him, and in him shall they glory. (v1-2)

This isn't going to happen. A great army will come and destroy the unrepentant Jerusalem.

Ch. 5
Jeremiah is asked to go through the city to search for any righteous man but he can find none. None even know who YWHW is (verse 4). The prophets lie (verse 13 & 31). An army from the North is coming (Babylonian) they will destroy the city. The people do not trust in YHWH at all.

---

[a] The kingdoms of Judah and the northern kingdom of Israel. Jeremiah refers to them as two sisters (v7)
[b] Verse 18

With the sword they will destroy the fortified cities in which you trust. (v17)

G-d promises that He will not completely destroy everything, some people will remain.

Ch 6

Zion and Jerusalem will be destroyed for all the idolatry going on. Jeremiah continues to warn them, but the people refuse to listen to him.

Ch 7

Jeremiah is told to stand in the gateway to the Temple and warn the people against their corrupt ways. The temple will also be destroyed as was Shiloh, if they do not listen. There is idolatry even in the Temple.

Therefore pray not thou for this people, neither lift up cry nor prayer for them,
neither make intercession to me; for I will not hear thee.
Don't you see what they do in the cities of Judah and in the streets of Jerusalem?
The children gather wood, and the fathers kindle the fire, and the women knead the dough,
to make cakes to the queen of heaven, and to pour out drink-offerings unto other gods,
that they may provoke me to anger. Do they provoke me to anger? Says YHWH;
do they not provoke themselves, to the confusion of their own faces? (v16-19)

YHWH reminds them of how he saved them from Egypt and of His commandments and especially the commandment..

Obey me, and I will be your God and you will be my people (v23)

But, *Truth has perished; it has vanished from their lips*. (v28)

The people have even committed child sacrifice..

They have built the high places of Topheth in the Valley of Ben Hinnom
to burn their sons and daughters in the fire;
something I did not command, nor did it enter my mind. (v31)

Ch 8

No one is listening. Jerusalem has *turned away* and doesn't care for the word of YHWH or know what He wants. The leaders proclaim that there will be peace; the priests and prophets deal falsely; the people are left without healing.

Ch 9

All the advisers within Jerusalem are deceivers. The city will be laid waste. The people have not followed the Torah (Law). They will be scattered into all the uncircumcised world.

YHWH says...

I will punish all who are circumcised only in the flesh.
Egypt, Judah, Edom, Ammon, Moab and all who live in the wilderness in distant places.
For all these nations are really uncircumcised,
and even the whole house of Israel is uncircumcised in heart." (v25-26)

Ch 10

Jeremiah advises the people not to worship idols or fear them. YHWH is the king of the nations. The Living G-d, Eternal King, who rules the Heavens and the Earth. Still the people are unreceptive. The people of Jerusalem are to be cast out. Jeremiah prays…

I know, YHWH, that the way of man is not in himself;
it is not in man that walks to direct his steps.
Correct me, YHWH, but in measure; not in thine anger, lest thou bring me to nothing.
Pour out thy wrath upon the nations that know thee not,
and upon the families that call not on thy Name;
for they have devoured Jacob, yea, they have devoured him and consumed him,
and have laid waste his habitation. (v23-25)

Ch 11

Jeremiah implores them to swear by the covenant again, but still none listen. YHWH brings the curses of Deuteronomy 11.26-28 on the people ..

For YHWH of hosts, who planted thee, has pronounced evil against thee,
because of the evil of the house of Israel and of the house of Judah,
which they have wrought for themselves in provoking Me to anger
by offering incense unto Baal. (v17)

And YHWH gave me knowledge of it, and I knew it: then thou showed me their doings.
But I was like a gentle lamb that is led to the slaughter;[a]
and I knew not that they had devised devices against me,
saying, Let us destroy the tree with the fruit thereof,
and let us cut him off from the land of the living,
that his name may be no more remembered. (v18-19)

Some from Anathoth become indignant against Jeremiah and plot to kill him. YHWH says it is they who will be destroyed.

---

[a] A parallel with Isaiah 53.8

Ch 12
Jeremiah wonders why evil people seem to prosper. YHWH advises Jeremiah that His justice will prevail eventually, both within Israel and within all the nations.

Ch 13
Jeremiah is directed to get a linen girdle and to ruin it. YHWH has worn Israel as a girdle but now Jerusalem, like the girdle, will be ruined and humbled. She is to go into exile for her shameless acts.

Ch 14
The drought becomes more serious. Jeremiah asks for YHWH to help. YHWH says that these wicked people are being punished and also advises Jeremiah not to pray for them as they are soon to be destroyed. Other prophets proclaim there is no problem with Jerusalem and to that advice the people listen. YHWH condemns them as liars (v14).
Jeremiah begs YHWH for help.

Ch 15
YHWH says no to Jeremiah's request.

Then said YHWH unto me, Though Moses and Samuel stood before Me,
yet My mind would not be toward this people:
cast them out of My sight, and let them go.
And it shall come to pass, when they say unto thee, Where shall we go?
then thou shall tell them, thus says YHWH:
Such as are for death, to death; and such as are for the sword, to the sword;
and such as are for the famine, to the famine;
and such as are for captivity, to captivity.'
And I will appoint over them four kinds, says YHWH:
the sword to slay, and the dogs to tear, and the birds of the heavens,
and the beasts of the earth, to devour and to destroy.
And I will cause them to be tossed to and fro among all the kingdoms of the earth,
because of Manasseh, the son of Hezekiah, king of Judah,
for that which he did in Jerusalem.[a] (v1-4)

Jeremiah is despondent and curses his own life but YHWH encourages him on and promises further protection.

Ch 16
Jeremiah is told not to marry or have children as the people of Jerusalem are all destined to die by the sword. YHWH has withdrawn his pity for them. The people still don't seem to know why Jeremiah is so harsh on them. Jeremiah reminds them..

[a] He sacrificed his own son to Molech and instituted extensive idol worship (2 Kings 21)

because your fathers have forsaken me, says YHWH,
and have walked after other gods, and have served them,
and have worshipped them, and have forsaken me, and have not kept my law;
and ye have done evil more than your fathers;
for, behold, ye walk every one after the stubbornness of his evil heart,
so that ye hearken not unto me (v11-12)

YHWH will punish them, but eventually they will come to know the power of YHWH.

Therefore, behold, I will cause them to know, this once will I cause them to know my hand and my might; and they shall know that my name is YHWH (v21)

Ch 17
The people's sin is engraved on their hearts (of stone). They are about to lose their inheritance. Those whose trust is *in men* are cursed. Those who trust in YHWH are blessed.

YHWH says..
The heart is deceitful above all things, and it is exceedingly corrupt:
who can know it? I, YHWH, search the mind,
I try the heart, even to give every man according to his ways,
according to the fruit of his doings.
As the partridge that sits on eggs which she has not laid,
so is he that gets riches, and not by right;
in the midst of his days they shall leave him, and at his end he shall be a fool. (9-11)

Jeremiah again makes a sorrowful plea..

Heal me, YHWH, and I shall be healed;
save me, and I shall be saved: for thou are my praise.
Behold, they say unto me, Where is the word of YHWH? let it come now. (v 14-15).

Jeremiah is directed to stand at one of the Jerusalem gates and then tell people not to work on the Sabbath. They are then told if they obey this commandment all will be well and..

then shall there enter in by the gates of this city
kings and princes sitting upon the throne of David, riding in chariots and on horses,
they, and their princes, the men of Judah, and the inhabitants of Jerusalem;
and this city shall remain for ever (v 25)

..but if not then the city will be burnt down (v27)

Ch 18

Jeremiah is called to go to the potter's house where he watches a pot being made. Before the pot is finished it spoils in the potter's hand and is then reformed. YHWH says…

> *Behold, as the clay in the potter's hand, so are ye in my hand, O house of Israel. In one instant I shall speak concerning a nation, and concerning a kingdom, to pluck up and to break down and to destroy it.* (v 6-7)

The people are still not listening and are therefore destined to suffer the calamity about to unfold.

Ch 19

Jeremiah is told by YHWH to take an earthen pot and then invite the elders down to the valley of Ben Hinnom[a] where he will Prophesy to them the terrible events which are to overcome Jerusalem and its people. He is then to smash the pot into pieces and declare so it will be with the city.

Ch 20

Jeremiah is placed in the stocks by the chief officer of the Temple, Pashur, for prophesying against Jerusalem and its leaders. Jeremiah then tells Pashur that the city will fall into the hands of the Babylonians and all of its people and its treasures will be carried off. Jeremiah has become a laughing stock within Jerusalem. No one listens to him not even his own friends and family. He knows he can't do anything but bring the prophesies to the people from G-d, but curses his life nonetheless (v 14-18) in a way very similar to Job.[b]

Ch 21

King Zedekiah[c] sends an envoy[d] to Jeremiah. The king of Babylon has come to make war on Jerusalem. Zedekiah wants to know if G-d will help them. Jeremiah is told by G-d to inform Zedekiah that the city will fall to the Babylonians. YHWH Himself will fight against Jerusalem for its corruption. Jeremiah advises those who wish to live, to hand themselves over to the Babylonians otherwise they will die from famine pestilence and the sword. Jeremiah puts his hand out and touching the house of the king, condemns the monarchy (House of David) for oppressing the people and believing they can never be overrun.

Ch 22

Jeremiah again prophesies to Zedekiah informing him that if only he repent and return to YHWH and His ways the Babylonian capture can be averted, but if not then destruction.

---

[a] Where child sacrifice had been taking place.

[b] Job chapter 3

[c] 2 Kings 25.1 *So in the ninth year of Zedekiah's reign, on the tenth day of the tenth month, Nebuchadnezzar king of Babylon marched against Jerusalem with his whole army.*

[d] Zedekiah ruled 597-587BC. This envoy sent then at the end of his reign

And many nations shall pass by this city,
and they shall say every man to his neighbour,
Why has YHWH done thus unto this great city?
Then they shall answer, Because they forsook the covenant of YHWH their God,
and worshipped other gods, and served them. (v8-9)

Jeremiah also prophesies against the last kings of Judah. Shallum,[a] who reigned for 3 months after King Josiah was killed by Pharaoh. Jehoiakim[b] … *shall be buried with the burial of an ass* (v19). Jehoiachin[c] son of Jehoiakim son of Josiah is also to be handed over to the Babylonians..

Is this man Coniah [d] *a despised broken vessel? is he a vessel wherein none delights?*
why are they cast out, he and his seed, and are cast into a land which they know not?
O earth, earth, earth, hear the word of YHWH.
Thus Says YHWH, Write ye this man childless, a man that shall not prosper in his days;
for no more shall a man of his seed prosper,
sitting upon the throne of David, and ruling in Judah. (v28-30)[e]

Ch 23
Woe unto the shepherds who have led the people astray. But YHWH will still return a remnant of His people, to abide and multiply in the land with new shepherds over them.

Behold, the days come, says YHWH,
that I will raise unto David a righteous Branch,
and he shall reign as king and deal wisely,
and shall execute justice and righteousness in the land.
In his days Judah shall be saved, and Israel shall dwell safely;
and this is his name whereby he shall be called:

YHWH Siḏqēnû (YHWH our righteousness) [f] (v5-6)

YHWH will be known not as he who led the people out of Egypt but he who led them home from all the nations where they were captives. YHWH concludes by condemning the lying prophets. They could have helped but only deluded the people.

[a] Also called Jehoahaz son of Josiah
[b] Ruled before Zedekiah 608-597BC
[c] Ruled during 597BC only
[d] AKA Jehoiachin
[e] Jehoiachin, however, is given special honourable treatment by the king of Babylon (2 Kings 25.27-30). He is after all the last hope of a continuance of the Davidic line should they return to Jerusalem
[f] Also in Jeremiah 33.16

Ch 24
The Babylonians have already entered the city and taken captive Jehoiachin the son of Jehoiakim, and the leaders of Judah, with all the city's craftsmen.
Jeremiah sees two baskets of figs outside the Temple, one good and the other bad. He prophesies..

Thus says YHWH, the God of Israel:
Like these good figs, so will I regard the captives of Judah,
whom I have sent out of this place into the land of the Chaldeans, for good.
For I will set mine eyes upon them for good, and I will bring them again to this land:
and I will build them, and not pull them down; and I will plant them, and not pluck them up.
And I will give them a heart to know me, that I am YHWH:
and they shall be my people, and I will be their God;
for they shall return unto me with their whole heart. (v5-7)

The bad figs are those who will not return but will die in captivity.

Ch 25
This chapter moves back to the rule of Jehoiakim..

The word that came to Jeremiah concerning all the people of Judah, in the fourth year of Jehoiakim the son of Josiah, king of Judah (the same was the first year of Nebuchadnezzar king of Babylon), which Jeremiah the prophet spoke unto all the people of Judah, and to all the inhabitants of Jerusalem, saying:
From the thirteenth year of Josiah the son of Amon, king of Judah,
even unto this day, these three and twenty years, the word of YHWH has come unto me,
and I have spoken unto you, rising up early and speaking; but ye have not hearkened. (v 1-3)

The people have continued in their idolatry as described above, but..

.. it shall come to pass, when seventy years are accomplished,
that I will punish the king of Babylon, and that nation, says YHWH,
for their iniquity, and the land of the Chaldeans; and I will make it desolate for ever. (v12)

Jeremiah is told..

Take this cup of the wine of wrath at my hand, and cause all the nations,
to whom I send thee, to drink it. And they shall drink, and reel to and fro, and be mad,
because of the sword that I will send among them (v 15-16)

He is to take it to all the kings of the world and say..

Thus says YHWH of hosts, the God of Israel:
Drink ye, and be drunken, and spew, and fall, and rise no more,

because of the sword which I will send among you.
And it shall be, if they refuse to take the cup at thy hand to drink,
then shall thou say unto them, Thus says YHWH of hosts:
Ye shall surely drink, for lo, I begin to work evil at the city which is called by my name;
and should ye be utterly unpunished? Ye shall not be unpunished;
for I will call for a sword upon all the inhabitants of the earth,
says YHWH of hosts. (v27-29)

An apocalyptic day is then described when people from the entire earth are killed and left with no one to bury them.

Ch 26
At the beginning of Jehoiakim's rule, Jeremiah is commanded to go to the courtyard of the Temple and say..

If ye will not hearken to me, to walk in my law, which I have set before you, to listen to the words of my servants the prophets, whom I send unto you, even rising up early and sending them, but ye have not listened; then will I make this house like Shiloh,[a] *and will make this city a curse to all the nations of the earth.* (v4-6)

All the people there take hold of him and want to kill him. They take him to the leaders and say he should die. Jeremiah exclaims that he is only bringing the word of G-d and after all if only the people and leaders of Jerusalem repent, then none of this need happen. Some of the leaders defend Jeremiah saying that the people should listen to him to avert disaster. Jeremiah is saved from them.

Ch 27
Moving forward again to Zedekiah's rule, Jeremiah puts a yoke around his neck and proclaims to all the kings of the earth that they will be ruled by the Babylonians by the order of YHWH. He gives the message to Zedekiah and tells him that every nation which accepts the yoke of the king of Babylon will remain in their land. Jeremiah warns him not to listen to the 'lying' prophets who say that he should not serve the king of Babylon.
Jeremiah also speaks to the leaders and the people telling them not to listen to false prophets who are saying that the items removed from the Temple by Nebuchadnezzar when he took Jehoiachin away to Babylon will soon be returned. Jeremiah says even the remaining vessels will be taken away to Babylon until such times as YHWH decrees their return.

Ch 28
In that same year Hananiah the prophet proclaims in the presence of the priests and people at the Temple that the yoke of Nebuchadnezzar will be broken..

---

[a] Destroyed

Within two full years will I bring again into this place all the vessels of YHWH's house, that Nebuchadnezzar king of Babylon took away from this place, and carried to Babylon: and I will bring again to this place Jehoiachin the son of Jehoiakim, king of Judah, with all the captives of Judah, that went to Babylon, says YHWH; for I will break the yoke of the king of Babylon. (v 3-4)

Jeremiah says amen to that, but he says we will have to wait and see which of them is truly speaking the word of YHWH. Hananiah takes the yoke off Jeremiah and breaks it saying..

Thus says YHWH: Even so will I break the yoke of Nebuchadnezzar king of Babylon within two full years from off the neck of all the nations (v11)

YHWH tells Jeremiah to go to tell Hananiah that Nebuchadnezzar's yoke will now be made of iron. Jeremiah also tells him he will soon die for this rebellion. Hananiah dies the same year.

Ch 29
Jeremiah sends a letter to the exiles telling them to settle down and be at peace wherever they are and in 70 years YHWH will bring them back and restore them.

And ye shall call upon me, and ye shall go and pray unto me, and I will hearken unto you. And ye shall seek me, and find me, when ye shall search for me with all your heart. (v12-13)

Jeremiah warns that there are yet more people still in Jerusalem who will go into captivity. A 'prophet' of the exiles, Shemaniah, sends another letter back saying Jeremiah should be punished for sending such a letter. Jeremiah pronounces doom on Shemaniah for this new rebellion.

Ch 30
Jeremiah is told to write everything YHWH has spoken down on a scroll.
A great day is coming in which..

I will break his yoke from off thy neck, and will burst thy bonds;
and strangers shall no more make him their bondman;
but they shall serve YHWH their God, and David their king, whom I will raise up unto them.
Therefore fear thou not, O Jacob my servant, says YHWH;
neither be dismayed, O Israel: for, lo, I will save thee from afar. (v8-10)

YHWH promises to heal them and punish their oppressors. The cities and palaces will be rebuilt and the people will have leaders of their own.

And ye shall be my people, and I will be your God. (v22)

The fierce anger of YHWH shall not turn back, until he has executed,
until he has performed the intents of his heart: in the latter days ye shall understand it. (v24)

Ch 31

At that time, says YHWH, will I be the God of all the families of Israel,
and they shall be my people (v1)

YHWH says he will give rest to Israel and will rebuild the land..

For there shall be a day, that the watchmen upon the hills of Ephraim shall cry,
Arise ye, and let us go up to Zion unto YHWH our God. (v6)

The remnant shall return..

They shall come with weeping; and with supplications will I lead them:
I will cause them to walk by rivers of waters,
in a straight way wherein they shall not stumble;
for I am father to Israel, and Ephraim is my first-born. (v 9)

They will return and all their mourning will be changed to joy and their sorrow into rejoicing. There has been the sorrow of the exile..

Thus says YHWH: A voice is heard in Ramah,[a] *lamentation, and bitter weeping,*
Rachel weeping for her children; she refuses to be comforted for her children,
because they are not. (v15)

But now the people must refrain from weeping as they are to return to the Land. This includes all of Israel (Ephraim also)..

Is Ephraim my dear son? is he a darling child? for as often as I speak against him,
I do earnestly remember him still: therefore my heart yearns for him;
I will surely have mercy upon him, says YHWH (v20)

Set thee up waymarks, make thee guide-posts;
set thy heart toward the highway, even the way by which thou went:
turn again, O virgin of Israel, turn again to these thy cities. (v21)

Behold, the days come, says YHWH,
that I will make a new covenant with the house of Israel, and with the house of Judah: (v31)

---

[a] Ramah will be where the Exiles are first gathered after they are removed from Jerusalem by the Babylonians (Jer 40.1)

I will put my law in their inward parts, and in their heart will I write it;
and I will be their God, and they shall be my people.
And they shall teach no more every man his neighbour, and every man his brother,
saying, Know YHWH; for they shall all know me,
from the least of them unto the greatest of them, says YHWH:
for I will forgive their iniquity, and their sin will I remember no more. (v33-34)

YHWH's eternal promise to Israel.

Thus says YHWH, who gives the sun for a light by day,
and the ordinances of the moon and of the stars for a light by night,
who stirs up the sea, so that the waves thereof roar; YHWH of Hosts is his name:
If these ordinances depart from before me, says YHWH,
then the seed of Israel also shall cease from being a nation before me for ever.
Thus says YHWH: If heaven above can be measured,
and the foundations of the earth searched out beneath,
then will I also cast off all the seed of Israel
for all that they have done, says YHWH. (v35-37)

Ch 32
In the 10th year of Zedekiah Jerusalem was under siege. Jeremiah was confined to the courtyard of the guard and Zedekiah asks Jeremiah why it is that he says the city will be captured. Jeremiah does not answer that but says a family member of his will come and ask Jeremiah to buy some land. Indeed Jeremiah's uncle comes to offer the land. Jeremiah buys the land as YHWH had said to him, as a sign, that land will be bought and sold again when the captives return.
Jeremiah then answers Zedekiah with a list of all the wrongdoing of the people of Jerusalem which is to result in its destruction. However the people will return to safety again and..

.. they shall be my people, and I will be their God
and I will give them one heart and one way, that they may fear me for ever,
for the good of them, and of their children after them:
and I will make an everlasting covenant with them,
that I will not turn away from following them, to do them good;
and I will put my fear in their hearts, that they may not depart from me. (v 38-40)

YHWH says..
Just as I have brought all this great evil upon this people,
so will I bring upon them all the good that I have promised them (v 42)

Ch 33

Jeremiah is still in the courtyard of the guard. Buildings from within the city are being torn down and their materials used in the fight against the besieging Babylonians. Amongst all this destruction YHWH promises to Jeremiah that he will forgive the people of Jerusalem and return them which will amaze the nations and leave them in awe. YHWH says He will fulfil his promise..

In those days, and at that time,
will I cause a Branch of righteousness to grow up unto David;
and he shall execute justice and righteousness in the land.
In those days shall Judah be saved, and Jerusalem shall dwell safely;
and this is the name whereby she shall be called: YHWH our righteousness. (v 15-16)

YHWH says David shall always have someone to sit on the throne and the Levites will always have someone to operate the Temple sacrificial system.

Thus says YHWH: If ye can break my covenant of the day,
and my covenant of the night, so that there shall not be day and night in their season;
then may also my covenant be broken with David my servant,
that he shall not have a son to reign upon his throne;
and with the Levites the priests, my ministers. (v 20-21)

YHWH again confirms his covenant with David with Abraham, Isaac and Jacob and says the exiles will return.

Ch 34

King Zedekiah makes a covenant with all the people that they are to free their Hebrew slaves. They all do but soon after enslave them all again. Jeremiah reminds them of the Law which stated that the Hebrew slaves were to be freed every 7th year.[a] He says that the ancestors also failed to do this and now they have profaned His name (YHWH) by doing this again.
And so the destruction of Jerusalem goes ahead.

Ch 35

Jeremiah is commanded to go and invite some of the Rechabites[b] to come to a chamber within the Temple and offer them some wine. He does this and the Rechobites refuse to obey Jeremiah citing the commands of their founding fathers. Jeremiah then speaks to the people of Jerusalem and asks why it is *they* can't listen to the voice of *their* father (YHWH) when He speaks to them through the prophets. YHWH continues with His plan towards Jerusalem and Judah.

---

[a] Deut. 15.12; Exo. 21.2. 2) The general freeing of Hebrew slaves was to occur in the Jubilee year- 7x7 years (Lev 25.8-11)

[b] 1 Chron 2.55. A nomadic family of the Kenite people living nearby who were commanded not to drink alcohol. They were in the city of Jerusalem because of the invading Babylonians.

Ch 36

We move back again to the 4th year of Jehoiakim, Jeremiah is commanded to have a scroll written up with all the words he has prophesied to the people of Jerusalem since he began prophesying in the days of Josiah. Jeremiah gets Baruch, a scribe to do this. Baruch is asked to go to the temple on a *fast-day*[a] to read it out loud for all to hear, which he does in the 5th year 9th month when all the people of Jerusalem and the surrounding cities come for the fast. Baruch is asked by a Temple official to bring the scroll to the kings house at the scribes chamber where he reads again before all the leaders. They are scared by the words therein and say they must tell the king. They then read it before the king but he doesn't care and has the scroll burnt. Jeremiah has another scroll written at the behest of YHWH. Jehoiakim is condemned for his act.

Therefore thus says YHWH concerning Jehoiakim king of Judah: He shall have none to sit upon the throne of David. (v30)

Ch 37

Moving forward again to Zedekiah's rule we are reminded that he was placed on the throne by Nebuchadnezzar when Jehoiachin was disposed.

The Egyptian army has moved out of Egypt with intent of attacking the Babylonian army at Jerusalem. The Babylonians have consequently decamped in fear of the larger forces facing them.

Zedekiah sends word to Jeremiah saying *Pray now unto YHWH our God for us.* (v5). Jeremiah tells him Pharaoh's army will not attack but will return to Egypt and so too will the Babylonians return to besiege Jerusalem. Jeremiah takes this opportunity to see the land he bought earlier. He is arrested at the gate and accused of defecting. And is brought to the leaders who have him beaten and imprisoned. Jeremiah *remained there many days* (v16) but then Zedekiah, secretly, brought him up to the kings house and enquires if there is news from YHWH. Jeremiah says there is and that surely Jerusalem will fall to the Babylonians. Jeremiah requests he be kept within the kings house as he expects he may die in the prison. Zedekiah agrees and Jeremiah thereafter stays in the court of the guard.

Ch 38

The words of Jeremiah spoken earlier[b] seem to be in view here. Some of the leaders hear what he has said..

Thus says YHWH, He that abides in this city
shall die by the sword, by the famine, and by the pestilence;
but he that goes forth to the Chaldeans shall live,
and his life shall be unto him for a booty, and he shall live. (v2)

---

[a] The particular fast day is not unspecified. Probably related to the threat to the city from the Babylonians

[b] And unto this people thou shall say, Thus says YHWH: Behold, I set before you the way of life and the way of death. He that abides in this city shall die by the sword, and by the famine, and by the pestilence; but he that goes out, and passes over to the Chaldeans that besiege you, he shall live, and his life shall be unto him for booty (Chapter 21.8-9)

The leaders say that Jeremiah should die for this as he is weakening their position against the Babylonians. King Zedekiah agrees to this and Jeremiah is lowered into an cistern without food or water. King Zedekiah changes his mind when he finds out where Jeremiah is and he returns him to the court of the guard. Zedekiah again asks of Jeremiah news from YHWH and promises not to harm Jeremiah no matter what the news is.

Then said Jeremiah unto Zedekiah, Thus says YHWH, the God of hosts, the God of Israel:
If thou will go forth unto the king of Babylon's princes,
then thy soul shall live, and this city shall not be burned with fire;
and thou shall live, and thy house.
But if thou will not go forth to the king of Babylon's princes,
then shall this city be given into the hand of the Chaldeans,
and they shall burn it with fire, and thou shall not escape out of their hand. (v17-18)

Zedekiah says he is afraid of the Jews who have already defected. He thinks they will harm him. Jeremiah tells him not to worry as no harm will come to him. Zedekiah asks Jeremiah

not to say what has just been said to anyone.
Last verse reads..

So Jeremiah abode in the court of the guard until the day that Jerusalem was taken. (v28)

Ch 39
Now in the fifth month, in the tenth day of the month, which was the nineteenth year of king Nebuchadnezzar, king of Babylon,

In the ninth year of Zedekiah king of Judah, in the tenth month,
came Nebuchadnezzar king of Babylon and all his army against Jerusalem, and besieged it;
in the eleventh year of Zedekiah, in the fourth month, the ninth day of the month,
a breach was made in the city, that all the captains of the king of Babylon came in; (v1-3)

When king Zedekiah sees this unfolding, he and all the men of war escape along a secret passage to the countryside at night. However the Babylonians pursue them and Zedekiah is captured and brought to the king of Babylon who kills all his sons and the captured nobles. Then he has Zedekiah blinded before taking him off to captivity. The Babylonians then destroy Jerusalem.

And the Chaldeans burned the king's house, and the houses of the people, with fire, and broke down the walls of Jerusalem (v8) [a]

Then Nebuzaradan the captain of the guard carried away captive into Babylon the residue of the people that remained in the city, the deserters also that fell away to him, and the residue of the people that remained.
But Nebuzaradan the captain of the guard left of the poor of the people, that had nothing, in the land of Judah, and gave them vineyards and fields at the same time. (v 9-10)

Nebuchadnezzar tells Nebuzaradan to find Jeremiah and release him to the newly instated governor Gedaliah[b] for safe passage home.

Ch 40
Nebuzaradan meets Jeremiah amongst the Exiles, now being held in Ramah, and says..

YHWH thy God pronounced this evil upon this place;
and YHWH has brought it, and done according as he spoke:
because ye have sinned against YHWH, and have not obeyed his voice,
therefore this thing is come upon you. (v2-3)

Jeremiah stays with Gedaliah at Mizpah[c] and with the people who were left in the land by Nebuchadnezzar / Nebuzaradin. Now some of Zedekiah's men who had escaped when Zedekiah was captured hear about the new governor Gedaliah and come to see him. Gedaliah promises they will not be harmed and recommends they take some land in the cities and become vinedressers for Babylon. More Jews living in Moab, Ammon and Edom and all countries to where they had been scattered also hear about Gedaliah and the remnant remaining in the land and make their return and do in fact begin harvesting summer fruits. Johanan one of the escaped captains, warns Gedaliah that Ishmael,[d] another of these captains, is planning to kill him. Johanan says..

Let me go, I pray thee, and I will slay Ishmael the son of Nethaniah,
and no man shall know it. Why should he take thy life,
that all the Jews that are gathered unto thee should be scattered,
and the remnant of Judah perish? (v14-15)

Gedaliah refuses as he thinks Johanan is lying.

---

[a] Chapter 52 verse 12-13 adds in the fifth month, in the tenth day of the month, Nebuzaradan burned the house of YHWH, and the king's house and all the houses of Jerusalem
[b] Son of Ahikam who saved Jeremiah from death (Jer. 26.24)
[c] Mizpah in Benjamin (near Ramah) where many important meetings took place amongst the Israelites
[d] Also 2 Kings 25. Ishmael is of royal seed. Perhaps he is jealous of Gedaliah's position or that he felt Gedaliah was a collaborator

Ch 41

In the 7th month Ishmael[a] and some of his men come to dine with Gedaliah at Mizpah. They kill him at the meal. They also kill every other Judean there and all the Babylonian soldiers. Ishmael also comes across a group of pilgrims on their way to the Temple whom he also kills excepting a few who had food supplies. He then took captive all the remaining people who were left in the land and departed with intent to go to the land of Ammon.

Johanan and his men hear about it and go after him. Johanan catches up with him near Gibeon.[b] All the captives are happy to see Johanan and leave Ishmael to go over to him. Ishmael escapes with some of his men to Ammon. Johanan brings everyone to a place near Beth-lehem with the intention of continuing their journey on to Egypt as they were fearing repercussions from the Babylonians for the killing of his Governor.

Ch 42

Then in an amazing event somewhat resembling Exodus 24 (na'aseh v'nishma)

Then all the captains of the forces, and Johanan the son of Kareah, and Jezaniah the son of
Hoshaiah, and all the people from the least even unto the greatest, came near,
and said unto Jeremiah the prophet,
Let, we pray thee, our supplication be presented before thee,
and pray for us unto YHWH thy God, even for all this remnant,
(for we are left but a few of many, as thine eyes do behold us),
that YHWH thy God may show us the way wherein we should walk,
and the thing that we should do. (v 1-3)

After 10 days Jeremiah gets the reply..

Thus says YHWH, the God of Israel,
unto whom ye sent me to present your supplication before him:
If ye will still abide in this land,
then will I build you, and not pull you down,
and I will plant you, and not pluck you up;
for I repent me of the evil that I have done unto you.[c]
Be not afraid of the king of Babylon,
of whom ye are afraid; be not afraid of him, says YHWH:
for I am with you to save you, and to deliver you from his hand. (v 9-11)

but if they decide otherwise..

---

[a] Ishmael really lives up to his name as stated in Gen 16.12 *And he shall be as a wild ass among men; his hand shall be against every man, and every man's hand against him; and he shall dwell over against all his brethren.*

[b] Also in Benjamin. Another site of major events in Israeli history

[c] *For I will set mine eyes upon them for good, and I will bring them again to this land:*
and I will build them, and not pull them down; and I will plant them, and not pluck them up. (Jer 24.6)

Thus says YHWH of hosts, the God of Israel,
If ye indeed set your faces to enter into Egypt, and go to sojourn there,
then it shall come to pass that the sword, which ye fear,
shall overtake you there in the land of Egypt;
and the famine, whereof ye are afraid, shall follow hard after you there in Egypt;
and there ye shall die. (v14-15)

And just as YHWH's anger has poured on Jerusalem it will then be poured on them. Jeremiah pleads with them, but even though they have just said they will do what YHWH says, they are in fact intent on going, *their own way*, to Egypt. Jeremiah says very well but it is to your death you go.[a]

Ch 43
Then all the leaders, proud men, including Johanan stand up to speak and accuse Jeremiah of lying and say he is just trying to hand them over to the Babylonians. Then the whole people set off for Egypt and take Jeremiah and Baruch with them. Upon arrival YHWH tells Jeremiah to take some stones and hide them in the walling of Pharaoh's house and say..

Thus says YHWH of hosts, the God of Israel:
Behold, I will send and take Nebuchadnezzar the king of Babylon, my servant,
and will set his throne upon these stones that I have hid;
and he shall spread his royal pavilion over them.
And he shall come, and shall smite the land of Egypt;
such as are for death shall be given to death,
and such as are for captivity to captivity,
and such as are for the sword to the sword. (v10-11)

Egypt will also be destroyed with fire and carried captive.

Ch 44
Whilst in Egypt Jeremiah reminds the people of all the idolatry which was done in Jerusalem and all the worshiping of foreign gods and other wickedness; how YHWH sent prophets to warn them; how Judah was destroyed and the people exiled because they would not listen. Jeremiah asks why do you do this to yourselves? Is it that they have forgotten all the evil that was done in Judah or is it that they simply refuse to humble themselves and obey the commandments. YHWH informs them that they will all die there in Egypt from *the sword, by the famine, and by pestilence*; none will return.

Then, in an amazingly defiant and idolatrous standpoint,[b] all the people men and women say

[a] Israel had been commanded never to return to Egypt anyway. Exo 14.13; Deut 17.16; 28.68
[b] In opposition to the people's position of chapter 42. The influence of the intense idolatry of Egypt affecting them now

..even all the people that dwelt in the land of Egypt, in Pathros, answered Jeremiah, saying,
As for the word that thou have spoken unto us in the name of YHWH,
we will not hearken unto thee.
But we will certainly perform every word that is gone forth out of our mouth,
to burn incense unto the queen of heaven. [a] (v16-17)

Because, they noted, it was since they stopped worshiping her that all their troubles began. Jeremiah simply states that such sentiment is exactly the reasons why they were exiled. Jeremiah then gives this word from YHWH saying no longer will the name of YHWH be heard of any man of Judah in Egypt. YHWH will now be out, not to protect Judah, but to harm them and all the people will know whose word is true. The sign for this will be that Pharaoh will be handed over to Nebuchadnezzar just as Zedekiah was handed over.

Ch 45
Jeremiah gives a prophecy concerning Baruch. He should not worry about his life; although there is disaster everywhere he shall not suffer from it in his life.

Ch 46
A new section opens concerning the nations. Jeremiah is given prophecies for their future. Egypt is first. Beginning by recounting the battle of Charchemish,[b] they will continue to fight Babylon but will be utterly defeated. All who trust in them will fail. They are to be handed over to Nebuchadnezzar. Egypt and her people will however be allowed to emerge again. Another message is given to Israel..

But fear not thou, O Jacob my servant, neither be dismayed, O Israel:
for, lo, I will save thee from afar, and thy seed from the land of their captivity;
and Jacob shall return, and shall be quiet and at ease, and none shall make him afraid
Fear not thou, O Jacob my servant, says YHWH; for I am with thee:
for I will make a full end of all the nations where I have driven thee;
but I will not make a full end of thee, but I will correct thee in measure,
and will in no way leave thee unpunished. (v27-28)

Ch 47
Prophecy against the Philistines. A great army (Babylonian) like a river will flood over them.

---

[a] A title given to a number of sky goddesses including Inanna, Anat, Isis, Nut, Astarte, Asherah (as they did in chapter 7. 16-19

[b] Battle of Charchemish (609BC) Pharaoh and his army travel north to try to curtail the land being ceded to the Babylonians from the now defeated Assyrian Empire. They meet Josiah on the way and he is killed. Pharaoh will be unsuccessful with the Babylonians but, on his return home, will turn Jerusalem/Judah to a vassal state

Ch 48

Moab is next.. She has trusted with pride in her works and wealth. She will be destroyed and her people taken into captivity. Moab will however be allowed to rebuild herself later.

Ch 49

Ammon will be a desolate heap of ruins, burnt by fire. They grabbed lands belonging to Israel. Israel will own Ammon's land and *she* will go into captivity.
Edom will be destroyed; their punishment has come. Damascus[a] will be burnt down. Of Kedar,[b] and of the kingdoms of Hazor, they are nations at peace with no apparent enemies, but they will be robbed of everything by Nebuchadnezzar. Elam[c] will be destroyed but allowed to recover later.

Ch 50

Prophecy against Babylon; another country from the North will come to destroy them. Another prophecy for Israel…

In those days, and in that time, says YHWH,
the children of Israel shall come, they and the children of Judah together;
they shall go on their way weeping, and shall seek YHWH their God.
They shall inquire concerning Zion with their faces facing there, saying,
Come ye, and join yourselves to YHWH in an everlasting covenant
that shall not be forgotten.
My people have been lost sheep: their shepherds have caused them to go astray;
they have turned them away on the mountains; they have gone from mountain to hill;
they have forgotten their resting-place.
All that found them have devoured them; (and their adversaries said, We are not guilty)
because they have sinned against YHWH, the habitation of righteousness,
even YHWH, the hope of their fathers. (v4-7)

Israel is told to come out of Babylon because she is soon to be utterly destroyed in repayment for the way she has treated YHWH's people. Israel has been like a hunted sheep, first by Assyria until the Babylonians were sent to punish them. Now it is Babylon's turn to be punished. Israel will be brought back to her land..

In those days, and in that time, says YHWH,
the iniquity of Israel shall be sought for, and there shall be none;
and the sins of Judah, and they shall not be found:
for I will pardon them whom I leave as a remnant. (v20)

[a] Capital of (commonly interpreted as Syria, actually Aram)
[b] Of Ishmael
[c] Of Persia

Babylon was caught unawares; the time of her visitation has come. Israel departs..

The voice of them that flee and escape out of the land of Babylon, to declare in Zion the vengeance of YHWH our God, the vengeance of his temple. (v28)

YHWH declares He is against Babylon; but as for Israel..

Their Redeemer is strong; YHWH of hosts is his Name:
He will thoroughly plead their cause that He may give rest to the earth,[a] (v34)

A sword is over all that is Babylon, she will be destroyed like Sodom and Gomorrah; a nation will come to destroy her..

and whoso is chosen, him will I appoint over it: for who is like me?
and who will appoint me a time? and who is the shepherd that can stand before me?
Therefore hear ye the counsel of YHWH, that he has taken against Babylon;
and his purposes, that he has purposed against the land of the Chaldeans:
Surely they shall drag them away, even the little ones of the flock;
surely he shall make their habitation desolate over them.
At the noise of the taking of Babylon the earth trembles,
and the cry is heard among the nations. (v44-46)

Ch 51
Babylon will be destroyed. Israel and Judah have not been forgotten by their G-d, but they must flee from out of her.

Babylon has been a golden cup in YHWH's hand, that made all the earth drunken: the nations have drunk of her wine; (v7)

Babylon is fallen and there is no remedy for her. The righteousness of YHWH has arrived and the Israelites will declare it in Zion. YHWH has created everything in the Heaven and on the Earth; all this idol worship is futile, it too will perish. Israel though is the inheritance of YHWH.
There then follows an extensive description (v11-58) of the destruction of Babylon.
Another prophecy of Jeremiah follows in which he has written all the things that would happen to Babylon on a scroll. When Zedekiah visits Babylon in his 4th year,[b] Seraiah the kings chief chamberlain is given the scroll and told to read it out there; then bind the scroll to a stone and throw it in the Euphrates and say so will Babylon sink never to return!

---

[a] Israel's primary position of bringing knowledge of YHWH to the nations
[b] Before he had rebelled against Nebuchadnezzar

Ch 52

Describes more of Zedekiah's life and then recounts the destruction of Jerusalem again in more detail.

Now in the fifth month, in the tenth day of the month,
which was the nineteenth year of king Nebuchadrezzar, king of Babylon,
came Nebuzaradan the captain of the guard,
who stood before the king of Babylon, into Jerusalem.
And he burned the house of YHWH, and the king's house;
and all the houses of Jerusalem, even every great house, burned he with fire. (v12-13)

Also the last 4 verses describe the removal from prison of Jehoiachin by the new king of Babylon to sit at the kings table; therefore leaving hope for the continuance of the Davidic line.[a]

Lamentations[b]

The Hebrew name for this book is אֵיכָה, ['Êykhôh] How? In reference to the now complete destruction of Israel, Judah, the monarchy, Jerusalem and the Temple; all gone. The remaining people now taken into exile. Echoing the expulsion of Adam from Eden, the book goes on to document the overwhelming suffering of the survivors. All the promises made to Abraham and the great nation Israel became with David and Solomon, now in complete ruins. The city of Jerusalem thought of as impregnable, overrun and burnt down.
Lamentations has been *traditionally* ascribed to Jeremiah. Although there is no mention of him within the book, he is known as the 'weeping prophet' and was noted as being involved in the formation of certain *laments* concerning the death of King Josiah (2 Chron 35.25). Lamentations ch 3 (*The servants response*) does however have a very close affinity with Deutero Isaiah, (*The Servant of YHWH,* ch 40-55).
The 5 poems (chapters) of Lamentations are highly organised; all the chapters have a length based upon the Hebrew Alphabet (22 letters). Chapters 1-4 are acrostic.[c] Chapter 3 has three lines[d] for each letter of the alphabet therefore giving 66 verses.[e] Chapter 5 has 22 verses but not in acrostic form. The main chiastic structure looks like this :-

---

[a] Also 2 Kings 25.27-30

[b] Placed within the Ketuvim, [Writings] in the Torah

[c] Each verse starting with a successive letter of the alphabet. 2) Acrostics are used often to indicate completeness as here with complete destruction. Chapters 1-4 also have a well defined **qinah** (dirge) rhythm

[d] Each starting with the correct alphabet letter

[e] Therefore Lamentations actually has 6 acrostics. Many scholars have searched within chapter 5 for some kind of acrostic with limited success. If Lamentations did have 7 acrostics then there would be a complete number (of 7) perhaps it is that which the writer avoids as clearly something is broken

ch 1 Jerusalem's desolation

ch 2 YHWH's judgement

ch 3 The Servant's response

ch 4 YHWH's anger

ch 5 Survivor's (Remnant) response

Ch 1

Referred to as 'she' and 'her' throughout, Jerusalem's present situation is detailed. Empty and alone she weeps, her people in exile, delivered into the hands of the gentile nations. YHWH's judgement has come about because of her great sin.

Ch 2

YHWH has mercilessly brought her down..

All that pass by clap their hands at thee;
They hiss and wag their head at the daughter of Jerusalem, saying,
Is this the city that men called The perfection of beauty, The joy of the whole earth? (v5)

Her plea to YHWH to take note of what is happening as..

Shall the women eat their offspring, the infants that are dandled in the hands?
Shall the priest and the prophet be slain in the sanctuary of YHWH?
The youth and the old man lie on the ground in the streets;
My virgins and my young men are fallen by the sword: (v20-21)

Ch 3

A male voice speaks to tell how he has been afflicted. He sees that as, at least, there are survivors then there is still hope from YHWH's loving-kindness for help. The events are YHWH's righteous judgement against the people's sin. His call is for help from YHWH both for himself and against the enemies who have overrun them.

Ch 4

The scene now is within Jerusalem during the height of the siege. Gold and Jewels are useless, scattered in the streets; children are abandoned to die from starvation; There are no visible leaders; cannibalism is taking place..

The kings of the earth believed not, neither all the inhabitants of the world,
That the adversary and the enemy would enter into the gates of Jerusalem.
It is because of the sins of her prophets, and the iniquities of her priests,
That have shed the blood of the just in the midst of her. (v12-13)

Blame here directed at the prophets and priests who failed to warn the people. Disbelief that such a thing could happen. Now the people are scattered amongst the nations and hated therein; they are pleased with Jerusalem's downfall. A warning is given to the nations that they will also be punished. Verse 22 has the only optimistic words from the entire book and says...

The punishment of your iniquity is accomplished, O daughter of Zion;
he will no more carry thee away into captivity.

The chapter ends with the warning that the sin of Edom[a] will soon be addressed by YHWH.

Ch 5

Remember, YHWH, what is come upon us: Behold, and see our reproach. (v1)

How the people have been handed over to the nations.[b] Now they are slaves in their own land and city; servants rule over them. There is no help from anywhere.

The crown is fallen from our head: Woe unto us! for we have sinned.
For this, our heart is faint; For these things, our eyes are dim;
For the mountain of Zion, which is desolate: The foxes walk upon it.
Thou, YHWH, abides for ever; Thy throne is from generation to generation.
Why do You forget us for ever, And forsake us so long?
Turn thou us unto thee, YHWH, and we shall be turned. Renew our days as of old.
But thou have utterly rejected us. Your anger is great against us. (v16-22)

So the chapter ends, without any answer from YHWH as to the plea of verse 1 and to what will be the fate of Israel.

Ezekiel

Ch 1

Ezekiel was amongst the exiles after the siege of Jerusalem (597BC) at the end of Jehoiakim's reign and the beginning of Jehoiachin's. Ezekiel's book begins by giving the date as the..

fifth day of the month,[c] which was the fifth year of king Jehoiachin's captivity [d] (v2)

---

[a] Edom's involvement with the destruction of Jerusalem. 2) Emblematic of 'the nations'

[b] Verse 7. *Our fathers sinned, and are not; And we have borne their iniquities.* (see Jeremiah 31.29; Ezekiel 18.2). However as read in Jeremiah, although their fathers had sinned, the offer to avert disaster had been made recently (Jer 17.10; Jer 22.4); <u>they had</u> sinned. (2) Although it could be that the present people are projecting their sin onto their fathers it is also possible that a later redactor's voice is heard here

[c] Of the fourth month (as just specified in verse 1)

[d] Jehoiachin was taken with the main Jerusalem population as captives, including Ezekiel (2 Kings 24.10-17)

So he has now been in Babylon for 5 years and he is 30 years[a] old (the age of which he would have entered service to the priesthood (Num 4.3). A vision comes to him and he sees an amazingly detailed manifestation of G-d, in three parts - wheels, cherubim and throne..

..and upon the likeness of the throne
was a likeness as the appearance of a man [b] *upon it above (v26)*

All around this is glowing brilliance of light, fire and colour..

This was the appearance of the likeness of the glory of YHWH.
And when I saw it, I fell upon my face, and I heard a voice of one that spoke.[c] (v28)

Ch 2
YHWH speaks to Ezekiel referring to him as *Son of man.*[d] He is commissioned as a prophet to the exiles.

And he said unto me, Son of man, I send thee to the children of Israel,
to nations [e] *that are rebellious, which have rebelled against Me:*
they and their fathers have transgressed against Me even unto this very day. (v2)

Ezekiel is to speak to the people on behalf of YHWH; whether they listen or not, they will know a prophet has been amongst them. Ezekiel is told not to be afraid of them..

But thou, son of man, hear what I say unto thee;
be not thou rebellious like that rebellious house:[f]
open thy mouth, and eat that which I give thee.
And when I looked, behold, a hand was put forth unto me;
and, lo, a roll of a book was therein; and he spread it before me:
and it was written within and without;
and there were written therein lamentations, and mourning, and woe. (v8-10)

Ch 3
Ezekiel eats the scroll and finds the taste sweet. He is told again to go to the house of Israel, not to other nations, even though they would listen, and speak to them. *They* will not listen but Ezekiel is told to confront them anyway and not to be afraid of them.
Then he sees again the first vision of the *Glory of YHWH* and is left overwhelmed for seven days. After that the word of YHWH comes to Ezekiel and tells him to warn the people, good

---

[a] Verse 1 states... *It came to pass in the 30th year,* but does not specify the starting point, only saying that was the time when the heavens were opened and he saw visions of G-d. Presumably Ezekiel's 30th birthday
[b] A man (אָדָם Adam)
[c] The Presence of YHWH has followed the Exiles to Babylon
[d] Hebrew ben – Adam; Greek Vios - Anthropos
[e] Of Israel and Judah
[f] House of Israel

and bad; if he warns them and they still don't listen then the sin is upon them but if he does not warn them he will get the blame for their sin.
Ezekiel is told to go out into an unspecified valley[a] where YHWH will talk to him. He again sees the Glory of YHWH and is then told to stay in his house and not speak unless YHWH gives him a message..

and thou shall say unto them, Thus says the Lord YHWH:
He that can hear, let him hear; and he that rejects, let him reject:
for they are a rebellious house (v27)

Ch 4
Ezekiel is told to act out certain scenarios[b] all indicating to the people that Jerusalem will be besieged and there will be scarcity of food.

Ch 5
He is told to shave his head and beard. Part of the hair he is chop again with the sword, part to throw to the wind and the last part into a fire as an indication as to what will happen to the House of Israel. The people have been just as sinful as the nations around. Soon judgement is to be executed against Jerusalem and it will be destroyed.

Ch 6
Ezekiel is to prophesy against the mountains, the valleys and the rivers of the land. This may seem rather odd to prophesy to land not people, but it gives an indication to the importance of *the land itself* rather than it being just an area where the Israelites are, the land is also holy to YHWH. Because of all the idolatry Jerusalem shall be destroyed. A remnant however shall escape death and they will remember their G-d and be sorry.

Ch 7
Again Ezekiel prophesies against the Land.

And thou, son of man, thus says the Lord YHWH unto the Land of Israel,
An end: the end is come upon the four corners of the Land.
Now is the end upon thee, and I will send mine anger upon thee,
will judge thee according to thy ways; (v2-3)

A day of Judgement is coming and there will be no one spared or pitied; the whole land is to lie desolate and the people who survive will be in mourning.

Ch 8
And it came to pass in the sixth year, in the sixth month, in the fifth day of the month,[c]

---

[a] בִּקְעָה [bik-aw'] from H1234; properly, a split, a level pace as opposed to uneven places (mountains)
[b] As had Jeremiah

Ezekiel is in his house with some of the elders sat before him, when ...

the hand of the Lord YHWH fell there upon me, Then I beheld, and, lo,
a likeness as the appearance of fire; from the appearance of his loins and downward, fire;
and from his loins and upward, as the appearance of brightness, as it were glowing metal.[a]

He is taken, in the vision, to the Temple in Jerusalem; to an inner court where there is an idol being worshipped. The Glory of YHWH, as seen earlier is also there who then directs him to see the idolatry within the Temple. He is further directed to look into another room..

So I went in and saw; and behold, every form of creeping things, and abominable beasts,
and all the idols of the house of Israel, portrayed upon the wall round about.
And there stood before them seventy men [b] *of the elders of the house of Israel* (v10-11)

The 70 elders of the House of Israel are worshiping the idols. He is then shown in another place women worshiping Tammuz.[c] Still further in the temple and there are people worshiping the sun.

Therefore will I also deal in wrath; mine eye shall not spare, neither will I have pity;
and though they cry in mine ears with a loud voice, yet will I not hear them. (v18)

Ch 9

Then He cried in mine ears with a loud voice, saying, Cause ye them that have charge over the city to draw near, every man with his destroying weapon in his hand. And behold, six men came from the way of the upper gate, which lies toward the north, every man with his slaughter weapon in his hand; and one man in the midst of them clothed in linen, with a writer's inkhorn by his side. And they went in, and stood beside the brazen altar. (v1-2)

YHWH then directs the man in linen to *set a mark upon the foreheads* (v4) of all those people who are dismayed by the events within the Temple. The men with the *destroying weapon* then go about the city and kill everyone else.

Ch 10
Ezekiel is looking at the Glory of YHWH, there appears something like a throne and a voice either of or from the throne which tells the man in linen to get some live coals from the Cherubim,[d] within the appearance of the Glory of YHWH. They are to be scattered on the city. He goes in and gets some.

---

[c] Of Jehoiachin's captivity (chapter 1 verse 2)
[a] From his first vision of the Glory of G-d (1.27)
[b] As a representation of <u>all</u> the leaders
[c] Fertility god. Likely to be the same as Jeremiah's Queen of Heaven (chapter 7)
[d] From chapter 1

Ch 11

The lesders are to be put out of the city and delivered to strangers. No one had walked in the statutes of YHWH. Ezekiel cries to YHWH and asks if he is to put an end to remnant of Israel. G-d explains the people will be scattered but later brought back to the land again.

And I will give them one [a] heart, and I will put a new spirit within you;
and I will take the stony heart out of their flesh, and will give them a heart of flesh;[b]
that they may walk in my statutes, and keep mine ordinances, and do them:
and they shall be My people, and I will be their God.
But as for them whose heart walk after the heart of their detestable things and their abominations, I will bring their way upon their own heads, says the Lord YHWH (v19-21)

The Glory of YHWH then moves away to the mountain at the east side of the city.[c] Ezekiel is returned to Babylon where he tells the captives what YHWH had shown him.

Ch 12

YHWH tells Ezekiel to make another sign for the people, perhaps they will take heed. He is to remove his belongings from his house in view of the people and place them elsewhere. He is to dig through the wall to do this. This is a sign that the remaining people are to be taken into captivity. Only a few will be left in the land. He also is to eat food with trembling and fearfulness as a sign that the people will be scared when they finally realise they are to lose the Land. There has come a saying amongst the people *The days are prolonged, and every vision fails?* Meaning a long time is passing and none of the prophecies are coming true. Ezekiel is to inform the people every prophecy is about to come true. The prophecies are not of the distant future but now.

Ch 13

Ezekiel is to warn the other 'prophets' who are just making up the imaginations of their hearts. They will not return to the Land. They prophesy that there will be peace. They are like a wall built with defective mortar; it will crash down.
Also women diviners are making charms and every type of talisman; they do this just to feed themselves but they cause the people to sin and feel confident in their ways. They have saddened the righteous and encouraged the wicked. YHWH says that He will free His people from their divinations.

Ch 14

Some of the Elders come to Ezekiel to hear him but really in their hearts they are heavy idol worshipers and remain estranged from YHWH. They will all be cut off and destroyed.

---

[a] LXX has ἑτέραν [heteros] another. (as different/ opposite from a stone heart)

[b] Also 18.31; 36.26

[c] Mount of Olives

YHWH says that even if Noah, Daniel[a] and Job[b] were there they would only be able to save their own souls this time and not be able to save their family or friends (as they had in their own time). Still a righteous remnant of the people in Jerusalem will be saved..

And they shall comfort you, when ye see their way and their doings;
and ye shall know that I have not done without cause all that I have done in it,
says the Lord YHWH (v23)

Ch 15

A vineyard parable. Israel is often compared to a vineyard, that is the fruit of the vineyard, but in this case there is no produce from the vine. Ezekiel is looking now only at the value of the wood and branches of the vine tree itself. There is nothing you can do with the wood thereof, not even to make a peg. Its only use is as fuel for a fire and so the inhabitants of Jerusalem will be used as fuel in Jerusalem's destruction.

Ch 16

Ezekiel is given a parable to tell to the people (she) of Jerusalem. On the day she was born in Canaan, of Canaanite descent, she was abandoned by her Canaanite parents and left to die. YHWH passed by and saved her, cared for her as she grew in excellence.

Now when I passed by thee, and looked upon thee, behold, thy time was the time of love,
and I spread my skirt over thee, and covered thy nakedness:
yea, I swore unto thee, and entered into a covenant with thee,
says the Lord YHWH, and thou became Mine. (v8)

Then YHWH adorned her with beautiful garments / jewellery and her fame of perfect beauty through the majesty of YHWH went out amongst the nations.

But thou did trust in thy beauty, and played the harlot because of thy renown,
and poured out thy whoredom; on every one that passed by, his it was (v15)[c]

All of the gifts YHWH had given her she used in her acts of idolatry and even sacrificed the children born to YHWH to them. In all this she did not remember her youth and how YHWH

---

[a] Daniel is a contemporary with Ezekiel being exiled also from Jerusalem. Seems unusual the Daniel, from the Book of Daniel would be mentioned here. Daniel, however, was of the nobility that were taken by Nebuchadnezzar when the Babylonians besieged Jerusalem 598BC and therefore had been in the Babylonian court for 5 years before Ezekiel's commission. (First siege [against Jehoiakim] 598BC (2 Kings 24.8-12)) He therefore may have had some renown amongst the people by then. 2) Noah and Job were said to be righteous (Gen 6.9 & Job 27.6). Daniel is not directly said to be, however his insistence, on pain of death, to worship only YHWH and adhere to His law (Torah) is an exemplary example of faithful obedience whilst in exile in accordance with the central message of Ezekiel

[b] Like Jeremiah 15.1 ...*Even if Moses and Samuel stood before me...*

[c] Her beauty. 2) Ezekiel now uses the language of sexual immorality as had Jeremiah

had saved her. She only increased the lewd and abominable behaviour and in somewhat graphic language her lewd acts with the nations roundabout are described. She never returns, she *takes strangers instead of her husband.* Only now it is worse, she is the one paying them to come to her. In judgement YHWH says He will bring her lovers back only to utterly destroy her. A proverb will be used against her *..As is the mother, so is her daughter.* The mother hated her husband and her daughter will hate her husband.
She is then described as having an elder sister[a] *Samaria* and a younger sister *Sodom.* Yet even they never fell to these levels of corruption and immorality. Now…

they are more righteous than thou:
yea, be thou also confounded, and bear thy shame, in that you have justified thy sisters (v52)

She *has despised the oath in breaking the covenant.* and will be judged for that. However..

I will remember my covenant with thee in the days of thy youth,
and I will establish unto thee an everlasting covenant.
Then shall thou remember thy ways, and be ashamed, (v60-61)

Ch 17
Ezekiel is to tell a riddle. A great eagle (Babylon) comes to Lebanon (Jerusalem) and removes a top branch of a cedar tree (the monarchy) it also carries some seed and plants a vine (rules the land with a puppet king). Another great eagle (Egypt) is also interested in the area; the vine (puppet king) deserts to him.
Jehoiakim (puppet king) has deserted from his oath with Babylon in the same way he deserted from the Covenant with YHWH, and for this Jehoiakim has brought the calamity about to befall Jerusalem.
However ultimately YHWH will again take a sprig from the top branch of the cedar tree and plant it Himself u*pon a high and lofty mountain* (v22) in Israel; it will bear fruit and all the nations will know that it was YHWH who did this.

Ch 18
Another proverb has become commonly used by the people. They suggest that what is happening is not their fault..

the fathers have eaten sour grapes, and the children's teeth are set on edge?[b]

The proverb concerns the notion of the sin of fathers being passed down and judgment inflicted onto their children. (Num 14.18). This is here rejected; sin or righteousness is credited to the individual only. The House of Israel is then encouraged to..

---

[a] An analogy also used by Jeremiah (Jer 3.7)
[b] Also Jeremiah 31.29. Same topic

Cast away from you all your transgressions, wherein ye have transgressed;
and make you a new heart and a new spirit:
for why will ye die, O house of Israel?
For I have no pleasure in the death of him that dies, says the Lord YHWH:
therefore turn yourselves, and live. (v31-32)

Ch 19

Ezekiel is to make a lamentation for the leaders[a] of Israel. An analogy is made of a mother lion and her offspring. The first young lion comes to power (Jehoiakim) but he was corrupt and is taken away to Egypt. Another young lion replaces him (Zedekiah) he is also corrupt and is taken away by the Babylonian king.

In a second analogy their mother is a strong vine, exalted by all the plants around it. It is now torn down, thrown into a dry wilderness.

Ch 20

And it came to pass in the seventh year, in the fifth month, the tenth day of the month (v1)

The elders again visit Ezekiel. Nothing has changed with them. YHWH tells Ezekiel to remind them of the day they were chosen in Egypt (at the time of Moses) to be brought to a beautiful land. They were supposed to abandon the idols of that place but even before they left Egypt, they rebelled against YHWH, even there YHWH was about to destroy them but held back for His Name's sake. YHWH then brought them to the wilderness where He gave them His Law (Torah) and His Sabbath. But they again rebelled against Him and disregarded YHWH's statutes and again YHWH was to destroy them and again he held back because of His Name.

YHWH says that ultimately *He will be their king* (v33) He will judge every one of them and the rebels will be removed from the land. The faithful shall remain..

For in my holy mountain, in the mountain of the height of Israel, says the Lord YHWH,
there shall all the house of Israel, all of them, will serve me in the land:
there I will accept them. (v40)

YHWH will be sanctified in the sight of the nations and the people of Israel will be truly sorry for their former transgressions. Ezekiel is then told to prophesy to the *forest of the south* (Judah) that YHWH is to set fire to it.

The people ridicule Ezekiel for speaking in parables and refuse to understand.

Ch 21

Ezekiel is again to tell the exiles that YHWH is against them. The people of Jerusalem are to be cut down by the sword. Ezekiel is told to..

[a] nāśîʾ[nasi] one lifted up, chief, prince, captain, leader

sigh therefore, thou son of man;
with the breaking of thy loins and with bitterness shall thou sigh before their eyes. (v6)

When people ask of him why he sighs he is to say..

Because of the tidings, for it comes; and every heart shall melt, and all hands shall be feeble, and every spirit shall faint, and all knees shall be weak as water: (v7)

A sword (Babylon) has been prepared for the purpose of destroying Jerusalem and the monarchy overturned.

And thou, O deadly wounded wicked one, the leader of Israel,
whose day is come, in the time of the iniquity of the end,
thus says the Lord YHWH: Remove the mitre, and take off the crown;
this shall be no more the same; exalt that which is low, and abase that which is high.
I will overturn, overturn, overturn it: this also shall be no more,
until he come whose right it is; and I will give it him. (v25-27)

Ch 22
The time of Jerusalem's destruction draws near. No one in her does the right thing.

And I sought for a man among them who would repair her boundaries,
to stand before me in the breach - for the land, that I should not destroy it; but I found none.
Therefore have I poured out mine indignation upon them;
I have consumed them with the fire of my wrath:
their own way have I brought upon their heads, says the Lord YHWH. (v30-31)

Ch 23
The *two daughters* analogy is revisited. They play the harlot in Egypt.

And the names of them were Oholah [a] *the elder, and Oholibah* [b] *her sister:*
and they became mine, and they bare sons and daughters.
And as for their names, Samaria is Oholah, and Jerusalem Oholibah. (v4)

Oholah became a harlot in Assyria and her acts are described with some serious sexual misconduct analogy. A point to be noted here is that these acts are not now described as with foreign gods but with the political powers of those lands as the sisters turn to idolizing the power of the nations.

---

[a] Meaning **in her own tent** (not worshiping YHWH)
[b] Meaning **my tent in her** (in reference to the Tabernacle)

Oholibah sees what her sister is doing and she then becomes even worse than her in Babylon. Again YHWH's judgement is to fall on them and these same nations will come to destroy the two sisters and remove their lewdness from the land.

Ch 24
A clear emphasised date given, in the ninth year, in the tenth month, in the tenth day of the month..

the word of YHWH came unto me, saying,
Son of man, write thee the name of the day, even of this self-same day:
the king of Babylon drew close [a] *unto Jerusalem this self-same day.*

The siege of Jerusalem begins.

Ezekiel is to tell a parable. A copper caldron cooking pot is to be made ready with water then filled with choice meat cuts, still with bones.[b] The pot's contents are then emptied into the fire and burnt. The empty cauldron is then set on the fire again and heated in an attempt to cleanse the interior of the pot. The pot cannot be made clean and is also burnt.
The meaning being that the leaders are very sure that Jerusalem is unassailable and has divine protection as according to the prophets whom they decide to listen to. This however is not the case and Jerusalem is to be destroyed in judgement of all the bloodshed and idolatry committed within her.
In another prophecy he is informed that YHWH is to take away the *delight of Ezekiel's eyes* (his wife). Ezekiel is not to mourn in any way for her. Ezekiel's wife dies that day; he does not mourn for her. The people ask what Ezekiel means by this and he tells them that the Sanctuary, the desire of *their* eyes, is to be profaned and the people will be either exiled or will die by the sword. On that day (that Jerusalem falls to the Babylonians) a fugitive will escape from the destruction of the city and bring the news to Ezekiel; Ezekiel will then regain his power to speak[c] for himself as a sign to the people.[d]

Ch 25
A new section opens here. Jerusalem's judgement has come; there is no need for further warnings. Ezekiel now continues with the condemnation of the nations.
These prophecies appear to condemn the nations for their actions after Jerusalem falls to the Babylonians some 18 months later.
Ammon is first. They are condemned for being happy at Judah's exile. Ammon will also be besieged and destroyed.

---

[a] סָמַךְ [sāmaḵ] a primitive root;, to lean upon or take hold of
[b] This image is taken directly from 11.3 where the leaders *say this city is the caldron, and we are the flesh*, (an idiomatic saying referring to their feeling of safety against the Babylonian threat). Verse 6 & 7 (of chapter 11) follow with condemnation of this position, reinterpreting the idiom as to the bloodshed within Jerusalem
[c] Ezekiel had been unable to speak unless delivering what YHWH had told him say (since 3.26-27)
[d] Warnings have ended and judgement has been executed

Edom and the Philistines also took the opportunity to seek revenge on Judah. They also will have the revenge of YHWH taken on them.

Ch 26
Tyre is condemned for her glee at the downfall of Jerusalem/Judah. She said..

Aha!, she is broken that was the gate of the peoples; she is turned unto me;
I shall be replenished, now that she is laid waste (v2)

Tyre will also to be destroyed by the Babylonians.

Ch 27
A lamentation for Tyre. She was a beautiful city, filled with all the produce of her sea trading. People are amazed at her downfall.

Ch 28
A continuing condemnation of Tyre, she has considered herself a god and not realised that it was YHWH who made her great in the first place. Sidon , a city near to Tyre is then condemned.
Israel's return to the land is prophesied..

And they shall dwell securely therein;
yea, they shall build houses, and plant vineyards, and shall dwell securely,
when I have executed judgments upon all those that do them despite round about them;
and they shall know that I am YHWH their God. (v26)

Ch 29-30
Egypt is condemned to destruction.[a] Nebuchadnezzar shall own her as a gift from YHWH for his *service* (to YHWH) against Tyre. She is given a 40 year exile after which she will return to rebuild her nation, but none of her former glory will return; it will be Israel who looks after her.

Ch 31
Egypt is further condemned by reminding Pharaoh of the former Assyrian empire. That Empire is described as having been a great tree, a *cedar in Lebanon,* under which all the nations took shelter; but just as that tree was uprooted and thrown down, so shall Egypt be thrown down.

Ch 32
A lamentation for Egypt. The smaller nations that surround her are also condemned including Edom.

[a] Egypt has been a great power in the region vying against Assyria and Babylon

Ch 33
An analogy of watchmen follows. Watchmen are normally chosen by the people to warn them of impending danger, which the watchman does by sounding the alarm (blowing a trumpet). Now if the watchman sees the danger and sounds the alarm but the people choose not to act (turn from their sin) then it is their own fault. However if the watchman does not sound the alarm then the watchman would be blamed. Ezekiel is the watchman of Israel now. The people complain that former sin is stacked against them and consequently they have no chance. YHWH tells Ezekiel to inform the people that former sin will not be held against them if they now turn away from evil. The people hear this and complain against YHWH's justice; that someone who has been righteous in their life, but ends it living sinfully is condemned yet someone who was wicked and ends their life in righteousness is saved. YHWH replies *O house of Israel, I will judge you every one after his ways.* (v20)

Jerusalem falls to the Babylonians.

> *.. in the twelfth year of our captivity, in the tenth month, in the fifth day of the month, one that had escaped out of Jerusalem came unto me, saying, The City is smitten.* (v21)

Ezekiel is then able to speak of his own again as indicated in chapter 24.
The people who are left in the land after Jerusalem falls are confident that in the same way that Abraham was one man and yet became many, they are few but will eventually become many again. Ezekiel prophesies to them that because they continue in their sinful ways they will all be picked off by disease, wild beasts and the sword; none will remain. Many people hear the prophesies of Ezekiel but pay no attention to him at all. For them it is just a bit of entertainment. They will find out when the prophecies come true that he truly was a prophet.

Ch 34
Ezekiel is to prophesy against the shepherds (leaders) of Israel. They are only interested in self-gain.

Ye eat the fat, and ye clothe you with the wool,
ye kill the fatlings; but ye feed not the sheep.
The diseased have ye not strengthened, [a]
neither have ye healed that which was sick,
neither have ye bound up that which was broken,
neither have ye brought back that which was driven away,
neither have ye sought that which was lost;
but with force and with rigor have ye ruled over them (v3-4)

---

[a] The following, saying something of Jesus, the true shepherd ministry 2) Isaiah 61

The sheep (people) have been thus scattered throughout the nations with no one to gather them. YHWH says He will bring them all back. He will judge them and bring them back to the pleasant land of a restored Israel. Then He will place a shepherd over them..

And I will set up one shepherd over them, and he shall feed them,
even my servant David; he shall feed them, and he shall be their shepherd.
And I, YHWH, will be their God, and my servant David prince among them;
I, YHWH, have spoken it. (v23-24)

And they shall live in peace and abundance in the land..

And they shall no more be a prey to the nations,
neither shall the beasts of the earth devour them;
but they shall dwell securely, and none shall make them afraid.
And I will raise up unto them a plantation for renown,
and they shall be no more consumed with famine in the land,
neither bear the shame of the nations any more. [a]
And they shall know that I, YHWH, their God am with them,
and that they, the house of Israel, are my people, says the Lord YHWH.
And ye my sheep, the sheep of my pasture, are men,
and I am your God, says the Lord YHWH. (v28-31)

Ch 35
A return to judgement of the nations here as Mount Sier (Edom) is condemned for her part in the destruction of Jerusalem..[b]

Because thou have had a perpetual enmity, and have given over the children of Israel
to the power of the sword in the time of their calamity, (v5)

Because thou have said, These two nations and these two countries shall be mine,
and we will possess it (v10)

Mount Sier will be destroyed just as Jerusalem has been.

Ch 36
Ezekiel is told to prophesy unto the mountains, to the hills, to the watercourses and to the valleys of Israel.[c] The enemies have surrounded and want to take possession of the Land. YHWH says..

because ye have borne the shame of the nations:

---

[a] Israel bears the shame of the nations (Isa 53.5)
[b] The book of Obadiah also covers Edom's involvement with the Babylonians in Jerusalem's destruction
[c] The importance of the land as also being Holy

therefore thus says the Lord YHWH: I have sworn, saying,
Surely the nations that are round about you, they shall bear their shame. (v 6-7)

The Land will be restored and bear fruit to the Israelites again. The Land will be farmed and the cities rebuilt. Israel will prosper and multiply again to a nation even better than before..

Yea, I will cause men to walk upon you, even my people Israel;
and they shall possess thee, and thou shall be their inheritance, (v12)

Thus says the Lord YHWH: Because they say unto you,
Your land is a devourer of men, and has been a bereaver of thy nation;
therefore you shall devour men no more, neither bereave thy nation any more, (v13)

YHWH says that Israel had defiled the Land and was therefore scattered in judgement, but wherever they went the people knew how they had been thrown off the Land by their G-d. This had resulted in the name of YHWH being profaned. Israel will be restored to the Land, but not for their own sake but for the sake of YHWH's Holy Name.

And I will sprinkle clean water upon you, and ye shall be clean:
from all your filthiness, and from all your idols, will I cleanse you.
A new heart also will I give you, and a new spirit will I put within you;
and I will take away the stony heart out of your flesh, and I will give you a heart of flesh.
And I will put my Spirit within you, and cause you to walk in my statutes,
and ye shall keep mine ordinances, and do them.
And ye shall dwell in the land that I gave to your fathers;
and ye shall be my people, and I will be your God (v25-28)

The Israelites will remember their wrongdoing and be ashamed. The Land cleansed and restored. Passers-by will say..

His land that was desolate, is become like the garden of Eden;
and the waste and desolate and ruined cities are fortified and inhabited. (v35)

Then the nations that are left round about you shall know
that I, YHWH, have built the ruined places, and planted that which was desolate: (v36)

Ch 37
Ezekiel is brought by the spirit of YHWH to a valley. The valley is filled with human bones. Ezekiel is told to prophesy to the bones so that they live again, first with flesh and then with *Breath.*
YHWH says these are the house of Israel, and though the people say their hope is lost (like these bones), YHWH is able restore them.

And I will put my Spirit in you, and ye shall live, and I will place you in your own land: and ye shall know that I, YHWH, have spoken it and performed it (v14)

Ezekiel is told to take two sticks. On one he is to write *for Judah, and for the children of Israel, his companions*: on the other he is to write *for Joseph, the stick of Ephraim, and for all the house of Israel, his companions*: (v16). Ezekiel is to join the sticks together as a symbolic statement that Israel will be reunited and returned to the Land..

and I will make them one nation in the land, upon the mountains of Israel;
and one king shall be king to them all; and they shall be no more two nations,
neither shall they be divided into two kingdoms any more at all; (v22)

The Israelites will not err again and will be saved and cleansed to be the people of YHWH. They will obey the Torah and shall remain in the Land. YHWH's servant David will be their king and shepherd. An everlasting covenant of peace will be made and YHWH's sanctuary will be set in the midst of them, then..

My tabernacle also shall be with them; and I will be their God, and they shall be my people.
And the nations shall know that I am YHWH that sanctifies Israel,
when my sanctuary shall be in the midst of them for evermore. (v27-28)

Ch 38-39
Ezekiel is to prophesy against the nation of Gog.[a] They are to be crushed. They will be allowed by YHWH to come up against Israel only to be defeated. Thus leaving Israel in the Land in peace.

And I will set my glory among the nations;
and all the nations shall see my judgment that I have executed,
and my hand that I have laid upon them.
So the house of Israel shall know that I am YHWH their God, from that day and forward.
And the nations shall know that the house of Israel went into captivity for their iniquity;
because they trespassed against me, (v21-23)

Ch 40-42
A new section begins with some of the latest material of the book, some 14 years after the fall of Jerusalem. The day is given as the 10th day of the first month, so probably the Day of Preparation for Passover (as noted in Exodus 12.1). Ezekiel has a vision in which he is transported by YHWH to the land of Israel and set upon a high mountain. On it, to the south, he sees an apparent outline of a city..

[a] The archetypical enemy of G-d and His people who come to despoil the land

And He brought me there; and, behold, a man,
whose appearance was like the appearance of brass,
with a line of flax in his hand, and a measuring reed; and he stood in the gate. (40.3)

Ezekiel is told to listen carefully and report all back to the house of Israel. The man then gives a very detailed description of the Temple courtyard with all its porches, doors, windows, gates, arches and inner courtyards, apparent in the vision.

Ch 43
The Glory of YHWH enters the Temple.

I heard one speaking unto me out of the house; and a man stood by me. And he said unto me
Son of man, this is the place of My throne, and the place of the soles of My feet,
where I will dwell in the midst of the children of Israel for ever. (v6-7)

Israel is warned not to defile the Temple by burying[a] former kings near the Temple.
The altar is described in detail and the sacrifices done there by the priests of Levi and Zadok who make them.

Ch 44-46
Further descriptions of the Temple courtyard and its management. Areas surrounding the Temple complex allocated to priests and Levites. (ch45) More Temple organisation / sacrificial rules (ch 46) More rules on coming to the Temple and making sacrifices.

Ch 47
The man then takes Ezekiel to the front of the Temple where water is pouring out from it via the Altar. Ezekiel and the man then follow the water along its course which then becomes progressively deeper, turning into a great river flowing into the world. Many trees producing fruit and food are on the banks of the river and all the creatures come to drink the healing water and *live* by it.
Verse 13 on continues with a description of the borders of Israel and the specific allotment of the land within to the Twelve Tribes. Strangers[b] within their land will also inherit a portion..

And it shall come to pass, that ye shall divide it by lot for an inheritance unto you
and to the strangers that sojourn among you, who shall beget children among you;
and they shall be unto you as the home-born among the children of Israel;
they shall have inheritance with you among the tribes of Israel.

---

[a] Verse 7b-8. פֶּגֶר peger; carcass of a once living body. The practice of burying kings within holy areas just a short distance from where the Presence of YHWH was. Used 22 times in the OT (dead bodies). Lev 26.30 has, in reference to idolaters, *Cast your remains upon the remains of your idols.* A play on words (idols never having life in the first place). 2) An awkward position for Christian translators, whose kings were buried in holy places
[b] גֵּר [gêr]; a guest; by implication, foreigner, alien, sojourner.

And it shall come to pass, that in whatever tribe the stranger sojourns,
there shall ye give him his inheritance, says the Lord YHWH. (v22-23)

Ch 48

The division of the land amongst the Tribes is further described. The allocations of land for priests and Levites and the land allocated to the city Jerusalem itself is described. The priests (sons of Zadok) have land surrounding the Temple/city and the Levites have land surrounding the priests. The area allocated for the leader of Israel is also described as between the borders of Judah and Benjamin.
The city border is then described as having one border[a] area for each Tribe (three for Joseph as his lot includes Manasseh and Ephraim).
Verse 35 concludes with

...and the name of the city from that day shall be, YHWH is there.[b]

Daniel [c]

The Book of Daniel explores the limited control various empires and their kings exert in the world. Ultimately it is G-d who is found to have full control of events and history.

Ch 1

When Nebuchadnezzar returned to re-establish his rule of Jerusalem/Judah, (after Jehoiakim rebelled against him; 2 Kings 24), Daniel is among the first people to be taken to Babylon.

And the king spoke unto Ashpenaz (the master of his eunuchs),
that he should bring in certain of the children of Israel,
even of the royal seed and of the nobles; youths in whom was no blemish, but well-favoured,
and skilful in all wisdom, and endowed with knowledge,
and understanding science, and such as had ability to stand in the king's palace;

---

[a] תּוֹצָאָה tôwtsâ'âh, exit, (geographical) boundary, outgoings.

[b] Jeremiah renames Jerusalem **YHWH our Righteousness** (Jer 23.6). Isaiah (62.4) renames her **Hephzibah (in whom is my delight)** [and your land Beulah (married)]

[c] Daniel, numbered with the 'major prophets' in the LXX but numbered with the Ketuvim, [Writings] in the Torah of (what is now referred to as) Judaism. Daniel chapter 9 as the central scripture of this 'promotion.' The Jewish Torah understanding of what qualifies a prophetic book is a somewhat simple one. A prophet will have direct interaction with G-d, on a level above his normal senses, in which information is given (*...this is what the LORD says*) to be relayed to various persons/groups. Other 'writings' Ketuvim will had have access to a lower level, known as the 'ruach ha-kodesh' (Hebrew for "divine inspiration' or spirit of the divine) in which the 'writings' are divinely inspired or are relayed indirectly by one of G-ds messengers (angels). The book of Daniel falls into this latter category. Most of Daniel is the interpretation of dreams and visions. Chapter 9 as a revelation from Gabriel, and is not so much divine dictation as it is an invitation to a study requiring mathematical insight. 2) Placing Daniel amongst the 'minor prophets' (The Book of the Twelve) would increase their number to an unfortunate 13

and that he should teach them the learning and the tongue of the Chaldeans (v3-4)

Daniel and his three companions, Hananiah (Shadrach[a]) Mishael (Meshach[b]) Azariah (Abed-nego[c]) are among these placed for training within the king's palace. Daniel resolves in his heart that he is to remain faithful to YHWH and the law (Torah) beginning with the diet offered. Daniel and his companions, on their simple diet, become more healthy than those around them.

Now as for these four youths, God gave them knowledge and skill in all learning and wisdom: and Daniel had understanding in all visions and dreams.
And at the end of the days which the king had appointed for bringing them in, the prince of the eunuchs brought them in before Nebuchadnezzar. And the king communed with them; and among them all was found none like Daniel, Hananiah, Mishael, and Azariah: therefore stood they before the king.
And in every matter of wisdom and understanding, concerning which the king inquired of them, he found them ten times better than all the magicians and enchanters that were in all

his realm. And Daniel continued even unto the first year of king Cyrus. (v17-21)[d]

Ch 2[e]
Nebuchadnezzar has a dream which disturbs him, he is however unable to recount the dream. He calls all his diviners, astrologers and sorcerers to interpret the dream. They say[f] they cannot tell the king anything of his dream unless he recounts it to them. The king is angered by this and orders the death of all the wise men of Babylon (including Daniel and his companions). Daniel hears of what is about to happen and requests a chance to see the king. He then meets with his companions and they ..*desire mercies of the God of heaven concerning this secret* (v18). Daniel receives a vision and the dream is revealed to him.

Daniel answers the God of heaven with this blessing..

Blessed be the name of God for ever and ever; for wisdom and might are his.
And he changes the times and the seasons; he removes kings, and sets up kings;
he gives wisdom unto the wise, and knowledge to them that have understanding;
he reveals the deep and secret things;
he knows what is in the darkness, and the light dwells with him.
I thank thee, and praise thee, O thou God of my fathers,

---

[a] Shadr Aku. Meaning of the command of Aku (Babylonian Moon god)
[b] Mesh Aku Meaning (?) of Aku (Babylonian Moon god)
[c] Abed Nebu. Meaning servant of Nebu. A Babylonian god. 2) also Nebu-chadnezzar; Nebu-nidus
[d] Daniel who is taken captive as a young man in 598BC and 'continues' until the 1st year of Cyrus which will be 539BC. Daniel is therefore approximately 80 years of age in the 1st year of Cyrus
[e] This chapter verse 4 begin an Aramaic section; through to chapter 7.28. 2) Paired with chapter 7, Daniel's dream
[f] Here begins the Aramaic section (verse 4) of Daniel up to 7.28

who hast given me wisdom and might,
and has now made known unto me what we desired of thee;
for thou has made known unto us the king's matter. (v20-23)

Daniel makes a plea for the wise men not to be killed and goes to see the king. He firstly explains to the king that it was not by his own wisdom he has known the dream but by the *God of Heaven* who revealed the dream to him. Daniel explains the dream…

The king saw a great (human like) image…*its head was of fine gold, its breast and its arms of silver, its belly and its thighs of brass, its legs of iron, its feet part of iron, and part of clay.*[a] A great stone comes and hits the feet and smashes the entire image into dust, blown away by the wind; the stone however becomes a great mountain that fills the whole earth.

Daniel explains the meaning as four kingdoms. The head of gold is Nebuchadnezzar and his kingdom. Three more great kingdoms will follow his. The last being a divided kingdom of two elements iron and clay, which fundamentally cannot mix. In the time of that kingdom the God of Heaven will set up an eternal kingdom and all other kingdoms will end.
The king praises Daniel and his God and then makes Daniel a ruler alongside himself.[b]
Daniel requests that his companions become rulers in the affairs of Babylon also.

Ch 3[c]
Nebuchadnezzar sets up a sixty cubit[d] high image of gold and orders that it be worshipped by everyone in his kingdom. Word is brought to the king that some of the Judeans, namely Shadrach, Meshach and Abed-nego, were refusing to do so. The king calls them before him and demands their worshipping of the image or they will be killed. The three answer him that their God will save them from him; they will not worship the image.
The king orders them to be burnt in an extra hot furnace. They are thrown in. The king then notices they are unharmed within the fire and also the appearance of a fourth *like a son of Elohim* could be seen walking with them. The king calls for them to come out and they do totally unaffected by the flame..

Nebuchadnezzar spoke and said, Blessed be the God of Shadrach, Meshach, and Abed-nego,
who has sent his angel, and delivered his servants that trusted in him (v28)

The king then makes a decree that nothing should be done or said against their God anywhere in the Empire. Shadrach, Meshach, and Abed-nego are promoted.

---

[a] An Aramaic word used only here (between 2-33 & 2.35) to describe 'clay' The Hebrew cognate חַסְפַּס [chaçpaç] used only once in the OT to describe manna. (Exodus 16.14)

[b] Daniel's position now parallels Joseph's in Egypt

[c] Paired with chapter 6 The lion's den

[d] Cubit: Elbow to fingertips length

Ch 4[a]

Nebuchadnezzar narrates this chapter. It is a story of how he came to acknowledge God as the true ruler in the affairs of men.

He has another dream. A great tree grows, reaching right up unto the heavens. The tree becomes a source of food and shelter to all birds beasts, to all flesh. Then *a holy one* comes down from heaven and calls for the tree to be cut down. The stump is to remain but it's heart changed from a man to an animal. *The holy one* says this is a lesson to show that The Most High is ruler over the kingdom of men.

Again no one can interpret the dream except Daniel, who is somewhat afraid to tell the king the meaning. The king encourages Daniel to interpret the dream. Daniel explains that the tree is Nebuchadnezzar and that he will become like an animal living in the fields for seven years until he has acknowledged that it is the Most High God who actually rules. The dream comes true and the king lives in the fields for seven years as an animal *..and thou shall be made to eat grass as oxen ..*(v25).[b] Eventually the king does acknowledge the Most High God and gives praise to Him. (Nebuchadnezzar's blessing (v34-37)

Now I, Nebuchadnezzar, praise and extol and honour the King of heaven;
for all his works are truth, and his ways justice;
and those that walk in pride he is able to abase. (v37)

He is then restored as king.

Ch 5

Belshazzar[c] becomes king after Nebuchadnezzar. This chapter relays how his defiance of God's ultimate rule brings about his downfall.

Belshazzar orders a great feast and also orders that all of the vessels, taken by his father from the Temple at Jerusalem, be used by those attending.

In the same hour came forth the fingers of a man's hand,
and wrote over against the candlestick upon the plaster of the wall of the king's palace:
and the king saw the part of the hand that wrote (v5)

The king is terrified by this and brings in the enchanters, soothsayers and other wise men to interpret the words written by the hand, but no one can. His queen reminds him of Daniel who had resolved many mysteries for Nebuchadnezzar. Daniel is called and promised a high

---

[a] Paired with chapter 5 Belshazzar's unrepentance

[b] Psalm 106 20. Lost glory

[c] Belshazzar ruled on behalf of his father (Nebu-nidus) in his absence. Nebu-nidus came to power, helped by his son Belshazzah, in 556BC. He was the fourth king to rule (in just 6 years) after Nebu-chadnezzar's death in 562BC. He was king until Cyrus overpowered his empire (539BC). Three years into his rule he was self-exiled and remained so until the last three years before Cyrus. Since it appears that Nebu-nidus was 'unwell' during this time of self-exile and did return bringing something of a religious revival to Babylon, it is speculated that he is the king of Daniel chapter 4

place in the kingdom if he can interpret the words. Daniel refuses the gifts but agrees to interpret the words. He goes on to recount the events of Nebuchadnezzar in the last chapter and how he humbled himself before God; but Belshazzar has not taken to heart the events in his father's life and has *lifted himself up against God.*
Daniel then interprets..

And this is the writing that was inscribed: mene, mene, tekel, peres.
This is the interpretation of the thing:
mene; God has numbered thy kingdom, and brought it to an end;
tekel; thou are weighed in the balances, and are found wanting;
peres thy kingdom is divided, and given to the Medes and Persians. (v25-28)

Then commanded Belshazzar, and they clothed Daniel with purple,
and put a chain of gold about his neck, and made proclamation concerning him,
that he should be the third ruler in the kingdom.
In that night Belshazzar the Chaldean king was slain. And Darius the Mede [a]
received the kingdom, being about threescore and two years old. (v29-30)

Ch 6
Darius sets Daniel as the top man of three presidents and 120 provincial governors (satraps) for the entire kingdom. These leaders were against Daniel and colluded to find a way to have him removed. They could not find any corruption in him so they made a plan and put it before Darius that no one in the entire kingdom should worship any god, but worship Darius only, for 30 days. Darius agrees. However..

And when Daniel knew that the writing was signed, he went into his house (now his windows were open in his chamber toward Jerusalem); and he kneeled upon his knees three times a day, and prayed, and gave thanks before his God, as he did from before this. (v10-11)

The leaders find Daniel praying and go straight to Darius to tell him his decree is being ignored. Darius is actually not bothered by it as he knows how valuable Daniel is to him, but the leaders remind Darius that a decree from the king cannot be overruled. So Darius reluctantly allows Daniel to be put into a lion's den. The king fasts for Daniel during the night. In the morning the king goes to the lion's den and calls out to Daniel. He is overjoyed when he hears Daniel answer him and that he has not been harmed. Darius then has the leaders who accused Daniel thrown into the lion's den.

Then king Darius wrote unto all the peoples, nations, and languages,
that dwell in all the earth:

---

[a] Darius the Mede holds the Median throne. The name Darius being a title for a ruler. The actual Median ruler is believed to be Cyaxares II. although Cyrus personally defeats the Babylonian king Nebu-nidus 539BC it is Darius (Cyrus' uncle) who rules the larger Median Empire and takes the title. Darius will die within 2-3 years (without an heir) leaving the entire Persia-Median Empire to Cyrus

Peace be multiplied unto you. I make a decree,
that in all the dominion of my kingdom men tremble and fear before the God of Daniel;
for he is the living God, and steadfast for ever,
And his kingdom that which shall not be destroyed;
and his dominion shall be even unto the end.
He delivers and rescues, and he works signs and wonders in heaven and in earth,
who has delivered Daniel from the power of the lions. (v25-27)

So this Daniel prospered in the reign of Darius, and in the reign of Cyrus the Persian. (v28)

Ch 7
The time frame now moves back into Babylonian Empire. Daniels own visions are now described. His first vision closely follows the framework of Nebuchadnezzar's dream in chapter 2 with four kingdoms followed by the establishment of G-d's Kingdom.

The first vision appears to him in the 1st year of Belshazzar's rule.[a] The first vision…
The four great winds of heaven blow on the great sea and four great beasts come out of the water.

The first was like a lion, and had eagle's wings;[b] *I beheld till the wings thereof were plucked,*
and it was lifted up from the earth, and made to stand upon two feet as a man;
and a man's heart was given to it.[c]
...a second, like to a bear; and it was raised up on one side,[d]
....and, lo, another like a leopard, which had upon its back four wings of a bird;
the beast had also four heads;[e]
....a fourth beast, terrible and powerful, and strong exceedingly; and it had great iron teeth..
it devoured and broke in pieces, and stamped the residue with its feet:[f] *and it was diverse* [g]
from all the beasts that were before [h] *it; and it had ten horns.*[i] (v4-7)

A further 'little horn' becomes apparent, it has…*eyes like the eyes of a man, and a mouth speaking great things.* Upon the appearance of this last 'horn' God's throne appears reminiscent of Ezekiel's throne with the Ancient of days seated. Tens of thousands minister

---

[a] 553BC
[b] Babylonian emblem (artefacts held in the British museum)
[c] *let his heart be changed from man's, and let a beast's heart be given unto him;* (ch 4.16) Nebuchadnezzar
[d] Persia, Media 559BC-323BC
[e] Greek (as described in chapter 8) with the Ram and the he Goat
[f] *And the fourth kingdom shall be strong as iron, forasmuch as iron breaks in pieces and subdues all things; and as iron that crushes all these, shall it break in pieces and crush.* (ch 2.40). A return to the framework of Nebuchadnezzar's colossus
[g] שְׁנָא [sh?nâ]; to change, alter 2) divided as with chapter 2?
[h] קֳדָם [qŏdâm]; in front of; in the presence of. (not used of time)
[i] An empire derived from the Greek before it

to Him. Judgement is to take place. The fourth beast is slain whilst the others are disempowered. Then..

I saw in the night-visions,
and, behold, there came with the clouds of heaven one like unto a son of man,
and he came even to the ancient of days, and they brought him near before him.
And there was given him dominion, and glory, and a kingdom, that all the peoples, nations,
and languages should serve him: his dominion is an everlasting dominion,
which shall not pass away, and his kingdom that which shall not be destroyed. (v13-14) [a]

Daniel asks one of those present in the vision what this all means and is told that four great kings will come to power but the holy-ones of G-d *will* inherit the kingdom as *their* possession.

Ch 8
Daniel's 2nd vision appears in the 3rd year [b] of Belshazzar. Daniel is in the palace at Shushan, in Elam, the administrative capital of the Persian Empire. Daniel's vision sees a ram with two horns (kings), one bigger than the other.

I saw the ram[c] *butting westward, and northward, and southward;*
and no beast could stand before him,
neither was there any that could deliver out of his hand;
but he did according to his will, and magnified himself. (v4)

A he goat,[d] with a single horn, now comes from the west *over the face of the whole earth* and with great power and fury, kills the ram.

And the he-goat magnified himself exceedingly:
and when he was strong, the great horn was broken;
and instead of it there came up four notable horns toward the four winds of heaven.
And out of one of them came forth a little horn, which waxed exceeding great,
toward the south, and toward the east, and toward the glorious land.
And it waxed great, even to the host of heaven;
and some of the host and of the stars it cast down to the ground, and trampled upon them. [e]
(v8-10)

It magnifies itself against G-d and puts an end the sacrifices of the Temple Sanctuary. Daniel wants to understand the vision and Gabriel come near to him and says..

---

[a] The final kingdom, as stated in Nebuchadnezzar's Colossus. 2) Darius words also 6.25-27
[b] 551BC
[c] Aries (Persian association)?
[d] Capricorn (Greek association)?
[e] ..and stamped the residue with its feet: (see ch 7.7). Again the actions of the fourth kingdom

Understand, O son of man; for the vision belongs to the time of the end (v17)

Gabriel then explains the vision.
The ram was the two kings of Media[a] and Persia. The he goat is Greece with their first king. He is cut off. Then four more kingdoms will emerge from that. One of those kings will become dominant and he will fight against G-d and His people.[b] He also will be broken eventually. Daniel is told to shut up the vision as it refers to the many days in the future. When Daniel recovers from the trauma of the vision he continues with his work for the king.

Ch 9
In the first year of Darius[c] (v1) Daniel is studying the book of Jeremiah, specifically the 70 year prophecy.[d] Daniel begins to pray to G-d and makes a lengthy confession for the sins of Israel. He then makes a plea for Jerusalem, the Temple and the people who bear G-d's name.

O my God, incline thine ear, and hear; open thine eyes,
and behold our desolations, and the city which is called by thy name:
for we do not present our supplications before thee for our righteousness,
but for thy great mercies' sake. O Lord, hear; O Lord, forgive;
O Lord, hearken and do; defer not, for thine own sake,
O my God, because thy city and thy people are called by thy Name (v18-19)

As Daniel is praying, the angel Gabriel who had appeared in his earlier visions, returns and says to him…

I am now come forth to give thee wisdom and understanding.
At the beginning of thy supplications the commandment went forth,
and I am come to tell thee; for thou are greatly beloved:
therefore consider the matter, and understand the vision. (v22-23)

Gabriel gives Daniel the prophecy of the 70 weeks [e] thus..

---

[a] Media being controlled by Persia since the time of Cyrus.
[b] Again the actions of the fourth kingdom
[c] The Mede 539BC, when he took the throne (alongside Cyrus) after Belshazzar (AKA Nebu-nidus) died (Dan. 5.30).
[d] Jeremiah's 70 year prophecy is now approaching its end. Daniel being of the first exiles in 598BC has now been in Babylon 59 years (up to the year 539BC). 2) Jeremiah's prophecy itself being related to the Blessings & Curses of Lev 26 (specifically Lev 26.31-35), that is, 70 years worth of Sabbaths.
This first year of Darius (v1) (539BC) marks the beginning of another possible 70 year period, (the first being from destruction of the 1st Temple to the dedication of the 2nd Temple 586/7BC to 516BC = 70)
This second possibility (of weeks [70 x 7]), gives a 49 year period (7 weeks [v25]) between the Temple's destruction and the Decree of Cyrus (587BC to 538BC = 49). It also gives the date 104BC for the end of the 62 weeks (538BC minus 434 (62x7), the year when Aristobulus became the first king (and high priest) of a restored Israel since Zedekiah at the fall of Jerusalem. 3) Josephus also notes that Aristobulus became the first king of Israel 483 years (7 weeks + 62 weeks) after Zedekiah. 2) Aristobulus and his brother Antigonus (the next in line to the throne) will both die within 1 year.
[e] 70 x 7 years =490

..to finish transgression, and to make an end of sins,
and to make reconciliation for iniquity, and to bring in everlasting righteousness,
and to seal up vision and prophecy, and to anoint the most holy (v24)

Know therefore and discern,
that from the going forth of the commandment to restore and to build Jerusalem[a]
unto the anointed one, the prince, shall be seven weeks,
and threescore and two weeks: it shall be built again,
with street and moat, even in troubled times.
And after the sixty-two weeks shall the anointed one [b] *be cut off, and shall have nothing:*
and the people of the prince that shall come shall destroy the city and the sanctuary;
and the end thereof shall be with a flood,
and even unto the end shall be war; desolations are determined
And he shall make a firm covenant with many for one week:
and in the midst of the week he shall cause the sacrifice and the oblation to cease;
and upon the wing of abominations shall come one that makes desolate;
and even unto the full end, and that determined,
shall wrath be poured out upon the desolate. (v25-27)

A fairly complex piece of prophecy which covers the happenings within the 70 weeks in which it says that 490 [c] years are in fact decreed and it is in that time period which ultimately the promise of YHWH are to be realized *...to make reconciliation for iniquity, and to bring in everlasting righteousness* to Israel as just stated above (v24)

---

[a] This *commandment to restore* could relate to 1) The 70 years prophecy of Jeremiah, beginning with the destruction of Jerusalem and the Temple 2) The decree of Cyrus (539BC); 3) Artaxerxes gives permission for Ezra to go to Jerusalem (Ezra 7.13); 4) a king named Artaxerxes gives Nehemiah permission to go (Neh 2); 5) or as just stated in Daniel 9 verse 23 *At the beginning of thy supplications* ***the commandment went forth***, and verse 25 *Know therefore and discern, that from the* ***going forth of the commandment***.. Therefore the prophecy could begin with Daniel's confession (and ultimately set in motion the Cyrus Decree).
One of the main argument for deciding between these options for where the prophecy is to begin is with the words of Gabriel '*to restore and to build Jerusalem'* These words are compared to the wording of the other decrees to find which one fits the wording of Gabriel. However even with Jeremiah the prophecy is aimed ultimately at the restoration of the Israelites and as such any of the decrees can fit the restoration position. It should also be said that it is highly unlikely that the restoration process was aimed solely at the Temple as it would be bizarre to rebuild a functioning Temple in the midst of a desolated unpopulated Jerusalem.
[b] LXX refers to Jerusalem not the Messiah
[c] 490 years is apparently a full era in G-ds accounting. If for instance we look at the genealogy of Matthew's Gospel (of the Jewish Church) where we have the 14 generations from Abraham to David; 14 from David to the exile and 14 from the exile to the coming of the messiah. The point here being that 14 generations equal 490 years. {The lifespan of a man is 70 years (psalm 90.10) therefore a generation is 35. Also in Job, when eventually restored (42.16) lives a further 140 years and sees his children to the fourth generation (4 X 35). So 14 x 35 = 490}. G-ds soteriological actions on earth revolve around this number. Looking at some other Bible history we have..
490 years. (The new generation to the promised son) The time from the birth of Shem to the birth of Isaac.

Ch 10
This chapter returns to the third[a] year of Cyrus.[b] Daniel has another vision, this time he understands it. It's about spiritual warfare.
This leads Daniel to mourn and fast for *three whole weeks*. It's the 24th day of the first month and he's by the river Hiddekel, (Tigris), one of the great rivers of Eden.[c]

Then, Daniel says..

I lifted up mine eyes, and looked, and, behold, a man clothed in linen,
whose loins were girded with pure gold of Uphaz: his body also was like the beryl,
and his face as the appearance of lightning, and his eyes as flaming torches,
and his arms and his feet like unto burnished brass,
and the voice of his words like the voice of a multitude. (v5-6) [d]

Daniel is with other men, they don't see the vision but they feel scared and hide. Daniel himself is without any strength and falls face down in a deep sleep. A hand touches him and sets him up. The messenger tells Daniel…

Fear not, Daniel; for from the first day that thou did set thy heart to understand,
and to humble thyself before thy God,
thy words were heard: and I am come for thy words' sake.
But the prince of the kingdom of Persia withstood me one and twenty days;
but, lo, Michael, one of the chief princes, came to help me:[e]
and I remained there with the kings of Persia (v12-13)

A rather interesting point here is that the angel has been somehow battling against the prince of the kingdom of Persia on a spiritual level, for twenty one days, exactly the three weeks that

---

490 years. (Isaac's blessing of Jacob until YHWH's decent on mount Sinai) From the time Jacob received the blessing from Isaac (age 70. Book of Jubilees chapter 26) to his arrival in Egypt age 130 (Gen 47.9) 130-70=60. Plus the 430 years in Egypt ending with Moses at Sinai, (Exo. 12.40)
487 years. (YHWH's presence in the Tabernacle) From Mount Sinai to Solomon's 4th year (1 Kings 6.1) 480 plus the building of the Temple 7 years (1 Kings 6.38).
So now Daniel has enough biblical history before him to see the 'pattern.' Now he is told by Gabriel that...*Seventy sevens are decreed for your people..* Thus it is the end of this next era where G-d has decreed that His planned kingdom is to be set up. 2) Daniel's meeting with Gabriel is one requiring some mathematics (*know and understand this* (v25) therefore not necessarily prophecy. This may explain why Judaism does not hold Daniel as a prophet. 3) see further commentary in Ezra 4; Ezra 7; Nehemiah 1
[a] Some LXX versions read 1st year
[b] Dan 1. 21 states ..*And Daniel continued even unto the first year of king Cyrus.*
[c] Daniel now has a vision of YHWH in the same way that Ezekiel did (Ezekiel 1.1) also by a river. Daniel's vision has him in the palace of Susa (Elam). 2)Nehemiah is also noted as being there at some point (Neh 1.1)
[d] A vision of The Living G-d (as opposed to the earlier vision of the metal colossus/Empire idol of Nebuchadnezzar)
[e] One of the chief angels, Michael, [Mi-cha-el]; meaning who-is like-God. The defender/ angelic warrior of Israel is introduced here

Daniel has been mourning and fasting. It would appear that the actions of Daniel during this time have in fact empowered the angels.
The angel then goes on to say he is there to let Daniel know what will befall his people in the latter days. One having the appearance of a man says to him..

O man greatly beloved, fear not:
peace be unto thee, be strong, yea, be strong. (v19)

Do you understand why I came unto thee?[a]
and now will I return to fight with the prince of Persia:
and when I go forth, lo, the prince of Greece shall come.
But I will tell thee that which is inscribed in the writing of truth:
and there is none that holdeth [b] *with me against these, but Michael your prince.* (v20-21)

Daniel is informed that the angel is fighting against the ruler of Persia in the spiritual realm. The king of Persia, or other Empires, being apparently strongly influenced by spiritual beings (demonic). The angel also states that the angel Michael, alone, (of Israel) is helping in this.

Ch 11
Verse 1 continuing with what was just spoken of Michael..

And as for me,[c] *in the first year of Darius the Mede,*
I stood up to confirm and strengthen him.[d]

The angel has been assisting Israel since then to ensure a positive outcome for them from within the turmoil of the passing of Empire.
The angel then begins to tell Daniel about the events of the (four) kings who arise from the Greek Empire and will be against G-d and His people, as described in the earlier visions. One of the kings will cause much trouble but will eventually be destroyed.

Ch 12
Verse 1 continues..

And at that time shall Michael stand up,
the great prince who stands for the children of thy people;
and there shall be a time of trouble,
such as never was since there was a nation [e] *until that time;*
and at that time your people shall be rescued, everyone who is found written in the scroll,

---

[a] The angel is there to encourage Daniel to continue fasting as there's more fighting to do
[b] Assist; stand firmly with
[c] The angel
[d] To strengthen either Michael or Darius
[e] LXX adds *on earth*

And many of them that sleep in the dust of the earth shall awake,
some to everlasting life, and some to shame and everlasting contempt. (v2)

Those who assist the people to turn to righteousness..

And they that are wise shall shine as the brightness of the firmament;
and they that turn many to righteousness as the stars for ever and ever. (v3)

But thou, O Daniel, shut up the words, and seal the book, even to the time of the end:
many shall go forth and knowledge shall be increased. (v4)

Daniel then sees two 'others' (angelic beings) one on each of the riverbanks.[a] One of them speaks to the '*man clothed in linen*' (from 10. 5-6) who is now above the *waters of the river*, and asks him when will these things happen. The '*man clothed in linen*' replies by lifting up his hands to heaven swearing *by Him that lives for ever..*

..that it shall be for a time, times, and a half;[b]
and when they have made an end of breaking in pieces the power of the holy people,[c]
all these things shall be finished (v 7)

Daniel does not understand and asks of the meaning of it but is told..

Go thy way, Daniel; for the words are shut up and sealed till the time of the end

The angel then returns to the theme of verse 2 with the fate of the righteous, the wicked and the wise. A last calculation is given as the days which make up the two 3½ years periods of the last 'year' given as 1290 and 1335. [d]

Daniel is then told..

But go thou thy way till the end be; for thou shall rest,
and shall stand in thy lot, at the end of the days. (v13)

---

[a] This single vision continuing on from ch 10.4

[b] Also 7.25 & 9.27, the middle point of the last week (7 years) until the end (3 ½ years). The period during which the holy-ones are trampled and the sacrifices ceased

[c] The 'trampling' of the fourth kingdom. (ch 7)

[d] These two numbers together minus 70 equal 7 x 365. 70 is a number of judgement

Hosea [a]

YHWH begins to speak to Hosea within the Northern kingdom at some point after king Jehu of Israel or shortly thereafter.[b] He is told..

Go, take unto thee a wife of whoredom and children of whoredom;
for the land doth commit great whoredom, departing from YHWH. (v2)

Hosea is to take a prostitute as a wife. He takes Gomar[c] and has a first child. YHWH tells him to name the child Jezreel. He is named as such because YHWH is to..

avenge the blood of Jezreel [d] upon the house of Jehu, [e]
and I will cause the kingdom of the house of Israel to cease.[f] (v4)

Hosea's wife conceives again and YHWH tells Hosea..

Call her name Lo-ruhamah;[g] for I will no more have mercy upon the house of Israel,
that I should in any wise pardon them. (v6)

Gomer gives birth again.

And YHWH said, Call his name Lo-ammi;[h]
for ye are not my people, and I will not be your God. (v9)

However YHWH continues with words of later restoration..

Yet the number of the children of Israel shall be as the sand of the sea,
which cannot be measured nor numbered;
and it shall come to pass that, in the place where it was said unto them,
Ye are not my people, it shall be said unto them, Ye are the sons of the living God.
And the children of Judah and the children of Israel shall be gathered together,
and they shall appoint themselves one head,[i] and shall go up from the land;[j]

---

[a] 760-720 BC. The name Hoshea comes from the root ישע [yasha'] meaning to be saved, delivered. 2) The first book of the Twelve Prophets which now follow. 3) This book within the Hebrew Bible contains the 12 minor prophets: Hosea, Joel, Amos, Obadiah, Jonah, Micah, Nahum, Habakkuk, Zephaniah, Haggai, Zechariah, and Malachi.

[b] The events within Hosea match with those described in 2 Kings 11-15, that is after the actions of king Jehu but before the arrival of the Assyrians; also (Hosea 11.12) during the reign of some of the better kings in Judah (Jehoash and Uzziah)

[c] Meaning to complete or bring to an end.

[d] The city where king Ahab's sons were. 2) Jezreel , meaning that which G-d planted. 3) Jezreel [yizr?ʿel } play on words yiśrā'ēl Israel 4) Jezreel is used in condemnation here but will later be blessed

[e] Jehu had massacred Ahab's family when he ascended to the throne. (2 Kings 10)

[f] The northern kingdom to cease and be united again with Judah

[g] Meaning No mercy

[h] Not my people

for great shall be the day of Jezreel.[a] (v10-11)

After the judgement (causing Israel to cease) will be mercy and restoration.

Ch 2
Verse 1 begins..

Say ye unto your brethren, Ammi; and to your sisters, Ruhamah.

The children now named without the negative prefix are told to rebuke their mother for her actions. YHWH has rejected her (Israel). Israel will be punished for these adulterous actions she has taken (v 8-13).
Verse 14-20 Israel will again be forgiven and restored to YHWH as a wife

And I will betroth thee unto Me for ever;
yea, I will betroth thee unto Me in righteousness,
and in justice, and in loving-kindness, and in mercies.
I will even betroth thee unto Me in faithfulness; and thou shall know YHWH (v19-20)

The cosmic order restored.

And it shall come to pass in that day, I will answer, says YHWH,
I will answer the heavens, and they shall answer the earth;
and the earth shall answer the grain, and the new wine, and the oil;
and they shall answer Jezreel. And I will sow her unto me in the earth;
and I will have mercy upon her that had not obtained mercy;
and I will say to them that were not My people, Thou are My people;
and they shall say, Thou are my God (v21-23)

Ch 3
Hosea is told to get back his wife from her lovers to show her that she is still loved. He pays a hefty price to keep her with him '*for many days*'. She is now to remain without lovers as a sign that Israel will be without king or leader or religious freedom in the soon to come captivity by the Assyrians. However..

afterward shall the children of Israel return,
and seek YHWH their God, and David their king,
and shall come with fear unto YHWH and to His goodness in the latter days. (v5)

---

[i] Use of this word here remembering what had happened at Jezreel to Ahaz' sons
[j] As a united people to ultimately fulfil their divinely appointed purpose. Meaning that which G-d planted
[a] When Israel are restored as a single people with a single ruler.

Ch 4
Israel is lost in her unfaithfulness. They are too stubborn to listen to their G-d.

Ch 5
A warning is given to the priests, royal leaders and tribal leaders (Ephraim); their deeds do not go unnoticed. Judah is also included in this warning. Their sickness cannot be cured by reliance on Assyria.

When Ephraim saw his sickness, and Judah saw his wound,
then went Ephraim to Assyria, and sent to king Jareb:[a]
but he is not able to heal [b] *you, neither will he cure you of your wound.* (v13)

They will be carried off with none who can help them as it will be at YHWH's behest.

For I will be unto Ephraim[c] *as a lion, and as a young lion to the house of Judah:*
I, even I, will tear and go away; (v14)

He will abandon them until such time as they realize their mistake.

I will go and return to My place,[d] *till they acknowledge their offence,*
and seek My face: in their affliction they will seek Me earnestly (v15)

Ch 6
Verse 1, following closely the ending of chapter 5, begins with a message of hope..

Come, and let us return unto YHWH;
for he has torn, and he will heal us; he has smitten, and he will bind us up.
After two days will he revive us: on the third day he will raise us up,
and we shall live before him. And let us know, let us follow on to know YHWH:
his going forth is sure as the morning; and he will come unto us as the rain,
as the latter rain that waters the earth. (v1-3)

YHWH has loved Judah and Ephraim and has consequently sent prophets to speak to them, but they have not listened and have continued in their transgressions.

For I desire goodness, and not sacrifice;
and the knowledge of God more than burnt-offerings.
But they, like Adam, have transgressed the covenant:

---

[a] An epithet for an Assyrian king. From the verb רבב (rabab), to be great or many.

[b] The notion of YHWH healing Israel/Judah being returned to in 7.1 & 11.3

[c] House of Israel

[d] Heavenly abode (Micah 1.3; Isaiah 6.1; Isaiah 18.3-4)

there they have dealt treacherously against me. (v6-7)

YHWH will however eventually restore them from the captivity of their sin.

Ch 7
There is great sin amongst the people. G-d wonders when they will be ready for healing. They are compared to an oven with their passions burning, ready for the next thing to be 'cooked' within them. Ephraim is as a cake improperly cooked and eaten by strangers. The people have rebelled and make much mischief. But..

..their princes shall fall by the sword for the rage of their tongue:
this shall be their derision in the land of Egypt.[a] (v16)

Ch 8
Israel is warned get ready for an enemy is coming to overtake them. They have set their own kings and rulers not the ones chosen by YHWH. They have worshipped idols, all the while claiming innocence. It will be no good to cry out for help to YHWH when the enemy arrives. They have made their friendship with Assyria, but Assyria will come against them. They have completely forgotten the Law. Judgement is soon to be upon them. Israel will return to Egypt and their cities burned.

Ch 9
The Land will no longer feed Israel. They shall return to Egypt and Assyria. Their sacrifices are not accepted and their Feast Days are a waste of time. YHWH had found them as a beautiful thing but now they are a shameful thing. Their ability to raise children will be taken from them. They will bear no fruit. Hosea laments..

My God will cast them away, because they did not hearken unto him;
and they shall be wanderers among the nations. (v17)

Ch 10
Israel's land has been very fertile, but they have not given thanks to YHWH for this but have instead built altars to idols. They respect neither YHWH nor their kings. Their idols will be carried away to Assyria. When YHWH is ready He will chastise them for their breaking away from Judah and worshipping idols. The people are told..

Sow to yourselves in righteousness, reap according to kindness;
break up your fallow ground; for it is time to seek YHWH,
till he come and rain righteousness upon you.(v12)

but...

---

[a] Of captivity/slavery

ye have ploughed wickedness, ye have reaped iniquity; ye have eaten the fruit of lies (v13)

They have trusted in their own power; now the nations will come and destroy them.

Ch 11
YHWH laments his love for Israel..

When Israel was a child, then I loved him, and called my son out of Egypt.
The more the prophets called to them, the more they went away from them:
they sacrificed unto the Baalim, and burned incense to graven images. (v1-2)

YHWH has raised Ephraim as a child, caring, feeding and healing him. They will not return to Egypt but in fact Assyria will rule them and destroy their cities.

YHWH then reconsiders his judgement against them.

How shall I give thee up, Ephraim? how shall I cast thee off, Israel?
how shall I make thee as Admah? how shall I set thee as Zeboiim? [a]
my heart is turned within me, my compassions are kindled together.
I will not execute the fierceness of mine anger, I will not return to destroy Ephraim:
for I am God, and not man; the Holy One in the midst of thee;
and I will not come in wrath. (v8-9)

He finds the prospect too saddening. Instead He says he will save them and they will return to Him in humbleness and live in the Land. The chapter ends stating that Judah, unlike Israel, has still been somewhat faithful to Him.

Ch 12
Ephraim does nothing now for YHWH. His alliances are with Egypt and Assyria. YHWH also has a case against Judah and Jacob:[b] Jacob their father had really struggled to get the blessings for the people of Israel and now they should do as he did..

Therefore turn thou to thy God: keep kindness and justice,
and wait for thy God continually. (v6)

But now Jacob[c] is full of deceit and oppression. Ephraim trusts in his wealth. YHWH says He will again make Ephraim repentant. YHWH has sent many prophets with visions for them but they don't listen. Gilead and Gilgal [d] were two great centres for idolatry; Jacob is noted as

[a] Admah – Zeboiim, Cities destroyed, like Sodom and Gomorrah by YHWH (Deut 29:23)
[b] Judah and the whole nation
[c] Israel
[d] They will be the first areas to be taken by the Assyrians.

fleeing from such areas (Gen 27-28) to avoid any such compromise with foreign influences (as Esau had involved himself with) and to preserve the promises made to Abraham.

And Jacob fled into the field of Aram, and Israel served for a wife,
and for a wife he kept sheep. (v12)

YHWH's prophets had saved Israel from Egypt in the past. Ephraim[a] had forgotten all what YHWH has done. His coming punishment is well deserved.

Ch 13
Ephraim's once exalted position within Israel is over. He is now an idol worshipper and has become worthless. YHWH reminds him that He has always protected them..

Yet I am YHWH thy God from the land of Egypt;
and thou shall know no god but Me, and besides Me there is no saviour (v4)

Ephraim has forgotten, now YHWH will be as a lion come to attack them. Israel asked for a king when they rejected YHWH (1Sam 8) to rule them, now their kings have failed. For Ephraim's sin he will be held accountable. As a woman in labour and the child yet unborn,[b] now is the moment; the last chance to repent is here but Israel is in the wrong place.

The sorrows of a travailing woman shall come upon him: he is an unwise son;
for it is time he should not tarry in the place of the breaking forth of children[c] (v13)

Shall I ransom them from the power of Sheol? Shall I redeem them from death?
O Death, where[d] *are your thorns? O Sheol, where is your sting?*
Compassion shall be hidden from My sight. (LXX v14)[e]

But now YHWH is to hide His mercy and call for destruction to befall Israel. By the breath of YHWH the East wind (Assyria) will now come and mercilessly destroy them.

Samaria shall bear her guilt; for she has rebelled against her God:
they shall fall by the sword; their infants shall be dashed in pieces,
and their women with child shall be ripped up. (v16)

---

[a] Another name given to the Northern kingdom
[b] In contrast to Jacob's birth with his desire/struggle for the blessing of G-d
[c] Or as the Berean Study Bible interprets *Labour pains come upon him, but he is an unwise son. When the time arrives, he fails to present himself at the opening of the womb.*
[d] In the sense of bring it now forth. 2) The Hebrew text has **plagues; destruction** (for **thorns; sting**)
[e] The meaning of this verse can easily change from condemnation to forgiveness by the interpretation **I shall** or **shall I** . 2) Paul's interpretation reflecting a modified understanding relating to the resurrection of Christ

Ch 14

Another plea is made for Israel to return to YHWH. Ask Him to ..*take away all iniquity,* and then... *accept that which is good* (v2). Assyria will not save them; their idols; cannot help them.

YHWH's last message of hope..

I will heal their backsliding,
I will love them freely; for mine anger is turned away from him.
I will be as the dew unto Israel; he shall blossom as the lily,
and cast forth his roots as Lebanon. (v4-5)

The chapter ends with an editorial note..

Who is wise, that he may understand these things? Prudent, that he may know them?
For the ways of YHWH are right, and the just shall walk in them;
but transgressors shall fall therein. (v9)

Joel [a]

Ch 1

In Joel's vision, a great catastrophe, never seen before, is to come upon the land. A calamity described first as a swarm of locusts, then a strong innumerable nation, then as a fire, has devoured every growing thing, crop, fruit tree, even the grass. The people are called to fast and assemble before YHWH and cry for help..

Alas for the day! for the day of YHWH is at hand, [b]
and as destruction from the Almighty shall it come. (v15)

Ch 2

Verse 1 continues..

Blow ye the trumpet in Zion, and sound an alarm in my holy mountain;
let all the inhabitants of the land tremble:
for the day of YHWH is coming, for it is nigh at hand

---

[a] Meaning YHWH is G-d 2) A prophesy likely referring to the Babylonian destruction of Jerusalem (3.5-6)
[b] Isaiah 13.6; Ezekiel 30.2-3; Zephaniah 1.14-16; Amos 5.18-20. The point at which YHWH finally executes judgment against wrongdoing

A great never seen before or likely to be seen again nation/army is described. A fire goes before and behind them devouring everything; leaving only a desolation of wilderness. The army has the appearance of horsemen and chariots as they come crashing forward straight into the city over the walls and in through windows. They are in fact YHWH's army and…

The earth quakes before them; the heavens tremble;
the sun and the moon are darkened, and the stars withdraw their shining.
And YHWH utters his voice before his army; for his camp is very great;
for he is strong that executes his word;
for the day of YHWH is great and very terrible; and who can abide it?[a] (v10-11)

YHWH says even now if only the people would repent sincerely..

..turn ye unto me with all your heart,
and with fasting, and with weeping, and with mourning:
and rend your heart, and not your garments. (v12-13)

He may relent as He *is gracious and merciful, slow to anger.* (v13) [b]

The people are again called to gather for a fast in which they will exhibit truthful repentance for their wrong doing - from the heart.

Let the priests, the ministers of YHWH, weep between the porch and the altar,
and let them say, Spare thy people, O YHWH,
give not thy heritage to reproach, that the nations should rule over them:
why should they say among the peoples, Where is their God? (v17)

YHWH then relents and sends food to them. He also removes the invading army away to its destruction. YHWH then tells the Land to rejoice, the animals not to fear and the people to rejoice as the rain is to be returned and their food plentifully restored. [c]
The people will praise the Name of YHWH and will know that He is amongst them.
YHWH further promises..

And it shall come to pass afterward, that I will pour out my Spirit upon all flesh;
and your sons and your daughters shall prophesy, your old men shall dream dreams,
your young men shall see visions and also upon the servants and upon the handmaids
in those days will I pour out my Spirit.[d] (v28/29)

---

[a] Malachi 3.2. *But who can abide the day of his coming? and who shall stand when he appears?*
[b] Exo 34.6 And YHWH, a God merciful and gracious, slow to anger, and abundant in loving-kindness and truth
[c] A restoration similar to Isaiah 35 & Ezekiel 38-39; Ezekiel 47; Zechariah 14
[d] Pouring out of His Spirit. Isaiah 32.15; Isaiah 44.3; Jeremiah 31.31-34; Ezekiel 36.23-28

YHWH will show many great wonders on the Earth before His day of judgment, but only those who truly call upon His Name will be saved.

Ch 3
Verse 1 begins giving a time reference for this book.

For, behold, in those days, and in that time,
when I shall bring back the captivity of Judah and Jerusalem,

Then YHWH will gather all the nations to the *valley of Jehoshaphat,* [a] where they are to be judged for all the wrongdoing they have done to Israel and repaid for their acts against her people. The nations are then told to prepare for war and to..

Beat your ploughshares [b] *into swords, and your pruning-hooks into spears:*[c] (v10)

They will be cut down as a crop at harvest time as repayment for their wickedness..

Multitudes, multitudes in the valley of decision!
for the day of YHWH is near in the valley of decision.
The sun and the moon are darkened, and the stars withdraw their shining. (v14-15)

The nations will be destroyed but Israel will be saved. YHWH their G-d will dwell in Zion, in Jerusalem, the holy city and she shall never be invaded again. The land will be overflowing with produce and water. Egypt and Edom will lie deserted. Judah and Jerusalem will be inhabited forever.

Amos

Amos is described as a shepherd of Tekoa.[d] His call to prophecy is during the rule of Jeroboam II.[e]
Chapters 1 & 2 concern the kingdom of Israel and the neighbouring nations.
Chapters 3 to 6 are directed at Israel and its leaders.
Chapters 7 to 9 are a series of Amos' visions concerning YHWH's coming judgement on Israel.

---

[a] Meaning G-ds Judgement
[b] The cutting blade of the plough
[c] Opposing Isaiah 2.4; Micah 4.3
[d] In northern Judea. The name meaning a sudden loud noise (such as a trumpet call)
[e] Amos 7.10 Jeroboam is informed of the actions of Amos

Ch 1

Amos begins by delivering YHWH's condemnation of the inhumane actions of the nations which surround Israel geographically. Damascus (Syria/Aram) [violence]. Gaza (Ashdod and the Philistines) [enslavement of people] Tyre [enslavement of people] Edom [unrelenting hatred for their enemies] and Ammon [murder of women and children] are mentioned.

Ch 2

Moab [unrelenting hated for their enemies] then Judah [abandoning the Law of YHWH and idolatry] are condemned.

Verse 6 continues with a condemnation of Israel for their gross mistreatment of the poor and needy, sexual misconduct and idol worship. YHWH recalls the fact that they were brought out of slavery to the freedom of the Promised Land. YHWH continues..

And I raised up of your sons for prophets, and of your young men for Nazirites.
Is this not so, O ye children of Israel? Says YHWH.
But ye gave the Nazirites wine to drink,
and commanded the prophets, saying, Prophesy not. (v11-12)

Israel is to be crushed like a seed under a cartwheel; no one will escape.

Ch 3

Amos continues with YHWH's message against Israel and Judah..

You only have I known of all the families of the earth:
therefore I will visit upon you all your iniquities. (v2)

But the companionship the family of Israel has with YHWH is ignored and now judgement is come against them, especially Israel. An enemy (Assyria) will be sent against them. Their idol worship temples and all the great houses of her leaders will be destroyed.

Ch 4

The people are warned they are to be enslaved. The sacrifices they give in their temples are for their own pleasure and are useless. YHWH has caused a drought but the people do not understand why it is happening. YHWH goes on to remind the people of all the disasters He had inflicted upon them as warnings (in the same way He did to the Egyptians at the time of Moses) but they had not taken heed. Israel have been saved many times but now..

Therefore thus will I do unto thee, O Israel; and because I will do this unto thee,
prepare to meet thy God O Israel! (v12)

Ch 5

A lament is then given..

The virgin of Israel is fallen; she shall no more rise:
she is cast down upon her land; there is none to raise her up. (v2)

Israel is to be decimated. Yet still there is hope if only the people would seek YHWH and live. Otherwise all of Israel's injustice and idolatry will be her downfall. Israel, unfortunately, will not listen and actually hates those who have come to warn her. There will be great mourning in the land when judgement comes.

Ch 6
The leaders of Israel and nobles are condemned for their luxurious ease of carefree living. Soon they will all be carried off and their great houses destroyed. They have trusted in their own strength and now a destroying nation will be brought up against them.

Ch 7
Amos is shown a series of visions. First a swarm of locusts readied to destroy the crops of the land. Amos pleads with YHWH to relent; YHWH relents.
YHWH then sends a great fire through the land and again Amos pleads for it to stop YHWH stops the fire. YHWH then shows Amos a plumb line which is a sign that they have been checked for uprightness and failed. There are no more chances for Israel. YHWH then says..

and the high places of Isaac shall be desolate,
and the sanctuaries of Israel shall be laid waste;
and I will rise against the house of Jeroboam with the sword. (v9)

After this vision, (v10) Amaziah a priest at Beth-El[a] sends a message to Jeroboam king of Israel saying that Amos was conspiring against him by his prophecies. Amaziah tells Amos to get back to Judah and prophesy there. Amos simply continues further to prophesy against Amaziah's family, they too will soon be ruined and the survivors taken into captivity.

Ch 8
YHWH then shows Amos a basket of summer fruit. There is some word play here as 'qaits' is the Hebrew for summer-fruit, and 'qêts' Hebrew for *end.* The 'harvest' time is near, YHWH will not overlook Israel's sin any more.
Again the corruption of the people is noted and their denial of the rights of the poor and needy. Judgement will bring great sorrow. YHWH is to send a famine, not a famine of food but of *His words* and the people will fall never to rise again.

Ch 9
Amos sees the Lord [b] standing next to the Altar (of Beth'El) where He orders its destruction, falling on those beneath. Anyone left alive is to die by the sword, none shall escape no matter

[a] The place of worship that Jacob had established

[b] אֲדֹנָי ['ăḏōnāy]

where they try to hide. Even though they are to go into captivity they will still be killed there by the sword. YHWH is only looking for their harm now not for good.
However YHWH will not utterly destroy the house of Jacob. They are to be shaken as grain in a sieve: only the solid grain will remain. With those remaining people YHWH will..

... raise up the tent of David that is fallen,
and close up the breaches thereof; and I will raise up its ruins,
and I will build it as in the days of old. (v11)

The remaining people will return and they will rebuild the farms and cities and no more will they be uprooted from the Land.

Obadiah

The short prophecy of Obadiah, just 19 verses. The prophecy concerns the people of Edom.[a] The Babylonian conquest and destruction of Jerusalem has recently taken place. The people of Edom were happy to see Judah destroyed and even took part in the pillaging.

For the violence done to thy brother Jacob, shame shall cover thee,
and thou shall be cut off for ever. (v10)

Edom stood by and watched from their high hills as Babylon laid siege and eventually destroyed Jerusalem. The Day of YHWH is near for all the nations and Edom to be judged. Edom will lose her land and it will be given to Judah. All the land of the Israelites will be returned to them..

..and the kingdom shall be YHWH's (v21)

Jonah

Jonah is an unusual prophet in that he runs away from his calling. His time period is around the reign of Jeroboam II[b] although his calling is not to the affairs of Israel (at least in this book) but to the Assyrian capital Nineveh, where he is called to warn the people there that unless they repent from their evil lifestyles they will be destroyed. For Jonah the calling to a gentile nation who are also threatening Israel, is a task that he finds somewhat distasteful.

Ch 1

Jonah tries to run away from YHWH's calling. He goes to the port of Joppa and pays a fare to take him to Tarshish[c] with the apparent belief that the influence of YHWH does not extend there.

---

[a] Edomite. They were descended from Esau, Jacob's brother. There was a long history of hatred by Esau for his brother

[b] The prophesies of Jonah (concerning Israel's borders) are mentioned in 2 Kings 14.25. Jeroboam II ruled 789–748BC. The Assyrian empire will go on to invade and destroy the kingdom of Israel in 720BC

The ship sets sail but YHWH sends a great storm which threatens to destroy it. The crew of the ship are afraid and pray to their various gentile gods. Jonah is not bothered; he has gone into the hold where he is soundly sleeping. The captain finds Jonah and tells him to also pray to his god to help them. The sailors somehow come to believe that the unfolding calamity is being caused by someone on board and cast a lot to find out who is responsible. The lot falls to Jonah and they realize what he is doing. The storm was getting worse and they ask him what they should do to be saved. Jonah replies..

"Pick me up and throw me into the sea," he replied, "and it will become calm.
I know that it is my fault that this great storm has come upon you. (v12)

The sailors don't want to do this and try even harder to save the ship, but the storm grows even worse than before. They then make a plea to YHWH not to hold them responsible for taking his life and they throw him into the sea. The storm then ends.

Then the men feared YHWH exceedingly;
and they offered a sacrifice unto YHWH, and made vows. (v16)

and then..

YHWH prepared a great fish to swallow up Jonah;
and Jonah was in the belly of the fish three days and three nights. (v17)

Ch 2

Now, within the fish, Jonah makes an impassioned prayer of thanks (for saving his life) and repentance to YHWH. After this prayer..

..YHWH spoke unto the fish, and it vomited out Jonah upon the dry land. (v10)

It is this repentance and salvation (lifesaving) which forms the central theme of the Book of Jonah and although the prayer just made by Jonah seems sincere enough we will find later that the boundary of that repentance is still personal, possibly national[a] but not universal[b]

Ch 3

Jonah is called a second time to go to Nineveh. This time he goes. He enters the city and says..

Yet forty days, and Nineveh shall be overthrown. [c] (v4)

At this declaration to the people of Nineveh they all immediately believe and repent, proclaiming a fast and wearing sackcloth even up to the king who also issues a decree that all,

---

[c] Tarshish the city famed for its wealth and merchant fleet (1 Kings 10:22) Location unknown but essentially, for Jonah, its location being about as far away as you can get from Israel

[a] As an Israelite

[b] As implied by the fish *vomiting* Jonah upon the dry land

[c] This statement is the entirety of Jonah's spoken prophecy in the book

even the animal livestock, (who must not be fed or watered) should fast and cry up to G-d in the hope that..

Who knows whether God will not turn and repent,
and turn away from his fierce anger, that we perish not? (v9)

The next verse continues with G-d's response to them..

And God saw their works; that they turned from their evil way;
and God repented of the evil which he said he would do unto them; and he did it not. (v10) [a]

Ch 4
When Jonah sees that his prophecy to the Ninevites has caused them to repent he is angry. He prays to YHWH complaining that he knew this would happen as..

that thou are a gracious God, and merciful, slow to anger,
and of great kindness, and repents thee of the evil (v2)[b]

Jonah wishes for his death. He now shows his inner intention that he has carried all along- his death wish, now turned on himself. YHWH simply asks if he is right to be angry. Jonah goes out of the city up on the east side and makes a tent for shade while he waits to see what will ultimately happen to the city.[c]
YHWH then begins a final lesson for Jonah. He appoints a leafy plant[d] to grow and shade Jonah's head to relieve some of his anger.[e] Jonah is indeed happy when the plant appears and shades him. Then G-d prepares a worm to come to kill the plant and it withers away; then G-d prepares a scorching east wind. The sun again beats down on Jonah's head and again he wishes for his death.
Again G-d asks if he is right to be angry (now about the plant) Jonah exclaims that he is so angry he wishes he were dead. YHWH says in His final response..

Thou have had regard for the gourd, for which thou have not laboured, neither made it grow;
which came up in a night, and perished in a night:
and should not I have regard for Nineveh, that great city,
wherein are more than six-score thousand persons that cannot discern
between their right hand and their left hand; (v10-11)

---

[a] Matthew 12:38-42, Mark 8:12, Luke 11:29-32. The Sign of Jonah - of repentance. Mark gives no further elaboration to the faithless request for a sign. Matthew mentions the time spent in the fish's stomach (Jonah's prayer) associating it first with the time of Jesus in the tomb, then mentioning the repentance of the Ninevites. Luke makes the direct statement that just as Jonah was the sign (call to repentance) to the Ninevites so was Jesus to his generation.
[b] Quoted from Exo. 34.6
[c] At the end of the 40 days?
[d] Gourd. Qîqāyôn. Probably a castor oil plant which grows in Palestine. A leafy quick growing plant that grows as tall as a tree
[e] Anger as stated at the beginning of the chapter

Micah

Micah's prophecy begins *in the days of Jotham, Ahaz, and Hezekiah, kings of Judah.*[a] Micah's prophecy is stated as toward Samaria[b] and Jerusalem. YHWH is about to bring His judgement upon them for their corruption, Israel first then Judah. They are to be destroyed and the people taken away into captivity as punishment. Micah however goes on to say that after that they will eventually be restored to the glorious future as YHWH had promised beforehand. The book consists of a brief introduction 1.1, then three sections -

1) 1.2--2.11 Oracles of judgment
   2.12-13 Oracles of restoration
2) 3.1-12 Oracles of judgment
   4.1--5.15 Oracles of restoration
3) 6.1--7.6 Oracles of judgment
   7.7-20 Oracles of restoration

This Judgement/restoration theme also forms the chiastic structure to the book which places chapters 4-5 (the glorious future) at the centre.

Ch 1

A theophany is described, in a way reminiscent of YHWH's appearance at Mount Sinai, but now His arrival is in judgement of the Israelites for the idolatry taking pace both in Samaria and reaching as far as Judah. The Assyrian empire is to be brought in to destroy Israel and the people taken into captivity.

I will yet bring unto thee, O inhabitant of Mareshah,[c] *him*[d] *that shall possess thee: the glory of Israel*[e] *shall come even unto Adullam.*[f] (v15)

Ch 2

With the sin of the people focused around the Land, Micah notes that the leaders have become land-grabbers and spend their time planning how to steal their next field from the poor. Micah tells them this is not the way of YHWH but they don't want to listen. They will listen only to the 'prophets' who tell them what they want to hear. They continue with their oppression whilst believing the 'lying' prophets who tell them that their increasing material wealth is a blessing from G-d.

---

[a] The same time period as Isaiah (as stated in Isaiah 1.1.)

[b] Capital of the kingdom of Israel

[c] A city in Judah. Play on words Mareshah sounds like Morashah, the Hebrew word for inheritance. Israel's inheritance of the Land

[d] A conquering nation - Assyria

[e] The people and it's rulers

[f] The caves where David took refuge

Verse 12-13, in an abrupt theme change, moves to the rescue of Israel by YHWH. He will gather the righteous remnant with a righteous leader together and lead them out of this 'captivity.'

Ch 3
Micah returns to the theme of condemnation of the leaders. They are supposed to know justice yet they are likened to cannibals of the people. The other 'prophets' too, with their prophecies of peace in the face of war, will be silenced. The spirit of prophecy will be removed from them, Micah says..

But as for me, I am full of power by the Spirit of YHWH,
and of judgment, and of might,
to declare unto Jacob his transgression, and to Israel his sin. (v8)

Micah again addresses the leaders of the people..

The heads thereof judge for reward, and the priests thereof teach for hire,
and the prophets thereof divine for money: yet they lean upon YHWH, and say,
Is not YHWH in the midst of us? no evil shall come upon us.
Therefore shall Zion for your sake be ploughed as a field, and Jerusalem shall become heaps,
and the mountain of the house as the high places of a forest. (v11-12)

Ch 4
Returning to the theme of restoration, in a reference to the aftermath of the coming destruction of the Temple / Jerusalem just mentioned.

..the mountain of YHWH's house shall be established again. (v1)

Verses 1-5[a] continue with the central position the Temple in Jerusalem will have on Earth. It will be a focal point for all the nations and peoples, who will come to be taught of YHWH's ways and follow in them. All people will live in peace and worship YHWH. The Israelites will be returned to the Land and the kingdom restored.
Verse 9 then continues with a prophecy of the capture of Jerusalem by the Babylonians. The Israelite king is removed and they are left without any councillor to help them. They will cry as a woman in labour as they are taken to Babylon. They will be saved eventually, but it will be YHWH who does this. The nations who have it in mind to conquer *the daughter of Zion* don't know they will be there at YHWH's behest as a judgement and punishment to His people. Eventually YHWH will restore them and those nations will be in their service. Israel will devote all their gain to YHWH.

---

[a] Verse 1-3 appears to directly quote Isaiah 2.2-4

Ch 5
A leader will come from the small town of Beth-lehem Ephrather[a] after the Israelites have been returned..

And he shall stand, and shall feed his flock in the strength of YHWH,
in the majesty of the name of YHWH his God:
and they shall abide; for now shall he be great unto the ends of the earth. (v4)

Invading nations will come to nothing as this leader will quickly remove them. The remnant of Israel (Jacob) will spread into all of the nations where they will be in charge of events. Idolatry and weaponry will be ended in Israel and in the nations.

Ch 6
YHWH then brings a kind of legal suit[b] against Israel. He says..

O my people, what have I done unto thee? and wherein have I wearied thee? (v3)

YHWH has saved the Israelites many times. What is it that YHWH wants from his people? Is it endless sacrifices? Verse 8 continues..

He has showed thee, O man, what is good; and what does YHWH require of thee?
but to do justly, and to love kindness, and to walk humbly with thy God?

YHWH begins a denunciation of the people. He says the wise man will understand what He is doing with the Assyrian invasion. Will the unjust continue unchecked? Can Jerusalem be cleansed? The people and its rulers are filled with deceit. Now they will be frustrated by YHWH in whatever they try to do. They have followed the ways of Omri and Ahab (who abandoned the worship of YHWH in favour of Baal), now they will be given over to ruin and derision.
Leviticus 26 gives a list of rewards for obedience and punishments for disobedience (similar in theme to Deuteronomy 26 (Blessings & Curses) Micah makes reference to these lists now connecting them to the present situation (v13-16)

---

[a] Meaning to bear fruit / be fruitful. Rachel died here giving birth to Benjamin (Gen 35.19). David's father came from here. A statement similar to Isaiah 11.1 *And there shall come forth a shoot out of the stock of Jesse, and a branch out of his roots shall bear fruit.*
[b] Similarities to Deuteronomy 32:1, Isaiah 1:2.

Ch 7.
There is terrible corruption in the land with the people, they only do evil; their leaders the same. YHWH's judgement has come and the people are in confusion..

Trust ye not in a neighbour; put ye not confidence in a friend;
keep the doors of thy mouth from her that lies in thy bosom.
For the son dishonours the father, the daughter rises up against her mother,
the daughter-in-law against her mother-in-law;
a man's enemies are the men of his own house. (v5-6)

Micah says he will wait for the salvation of his G-d even though Israel is downtrodden at the moment. However the enemies will be overcome and Israel's borders increased. Israel will be restored as of old. YHWH will send more marvellous signs as after the departure from Egypt. The nations will be ashamed of their hostility towards Israel.

The book ends with an ode in praise of God's mercy and faithfulness.

.

Who is a God like unto thee, that pardons iniquity,
and passes over the transgression of the remnant of His heritage?
He retains not his anger forever, because He delights in loving-kindness.
He will again have compassion upon us; He will tread our iniquities under foot;
and will cast all their sins into the depths of the sea.
You will perform the truth to Jacob, and the loving-kindness to Abraham,
which You have sworn unto our fathers from the days of old. (v18-20)

Nahum

Chapter 1 begins..

The burden of Nineveh. The book of the vision of Nahum[a] *the Elkoshite.* (v1)

There then follows a partial (half alphabet) acrostic hymn extolling the power and sovereignty of YHWH over the Earth and His enemies. (v1-8)[b]
Verse 9 continues. A nation (Assyria) has risen up against Him and His people. That nation will be cut down freeing YHWH's people.

Behold, upon the mountains the feet of him that brings good tidings that publishes peace![c]
Keep thy feasts, O Judah, perform thy vows;
for the wicked one shall no more pass through thee; he is utterly cut off. (v15)

---

[a] Meaning 'comfort'
[b] The remaining part of prophecy now highly poetic. The acrostic reserved for the Hymn to YHWH?
[c] A verse modelled upon Isaiah 52.7

Ch 2
The language here is highly poetic; it describes Nineveh the great and arrogant city now being besieged and captured by Babylon (and the Medes).[a]

Ch 3
The once proud city teaming with soldiers and their equipment is now destroyed and the people therein led off in captivity. The peoples of cities who have been under her rule now clap their hands with joy at her fall.

Habakkuk[b]

The burden [c] *which Habakkuk the prophet did see.* (v1)

Habakkuk's first two chapters follow a lament[d] structure whilst exploring the concept of theodicy.[e] The book does not address the Israeli people or her leaders, but is a personal enquiry into how a good G-d seems to stand by whilst allowing evil to run seemingly uncontrolled. The final chapter is a psalm; written on subject and following closely the structure of many of the psalms within the Book of Psalms.

Ch 1
Habakkuk is witnessing the corruption within Jerusalem and Judah at some point during the last years before the Babylonian conquest.[f]
Habakkuk complains to YHWH; the Law is neglected; there is violence and injustice everywhere and all is tolerated and propagated by the leaders. He cries out to YHWH and pleads for Him to do something.
YHWH then makes His reply, beginning with..

Behold ye among the nations, and look, and wonder marvellously;
for I am working a work in your days, which ye will not believe though it be told you. (v5)

---

[a] An event which took place in 612BC. The Battle of Nineveh
[b] Derived from the meaning 'to embrace'
[c] The Hebrew word מַשָּׂא [maśśā'] also meaning utterance, oracle [a weighty oracle against..]
[d] The lament structure begins with a turning to address G-d in communication. Then a complaint is put forward. The third element is then to ask G-d to intervene and the last part of the lament is of trust. Trust that G-d will act
[e] Why G-d allows evil
[f] The same time period of Jeremiah also

YHWH then goes on to explain that He is about to bring up the Chaldeans,[a] the cruel violent arrogant Chaldeans, to punish Jerusalem. Habakkuk then complains to YHWH, how can a good and righteous G-d enlist the help of such an unjust people to implement His judgements.

Ch 2
Verse 1 continues with Habakkuk's response..

I will stand upon my watch,[b] *and set me upon the tower, and will look forth to see what he will speak with me and what I shall answer concerning my complaint.*

YHWH does answer, and asks Habakkuk to write down the contents of His answer on a tablet in plain, easy to read language. Habakkuk, in chapter 1, has complained of the corruption of the leaders, presumably in Jerusalem, the answer now given focuses on the Babylonians and the punishment for *their corruption.* What is to be written concerns events of the near future. The prophecy begins with..

Behold, his soul is puffed up, it is not upright in him;
but the righteous shall live in His faith. (v4)

YHWH continues with a condemnation of Babylon.[c] The words are a prediction of her destruction by the very same people who she has oppressed. There are then five woes (condemnations) described of the typical actions of the nation driven by such a *puffed up soul*[d] which are unacceptable to YHWH and bring Judgement. The last verse (although sounding more as an interlude to the next chapter than what has just been said) follows on from the theme of idolatry introduced in v18-19.

But YHWH is in his holy temple: let all the earth keep silence before him. (v20)

Ch 3
The prayer of Habakkuk, written as a psalm, Habakkuk acknowledges YWHW's ultimate power and authority as to what happens on Earth and requests that He returns now as He has in the past to enact His Justice and save His people.

You went forth for the salvation of thy people, for the salvation of your anointed;
You wound the head out of the house of the wicked. (v13)

---

[a] Babylonians
[b] Prophets being regarded as 'watchmen' of Israel
[c] Reflecting the same arrogance of the Assyrians in the preceding book of Nahum 2) Also reflecting the call to faith of the following book of Zephaniah
[d] *Transgression by wine* (v5). The 'wine' being the adopted corrupt spirit

Habakkuk is frightened by the sheer power of what YHWH will do to both Israel and ultimately to the Babylonians. He now awaits the destruction that will come when they invade, however, *in faith*, he ends by saying..

Yet I will rejoice in YHWH, I will delight in the God of my salvation.
YHWH, the Lord, is my strength;
and he makes my feet like hinds' feet,
And will make me to walk upon my high places. (v18-19)

Zephaniah

Zephaniah is called to be a prophet during the days of King Josiah [a]
Although Josiah did try to bring back the worship of YHWH and the people to the adherence to the Law, his efforts would not be enough; Judgement is now cast upon Jerusalem and Judah for their continual corruption and idolatry. They are to be utterly destroyed.

The great day of YHWH is near; it is near and hastens greatly,
even the voice of the day of YHWH; (the mighty man cries there bitterly). (v14)

A great distress will befall the people and nothing will be able to save them out of its hand.

Ch 2
Zephaniah makes a plea to those righteous people who remain to continue in meekness and to seek YHWH in the hope that He will save them when the calamity arrives. All the peoples of the surrounding lands will be uprooted, but the faithful remnant will find themselves in safety in those new areas. The peoples of Moab and Ammon will be *made as Sodom* for their continuing aggression toward Judah and Jerusalem. YHWH will end all the idolatry of the nations and they all shall serve Him. The destruction will continue right up to the Assyrian city of Nineveh.

Ch 3
Condemnation is further directed at Jerusalem. She has not listened to the voice of YHWH. Her leaders are corrupt; her prophets traitors and her priests profane the Sanctuary. YHWH in the midst of her remains righteous. He has brought judgement on the nations before and their cities now lie as uninhabited ruins. YHWH continues..

I said, Only fear thou me; receive correction;
so her dwelling shall not be cut off,
according to all that I have appointed concerning her:

---

[a] (1.1). 2) Jeremiah is also noted as beginning his prophet hood in the thirteenth year of his reign (Jer 1.2)

but they rose early and corrupted all their doings. (v7)

YHWH again addresses the righteous and calls the remnant to wait for Him until He has assembled all the rebellious nations for their judgement.

For then will I turn to the peoples of a pure language,
that they may all call upon the name of YHWH, to serve him with one consent. (v9)

All of Israel including those of the diaspora will come back and be forgiven. All the proud and exulting ones shall be removed.

I shall leave among you a humble and lowly people,
and they shall take refuge in the name of YHWH [a]
The remnant of Israel shall not do iniquity, nor speak lies;
neither shall a deceitful tongue be found in their mouth;
for they shall feed and lie down, and none shall make them afraid. (v12-13)

Israel is then called to sing for joy as her judgements have been taken away and her enemies removed...

the King of Israel, YHWH, is in the midst of thee;
thou shall not fear evil any more. (v15)

Haggai [b]

The book of Haggai begins a subsection within *the Book of the Twelve* [c] which includes the books of Zechariah and Malachi. These three books, bringing the Old Testament to a close, are set in the period of the returned Exiles and cover the events and continuing prophetic revelation in their affairs with the promise of restoration. It is with this in mind that the three books can be read as a prophecy with a single story line.

The prophecy of Haggai covers a period of less than four months.[d] The first part of Haggai's prophecy[e] begins by informing Zerubbabel and Joshua that the time to finish building the Temple has come. The people should put themselves right before YHWH for this to happen, which they do. A modest Temple is being built but Haggai informs the people not to worry as eventually this new temple will be greater than the first. Haggai then speaks to the priests about the Law (Torah) and its application. If the people are in a state of ritual uncleanliness[f]

---

[a] LXX has.. And I shall leave behind among you people a gentle, and humble; and they shall show reverence at the name of YHWH

[b] Meaning celebration of festival (of YHWH)

[c] As it is known in the Hebrew. The twelve (minor) prophets

[d] The dates for this are unusually accurately stated in the text

[e] Refer to the events of Ezra 4.24 – 6.12

[f] טָמֵא [ṭâmê'] foul in a religious/moral sense

then all their work will be in the same state and it is this that has held them back. They need to turn their hearts to YHWH to succeed. Haggai's last prophecy is directed to Zerubbabel alone and is undoubtedly understood as royalist in orientation. The restarting of the building work alone had brought the attention of the Persian king; this last prophecy now would have again caused more consternation.[a]

Ch 1
On the 1st day of the 6th month of the second year of king Darius (520BC), Haggai brings the word from YHWH and informs Zerubbabel and Joshua that the time has come for the returned exiles to re-start the building of the Temple. They have been busying themselves with their personal projects since the order[b] preventing them from rebuilding it was issued. This restarting of work on the Temple is reported to Darius.[c] After searching for and then finding the original decree of Cyrus, Darius gives permission for the work to continue. Haggai informs the people that the restarting of the work on the Temple should be their priority but they have been content thus far in building their own houses. Haggai says it is this unwillingness to start the Temple building that has led to them being beset by numerous problems.

Now therefore thus says YHWH of hosts:[d] Consider your ways.
Ye have sown much, and bring in little; ye eat, but ye have not enough;
ye drink, but ye are not filled with drink; ye clothe you, but there is none warm;
and he that earns wages earns wages to put it into a purse with holes. (v5-6)

The people do then listen to Haggai and obey the voice of YHWH. Haggai then gives YHWH's message to the people, saying..

I am with you, says YHWH.
And YHWH stirred up the spirit of Zerubbabel the son of Shealtiel, governor[e] of Judah,
and the spirit of Joshua the son of Jehozadak, the high priest,
and the spirit of all the remnant of the people;
and they came and did work on the house of YHWH of hosts, their God (v13-14)

The work then restarts on the 24th of the 6th month in Darius 2nd year.

Ch 2
It's the 21st day of the 7th month,[f] and the new Temple is complete. Haggai has another message (his second) from YHWH. He asks the people to compare the new Temple with that

---

[a] The name Zerubbabel is last mentioned in chapter 5 of Ezra where Haggai and Zechariah inform him that the time has come to restart the building work of the Temple, which he does.
[b] Ezra 4.11-24
[c] Ezra 6.1-12
[d] A militaristic appellation for YHWH
[e] פֶּחָה [pechâh] Aramaic loan word used here by the Persians (a Persian governor for an area)
[f] This date coinciding with the last day of the Feast of Tabernacles. (Lev 23.33-36; Lev 23.39-43)

of the destroyed one and notes how this new Temple seems as nothing in their eyes. They are encouraged to be strong as YHWH is with them and that all the promises given to them in the past will soon come true and the glory of this present Temple will be greater than the first. On the 24th day of the ninth month comes Haggai's third prophecy; he speaks to the priests about ceremonial cleanliness and uncleanliness and how this state is passed from one person / thing to another. Haggai says it is this uncleanliness which has held the people back in their efforts so far; right from the laying of the foundation stones when they were released by Cyrus until the present, but..

....from this day will I bless you (v19)

The word of YHWH comes again to Haggai that same day asking him to speak to Zerubbabel, saying..

I will shake the heavens and the earth; and I will overthrow the throne of kingdoms;
and I will destroy the strength of the kingdoms of the nations;[a]
and I will overthrow the chariots, and those that ride in them;
and the horses and their riders shall come down, everyone by the sword of his brother.
In that day, says YHWH of hosts,
I will take thee, O Zerubbabel, my servant, the son of Shealtiel, says YHWH,
and will make thee as a signet; for I have chosen thee, says YHWH of hosts. (v21-23)

Zechariah

Zechariah begins his prophecy in the eighth month of the second year of Darius. He declares to the people that YHWH had been angry with their ancestors but now the message is..

Return unto me, says YHWH of hosts, and I will return unto you. (v2)

The people are urged to actually hear, listen[b] and act upon the words that YWWH gives to them through His prophets, something they have not done in the past. Ultimately this rebellious nature of their ancestors has led them to where they are today. YHWH's intentions will eventually come to be.

..and they returned and said, Like as YHWH of hosts thought to do unto us,
according to our ways, and according to our doings, so has he dealt with us.[c] (v6)

---

[a] Repeated again from verse 6-7
[b] Another *nah'say nishmah* moment
[c] Lam. 2.17 *YHWH has done that which he purposed;*
he has fulfilled his word that he commanded in the days of old;
He has thrown down, and has not pitied: And he has caused the enemy to rejoice over thee;
he has exalted the horn of thine adversaries.

Verse 7 begins a new section in the book with the first of eight visions which Zechariah receives. The general location of the visions seems to be in or around Jerusalem, although not in a physical sense. These visions, pictorially and symbolically give Zechariah's prophecy for the restoration of Israel, now in progress.
It should be noted here that Zechariah's prophecy (as well as those of Haggai) are announced to the returned exiles whilst they continue to be under the overarching control of a foreign power. The 70 years of Jeremiah's prophecy are almost up, and so what shape will this restoration take? With the limited authority to rebuild and operate the Temple, the hopes of restoring a monarchy fade but the role of the High Priest increase.
The 1st and 8th vision give information as to the state of the surrounding nations; visions 2 & 3 depict the restoration of Jerusalem; visions 4 & 5 (central visions) the restoration of the Temple and the priesthood; 6 & 7 the cleaning of the Holy Land.

The first vision. On the 24th day of the eleventh month[a] of Darius's 2nd year Zechariah sees a rider (the Angel of YHWH) on a red horse with other horses behind him. They have been sent by YHWH to travel throughout the Earth. They bring the report that the world is at peace. The angel enquires..

how long will thou not have mercy on Jerusalem and on the cities of Judah,
against which thou have had indignation these threescore and ten years?[b] (v13)

The angel says YHWH has a great jealousy for Jerusalem and Zion and also displeasure at the way the nations have exceeded YHWH's punishment. YHWH says He is now to return His Mercies and restore Jerusalem and the House of YHWH..

my house shall be built in it, says YHWH of hosts,
and a line shall be stretched forth over Jerusalem.
Cry yet again, saying, thus says YHWH of hosts:
My cities shall yet overflow with prosperity;
and YHWH shall yet comfort Zion, and shall yet choose Jerusalem. (v16-17)

Verse 18 begins the second vision. Zechariah sees four horns,[c] they are the powers who have been scattering Judah and Israel. Four artisans then arrive sent by YHWH; they are there to cast down the four horns.

---

[a] Exactly 5 months after the work on the Temple resumed
[b] A reference to Jeremiah's 70 year prophecy, now almost arrived at
[c] Earthly powers, nations

Ch 2

In the third vision Zechariah then sees a man with a measuring line. He is going to measure the city of Jerusalem. Another angel goes out to meet the man who is to measure and tells him..

Jerusalem shall be inhabited as villages without walls,
by reason of the multitude of men and cattle therein.
For I, says YHWH, will be unto her a wall of fire on every side,
and I will be the glory in the midst of her. (v4-5)

YHWH then pleads for the people to flee from the nations, for Zion to escape from the daughter of Babylon. They have been plunderers, now they will be plundered by those that served them. YHWH promises that His presence will again return.

Sing and rejoice, O daughter of Zion; for, lo, I come,
and I will dwell in the midst of thee, says YHWH (v10)

Many nations will join[a] themselves to YHWH and be his people.

And YHWH shall inherit Judah as His portion in the holy land,
and shall yet choose Jerusalem.
Be silent, all flesh, before YHWH; for He is aroused out of His holy habitation.[b] (v12-13)

Ch 3

In the fourth vision Zechariah is shown Joshua the high priest being initiated. Joshua is standing before the angel of YHWH. Satan is standing to his right as his adversary. YHWH speaks; He rejects Satan and choses Jerusalem. Joshua has been saved to be the High priest and exchanges his filthy clothes for rich apparel. The angel of YHWH then charges Joshua..

If thou will walk in my ways, and if thou will keep my charge,
then thou also shall judge my house, and shall also keep my courts. (v6-7)

Joshua's associates are then called to witness as the Angel of YHWH declares He will now bring forth His servant, *the Branch.*[c] Also a *stone with seven eyes,*[d] is set before Joshua,

---

[a] The Hebrew has 'join'; the LXX has 'take refuge'

[b] Deut 26 15 Look down from thy holy habitation, from heaven, and bless thy people Israel, and the ground which thou hast given us, as thou swore unto our fathers, a land flowing with milk and honey.

[c] Zerubbabel (of the Davidic monarchy). Also used as of a remnant of the people (Isaiah 4.2)

[d] 2 Chron 6.20 & 6.40. 2) the word [ayin] H5869 can also be translated as 'fountain' (11 times in the OT) therefore also in reference to the water & rock of Moses 3) Engraved- the word [patah] H6605 (also used in this verse) is commonly translated as 'open' as with Isa 41.18 *I will open rivers in high places and fountains in the midst of the valleys.* This makes more sense for the fountains to *remove the iniquity of the land.* 4) Zechariah 13.1 *there shall be a fountain opened [patah] to the house of David and the inhabitants of Jerusalem*

representing the Temple or the presence of YHWH within it. The Angel of YHWH then declares that He will remove the iniquity from the land and everyone will live in peace and happiness.[a]

Ch4

Zechariah's fifth vision has the seven branched candlestick (Menorah) with two olive trees, one either side which supply the oil.[b] Oddly when Zechariah asks the explanation for this vision it is given by the angel as..

Then he answered and spoke unto me, saying,
This is the word of YHWH unto Zerubbabel, saying,
Not by might, nor by power, but by my Spirit, says YHWH of hosts. (v6)

Here again, as in the second vision, YHWH becomes the personal protector of a Jerusalem which does not need a city wall nor an army. The builder of the Temple will also do so successfully by this power alone. Zerubbabel is then noted to have laid the first stone[c] of the Temple and now it is said that he will lay the last. The seven lights of the candlestick and the seven eyes of the stone[d] will rejoice in Zerubbabel's leadership of the building project.

Zechariah asks the meaning of the two olive branches and is told they..

are the two anointed ones, that stand by the Lord of the whole earth. (v14)

Which in the context of Zechariah would appear to be Zerubbabel and Joshua who will serve YHWH. Also possible as two spiritual beings which themselves empower Zerubbabel and Joshua or empower Zechariah and Haggai.

Ch 5

In the sixth vision Zechariah sees a 10 cubit by 20 cubit flying scroll which travels through the entire land. The scroll is described as..

This is the curse that goes forth over the face of the whole land:
for every one that steals shall be cut off on the one side according to it;
and every one that swears[e] shall be cut off. (v 3)

---

[a] As they had done in Solomon's time (1 Kings 4.25)

[b] Echoing Exodus 27.20-22 (the operation and design within the Tabernacle by Aaron and his sons) The Olive oil and the Menorah it supplies being central themes within the Tabernacle. 2) Olive oil being *the* Anointing oil of the OT 3) Ultimately the oil and the candlestick work together in the production of **light**

[c] Ezra 3.8. Zerubbabel leads the laying of the temple foundation

[d] YHWH and His people

[e] Falsely in the name of YHWH

The words written on the scroll[a] will therefore prevent the corruption of the people so that they do not sin against each other or against YHWH.

In the seventh vision Zechariah sees an 'ephah' of which there seems to be many in the land. Within the 'ephah' is a woman described as wickedness. Two other women with stork's wings then carry the 'ephah' back to Shinah (Babylon).
The vision itself concerns the removal of idolatry from the Land now being restored by YHWH.[b] The 'ephah' [c] here is unlikely to be a measure of grain as commonly understood but as an idol's throne/shrine in which is held a female idol (such as Ishtah or the Queen of Heaven.[d]) This idolatry and all idolatry is to be removed and returned to where it came from, in this case Babylon, where the appropriate house/temple/ziggurat will be made for it. The carrying by stork-winged women is mocking the movement of this 'ephah' as bringing to mind the Throne of YHWH carried by the cherubim in Ezekiel 1 / Isaiah 6.

Ch 6
Zechariah's eighth vision is of four chariots emerging from two mountains. This vision resembles the first vision (of horses) and its location the same, although described differently. In this vision chariots[e] are seen with the horses and they travel north and south.[f] The chariot going to the north country [g] is described as having 'quieted my spirit' (v8). This would give an indication that this vision relates to the Babylonians.[h] The southward travelling chariot would then be going to the Egyptians (who were also heavily involved in the events leading up to the exile of Judah).
In the first vision of horses of chapter 1 it is the red horse[i] which is at the forefront with the Angel of the YHWH upon it. In this vision the red horse is again at the forefront. This red horse-chariot is not described as moving off to any place. It could then be that the appearance of the 'bay[j] coloured horse of verse 7 is the red horse just described. The bay horse-chariot is then described as seeking[k] to walk throughout the entire Earth (rather than just north etc).

---

[a] The scroll is reminiscent of the Law. Perhaps Lev 26 / Deut. 28 Blessings and Curses 2) The Law fully active within the city

[b] Including possibly the problem of foreign wives

[c] A Sumerian word E-pa (housing for a female god)?

[d] Popular amongst the people of Judah according to Jeremiah 44

[e] Chariots although associated with warfare, are mostly described in the OT as used by dignitaries (Pharaoh, Joseph, Naaman)

[f] Several bible translations indicate the white horse going west. The word 'west' is not found in the Hebrew or the LXX. The white horse follows after the black

[g] Jeremiah refers to the Babylonians as the 'north country / from the north' some 25 times

[h] Recently subdued by the Persians

[i] אָד֖ם ['āḏōm] H122. The red horse is one of four horses described by colouring

[j] Reddish brown

[k] To strive after; desire to do

This horse-chariot is then given permission from the Angel to *walk to and fro through the earth.* (v6)[a]
Verse 9 returns to ongoing events in Jerusalem. Zechariah is directed to go to certain returned exiles who have gold and silver for him. He is then to ask a smith to make crowns (plural) with it and then..

.. set them upon the head of Joshua the son of Jehozadak, the high priest;
and speak unto him, saying, Thus speaks YHWH of hosts, saying,
Behold! the man whose name is the Branch:
and he shall grow up out of his place; and he shall build the temple of YHWH;
he shall build the temple of YHWH; and he shall bear the glory,
and shall sit and rule upon his throne; and he shall be a priest upon his throne;
and the counsel of peace shall be between them both. (v11-13)

The high priest is now to have a dual role including the monarchy. Joshua is here noted as being himself the branch, the one who will build the Temple and the one who will rule as a priest. Presumably the building here is of its function rather than its form (Zerubbabel's job) The chapter ends with..

And they that are far off shall come and build in the temple of YHWH;
and ye shall know that YHWH of hosts has sent me unto you.
And this shall come to pass, if ye will diligently obey the voice of YHWH your God. (v15)

As with many prophesies before, the people are warned that their future happiness and prosperity is dependent upon them obeying YHWH.

Ch 7
In the 4th day of the 9th month of the 4th year of Darius some of the leading people of Beth'El come to Jerusalem to make an enquiry as to whether the fast which they have been adhering to, in commemoration of the destruction of the Temple by Nebuchadnezzar, should be continued now that the new Temple is nearing completion.
Zechariah's response is that during the last 70 years they have fasted in vain for their own pleasure rather than in sorrow for what happened.[b] He gives YHWH's answer and says..

---

[a]The exact purpose of walking to and fro on the Earth is not clear. There are no indications of violent intentions for any of these horse-chariots. 2) In Job 1.7 Satan is described as הָלַךְ, אֶרֶץ שׁוּט [hālaḵ 'ereṣ šûṭ] going to and fro walking on the Earth. (The book of Job would have been known to Zechariah as Job is mentioned in Ezekiel 14) The exact reason of why Satan 'walks on the Earth' may have been clearer to Zechariah than it is to us
[b] In the fifth month the Babylonians had set fire to Jerusalem and the Temple (Jer.39.8; 2 Kings 25.9) 2) The seventh month, also mentioned is *The Fast of Gedeliah*. whose murder resulted in the remaining people, left behind by Nebuchadnezzar, leaving the Holy Land for Egypt (Jeremiah ch 40.7- ch 43.7)

Shouldn't you have heard the words which YHWH cried by the former prophets,
when Jerusalem was inhabited and in prosperity, and the cities thereof round about her,
and the South and the Lowland were inhabited? (v7)

Zechariah continues with YHWH's message saying it is not lip service which is required but a true turning to YHWH and the execution of true judgement to one another in kindness and compassion.

But they refused to hearken, and pulled away the shoulder,
and stopped their ears that they might not hear.
Yea, they made their hearts as an adamant stone, lest they should hear the Law,
and the words which YWHW of hosts had sent by his Spirit through the former prophets:
therefore there came great wrath from YWHW of hosts. (v11-12)

YHWH had cried to them they had not listened, then when they cried, He did not listen and ultimately scattered them amongst the nations.

Thus the land was desolate after them, so that no man passed through nor returned:
for they laid the pleasant land desolate.(v14)

Ch 8
YHWH reiterates[a] to Zechariah His great jealousy for Zion and says..

Thus says YHWH: I am returned unto Zion,
and will dwell in the midst of Jerusalem:
and Jerusalem shall be called The city of Truth;
and the Mountain of YHWH of hosts, The Holy Mountain. (v3)

The city of Jerusalem will be restored again with the old and young. All His people will be brought back to safety.

And they shall be my people, and I will be their God, in truth and in righteousness. (v8)

YHWH encourages the people to be strong and listen to His prophets for their troubles are over now. YHWH is with them..

For there shall be the seed of peace; the vine shall give its fruit,
and the ground shall give its increase, and the heavens shall give their dew;
and I will cause the remnant of this people to inherit all these things. (v12)

The house of Judah and the house of Israel will again be a blessing to the nations. YHWH has finished with His punishment and now seeks to do good for Judah and Jerusalem.

---

[a] Zech. 1.14 Thus says YHWH of hosts; I am jealous for Jerusalem and for Zion with a great jealousy.

Again[a] YHWH tells the people to be just and righteous to their neighbours..

And the word of YHWH of hosts came unto me, saying, thus says YHWH of hosts:[b]
The fast of the fourth month,[c] *and the fast of the fifth,*[d]
and the fast of the seventh,[e] *and the fast of the tenth,*[f]
shall be to the house of Judah joy and gladness, and cheerful feasts;
therefore love truth and peace. (v18-19)

Ch 9

A new section now begins. These chapters (9-14) are effectively the last prophecies of the Old Testament.[g] Often referred to as *Second Zechariah,*[h] but with very little within the remaining six chapters to indicate the exact timeframe.[i]

There is no further mention of the work to the establishment of the Temple or of Joshua and Zerubbabel.

The prophecy now changes to an apocalyptic nature, continuing the hope and expectation for the future of the remaining Israelites (centred now only on Jerusalem/Judea). Jeremiah's seventy years prophecy has long passed but still the people remain under the rule of imperial nations. Jerusalem and the Temple have been restored; prophecy still is being revealed showing YHWH's continuing concern, but now what is the future? When will Israel be restored to greatness and become *the light to the nations*? [j] When will the promises of YHWH through the ages to His people come to be?

Zechariah 9 now addresses this.

The burden of the word of YHWH upon the land of Hadrach [k] (v1)

Thus begins with prophecy against the surrounding nations bordering the sea to the north and west of Israel / Judah. They appear to be under attack. Judah doesn't need to worry as YHWH says..

---

[a] Zech 7.9-10

[b] Concerning the question of fasting beginning this prophetic section (ch 7)

[c] The running out of food within Jerusalem due to the siege and the breach of the city wall (Jer 52.6-7)

[d] The destruction of Jerusalem and the Temple (Jer 52.12-14)

[e] The Fast of Gedeliah. whose murder resulted in the remaining people, left by Nebuchadnezzar, leaving the Holy Land for Egypt (Jeremiah ch 40.7- ch 43.7)

[f] The siege of Jerusalem began (Ezekiel 24.2)

[g] Although the book of Malachi follows, Zechariah & Malachi are understood to relate to the same although later Post Exilic period.

[h] As with Isaiah. First Isaiah (the actions of the prophet in his lifetime 740-700BC apx); deutero or second Isaiah (prophecy during the exile (586-7 to 538 BC); trito or third Isaiah (the returned exiles 538-on)

[i] There is mention of Javani (H3120) Greece? Zech 9.13. 2) Joel 3.6 also has Javani (H3125) [Gentile nations]

[j] Isaiah 49 1-6

[k] An unknown name place person or idol relevant to the time of the prophecy's revelation. Likely to simply imply ' the nations '

And I will encamp about my house against the army,
that none pass through or return; and no oppressor shall pass through them any more:
for now have I seen with mine eyes.
Rejoice greatly, O daughter of Zion; shout, O daughter of Jerusalem:
Behold thy king [a] *comes unto thee; he is just, and having salvation;* [b]
lowly, and riding upon an ass, [c] *even upon a colt* [d] *the foal of an ass* [e] (v8-9)

A theme that will also occur later in this section, that YHWH now is personally involved in the leadership and defence of Jerusalem. This king will remove the equipment of warfare from the land proclaiming peace to the nations. Because of the *Covenant*, the captives of Jerusalem will be freed, returned and restored greater than before.
The sons of Judah and Ephraim (Israel united) will defeat the aggressors. YHWH himself will appear over Israel's 'army' and will go out to fight for them.

And YHWH their God will save them in that day as the flock of His people;
for they shall be as the stones of a crown, lifted on high over His Land. (v18)

Ch 10
Continuing the theme of restoration, YHWH is angry at the leaders (including the 'prophets' who advise them) of the people; they have led them astray and weakened them. YHWH *is with them* (v5). He will restore their strength as like mighty men ready for battle. Judah and Joseph[f] will be restored. YHWH will recall all of His people from the nations and they will fill the land. The nations themselves will be brought down.

Ch 11
Returning to the destruction of Jerusalem[g] and the enslavement of the people.
YHWH recounts how He had two staves (kingdoms of Judah and Israel) and how they rejected Him. The leaders (shepherds) did not take care of the people but left them to ruin.

---

[a] Zechariah's first mention of a king (a contentious issue for the returned exiles). Zechariah will return to the theme of YHWH as king in chapter 14. The humble, non-militaristic king who leads to victory. Zech 4.6 ...*This is the word of YHWH unto Zerubbabel, saying, Not by might, nor by power, but by my Spirit, says YHWH of hosts.*

[b] To save; saviour; deliver; preserve.

[c] חֲמוֹר [chămôwr] a male ass. The sons of David rode asses (2 Sa. 13 29) ; Solomon rode an ass to his coronation (1 Kings 1:38-40)

[d] עַיִר ['ayir] young, vigorous male ass

[e] אתון ['âthôwn] female ass; [from H386] enduring, patient, docile

[f] United Israel (verse 6)

[g] The Temple described as of the trees it was made with

Ch 12
A third section begins.

The burden [a] *of the word of YHWH concerning Israel.* (v1)[b]
Thus says YHWH, who stretches forth the heavens,
and lays the foundation of the earth,
and forms the spirit of man within him. (v1b)

Jerusalem will be protected by YHWH. All the nations around who attempt to attack her will be destroyed and the people strengthened.

In that day shall YHWH defend the inhabitants of Jerusalem;
and he that is feeble among them at that day shall be as David;
and the house of David shall be as God, as the angel of YHWH before them. (v8)

YHWH says..

And I will pour upon the house of David, and upon the inhabitants of Jerusalem,
the spirit of grace and of supplication;
and they shall look unto me whom they have pierced; and they shall mourn. (v10)

The people will really mourn when they realise how they have sinned in the past.

Ch 13
In that day..
YHWH will be as a cleansing fountain to the House of David (and all the people of Jerusalem). The idols, the prophets and the unclean spirits will be sent out of the land. Prophets will be rejected by their own parents and told not to prophesy (or be pierced through by them). The prophets will be ashamed of their visions and deny that they even are prophets. YHWH then calls for a sword to brought against the leaders also. The leaderless people will then be scattered, two thirds of them will die; but the remaining third will be purified in the same way gold and silver is purified then..

They shall call on my Name, and I will hear them:
I will say, It is my people; and they shall say, YHWH is my God. (v9)

Ch 14
A day of the Lord is coming. All the nations will be brought up to war against Jerusalem. The city will be captured and looted; half of the people taken away into captivity. Then YHWH will go out to war against the nations which have warred against her. YHWH will stand on

---

[a] A burdensome prophecy of judgement
[b]As opposed to Hadrach in chapter 9.1

the Mount of Olives; there will be an earthquake and the sun will fail to shine. On that day Living water will flow out from Jerusalem to the east and to the west.

And YHWH shall be King over all the earth:
in that day shall YHWH be One, and his name One. (v9)

The whole of the Promised Land from north to south will be levelled but the city of Jerusalem will be raised up on her place. There will be no more curses, Jerusalem will dwell in safety. All the nations who have warred against Jerusalem will be stricken with flesh rotting plagues. All their wealth, silver and gold, will then be gathered together for Jerusalem. All the remaining people of the nations..

..that came against Jerusalem shall go up from year to year
to worship the King, YHWH of hosts. (v16)

All the remaining people of the nations will also keep the Feast of Tabernacles.[a]

And it shall be, that whoso of all the families of the earth goes not up unto Jerusalem to worship the King, YHWH of hosts, upon them there shall be no rain. (v17)

In that day everything in Jerusalem will be holy. Even the headdresses of horses will be written HOLY UNTO YHWH as was the turban of the high priest. The pots in people's homes will be as holy as the Temple vessels. There shall be found no profane person in the House of YHWH.

Malachi

Rather than a personal name Malachi is an adjective meaning *my messenger*. This book being anonymous with the name being taken from the first verse..

The burden of the word of YHWH to Israel by the hand of my messenger. (v1)[b]

---

[a] Commemorating the Exodus and the dependence of the people of Israel on the Will of G-d.

Ye shall dwell in booths seven days; all that are home-born in Israel shall dwell in booths;
that your generations may know that I made the children of Israel to dwell in booths,
when I brought them out of the land of Egypt: I am YHWH your God. Lev 23. 42-43

[b] The interesting feature of this verse, noted by scholars is that the format '*the burden of the word of YHWH* ' only appears three times in the OT with the other two occurrences being the headings of the last prophecies in the book of (second) Zechariah, just read. Which are Zechariah 9 *The burden of the word of YHWH... upon the land of Hadrach;* and Zechariah 12 *The burden of the word of YHWH ...concerning Israel.*
Each section there with three chapters. As we now move into the next section (Malachi) also of three chapters (in the Hebrew) there again is the format *The burden of the word of YHWH*. This has led scholars to see the book of Malachi as a continuance of (second) Zechariah (ch 9-14) whilst maintaining the twelve books with,

Things had moved on some time now after Ezra-Nehemiah. The Temple has been built, Jerusalem restored, a new generation of people populate Jerusalem/Judah. None of the great promises to their ancestors and prophets have come to be and now their perspective has changed; they are sceptics who believe that G-d has no effect in human affairs. The old observances had been outgrown as seen in the public worship. Foreign cults were the order of the day. Despite this however, there still seems to be a group of people remaining faithful[a] to whom the prophecy is ultimately directed.
Chapter 1 through 3.15 explore the covenant violations of priests and the people in contrast to YHWH's faithfulness to it. YHWH has always been faithful to his people throughout the ages but the people don't see it that way. YHWH makes a series of statements each reflecting His faithfulness to the Israelites. They in turn reject each of these statements as untrue.
Chapter 3.16 through 4.6 forms a conclusion explaining that YHWH will return in Judgement. The wicked, like stubble[b] will be for the fire. The righteous who honoured YHWH will become His *treasured possession.*

Ch 1

I have loved you, says YHWH. Yet ye say, ***How have thou loved us?*** (v2a)[c]

The people complain that this is not true; from their perspective they can see that trouble has followed them everywhere throughout their history as a people, ultimately leading to the Exile and the destruction / desolation of the Land. They also still find themselves remaining under foreign rule and not in the privileged position they had expected according to the promises given them. YHWH's answer to this is…

Was not Esau Jacob's brother? Says YHWH:
yet I loved Jacob; but Esau I hated,
and made his mountains a desolation,
and gave his heritage to the jackals of the wilderness. (v2b-3)

That is to say Edom has met with trouble and they are now destroyed (as were many nations who have been known to the Israelites). Each time they try to raise themselves up they are beaten back down; yet the Israelite people, still continue as a nation in the Land.

---

perhaps, a *Zechariah II.* 2) The introduction of a chapter 4 in Malachi by the LXX is curious. There are only six verses to which the first three carry on the prophecy from the preceding chapter (beginning 3.16) ; and the last three verses form a general post script in regard to the Book of the Twelve and the Books of Moses. 3) Also chapter 4 verse 5 continuing the theme of YHWH, returning personally to Jerusalem as with Zech 9.9; 9.14 and 14.1 4) The twelfth prophet, un-named, perhaps beginning at Zechariah 9 ?

[a] Possibly a group that will later evolve to become the Pharisees?

[b] Dried out vegetative matter: straw, that which is left after harvesting crops: stalks, leaves

[c] In this first dispute the people clearly have not read, minimally, Deuteronomy in which their answer would be clarified

Verse 6 continues with a rebuke addressed to the priests for their gross misconduct, dishonouring YHWH and to the careless indifferent attitude of people for the sickly sacrifices being offered and accepted by the priests.

A son honours his father, and a servant his master:
if then I am a father, where is mine honour?
and if I am a master, where is my respect? Says YHWH of hosts unto you,
O priests, that despise my Name. And ye say, ***Wherein have we despised thy Name****?* (v6)

Both priest and layman have abandoned YHWH as they see that He doesn't really have any influence in their lives. Times have changed now YHWH's involvement with them was over with the exile; their worship in the Temple is just a part of social culture; for the priests it is just a job like any other. Thus they show no respect for G-d, the Temple or the people who rely on them as teachers. The priests and the people now engage in completely useless acts of worship. It would therefore be better if the Temple were closed.

Oh that there were one among you that would shut the doors,
that ye might not kindle fire on mine altar in vain! (v10)

YHWH reminds them that Israel were to bring knowledge of Him to all the people of the Earth and as such their actions are worse than useless.

For from the rising of the sun even unto the going down of the same
my Name shall be great among the nations;
and in every place incense shall be offered unto my Name, and a pure offering:
for my Name shall be great among the nations, says YHWH of hosts.[a] (v11)

Ch 2

The priests are further warned that a curse[b] will befall them if they continue like this. They are reminded of their covenant (of Levi) for service in the Temple and the way the Levi priests had once been..

My covenant was with him of life and peace;
and I gave them to him that he might fear; and he feared Me, and stood in awe of my Name.
The law of truth was in his mouth, and unrighteousness was not found in his lips
For the priest's lips should keep knowledge, and they should seek the Law at his mouth;
for he is the messenger [c] *of YHWH of hosts.* (v5-7)

---

[a] This verse attracting the attention of much exegesis. The future tense being used as a matter of *preference* as this verse does not indicate future or present. 2) Within the context though, there is also the position that only in Jerusalem is a G-d worshipped with such indifference. Throughout the ancient world in every place their own gods were worshipped with great reverence. 3) No doubt there were also pockets of YHWH worship around the ancient world by this time including the fervent diaspora

[b] Deut 27-28. Blessings & Curses

But now they have not even tried to obey the Law or bring it to the people. They have caused many to stumble.

Therefore have I also made you contemptible and base before all the people,
according as ye have not kept My ways, but have been partial [a] *in the Law.* (2.9)

The rebuke then continues against the unfaithfulness of the people..

Have we not all one father? [b] *has not one God created us?* [c]
why do we deal treacherously every man against his brother,
profaning the covenant of our fathers? (v10)

The men of Judah are again marrying foreign women[d] and have fallen back into idol worship..

Judah has dealt treacherously,
and an abomination is committed in Israel and in Jerusalem;
for Judah has profaned the holiness [e] *of YHWH which He loves,*[f]
and have married the daughter of a foreign god. (v11)

YHWH will cut off all who are doing this.
In verse 13 Malachi begins another of YHWH's complaints that the people offer their sacrifices with *tears, with weeping, and with sighing*. They are saddened by the fact that their prayers are left unanswered.

Yet ye say, Why?[g]
Because YHWH has been witness between thee and the wife of thy youth,
against whom thou have dealt treacherously,
though she is thy companion, and the wife of thy covenant. (v14)

Malachi gives YHWH's answer: it is because of their apostasy and unfaithfulness to their covenant..

And did he not make one,[h] *although he had the residue of the Spirit?*[i]

---

[c] The priests also referred to as măl'âk (messenger)

[a] Not interested in teaching/applying it

[b] Abraham

[c] YHWH

[d] Malachi's prophecy is understood to be written after Ezra-Nehemiah and as such there is the double understanding (of also abandoning YHWH as a wife) of the problems with intermarriage which are described there (Ezra 10; Nehemiah 9.14, 13.27)

[e] קֹדֶשׁ [qōḏeš] being separated, consecrated to G-d

[f] Holiness, which is loved by YHWH

[g] Why is this happening

[h] One flesh (Gen 2.23-24)

And why one? He sought a godly seed.[a] *Therefore take heed to your spirit,*
and let none deal treacherously against the wife of his youth
For I hate putting away,[b] *says YHWH, the God of Israel,*
and him that covers his garment with violence,[c] *says YHWH of hosts:*
therefore take heed to your spirit, that ye deal not treacherously. (v15-16)

Verse 17 continues with the peoples complaints as they have long noticed there is no profit in worshipping G-d, as all people good or bad seem to get the same treatment from Him. It seems that He does not intervene in human affairs. YHWH has now had enough.

Ye have wearied YHWH with your words. ***Yet ye say, How have we wearied Him?***
In that ye say, everyone that doeth evil is good in the sight of YHWH,
and He delights in them; ***or where is the G-d of justice****?* (v17)[d]

The answer to where the G-d of Justice is now is given in chapter 3. He is already on the way with His *intervention of Judgement.*

Ch 3

Behold, I send my messenger,[e] *and he shall prepare the way before me:*
and the Lord,[f] *whom ye seek, will suddenly come to his temple;*
and the messenger [g] *of the covenant, whom ye desire.* (v1)

YHWH's messenger will purify the priests. Offerings will then be done in righteousness as in the days of old. He will judge those people not adhering to His Law.

This continuing interest in the Israelites is stated as..

Because I, YHWH, have not changed,
you, descendants of Jacob, have not been destroyed. (v6)

YHWH's promises and faithfulness continue. Verse 7 follows with yet another chance for the unrepentant people.

---

[i] Did not make two spirits in the marriage
[a] In response to an argument that Abraham sent away Hagar
[b] Putting Away: a term used for divorce
[c] Against the purity and oneness just described
[d] Also 3.14-15 You have said: "It is useless to serve God. What have we gained by keeping His requirements and walking mournfully before the Lord of Hosts? So now we consider the arrogant to be fortunate. Not only do those who commit wickedness prosper, they even test God and escape."
[e] măl'âk (messenger)
[f] אדון ['āḏôn]
[g] măl'âk (messenger)

Since the days of your fathers, you have turned from My statutes; you have not kept them.
Return to Me! and I will return to you!" says YHWH of Hosts
But ye say: how shall we return?

Verse 8 follows on with the answer that if they were in fact following the Law (Torah) then they would treat YHWH, His Temple and His priests with reverence, in this case by giving tithes.

Will a man rob God? Yet you are robbing Me!
You ask: ***How do we rob You?*** (v8)

The people are defrauding YHWH. In the same way as their offerings are substandard they also do not pay the 'tithes' from their income for the upkeep of the Temple and the priests. It is because of this that YHWH has caused a drought,[a] which appears to be on-going at the time of the prophecy. If they would only pay their due into the Temple storehouses then the harvest would be great in their own storehouses.

And all nations shall call you happy; for ye shall be a land of delight,
says YHWH of hosts. (v12)

Malachi brings another complaint of YHWH..

Your words have been stout against me, says YHWH.
Yet ye say, ***What have we spoken against thee****?* (v13)

An amazingly oblivious remark, but the people have already concluded that their service to G-d ('ĕlōhîm) is in vain. Whether they are good or bad all people get the same treatment. And so they continue in their unrepentant unfaithfulness.
Verse 16 opens another section in which the chance for repentance is now replaced with a saving only of them that fear G-d.

Then they that feared YHWH spoke one with another;[b]
and YHWH hearkened, and heard, and a book of remembrance was written before him,
for them that feared YHWH, and that thought[c] *upon his name.* (v16)

And they shall be mine, says YHWH of hosts,
even mine own possession, in the day that I make;
and I will spare them, as a man spares his own son that serves him.
Then shall ye return and discern between the righteous and the wicked,

---

[a] A consequence of not adhering to the Covenant (Deut 11.13-17)
[b] After the statements of rejection by the people a last statement is made by those who accept YHWH. They discuss humbly amongst themselves. In the other disputes the people arrogantly dispute against YHWH.
[c] People who actually read Torah and meditate upon it as opposed to those who in the earlier disputations apparently have little or no knowledge of it

between him that serves God and him that serves Him not. (v17-18)

Ch 4 [a]

Continues with YHWH's final answer, which is that the correction will be made when His day of Judgement comes..

For, behold, the day comes, it burns as a furnace;
and all the proud, and all that work wickedness, shall be stubble;
and the day that comes shall burn them up, says YHWH of hosts,
that it shall leave them neither root nor branch
But unto you that fear my name shall the sun of righteousness arise with healing in its wings;
and ye shall go forth, and leap as calves of the stall.
And ye shall tread down the wicked;
for they shall be ashes under the soles of your feet in the day that I make,
says YHWH of hosts. (v1-3)

In the last addition to the book of Malachi, bringing to an end the 'Book of the Twelve' and the Old Testament, is the calling for the people to obey the Law of Moses [b] and to take heed of the prophets when sent to them. Elijah (the spirit of prophecy) will be sent again to bring the people back to YHWH.

Remember ye the law of Moses my servant,
which I commanded unto him in Horeb, for all Israel, even statutes and ordinances.
Behold, I will send you Elijah the prophet before the great and terrible day of YHWH come.
And he shall turn the heart of the fathers [c] to the children,[d]
and the heart of the children to their father[e]
lest I come and smite the Land [f] with a curse.[g] (v 4-6)

---

[a] The Hebrew Bible does not have a chapter 4 but continues chapter 3 until verse 24

[b] Something which, at least in Malachi, many do not

[c] The patriarchs of Israel

[d] The people of Israel

[e] LXX has

the one who shall restore the heart of the father to the son,
and the heart of a man to his neighbour, lest coming I strike the Land entirely.
Remember the law of Moses my manservant,
accordingly as I gave charge to him in Horeb for all Israel – orders and judgments

[f] Promised land

[g] In line with the decrees of Lev. 26 and Deut. 28. Blessings and curses

Printed in Great Britain
by Amazon

59569972R00163